Concurrences Books

Tributes

Eleanor M. Fox – Antitrust Ambassador to the World, *2021*

Herbert Hovenkamp – The Dean of American Antitrust Law, *2021*

Frédéric Jenny – Standing Up for Convergence and Relevance in Antitrust, (Vol. I & II), *2019 & 2021*

Albert Foer – A Consumer Voice in the Antitrust Arena, *2020*

Richard Whish – Taking Competition Law Outside the Box, *2020*

Douglas H. Ginsburg – An Antitrust Professor on the Bench (Vol. I & II), *2018 & 2020*

Wang Xiaoye – The Pioneer of Competition Law in China, *A. Emch, W. Ng (eds.), 2019*

Ian S. Forrester – A Scot without Borders (Vol. I & II), *A. Komninos (eds.), 2015*

William E. Kovacic – An Antitrust Tribute (Vol. I & II), *2013 & 2014*

Practical Books

Global Dictionary of Competition Law, *D. Healey, W. Kovacic, P. Trevisan, R. Whish, Forthcoming 2022*

Antitrust in the Pharmaceutical Sector, *M. Cowie, G. Gordon M. Thill-Tayara, Forthcoming 2022*

Competition Law Treatment of Joint Ventures, *B Bleicher, N. Campbell, A. Hamilton, N. Hukkinen, P. Khan, Forthcoming 2022 (in collaboration with the IBA)*

State Aid & National Enforcement, *J. Derenne, D. Jouve, C. Lemaire, F. Martucci (eds.), Forthcoming 2022*

Information Exchange and Related Risks – A Practical Guide, *Z. Marosi & M. Soares (eds.), Forthcoming 2022 (in collaboration with the IBA)*

Competition Case Law Digest – 5th Edition, *F. Jenny, N. Charbit (eds.), 2022*

Competition Inspections in 21 Jurisdictions – A Practitioner's Guide, *N. Jalabert-Doury (ed.), 2022*

Perspectives on Antitrust Compliance, *A. Riley, A. Stephan, A. Tubbs (eds.), 2022 (in collaboration with the ICC)*

Turkish Competition Law, *G. Gürkaynak, 2021*

Competition Law - Climate Change & Environmental Sustainability, *S. Holmes, D. Middelschulte, M. Snoep (eds.), 2021*

Merger Control in Latin America – A Jurisdictional Guide, *P. Burnier da Silveira, P. Sittenfeld (eds.), 2020*

Competition Inspections under EU Law – A Practitioner's Guide, *N. Jalabert-Doury, 2020*

Gun Jumping in Merger Control - A Jurisdictional Guide, *C. Hatton, Y. Comtois, A. Hamilton (eds.), 2019 (in collaboration with the IBA)*

Choice – A New Standard for Competition Analysis? *P. Nihoul (ed.), 2016*

PhD Theses

Competition & Regulation in Network Industries – Essays in Industrial Organization, *J-M. Zogheib, 2021*

The Role of Media Pluralism in the Enforcement of EU Competition Law, *K. Bania, 2019*

Buyer Power, *I. Herrera Anchustegui, 2017*

General Interest

Women and Antitrust – Voices from the Field (Vol I & II), *E. Kurgonaite & K. Nordlander, 2020*

Conference Proceedings

Antitrust in Emerging and Developing Countries – (Vol I & II), *E. Fox, H. First, 2015 & 2016*

Global Antitrust Law – Current Issues in Antitrust Law and Economics, *D. Ginsburg, J. Wright, (eds.) 2015*

Competition Law on the Global Stage – David Gerber's Global Competition Law in Perspective, *D. Gerber, 2014*

e-Book versions available for **Concurrences+** subscribers

Rulemaking Authority of the US Federal Trade Commission

106 West 32nd Street, Suite 144 New York, NY, 10001, USA
www.concurrences.com
book@concurrences.com

First Printing, June 2022
978-1-954750-86-9 (Hardcover)
Library of Congress Control Number: 2022909741

Cover Design: Yves Buliard, www.yvesbuliard.fr
Book Design and Layout implementation: Nord Compo

Rulemaking Authority of the US Federal Trade Commission

Foreword by J. Howard Beales III
and Timothy J. Muris

Edited by
Daniel A. Crane

Contributors

Alden F. Abbott
George Mason University

Jonathan M. Barnett
University of Southern California

Corbin Barthold
TechFreedom

Neil Chilson
Stand Together

James C. Cooper
George Mason University

Daniel A. Crane
University of Michigan

Marina Lao
Seton Hall University

Aaron L. Nielsen
Brigham Young University

Maureen K. Ohlhausen
Baker Botts

Richard J. Pierce, Jr.
George Washington University

James F. Rill
Baker Botts

Ben Rossen
Baker Botts

Berin Szóka
TechFreedom

Henry C. Su
Bradley Arant Boult Cummings

Overview

Foreword

J. Howard Beales III*
George Washington School of Business
Timothy J. Muris**
Antonin Scalia Law School and Sidley Austin

After decades of relative stability, change has come to the Federal Trade Commission (FTC), and to the broader antitrust and consumer protection firmament. The Biden administration filled each of the major policy positions, including the heads of the Antitrust Division and FTC, with neo-Brandeisians, who reject the world they inherit, believing that the economy needs a major overhaul. Echoing their sentiments, President Biden decried the failed forty-year experiment in economics-driven antitrust that he and his appointees now clearly plan to end.[1]

This book analyzes one of the major initiatives to fulfill the renewed progressive vision, rulemaking at the FTC. Following the sentiments of the President's rejection of the last forty years, the new leaders often speak glowingly of policy before those failed decades, including FTC's use of rulemaking. A historical tour of the FTC's use of rules will thus help introduce this volume.[2] Besides academic research, we have extensive personal experience, both generally at the agency and specifically with FTC rulemaking, having each held four jobs at the Commission, most recently as chairman (Muris) and director of the Bureau of Consumer Protection (Beales) from 2001 to 2004. Regarding rulemaking, from 1974 to 1987, one or both of us worked extensively on FTC rules, covering

---

* Emeritus Professor of Strategic Management and Public Policy at the George Washington University School of Business. Professor Beales has held four positions in the agency, in both the Bureau of Economics and the Bureau of Consumer Protection, most recently as Director of the Bureau of Consumer Protection in 2001–2004.

** George Mason University Foundation Professor of Law at the Antonin Scalia Law School, senior counsel at Sidley Austin. Professor Muris has held four positions in the agency, is the only person ever to direct both enforcement bureaus, and most recently was Chairman in 2001–2004.

1 Remarks by President Biden At Signing of An Executive Order Promoting Competition in the American Economy (July 9, 2021), https://www.whitehouse.gov/briefing-room/speeches-remarks/2021/07/09/remarks-by-president-biden-at-signing-of-an-executive-order-promoting-competition-in-the-american-economy.

2 We tell the story in more detail in a recently released report for the American Enterprise Institute. *See* J. Howard Beales III & Timothy J. Muris, *Back to the Future: How Not to Write a Regulation*, American Enterprise Institute (June 2022).

virtually every one of the major rules proposed then. In our most recent FTC tour, we led the agency when it enacted the rule that created the National Do Not Call Registry, one of the most popular consumer protection initiatives from any government agency. After that historical tour, we describe briefly the current FTC shift to rules, outline the book's chapters, and conclude with a cautionary tale of unintended consequences from a historic FTC rule.

I. Some FTC History

Rulemaking began, not at the agency's beginning in 1914, but in 1962, the agency having disclaimed any ability to issue substantive rules before then. New rules of practice, adopted in 1962 and effective the next year, provided for trade regulation rules that would resolve legal issues in subsequent enforcement proceedings. These were quite different rules than the modern rules that the FTC can write, in part because the agency's only authority to enforce them was to issue a cease and desist order, not obtain civil penalties.[3] Moreover, the 1962 rules envisioned that a respondent would have an opportunity in an enforcement proceeding to argue that the substantive rule should not apply to its particular circumstances.

Two years later, the Commission proposed one of the most significant rules in its history, requiring cigarette manufacturers to warn smokers of the health risks of their product.[4] For our current purposes, this important substance is not central; instead, it is the test for unfairness proposed in the Statement of Basis and Purpose (SBP) for that rule – a test significantly the brainchild of one who was to become a major figure in antitrust history, Richard Posner, then only twenty-five. Fresh from his stellar career at Harvard and having clerked for Justice William Brennan, Posner was an attorney advisor to Commissioner Philip Elman, an important figure in his own right for his role in the Cigarette Rule and, more notably in antitrust history, as one of the leaders in moving the FTC and the antitrust community from anticompetitive interpretations of the Robinson-Patman Act. The Cigarette Rule used a three-part test for an "unfair" act or practice: whether it "offends public policy," is "immoral, unethical, oppressive, or unscrupulous," or "causes substantial injury to consumers."[5]

Although the Commission continued to promulgate rules after 1964, it avoided using the Cigarette Rule unfairness test, perhaps because Congress had intervened, with its own, less restrictive cigarette warning.[6] On March 1, 1972, however,

3 The FTC's authority to obtain civil penalties for rule violations is specifically limited to rules that define unfair or deceptive acts or practices. *See* 15 U.S.C. § 45(m)(1)(A).

4 Cigarette Rule SBP, 29 Fed. Reg. 8325 (July 2, 1964).

5 *Id.* at 8355.

6 *See* An Act to regulate the labeling of cigarettes, and for other purposes, Pub. L. No. 89-92, 79 Stat. 282 (1965).

the Supreme Court decided the *Sperry & Hutchinson* (*S&H*) case.[7] Originally, the Commission had argued that S&H's restrictions on swapping its trading stamps were unfair methods of competition (UMC). On appeal, however, it advanced the new argument that S&H had committed unfair acts or practices.[8] Because this theory had not been litigated below, the Supreme Court remanded the case to the Commission. The opinion stated, in a passage that we were to read dozens of times in internal staff memoranda during the 1970s, that the FTC "does not arrogate excessive power to itself if, in measuring a practice against the elusive but congressionally mandated standard of fairness, it, like a court of equity, considers public values beyond those enshrined in the letter or encompassed in the spirit of the antitrust laws."[9] The sentence ended with a footnote that, in dicta, appeared to bless the unfairness analysis advanced in the Cigarette Rule.[10]

S&H inspired an effort to explore the outer limits of unfairness, particularly for use in rules. The then newly created Bureau of Consumer Protection devoted considerable resources and intellectual firepower to the effort, establishing a special unit to develop rule proposals.[11] While the staff was hard at work to implement an expanded vision of unfairness, they received renewed support from the September 1972 oral argument testing whether the FTC's Octane Rule, discussed below, would be sustained. With the panel containing two of the liberal giants of the D.C. Circuit, David Bazelon and J. Skelly Wright, Commission attorneys were confident of their prospects for success. Indeed, the opinion, issued in June 1973, blessed agency rulemaking authority, with the important inclusion of the "safety valve," based on the agency's 1962 rules, allowing any respondent an opportunity to argue in an enforcement proceeding that the rule should not apply to their particular circumstances.[12]

Concerned over the FTC's growing use of rules rather than cases, Congress acted to codify procedures for FTC rulemaking. Paramount among congressional concerns was the vagueness of the FTC's substantive statutory offenses, especially unfairness. To help ensure discretion was exercised wisely, rather than seeking substantive definitions, Congress adopted procedural constraints that require hybrid rulemaking between Administrative Procedure Act informal notice-and-comment rulemaking and the formal procedures of administrative litigation.

7 FTC v. Sperry & Hutchinson Co., 405 U.S. 233 (1972).

8 As passed in 1914, the FTC Act proscribed "unfair methods of competition." In 1938, Congress added "unfair or deceptive acts or practices."

9 *S&H*, 405 U.S. at 244.

10 The footnote stated that "The Commission has described the factors it considers in determining whether a practice that is neither in violation of the antitrust laws nor deceptive is nonetheless unfair," and quoted the unfairness test from the Cigarette Rule SBP.

11 The efforts to think creatively spawned a running joke among the staff that lasted for decades about the "unfair distribution of wealth" rule. Perhaps such a rule will yet emerge.

12 Nat'l Petroleum Refiners Ass'n v. FTC, 482 F.2d 672, 692 (D.C. Cir. 1973).

Passed late in 1974 and effective January 4, 1975,[13] section 18 of the FTC Act provided the Commission authority to write rules that "define with specificity" unfair or deceptive acts or practices (UDAP). The law did not change the Commission's authority regarding UMC rules.[14]

An extraordinary outburst of rulemaking followed. In a twelve-month period, beginning in April 1975, the Commission proposed sixteen transformative rules, touching myriad aspects of everyday life, including vocational schools, food and drug advertising, used cars, clothing care labels, hearing aids, funerals, mobile homes, and health spas, among others.[15] Not without cause was the Commission accused of seeking the mantle of the second most powerful legislature in Washington.

As we describe in detail elsewhere,[16] the rulemaking effort came undone, mostly of self-inflicted wounds, with the 1978 proposal to prohibit advertising to children prompting special hostility.[17] It signaled to many in Congress, the business community, and the media that the Commission was pursuing a personal vision, not addressing actual consumer harm. The *Washington Post*, no bastion of conservatism, editorialized that the FTC was becoming the "National Nanny."[18] Congress denied funding, closing the agency briefly – long before shutdowns became a recurring Washington phenomenon.

As multiple studies of 1970s FTC rulemaking documented, including one from the Administrative Conference of the United States, among the many failures, three stood out: (i) the lack of clear theories of illegality, (ii) substantive theories of why the practices were occurring and how to fix them, and (iii) systematic evidence to evaluate the extent of the problem and the efficacy of the remedies. Few of the proposals became final, and then usually after significant changes from the original.

Although the initial wave of proposals relied on defining UDAP, some had a competition rationale. The Eyeglass and Prescription Drug Rules, which would have preempted state bans on advertising, were based on the anticompetitive effects of such bans, for example.[19] The rationale for the surviving portion of the Eyeglass

13 Pub. L. No. 93-637, 88 Stat. 2183 (1975).

14 15 U.S.C. § 57a(a)(2).

15 *See* Admin. Conference of the U.S., Recommendation No. 79-1–Hybrid Rulemaking Procedures of the Federal Trade Commission (June 1979), https://www.acus.gov/recommendation/hybrid-rulemaking-procedures-federal-trade-commission, for a table listing the twenty rules proposed before 1979.

16 *See* Beales & Muris, *supra* note 2.

17 Although the FTC proponents thought they could achieve large reductions in the amount of advertising children saw by banning advertisements where children were a majority of the audience, in fact, that would have affected only one program – *Captain Kangaroo*, the cherished adult friend to millions of children who grew up before Mr. Rogers entered the neighborhood. Even had the Captain survived without advertising, the impact on the amount of advertising seen by children would have been trivial. Most of the advertising that children saw was in popular adults or family sitcoms, such as *Laverne & Shirley* or *Happy Days*, or reruns of older sitcoms such as *I Love Lucy* in the after-school hours on local television.

18 Editorial, *The FTC as National Nanny*, Wash. Post, Mar. 1, 1978.

19 The proposals to preempt state advertising bans were mooted when the Supreme Court extended First Amendment protection to commercial speech. *See* Va. Pharmacy Bd. v. Va. Consumer Council, 425 U.S. 748 (1976); Bates v. State Bar of Arizona, 433 U.S. 350 (1977).

Rule, requiring that the patient receive a copy of any prescription the doctor writes, is to encourage competition among eyewear and related providers. The Over-the-Counter Drug Rule, which would have required drug advertising to use precisely, and only, the words used to describe indications for use in Food and Drug Administration (FDA) regulations, addressed concerns that multiple terms for drug indications facilitated "spurious" product differentiation.[20]

Despite the fact that some rules were clearly aimed at competition problems, FTC antitrust attorneys did not want to join the rulemaking endeavor. They were preoccupied with their own effort to remake the American economy through a series of deconcentration cases and investigations, including litigation both to dismember vertical integration in the oil industry and to condemn the cereal industry for a shared monopoly (spurious product differentiation again!) as well as an extensive investigation to determine whether the auto industry should be dismembered.

In 1980, Congress stopped some specific rules and tightened section 18 procedures modestly. The Reagan administration arrived in October 1981 and disfavored rulemaking, as the new appointees proposed to move from unproductive and resource-intensive rules to cases. In consumer protection, the Reagan appointees created the program attacking fraud, which became a mainstay of FTC consumer protection, with the agency helping to coordinate a worldwide attack on the myriad aspects of fraud. In antitrust, they emphasized cases involving professions, trade associations, and restraints that misuse the government to stifle competition, as well as helping to develop the modern procedures for merger enforcement under the Hart-Scott-Rodino Act.

The problems caused by the FTC's aggressive use of its unfairness jurisdiction, primarily in section 18 rules, lead the agency to issue a letter in 1980 abandoning one of the prongs of the Cigarette Rule statement, regarding practices that were immoral, unscrupulous, or unethical, and relying principally on consumer injury to define unfairness. Nevertheless, the letter left independent use of public policy as a possible basis to find unfairness, an approach that the Commission abandoned in a 1982 codical to the 1980 letter. (The Reagan administration supported codification of the standard to limit the FTC's discretion.) The lack of agreement about an appropriate definition of unfairness delayed FTC reauthorization until 1994 when Congress finally enacted the current definition, in FTC Act section 45(n), combining both the 1980 and 1982 letters: A practice is only unfair if it causes or is likely to cause substantial consumer injury, without offsetting benefits to consumers or competition, that the consumer cannot reasonably avoid. Public policy can provide evidence to support the Commission's conclusions, but cannot serve as the sole basis for finding a practice unfair.[21]

---

20 The one rule that also included an explicit unfair methods theory involved standards and certification, discussed below.

21 We discuss the public policy and other issues of the unfairness debate in J. Howard Beales III & Timothy J. Muris, The Limits of Unfairness Under the Federal Trade Commission Act (Association of National Advertisers 1991).

One final piece of history relevant for today's debate was an effort in the late 1970s to use unfairness in competition cases, independent of the Sherman Act. The Commission lost all three cases litigated, in two different circuit courts.[22] In the intervening decades, only invitations to collude, beyond those that would give rise to attempted monopolization, have been the one area for use of so-called pure section 5, although the theory has yet to be tested in court.

II. Reliving History

Today's neo-Brandeisians seek to reverse the 1981 Reagan turn, shifting back from cases to rules. Unlike the 1970s, they propose to use rules under both UMC and UDAP. New Chair Lina Khan, writing with Rohit Chopra in 2020,[23] proposed UMC rulemaking, and it is uncertain whether the new FTC leadership will also use section 18 rulemaking to address competition issues. The *S&H* case, the use of section 18 rulemaking in the 1970s involving competition problems, and the increased emphasis in antitrust on consumer welfare since the 1970s all support an argument that no bright line necessarily exists between the "u" in unfair methods and that in unfair acts or practices. Moreover, section 18 rules have civil penalties and avoid the safety valve that is contained under existing precedent and FTC procedure. Most important, as discussed shortly, there are serious doubts that modern courts would sustain the D.C. Circuit's 1973 view that the FTC has the authority to issue UMC rules with the force of law.

Nevertheless, multiple reasons may move the current FTC towards UMC rules. Practically, they may fear section 45(n) because the statute reads in the consumer welfare language that they abhor – one of the principal causes they see of the alleged forty years of failure.[24] Substantively, although some of their proposals could be considered antitrust or consumer protection, others, perhaps aimed at redrafting Sherman Act principles, could not.[25] Section 45(n) does not apply to UMC, and, perhaps the

22 E.I. du Pont de Nemours & Co. v. FTC, 729 F.2d 128 (2d Cir. 1984); Boise Cascade Corp. v. FTC, 637 F.2d 573 (9th Cir. 1980); Official Airline Guides v. FTC, 630 F.2d 920 (2d Cir. 1980).

23 Rohit Chopra & Lina M. Khan, *The Case for "Unfair Methods of Competition" Rulemaking*, 87 U. Chi. L. Rev. 357 (2020). Chopra, then an FTC commissioner, is now director of the Consumer Financial Protection Bureau.

24 President Biden blamed the problem on Robert Bork and Chicago, ignoring the contributions of numerous other scholars, including those affiliated with Harvard, such as Phillip Areeda and Justice Stephen Breyer. *See* Biden Remarks, *supra* note 1. *See, e.g.*, William E. Kovacic, *The Intellectual DNA of Modern U.S. Competition Law for Dominant Firm Conduct: The Chicago/Harvard Double Helix*, 2007 Colum. Bus. L. Rev. 1 (2007). For extensive discussions, *see* Timothy J. Muris & Jonathan E. Nuechterlein, *Chicago and Its Discontents*, 87 U. Chi. L. Rev. 495 (2020); Bruce H. Kobayashi & Timothy J. Muris, *Chicago, Post-Chicago, and Beyond: Time to Let Go of the 20th Century*, 78 Antitrust L.J. 147 (2012).

25 Even if there is no general bright line between some practices for UMC and UDAP, they are two distinct statutory standards, arguably leaving some domain of unique cases for each. (The precise relation between the two standards is beyond our brief discussion here.) Agency use of UMC rules to apply different standards under section 5, then under the Sherman or Clayton Acts, for example to implement Chair Khan's desire to remove the recoupment requirement for predatory pricing (thereby chilling aggressive price-cutting) or to make mergers easier to challenge, would invite the conclusion that such rules were antitrust, not consumer protection or some hybrid. Section 18 could not be used for such rules.

new leadership is willing to take its chances with "pure" section 5 theories hoping for potential judicial deference to the FTC's interpretation of its organic statute.

III. The Book's Contents

This book's important set of essays addresses the myriad issues that the return to FTC rulemaking raise. Several chapters focus on UMC rules, both whether the FTC has this authority, and, if it does, whether and how that authority should be exercised. Questions include: In the fifty years since the D.C. Circuit endorsed FTC rulemaking, have courts changed their approach to the issue? What, if anything, can be read from the 1974 congressional authorization of only UDAP rules? How will the evolving Supreme Court limitations on regulatory agencies influence the FTC, a question that relates both to the agency's authority and how it uses that authority? Assuming the authority exists, how will "pure" section 5 coexist with the Sherman Act? What is the appropriate balance between substantive rules and traditional case-by-case adjudication in setting competition policy?

Arguing for FTC's boldness, Lao[26] emphasizes judicial precedent for the FTC to act beyond the Sherman and Clayton Acts, and believes that FTC rulemaking authority should survive even under modern judicial standards for supervising regulatory agencies. She finds it important that the FTC lead in setting substantive antitrust standards that would necessarily differ, at times, from the other laws. Specifically addressing the D.C. Circuit's 1973 opinion and its context, Ohlhausen and Rossen[27] argue that UMC rules are essentially a dead end. Not only finding that opinion inconsistent with modern standards of interpretation, they also reject arguments that Congress in 1974 ratified UMC rulemaking and, indeed, when it gave the FTC authority for the Octane Rule under a different statute in 1977, it did so only under UDAP, not UMC. Szóka and Barthold[28] also cast serious doubts on expanded FTC rulemaking powers, focusing in depth on what they believe was the well-reasoned district court opinion that the D.C. Circuit overturned in 1973 and the arguments in favor of the district court's position. Assuming that the agency has the power, Su[29] nevertheless opposes wide use of competition rulemaking. In support of adjudication over rulemaking, he emphasizes the practical difficulties of competition rulemaking, including developing a factual record encompassing an entire industry, protecting the due process rights of those charged with violations, and the necessity for coordination with the Department of Justice's Antitrust Division.

---

26 *See infra* Marina Lao, *Competition Rulemaking: The Case for Boldness*, pp. 1–29.

27 *See infra* Maureen K. Ohlhausen & Ben Rossen, *Dead-End Road:* National Petroleum Refiners Association *and FTC "Unfair Methods of Competition" Rulemaking*, pp. 31–48.

28 *See infra* Berin Szóka & Corbin Barthold, *The Constitutional Revolution That Wasn't: Why the FTC Isn't a Second National Legislature*, pp. 49–76.

29 *See infra* Henry Su, *Policing Anticompetitive Practices and Protecting the Competitive Process through Adjudication vs. Rulemaking*, pp. 77–100.

Other chapters are also critical of broad UMC rulemaking power. Pierce[30] joins those who believe that the 1973 D.C. Circuit opinion used statutory interpretation inconsistent with modern courts. As do other authors, he notes that were courts to allow UMC rules, they would likely use the developing major questions doctrine to prevent any FTC attempts to use rules to change antitrust law significantly. (He does believe that if, contrary to his arguments that the FTC lacks UMC rulemaking power, a court could well approve a rule consistent with the evidence and current antitrust interpretation.) Abbott[31] also doubts that the FTC's rulemaking effort will succeed legally, emphasizing the constitutional delegation doctrine, principles of statutory construction, and the general judicial trend toward reigning in administrative agencies. Finally, on the UMC rule issue, Ohlhausen and Rill[32] join in emphasizing the lack of statutory authority for such rules, and the problem that the rules will distract from the FTC's core mission of case-by-case expert adjudication.

Barnett[33] considers antitrust rulemaking through the lens of the principal-agent problem. He sees recent FTC policy shifts, in particular, the revocation of policy statements without any replacement, as attempts to expand agency discretion, an expansion likely to increase agency costs. He sees a significant risk that the agency is headed toward a repeat of the disastrous 1970s.

Several chapters consider the choice between writing rules and case-by-case enforcement from different perspectives. Chilson[34] places particular emphasis on keeping regulatory requirements in pace with rapid changes in technology. He argues that case-by-case enforcement creates fewer problems in fast-moving areas, and that the FTC should therefore embrace it. Cooper[35] notes the flexibility of the enforcement approach, and its ability to account for all relevant facts and circumstances surrounding a particular alleged violation. He also examines the need for section 18 rules to define unfair acts or practices "with specificity."

Nielsen[36] evaluates the consequences for the Commission if it does become a rulemaking agency. He points to three: (i) more White House oversight, increased judicial review, and ossification because of the difficulty of changing rules; (ii) more potential for policy flip-flops when administrations change (as with net neutrality); and (iii) more frequently becoming the victim of "administrative law as blood sport," with, for example, nominations held hostage over policy disputes.

---

30 *See infra* Richard J. Pierce, Jr., *Can the Federal Trade Commission Use Rulemaking to Change Antitrust Law?*, pp. 101–128.

31 *See infra* Alden F. Abbott, *Legal Constraints on FTC Competition Rulemaking*, pp. 129–154.

32 *See infra* Maureen K. Ohlhausen & James F. Rill, *Pushing the Limits? A Primer on FTC Competition Rulemaking*, pp. 155–176.

33 *See infra* Jonathan M. Barnett, *Regulatory Rents: An Agency-Cost Analysis of the FTC Rulemaking Initiative*, pp. 177–200.

34 *See infra* Neil Chilson, *Case-by-Case Rules! Old Statutes and New Tech at the FTC*, pp. 201–224.

35 *See infra* James C. Cooper, *Privacy Rulemaking at the FTC*, pp. 225–254.

36 *See infra* Aaron L. Nielson, *What Happens if the FTC Becomes a Serious Rulemaker?*, pp. 255–270.

Finally, as Crane[37] notes, the FTC's independence is under threat, both from the executive branch, with an executive order urging the Commission to address certain competition concerns of the administration, and from the judiciary, via decisions such as *Seila Law*[38] holding that executive branch officials must be subject to presidential removal at will. Because the FTC's current operations differ substantially from the characterization in *Humphrey's Executor*,[39] independence is at significant risk even if the Court follows that long-ago decision.

IV. The Pitfalls of Rulemaking: A Cautionary Tale of Unintended Consequences From the Historic FTC Octane Rule

We end with a reminder of the fallibility of rulemakers, discussing the rule on whose judicial blessing today's FTC relies for UMC rules. The Octane Rule itself illustrates the potential perils of rulemaking, and the risk of unintended side effects. As described in the rulemaking record, there were three measures of octane in use at the time: the research method, the road test method, and the motor method. For a given gasoline, research method octane numbers were generally eight to nine points higher than the motor method result, with the road test in between.

As originally promulgated in December 1970, the Commission declared it an unfair practice and an unfair method of competition to fail to disclose the research octane number. Before the rule took effect, however, Texaco provided evidence of an octane reversal problem: consumers who were dissatisfied with the anti-knock properties of their gasoline might, if they switched to a higher research octane gasoline, purchase a product with less road octane capability, rather than more. The Commission suspended the rule's effective date and reopened the record to reconsider the appropriate disclosure. The result was a decision to require retailers to post the average of the two most common measures: the research method, plus the motor method, divided by 2, or (R + M)/2. This requirement was promulgated in December 1971.[40]

The Commission never explained how this in fact solved the octane reversal problem. A gasoline with a higher research octane would also have a higher (R + M)/2, but could still have inferior road octane performance. But the "compromise" – if that was what the agency was attempting – created a different problem. At the time, owner's manuals frequently recommended octane requirements based on the research octane method. Most 1971–1974 model cars could

37 *See infra* Daniel A. Crane, *FTC Independence after* Seila Law, pp. 271–297.

38 Seila Law LLC v. Consumer Financial Protection Bureau, 591 U.S. ___, 140 S. Ct. 2183 (2020).

39 Humphrey's Executor v. United States, 295 U.S. 602 (1935).

40 36 Fed. Reg. 23,871 (Dec. 16, 1971).

use regular gas, with a research octane number of 91.[41] But with a motor octane number generally eight points lower, the new disclosure would identify the gasoline's octane rating as 87 – familiar today as the octane number for regular gas. The owner's manual, however, recommending 91 octane gas using a different scale,[42] could induce consumers to pay more for premium gasoline, even when their car did not need it. Consumer advocates estimated that consumers who purchased gasoline based on the car manufacturer's recommendations could pay an extra $35 per year[43] – or over $175 per year, in current dollars. In the name of helping consumers avoid needless expenditures for more octane than they needed, the rule created an incentive for those consumers who paid attention to buy more octane unnecessarily!

Of course, this is a transition problem – eventually, auto manufacturers would adjust their fuel recommendations to the new measurement system. But the extra consumer costs that result from the transition problem could easily overwhelm the presumed benefits of buying less octane that were thought to result from the required disclosure in the first place. The Commission never conducted sufficient analysis to determine whether consumers would actually save money, or, instead, spend more.

Perhaps ironically, the FTC's rule did not go into effect until it was repromulgated pursuant to the Petroleum Marketing Practices Act in 1978. Octane posting was instead required by the Cost of Living Council in 1973, and replaced by the same requirement from the Federal Energy Administration when the Council's authority expired in 1974.[44] Both agencies deferred to the presumed expertise of the FTC, requiring disclosure of (R + M)/2.

The current Commission seems determined to embark on a new rulemaking campaign. We hope it exercises more care than its progressive counterpart of the 1970s.

---

41 John D. Morris, *Octane Ratings Can Be Confusing*, N.Y. Times (Sept. 9, 1973), https://www.nytimes.com/1973/09/09/archives/octane-ratings-can-be-confusing-more-accuracy-testing-is-urged.html.

42 *Consumer Fuel Disclosure Act of 1975: Hearing on S. 1508 Before the Subcomm. for Consumers of the Senate Comm. on Commerce*, 94th Cong 1 (1975) (opening statement of Senator Hartke).

43 *Id.* at 42 (statement of Louis V. Lombardo, President, Public Interest Campaign).

44 Robert J. Gage, *The Discriminating Use of Information Disclosure Rules by the Federal Trade Commission*, 26 UCLA L. Rev. 1037, 1050 n. 36 (1979).

Competition Rulemaking: The Case for Boldness

MARINA LAO*
Seton Hall University School of Law

Abstract

This chapter makes the case for competition rulemaking and for boldness on the part of the FTC. Relevant statutory language, despite its terseness and generality, grants that authority; National Petroleum endorsed this reading of the provision, and the case was left undisturbed by subsequent congressional action with respect to competition rulemaking. Despite recent judicial trends concerning deference and the nondelegation doctrine, the agency's interpretation of the relevant statutory provision would likely continue to enjoy Chevron deference; moreover, the general grant of competition rulemaking authority in the FTC Act is unlikely to be categorically deemed unconstitutional. From a policy perspective, overcaution risks missing opportunities for the FTC to do more to fulfill its competition protection mandate. Predicting judicial reaction to agency "overreach" is difficult, and overthinking potential judicial backlash can be counterproductive. Using examples of past bold, and successful, rulemaking by other agencies, I argue there is precedent for pushing the limits in FTC rulemaking in exceptional and appropriate circumstances.

---

* Professor of Law, Seton Hall University School of Law. I am grateful to Peter Carstensen, Charles Sullivan, and Spencer Waller for their thoughtful comments.

I. Introduction and Background

Increasing concern over the size and economic power of some companies in the United States, particularly in the digital platform markets, has given rise to a movement for innovative competition reform. Globally, there is a growing sense that conventional, *ex post*, antitrust enforcement is insufficient to protect and promote competition in those sectors.[1] Both the EU and the UK have taken concrete steps to engage in *ex ante* regulation of certain digital platforms, through the proposal of the Digital Markets Act in the case of the EU[2] and the establishment of the Digital Markets Unit within the Competition and Markets Authority (CMA) in the UK.[3] In the United States, there are calls for the Federal Trade Commission (FTC) to supplement antitrust enforcement with regulation, while making greater use of its "unfairness" authority under section 5 of the Federal Trade Commission Act (FTC Act) to fill gaps in the Sherman Act.[4]

FTC Chair Lina Khan and former Commissioner Rohit Chopra, in particular, have advocated notice-and-comment rulemaking under the Administrative Procedure Act (APA)[5] as a means to give fuller effect to the agency's mandate to prohibit "unfair methods of competition" (UMC) under section 5.[6] Tim Wu, Special Assistant to the President for Technology and Competition Policy on the National Economic Council, likewise, supports the expansion of competition

---

1 *See, e.g.*, Jason Furman et al., Unlocking Digital Competition: Report of the Digital Competition Expert Panel (Mar. 2019) [hereinafter Furman Report], https://assets.publishing.service.gov.uk/government/uploads/system/uploads/attachment_data/file/785547/unlocking_digital_competition_furman_review_web.pdf; Margrethe Vestager, Statement by Executive Vice-President Vestager on the Commission Proposal on New Rules for Digital Platforms (Dec. 15, 2020), https://ec.europa.eu/commission/presscorner/detail/en/STATEMENT_20_2450 (stating her view that regulation is necessary because antitrust enforcement is insufficient); Eur. Comm'n, The Digital Markets Act: Ensuring Fair and Open Digital Markets (Dec. 14, 2020), https://ec.europa.eu/info/strategy/priorities-2019-2024/europe-fit-digital-age/digital-markets-act-ensuring-fair-and-open-digital-markets_en (proposing, in December 2020, the Digital Markets Act, which would impose extensive *ex ante* regulations on some digital platforms); Rohit Chopra & Lina M. Khan, *The Case for "Unfair Methods of Competition" Rulemaking*, 87 Chi. L. Rev. 357, 359 (2020) ("[R]eliance on case-by-case adjudication yields a system of enforcement that generates ambiguity, unduly drains resources from enforcers, and deprives individuals and firms of any real opportunity to democratically participate in the process."); William P. Rogerson and Howard Shelanski, *Antitrust Enforcement, Regulation, and Digital Platforms*, 168 U. Pa. L. Rev. 1911, 1922–24 (2020) (explaining the potential disadvantages of exclusive reliance on traditional antitrust adjudication in digital platform markets).

2 Eur. Comm'n, Proposal for a Regulation of the European Parliament and of the Council on contestable and fair markets in the digital sector (Digital Markets Act) (Dec. 15, 2020), https://eur-lex.europa.eu/legal-content/EN/TXT/PDF/?uri=CELEX:52020PC0842&from=en; *see* Adam Satariano, *E.U. Takes Aim at Big Tech's Power With Landmark Digital Act*, N.Y. Times (Mar. 24, 2022), https://www.nytimes.com/2022/03/24/technology/eu-regulation-apple-meta-google.html.

3 *See* Digital Markets Unit, https://www.gov.uk/government/collections/digital-markets-unit.

4 *See, e.g.*, Chopra & Khan, *supra* note 1; Sandeep Vaheesan, *Resurrecting "A Comprehensive Charter of Economic Liberty": The Latent Power of the Federal Trade Commission*, 19 U. Pa. J. Bus. L. 645 (2017). *See also* C. Scott Hemphill, *An Aggregate Approach to Antitrust: Using New Data and Rulemaking to Preserve Drug Competition*, 109 Colum. L. Rev. 629 (2009) (advocating FTC rulemaking with respect to pay-for-delay reverse settlement agreements); Rogerson & Shelanski, *supra* note 1 (recommending light-handed regulation for markets served by digital platforms); Daniel A. Crane, *Technocracy and Antitrust*, 86 Tex. L. Rev. 1159, 1206–09 (2008) (suggesting the possibility of, but also raising doubts about, FTC rulemaking).

5 5 U.S.C. §§ 551–559.

6 Chopra & Khan, *supra* note 1.

enforcement through rulemaking.[7] But there are opposing views, notably from former Acting FTC Chair Maureen Ohlhausen and former Assistant Attorney General for the Department of Justice James Rill, who argue against such a move, questioning both its legal basis and its appropriateness from a policy perspective.[8]

One major question that has been the subject of much debate is the agency's statutory authority to engage in substantive competition rulemaking in the first place, and the strength of that authority, assuming it exists. Perhaps because of a lack of confidence in its own authority and fearing judicial backlash against any perceived agency overreach, the agency has promulgated only one substantive antitrust rule, in 1968,[9] which it never enforced and subsequently rescinded.[10] More recently, on the administrative law front, a majority of the current Supreme Court justices have indicated a preference for tightening the nondelegation doctrine in the near future, which could potentially raise a constitutional issue as well.[11]

In light of these and other concerns, some say the agency would be wise to continue its longstanding policy of relying virtually exclusively on case-by-case adjudication, and litigation in Article III courts where appropriate, in exercise of its competition authority.[12] Otherwise, it might trigger an adverse judicial outcome, with the Supreme Court overruling the 1973 D.C. Court of Appeals decision in *National Petroleum*[13] and holding categorically that the FTC has *no* statutory authority to engage in competition rulemaking. Or it might hold that Congress's purported delegation of such authority to the agency was unconstitutional under a new and stricter nondelegation doctrine.[14]

I disagree with this perspective and argue for boldness on the part of the agency. First, though courts have rarely treated section 5 as a distinct source of competition liability, the provision in fact extends beyond the traditional boundaries

---

7 Tim Wu, *Antitrust via Rulemaking: Competition Catalysts*, 16 Colo. Tech. L.J. 33 (2017).

8 Maureen K. Ohlhausen & James Rill, *Pushing the Limits? A Primer on FTC Competition Rulemaking*, U.S. Chamber of Com. (Aug. 12, 2021), https://www.uschamber.com/assets/archived/images/ftc_rulemaking_white_paper_aug12.pdf. *See also* Lawrence J. Spiwak, *A Change in Direction for the Federal Trade Commission?*, 22 Federalist Soc'y Rev. 304 (Nov. 29, 2021), https://fedsoc.org/commentary/publications/a-change-in-direction-for-the-federal-trade-commission; Richard J. Pierce, Jr., *The Rocky Relationship Between the Federal Trade Commission and Administrative Law*, 83 Geo. Wash. L. Rev. 2026 (2015).

9 Discriminatory Practices in Men's and Boy's Tailored Clothing Industry, 16 C.F.R. pt. 412 (1968).

10 *See* Daniel A. Crane, *Debunking* Humphrey's Estate, 83 Geo. Wash. L. Rev. 1835, 1861 (2015).

11 *See, e.g.*, Gundy v. United States, 139 S. Ct. 2116, 2130–31 (2019) (Alito, J., concurring); *id.*, at 2135–37 (Gorsuch, J., dissenting); Paul v. United States, 140 S. Ct. 342 (2019) (Kavanaugh, J., statement respecting denial of cert.).

12 *See* Ohlhausen & Rill, *supra* note 8, at 16 ("It appears that the nondelegation doctrine may be poised for a revival . . . . This would create a challenging backdrop for the FTC to attempt aggressive new UMC rulemaking.").

13 Nat'l Petroleum Refiners Ass'n v. FTC, 482 F.2d 672 (D.C. Cir. 1973).

14 *See*, Ohlhausen & Rill, *supra* note 8, at 14–16 (discussing the nondelegation doctrine and the constitutional vulnerabilities of section 6(g) of the FTC Act), *See also infra* Part IV.

of the principal antitrust laws, the Sherman and Clayton Acts. In addition, rulemaking has merits, relative to adjudication, that make it a useful policy tool in addressing problems in certain markets that are especially hard to reach through adjudication under existing antitrust doctrines. Second, I argue that the FTC's statutory authority to engage in substantive competition rulemaking is quite strong. Relevant statutory language, despite its terseness and generality, grants that authority; *National Petroleum* endorses that reading; and subsequent congressional legislation leaves the case intact with respect to *competition* rulemaking. Furthermore, the agency's definition of section 6(g) should continue to enjoy judicial deference notwithstanding the current judicial trend toward circumscribing *Chevron*.[15] Third, while the Supreme Court may indeed be leaning toward stiffening the nondelegation doctrine, Congress's delegation of authority to the FTC to promulgate competition rules will likely withstand constitutional challenge even under the new tests favored by Justices Brett Kavanaugh and Neil Gorsuch.

Overcaution comes with distinct downsides: using rulemaking only to make refinements or minor technical changes is unlikely to adequately address the intractable market problems that have been identified in some markets currently dominated by the giant digital platforms.[16] Also, predicting judicial reaction to perceived agency overreach is an impossible task; thus, treading lightly so as not to trigger potential judicial backlash could risk missing opportunities to do what the FTC, as an expert agency, believes to be desirable in fulfilling its mission to protect competition. Two well-known instances of daring – and successful – adoption of rules by the Securities and Exchange Commission to override what were generally considered wrong decisions with significant impact, one by the Supreme Court in *Chiarella v. United States*[17] and the other by the Second Circuit Court of Appeals in *United States v. Chestman*,[18] illustrate well the potential benefits of agency boldness. Finally, the famous Cigarette Rule illustrates that even a "failed" rule (in that it never went into effect) is now widely lauded as one of the FTC's greatest successes because it spurred much-needed legislation by a Congress that learned from the expertise and painstaking work of the agency.[19] Notably, former Judge Richard Posner, not known for interventionist tendencies, has specifically credited the agency with drawing attention to "a serious issue of consumer welfare" in that proceeding.[20]

---

15 Chevron U.S.A., Inc. v. NRDC, 467 U.S. 837 (1984). *See infra* Part III.2.

16 *See, e.g.*, Furman Report, *supra* note 1, at 21–23, 32–37 (discussing the distinctive features of markets served by digital platforms and the reasons *ex post* antitrust enforcement alone is insufficient to reduce concentration and foster competition in those markets).

17 445 U.S. 222 (1980).

18 947 F.2d 551 (2d Cir. 1991), *cert. denied*, 503 U.S. 1004 (1992).

19 *See* Richard A. Posner, *The Federal Trade Commission: A Retrospective*, 72 Antitrust L.J. 761, 769–70 (2005) (noting that the cigarette rulemaking proceeding "had value in drawing attention to a serious issue of consumer welfare, though the rule that emerged from it was quickly preempted by Congress," and that the Commission's innovative effort "deserves credit for having… precipitated" federal legislation); *see also infra* Part V.3.

20 *Id.* at 769.

II. Looking Beyond *Ex Post* Antitrust Enforcement to *Ex Ante* Rulemaking, in Greater Reliance on Section 5 of the FTC Act

Commentators have proposed periodically that the FTC adopt competition (or UMC) rulemaking under the FTC Act to supplement antitrust enforcement by adjudication,[21] and there are sound reasons for that advocacy. Reliance on section 5 – either in the form of adjudication or rulemaking – would allow the agency to take advantage of the breadth of its "unfairness" mandate to expand its competition authority beyond the strictures of the principal antitrust laws, the Sherman and Clayton Acts. Furthermore, rulemaking has specific advantages that are especially helpful for the protection of competition in digital platform markets, primarily because the economic features of those markets often render conventional antitrust enforcement ineffective.[22]

1. The Breadth of Section 5 Relative to the Sherman and Clayton Acts

Section 5 of the FTC Act, in relevant part, simply declares "unfair methods of competition," or UMC, to be unlawful;[23] its statutory language neither explicitly nor implicitly ties UMC to either of the two main antitrust laws, the Sherman[24] and Clayton[25] Acts. However, courts have customarily treated section 5 as though it covered no more than the proscriptions of those two laws, and agency adjudications generally also follow the same approach.[26] Whether this treatment of UMC is correct or not was probably of little practical significance prior to the 1980s since the Sherman and Clayton Acts were interpreted very liberally at that time, which left little that might require coverage under a more expansive section 5.[27] Now that antitrust law, particularly doctrines governing dominant firm conduct and vertical restraints, are given very restrictive judicial interpretations, it has

---

21 *See supra* note 4; Rebecca Haw, *Amicus Briefs and the Sherman Act: Why Antitrust Needs a New Deal*, 89 Tex. L. Rev. 1247 (2011).

22 *See, e.g.*, Rogerson & Shelanski, *supra* note 1; Furman Report, *supra* note 1, at 32–37 (discussing economies of scale and scope, importance of data and incumbents' data advantage, network effects, switching costs, and the cumulative effects of these features on concentration and competition in those markets).

23 15 U.S.C. § 45(a)(1) ("Unfair methods of competition in or affecting commerce, and unfair or deceptive acts or practices in or affecting commerce, are hereby declared unlawful."). Because unfair or deceptive acts or practices (UDAP) implicate the consumer protection mandate of the FTC, rather than its competition-protection mandate, agency rulemaking with respect to UDAP will not be discussed in this chapter.

24 15 U.S.C. §§ 1, 2.

25 15 U.S.C. § 18.

26 *See* William E. Kovacic & Marc Winerman, *Competition Policy and the Application of Section 5 of the Federal Trade Commission Act*, 76 Antitrust L.J. 929, 933–34 (2010).

27 *See* Posner, *supra* note 19, at 765 (stating that the Sherman and Clayton Acts have been so broadly interpreted that "they no longer contain gaps" that might need to be filled by section 5 of the FTC Act); Kovacic & Winerman, *supra* note 26, at 934–35 (explaining the minimal utility of section 5 of the FTC Act when Sherman Act was "in a period of expansive Supreme Court readings").

become more important to determine whether section 5 is merely coextensive with the Sherman and Clayton Acts or whether it has a broader reach. Based on the legislative history of the FTC Act, its statutory language, and the circumstances that led to its enactment, I argue that the only reasonable answer is that section 5 was intended to be broader.

It is undisputed that Congress, in 1914, established the Federal Trade Commission and passed the FTC Act prohibiting "unfair methods of competition" in reaction to *Standard Oil*.[28] Specifically, though it did find a violation, the Supreme Court in *Standard Oil* had applied a rule-of-reason standard to evaluate the legality of the company's alleged anticompetitive conduct under the Sherman Act. Congress thought that resulted in an overly lenient application of the antitrust law.[29] And it passed the FTC Act to supplement the existing antitrust law, with authority to implement the new Act granted to the newly created Federal Trade Commission.[30] As the new FTC Act's main sponsor, Senator Francis Newlands, explained, the legislation was designed to be broader and to "cover[] every practice and method between competitors upon the part of one against the other that is against public morals... or is an offense for which a remedy lies either at law or in equity."[31] He further added that section 5 would "have such an elastic character that it [would] meet every new condition and every new practice that may be invented with a view to gradually bringing about monopoly through unfair competition."[32]

Also supporting the conclusion that section 5 and the main antitrust laws are not coextensive is the fact that Congress chose different ("unfair methods of competition") language for the new Act. Had Congress intended section 5 to cover no more than the *same* types of conduct and apply the *same* legal standards as the Sherman Act, it would logically have used identical, or at least very similar, language. What is more, since the Department of Justice's Antitrust Division already existed in 1914 to bring enforcement action under the Sherman Act, there was little reason for Congress to create a new agency only to grant it primarily duplicative authority and functions.[33] Therefore, although federal courts have customarily analyzed section 5 claims as though they were coextensive with Sherman Act claims, that treatment is contrary to congressional intent. Indeed, the Supreme Court has explicitly acknowledged that section 5 prohibits

---

28 Standard Oil Co. v. United States, 221 U.S. 1 (1911).

29 *See* Marc Winerman, *The Origins of the FTC: Concentration, Cooperation, Control, and Competition*, 71 Antitrust L.J. 1, 13–14 (2003).

30 *See* Neil W. Averitt, *The Meaning of "Unfair Methods of Competition" in Section 5 of the Federal Trade Commission Act*, 21 B.C. L. Rev. 227, 236 (1980); Justin (Gus) Hurwitz, Chevron *and the Limits of Administrative Antitrust*, 76 U. Pitt. L. Rev. 209, 227–28 (2014).

31 Averitt, *supra* note 30, at 272 (quoting 51 Cong. Rec. 11112 (1914)).

32 FTC Act, 63d Cong. 2d Sess. in 51 Cong. Rec. 12024 (July 13, 1914).

33 The original 1914 FTC Act did not include proscriptions against "unfair or deceptive acts or practices"; that was added in the Wheeler-Lea Amendment in 1938. Wheeler-Lea Amendment, Pub. L. No. 447, 52 Stat. 111 (1938).

"not only practices that violate the Sherman Act and other antitrust laws, but also practices that the Commission determines are against public policy for other reasons."[34]

2. Advantages of Supplementing Case-by-Case Adjudication with Rulemaking

Of course, the fact that section 5 should be given a broader construction than the main antitrust laws does not answer the question of why *rulemaking* is necessary or desirable. Those opposed to the FTC engaging in competition rulemaking could contend that any benefit of a broader section 5 standard can be achieved through the adjudication process. In other words, they may argue that the historical method of developing antitrust law through case-by-case decisions under a common law process is adequate.

The overall comparative merits of rulemaking versus adjudication in implementing law and policy is a subject that commentators have long debated,[35] and it is not my purpose to revisit that general discussion. Rather, my aim here is to focus on those advantages of rulemaking that are specifically pertinent to the agency's mission of protecting competition in the modern economy, particularly in markets served by digital platforms. One of the strengths of the common law process – that is, the evolution of law through adjudication or litigation – is that it promotes stability and predictability. Legal principles and standards do not change dramatically from one administration to another; instead, they are gradually refined (and occasionally reversed) over decades of judicial resolution of individual fact-specific cases.[36] The flip side of this virtue, however, is that when conditions exist that call for quicker and more fundamental corrections, gradual and incremental adjustments made through case precedents, characteristic of the common law process, tend to fall short.

For example, it is well understood that network effects, economies of scale, the importance of big data, and other distinct features of some digital platform markets increase their propensity to "tip" to a winner,[37] rendering the rule-of-reason standard particularly difficult to apply.[38] That, in turn, calls into question the effectiveness of the current analysis of anticompetitive conduct in those markets,

---

34 FTC v. Ind. Fed'n of Dentists, 476 U.S. 447, 454 (1986) (internal citation omitted); *see also* FTC v. Sperry & Hutchinson Co., 405 U.S. 233, 244 (1972) (stating that the FTC must "consider[] public values beyond simply those enshrined in the letter or encompassed in the spirit of the antitrust laws.").

35 *See, e.g.*, Chopra & Khan, *supra* note 1; William T. Mayton, *The Legislative Resolution of the Rulemaking Versus Adjudication Problem in Agency Lawmaking*, 1980 Duke L.J. 103, 103–04 (1980); Jeffrey J. Rachlinski, *Rulemaking Versus Adjudication: A Psychological Perspective*, 32 Fla. St. U. L. Rev. 529, 529–30 (2005); Todd Phillips, *A Change of Policy: Promoting Agency Policymaking by Adjudication*, 73 Admin. L. Rev. 495 (2021).

36 Jan M. Rybnicek & Joshua D. Wright, *Defining Section 5 of the FTC Act: The Failure of the Common Law Method and the Case for Formal Agency Guidelines*, 21 Geo. Mason L. Rev. 1287, 1293–98 (2014) (describing the virtues of development of law through the common law process).

37 *See generally* Furman Report, *supra* note 1.

38 *See* Rogerson & Shelanski, *supra* note 1, at 1914.

and the wisdom of judicial reluctance to take seriously certain exclusionary conduct claims and antitrust theories of harm.[39] Waiting for the law to evolve or change around the edges through a common law process may be too little too late when an industry is rapidly transforming or when new economic learning has exposed the errors of specific current doctrines. In those situations, in the absence of appropriate legislative action, rulemaking by an expert agency, backed by solid studies and careful analysis, could be one way to advance competition reform.

Relatedly, another advantage of administrative rulemaking is the relative flexibility of the process and the relative ease with which an agency can revise any rule if it believes that change is necessary. This is a particularly important factor in markets with rapidly changing, and often transformative, technologies. For example, assume the FTC promulgates a rule establishing criteria that would trigger a presumption of illegality under section 5 for specific types of conduct that harm competitors. If technologies, business models, or other conditions subsequently change such that the agency has good reason to believe that one or more of the criteria set forth are no longer apt, amending the rule to adjust to the change would generally be easier than waiting for the right result to emerge from case law evolution or from new legislation passed by Congress.[40] Although the process for notice-and-comment rulemaking, once quite informal, has become increasingly cumbersome,[41] this advantage has not completely disappeared.

Another well-known, general advantage of rulemaking is that it provides cost savings for all parties and thus allows an agency to do more with its limited resources.[42] This advantage is especially significant with respect to antitrust enforcement since antitrust trials are notoriously protracted and costly, with both sides having to incur steep expert fees and other litigation costs.[43] Promulgating rules *ex ante* and combining that with adjudication should help reduce those burdens because it would alleviate the need for experts to establish, in a laborious and costly process in each case, points that are the same in cases involving similar conduct based on similar theories of harm.[44] For this reason, even though promulgating a rule under the APA has become a more onerous process,[45] once a rule is established and has survived judicial review, using it in conjunction with adjudication should still generate real efficiencies.

---

39 *See id.*

40 *See* Nat'l Cable & Telecomms. Ass'n v. Brand X Internet Servs., 545 U.S. 967, 1000–01 (2005) (upholding a significant change in the Federal Communications Commission's interpretation of a statutory provision provided that a reasoned explanation is offered for the change). *See also* Hemphill, *supra* note 4, at 677 (noting that "the FTC is… less subject to the constraint of stare decisis.… The Supreme Court… is not quick to revisit antitrust doctrine… The FTC is freer to change course, provided that the new interpretation is a reasonable understanding of the FTC Act.")

41 *See* Phillips, *supra* note 34, at 498, 522–23.

42 *See Nat'l Petroleum Refiners*, 482 F.2d at 690.

43 *See* Chopra & Khan, *supra* note 1, at 368.

44 *See Nat'l Petroleum Refiners*, 482 F.2d 672 at 690.

45 *See* Phillips, *supra* note 34, at 498 (describing increased procedural requirements for agency rulemaking imposed by courts, Congress, and the White House).

Rulemaking would also allow the FTC to make better and more efficient use of its expertise and its full panoply of agency powers, including the power to collect market data from industry participants and conduct sector studies.[46] In rulemaking, the FTC can better harness the value derived from its many tools and deploy them to deal with problems that may be too large to address through individual enforcement actions. And it could potentially help open markets closed to effective competition by identifying the types of conduct most likely to harm competition that should be defined as UMC, though they may fall outside the scope of the Sherman Act's prohibitions under existing antitrust doctrines.

III. Statutory Authority for Competition (or UMC) Rulemaking

Of course, no matter how desirable rulemaking may be from a policy perspective, administrative agencies may engage in it only if authorized to do so in statutes passed by Congress,[47] and their powers are subject to any limitations that Congress may choose to impose. For example, Congress can statutorily grant an agency the authority to issue only procedural rules, as it did in Title VII of the Civil Rights Act.[48] In authorizing the Equal Employment Opportunity Commission (EEOC) to issue only procedural regulations,[49] Congress was implicitly withholding from it the power to issue substantive rules to further define the prohibitions on discrimination contained in Title VII. Of relevance to our discussion of competition rulemaking by the FTC is that Congress has clearly *not* placed a similar restriction on the FTC in the FTC Act.

Nevertheless, those who oppose or disfavor competition rulemaking by the FTC, including Ohlhausen and Rill, contend that the statutory basis for any such authority for the FTC is tenuous at best. Their arguments are based in part on the terseness and lack of specificity of section 6(g), the provision of the FTC Act that grants the agency rulemaking authority. Furthermore, they argue, the Supreme Court's recent decision in *AMG Capital Management*[50] reinforces this reasoning since *AMG* rejected the agency's broad construction of another provision of the FTC Act, section 13(b) – a provision on which the agency had based its authority for a longstanding enforcement practice. I disagree with this assessment.

---

46 *See* Chopra & Khan, *supra* note 1, at 358 (The FTC can "harness the value of an expert administrative agency to collect market data, analyze it rigorously, and use this analysis to inform enforcement and policymaking."); *but see* Crane, Debunking Humphrey's Estate, *supra* note 10, at 1856–58 (arguing that the FTC is not uniquely expert and has no more expertise than the Department of Justice, Antitrust Division, an executive branch agency).

47 *See* Thomas W. Merrill and Kristin E. Hickman, *Chevron's Domain*, 89 Geo. L.J. 833, 876–77 (2001).

48 Title VII of the Civil Rights Act of 1964, Pub. L. 88-352, 78 Stat. 241 (codified as 42 U.S.C. § 2000e).

49 42 U.S.C. § 2000e–12(a).

50 AMG Capital Management, LLC v. FTC, 593 U.S. __, 141 S. Ct. 1341 (2021). *See also* Steven A. Reed, Scott A. Stempel & Daniel S. Savrin, *The US Supreme Court holds that the FTC lacks the authority to seek equitable monetary relief in cases brought in federal court under FTC Act Section 13(b) (AMG Capital Management)*, e-Competitions April 2021, art. No. 100669.

1. Section 6(g), *National Petroleum*, Magnuson-Moss,[51] and Subsequent Legislation and Developments – All Pointing Toward Competition Rulemaking Authority

Opponents of competition rulemaking are indeed correct in noting that section 6(g) is terse and speaks in general terms. It generally grants the Commission authority to "make rules and regulations for the purpose of carrying out the provisions of [the FTC Act],"[52] and does not explicitly empower the agency to issue *substantive* rules giving content to section 5's prohibitions against "unfair methods of competition" or "unfair or deceptive acts or practices." But neither does it include any *limitation* on its rulemaking authority, unlike Title VII of the Civil Rights Act, which did place limits on the EEOC. The absence of any such limit in section 6(g) or in any other provision of the FTC Act, when Congress did include one for the EEOC in Title VII, strongly suggests that the FTC *is* authorized under section 6(g) to engage in both procedural and substantive UMC rulemaking subject only to the procedures of the APA. Unfortunately, because the FTC itself had seemed uncertain whether section 6(g) was limited in application to procedural rulemaking[53] and, therefore, rarely attempted to promulgate substantive rules, the issue was left unsettled until 1973, when the D.C. Circuit of Appeals decided *National Petroleum.*

In *National Petroleum Refiners Association v. FTC* – a case in which the FTC's authority for substantive rulemaking was directly challenged – the D.C. Circuit Court of Appeals held unequivocally that the FTC's rulemaking authority granted under section 6(g) covered not only procedural, but also substantive, rules.[54] More specifically, the court held that the general grant of rulemaking power in section 6(g) applied to section 5, allowing the agency to issue rules fleshing out the proscriptions of UMC and UDAP in section 5;[55] *National Petroleum* drew no distinctions between UMC and UDAP rulemaking.[56]

---

51 The Magnuson-Moss Warranty–Federal Trade Commission Improvements Act, Pub. L. No. 93-637, 88 Stat. 2183 (1975) (codified as amended at 15 U.S.C. §§ 2301–2312).

52 15 U.S.C. § 46(g).

53 *See* Pierce, *supra* note 8, at 2028 ("For the first fifty years of its existence, the FTC took the position that it lacked the power to issue legislative rules."); *Nat'l Petroleum Refiners*, 482 F.2d at 693 (remarking that "the agency itself did not assert the power to promulgate substantive rules until 1962 and indeed indicated intermittently before that time that it lacked such power," but still holding that the agency had such authority).

54 *Nat'l Petroleum Refiners*, 482 F.2d at 693 ("Section 6(g) plainly authorizes rule-making and nothing in the statute or in its legislative history precludes its use for [issuing substantive rules], the action of the Commission must be upheld."). For a critique of the case, *see* Thomas W. Merrill & Kathryn Tongue Watts, *Agency Rules with the Force of Law: The Original Convention*, 116 Harv. L. Rev. 467, 504–07 (2002).

55 *Nat'l Petroleum Refiners*, 482 F.2d at 676–77 (rejecting the argument that rulemaking power granted under section 6(g) "is limited to specifying the details of the Commission's nonadjudicatory, investigative and informative functions spelled out in the other provisions of Section 6 and should not be read to encompass substantive rulemaking in implementation of Section 5 adjudications. . . . Section 6(g) clearly states that the Commission 'may' make rules and regulations for the purpose of carrying out the provisions of Section 5.")

56 The Rule in question required gas stations to post octane rating numbers on their gasoline pumps, and declared that failure to do so was both an "unfair method of competition" and an "unfair or deceptive act or practice" under section 5 of the FTC Act. *Id.* at 674. The court of appeals held that the FTC's authority to issue rules under section 6(g) covered both procedural and substantive rules, without analyzing the two 'unfairness' bases separately.

Apparently in response to *National Petroleum*, Congress passed the Magnuson-Moss Warranty–Federal Trade Commission Improvements Act (Magnuson-Moss) in 1975. Magnuson-Moss affirmatively granted the FTC power to issue substantive rules with heightened procedural requirements (that is, beyond the notice-and-comment requirements demanded under the APA) with respect to UDAP. Magnuson-Moss expressly stated, however, that it does "not affect any authority of the [FTC] to prescribe rules... with respect to unfair methods of competition."[57]

Ohlhausen and Rill have argued that the Magnuson-Moss Act "is best read as [Congress] declining to endorse the FTC's UMC rulemaking authority and instead leaving the question open for future consideration by the courts."[58] A different interpretation, however, seems equally or more compelling. Magnuson-Moss is generally understood to be Congress's response to *National Petroleum*,[59] a case in which the court held that the FTC had the authority to promulgate substantive rules to give more specificity to section 5, which declares UMC and UDAP unlawful; the case did not draw distinctions between the two "unfairness" bases. The fact that the relevant provision of Magnuson-Moss expressly said that it applies only to UDAP and does not affect UMC strongly implies that *National Petroleum* stands, except to the extent that it has been modified *by* Magnuson-Moss. Since Magnuson-Moss did not touch on the FTC's rulemaking power with respect to UMC, *National Petroleum*'s holding with respect to UMC should remain intact. In other words, section 6 grants substantive competition rulemaking power to the FTC, and the APA's notice-and-comment procedures are sufficient, as Magnuson-Moss did not purport to modify them.

Subsequent related legislative actions by Congress also does not alter this reading of *National Petroleum*. In the late 1970s, the FTC had engaged in extensive regulation of advertising under its UDAP authority.[60] One proposed rule, the infamous KidVid Rule, sought to ban all advertising to young children and advertising of heavily sugared products to older children,[61] leading the *Washington Post* to deride the agency as the "national nanny."[62] Unhappy with what it perceived as the FTC's overzealousness,[63] Congress reacted by passing the FTC

57 Federal Trade Commission Act § 18(a)(2), 15 U.S.C. § 57a. Section 18 was added by the Magnuson-Moss Act in 1975 to add procedural requirements for rulemaking relating to UDAP.

58 Ohlhausen & Rill, *supra* note 8, at 11.

59 *See* Hurwitz, *supra* note 30, at 233–35 (providing legislative history of Magnuson-Moss).

60 *See* J. Howard Beales, The FTC's Use of Unfairness Authority: Its Rise, Fall, and Resurrection, The Marketing and Public Policy Conference (May 30, 2003), http:// www.ftc.gov/public-statements/2003/05/ftcs-use-unfairness-authority-its-rise-fall-and-resurrection (documenting those efforts).

61 The rule was proposed in 1978, Children's Advertising, 43 Fed. Reg. 17,967 (Apr. 27, 1978); and was withdrawn in 1981, Children's Advertising, 46 Fed. Reg. 48,710, 48714 (Oct. 2, 1981).

62 Editorial, *The FTC as National Nanny*, Wash. Post, Mar. 1, 1978.

63 *See* William MacLeod, Elizabeth Brunins & Anna Kertesz, *Three Rules and a Constitution: Consumer Protection Finds its Limits in Competition Policy*, 72 Antitrust L.J. 943, 955 (2005) (discussing the excesses of the proposed KidVid rules).

Improvements Act in 1980,[64] which further enhanced the procedural requirements for UDAP rulemaking and also added other safeguards against potential agency overreach with respect to UDAP.[65] Importantly, just as in Magnuson-Moss, the amendment did not implicate UMC (or competition) rulemaking; the conference report expressly noted that the section being amended "specifically addressed the [FTC's] rulemaking authority over 'unfair or deceptive acts or practices'" and disclaimed any change to the agency's authority with respect to "unfair methods of competition."[66] The more, and perhaps only, reasonable reading of the FTC Improvements Act, therefore, is that *National Petroleum's* holding – affirming the FTC's statutory authority under section 6(g) to engage in substantive rulemaking – remains intact and unchanged by Congress, *with respect to UMC.*

The last significant congressional action relating to the Commission is the 1994 FTC Reauthorization Act.[67] As with the FTC Improvements Act of 1980 and the Magnuson-Moss Act of 1975, the 1994 FTC Reauthorization Act affected only the FTC's UDAP authority, not its UMC (or competition) authority.[68] Thus, it is fair to conclude that section 6(g) does confer authority on the agency to engage in substantive competition rulemaking, subject only to the notice-and-comment requirements of the APA: it was so held in *National Petroleum*, and none of Congress's subsequent legislative actions limited *National Petroleum* with respect to UMC.

2. *Chevron*, Judicial Trend Toward Less Judicial Deference, and *AMG*

While a narrower interpretation of section 6(g) – that the agency is limited to procedural rulemaking – is not impossible, the agency's broader construction to cover substantive rulemaking should receive *Chevron*[69] deference. Discussion of the intricacies of the *Chevron* doctrine is outside the scope of this short chapter, but the doctrine generally states that where congressional intent is unclear, or Congress has specifically left a gap in a statute for the agency to fill, a court must defer to the agency's interpretation of the statute so long as the agency's statutory construction is reasonable or permissible.[70] Given the discussion above – the absence of limits on the FTC's authority in the language

64 Federal Trade Commission Improvements Act of 1980, Pub. L. No. 96-252, 94 Stat. 374 (1980) (codified at 15 U.S.C. § 57a).

65 *Id.* § 18(h) (stripping FTC authority relating to regulation of children's advertisements, among other things); § 21 (including a legislative veto for FTC rules for UDAP).

66 H.R. Rep. No. 96-917, at 1146–47.

67 Federal Trade Commission Act Amendments of 1994, Pub. L. No 103-312, 108 Stat. 1691 (1994).

68 *Id.* § 5(n) (codifying the agency's own policy statement adopted in 1980 defining unfair or deceptive acts or practices in a more limited fashion).

69 Chevron U.S.A., Inc. v. NRDC, 467 U.S. 837 (1984).

70 *Id.* at 842–43. For detailed discussion of *Chevron, see generally* Merrill & Hickman, *supra* note 47.

of section 6(g); the context of section 5; *National Petroleum*; and subsequent congressional actions relating to the FTC, all of which disclaimed any change to the FTC's *competition* authority – it would seem that the Commission's interpretation of section 6(g) as authorizing competition rulemaking would easily qualify for judicial deference under *Chevron*.

One point that has been made against this view is that the agency itself apparently believed it lacked such authority for well over fifty years.[71] But whatever the reason for the agency's earlier reticence, it clearly changed its thinking when it promulgated the rules that underlie the 1973 case of *National Petroleum*. And, in upholding the agency's authority to engage in substantive rulemaking against a legal challenge in *National Petroleum*, the Court of Appeals rejected that argument.[72] Moreover, the Supreme Court has more recently held that even where an agency (the Federal Communications Commission in that case) adopted a new interpretation of an ambiguous statute after years of adhering to a different one, the agency change was not "subjected to more searching review."[73] All that was required for *Chevron* deference was for the agency to "provide reasoned explanation" and "display awareness that it is changing position";[74] and "it suffices that the new policy is permissible under the statute, that there are good reasons for it, and that the agency believes it to be better."[75] This presents a low bar that the FTC should easily clear.

It is true that a majority of the current Supreme Court justices have expressed a more judge-centered view of statutory construction in recent years, and there is momentum toward circumscribing the application of *Chevron*. One limiting principle used, the "major questions doctrine," posits that Congress generally "does not alter the fundamental details of a regulatory scheme in vague terms or ancillary provision – it does not… hide elephants in mouseholes."[76] Nor does Congress intend to delegate to agencies decisions relating to questions of "economic and political significance" in a "cryptic" fashion.[77] Stated differently, under application of the major questions doctrine, *Chevron* deference would not be extended where an agency's interpretation of a vague or ancillary statutory provision would fundamentally alter the statutory scheme or have substantial economic and political significance.

---

71 *See Nat'l Petroleum Refiners*, 482 F.2d at 690.

72 *Id.* ("Our conclusion… is not disturbed by the fact that the agency itself did not assert the power to promulgate substantive rules until 1962 and indeed indicated intermittently before that time that it lacked such power." (footnotes omitted)).

73 FCC v. Fox Television Stations, 556 U.S. 502, 514 (2009).

74 *Id.* at 515.

75 *Id.*

76 Whitman v. Am. Trucking Ass'ns, 531 U.S. 457, 468 (2001). *See* Alison Gocke, Chevron*'s Next Chapter: A Fig Leaf for the Nondelegation Doctrine*, 55 U.C. Davis L. Rev. 955, 969 (2021) (discussing how the major questions doctrine limits *Chevron*).

77 FDA v. Brown & Williamson Tobacco Corp., 529 U.S. 120, 160 (2000).

Even under this limiting principle, it is reasonable to predict that an interpretation of section 6(g) that would authorize substantive competition rulemaking should enjoy *Chevron* deference. Empowering the FTC to issue substantive rules to help define what constitutes UMC can hardly be said to "alter the fundamental details of a regulatory scheme," since the core of the FTC Act declares UMC (and UDAP) to be unlawful and directs the FTC to prohibit them. As to whether such an interpretation would impact questions of "economic and political significance," no definitive answer seems possible. Much would depend on the details of the specific rule in question. The authority to engage in competition rulemaking, by itself, should not have the kind of economic or political impact that the Court assumes Congress could not have intended to delegate to an agency. However, if a proposed rule would effectively restructure an industry or require it to alter its fundamental business model, the major questions doctrine could well apply to deny *Chevron* deference.

A more challenging argument in support of a narrow interpretation of section 6(g) that has been asserted is that a broader construction would be in tension with the Supreme Court's 2021 *AMG Capital Management*[78] decision. In *AMG*, the Supreme Court unanimously rejected the FTC's reading of section 13(b), on which the agency had based its longstanding practice of filing section 5 suits directly in federal court to seek monetary relief.[79] Section 13(b) provides that the Commission may seek a "permanent injunction" in appropriate cases in federal court.[80] Other provisions in the regulatory scheme authorize the agency to seek monetary relief, such as restitution and disgorgement, in federal court only *after* a final cease-and-desist order has been issued in an administrative process, and the order is allegedly breached.[81] To bypass the administrative process set forth for eventually pursuing monetary relief, the FTC creatively construed the word "injunction" in section 13(b) to include equitable monetary relief, which would then permit the agency to proceed directly to federal court to file section 5 suit and request monetary relief. The Supreme Court rejected this statutory construction based primarily on the meaning of the word "injunction" and on the entire regulatory scheme.[82] The word "injunction" clearly does not cover monetary relief, and the regulatory scheme provides a specific path for obtaining monetary relief, which does not involve sidestepping the administrative process. Ohlhausen and others essentially argue that *AMG* shows the Court has become much stricter in its judicial review of agency interpretation of its governing statutes, and that to construe section 6(g) broadly to cover substantive rulemaking would be inconsistent with current judicial thinking.[83]

78 AMG, 141 S. Ct. 1341. *See also* Reed et al., *supra* note 50.

79 *Id.* at 1344.

80 15 U.S.C. § 53(b).

81 15 U.S.C. § 45(l).

82 *AMG*, 141 S. Ct. at 1347–49.

83 Ohlhausen & Rill, *supra* note 8, at 11–12. *See also* Reed et al., *supra* note 50 (discussing *AMG*).

Such a reading of the implications of *AMG* seems overbroad; judicial decisions on statutory challenges to rulemaking are not made in the abstract but depend on context and on the details of the rule in question. And there are substantial differences between *AMG* and the issue of the agency's rulemaking authority under section 6(g). In *AMG*, a key question was the meaning of the word "injunction" used in section 13(b). As the Court said, "[a]n 'injunction' is not the same as an award of equitable monetary relief."[84] Thus, permission to apply directly to federal court for an injunction, granted under section 13(b), cannot be read to include authorization to obtain *monetary* relief. Further supporting this conclusion is the structure of other sections of the FTC Act setting forth the process for obtaining monetary relief in federal court – it involves adjudication in an administrative proceeding to obtain a cease-and-desist order; and then, if such an order is violated, suit in federal court seeking monetary relief. Whatever one may think of the real-world implications (and the wisdom or lack thereof) of this two-step regulatory scheme in obtaining monetary relief, *legal* support for the agency's interpretation seems weak.

In contrast, support for the FTC's interpretation of section 6(g) is much stronger. The language in section 6(g) specifically states that the agency has the power "to make rules and regulations for the purpose of carrying out the provision of [the FTC Act]."[85] In the absence of any limits on that authority, an interpretation that it extends to *all* rulemaking, substantive and procedural, seems reasonable; it is certainly not peculiar or inexplicable as was the agency's construction of the word "injunction" to include monetary relief. Therefore, even in light of *AMG*, the FTC's statutory interpretation of section 6(g) as encompassing substantive competition lawmaking should receive *Chevron* deference.

IV. Constitutionality and the Nondelegation Doctrine

Aside from raising questions about statutory authority, those opposed to competition rulemaking by the FTC also contend that, given the vagueness and breadth of section 6(g), any rule promulgated pursuant to it could be vulnerable to a constitutional challenge under the nondelegation doctrine.[86] The argument is that, though the nondelegation doctrine has rarely stood as an impediment in the past, a majority of the justices on the present Supreme Court have signaled their dissatisfaction with the current test and their desire to modify and more aggressively apply the doctrine in the future.[87] While predictions about imminent changes to the nondelegation doctrine may be correct, warnings of their implications should the agency attempt to promulgate rules under section 6(g) are overstated.

84 *AMG*, 141 S. Ct. at 1347.

85 15 U.S.C. § 46(g).

86 *See* Ohlhausen & Rill, *supra* note 8, at 14.

87 *See id.*, at 14–16.

The nondelegation doctrine is derived from the principle that the U.S. Constitution vests legislative powers exclusively in Congress,[88] powers which Congress may not delegate to any other branch of the government or entity.[89] To operationalize this doctrine, the Supreme Court held long ago that if Congress sets forth "by legislative act an *intelligible principle* to which the person or body authorized [to legislate] is directed to conform, such legislative action [would not constitute] a forbidden delegation of legislative power."[90] In theory, that means that if no "intelligible principle" is found in a statute, then Congress's attempted delegation of legislative power in that statute to any agency (or any other branch of government) would be unconstitutional as a violation of the nondelegation doctrine. In practice, the doctrine has rarely been successfully invoked.[91] Congress has passed many statutes giving federal administrative agencies tremendous lawmaking-like authority, with little guidance, in connection with their implementation of statutes passed by Congress. Yet, except twice in 1935,[92] the Supreme Court has consistently rejected constitutional challenges based on the nondelegation doctrine.[93]

Recently, however, a majority of the justices on the Supreme Court have registered dissatisfaction with the doctrine and voiced a desire to replace the lax intelligible principle test with a formulation that would rein in the perceived boundless delegation of policymaking powers to agencies. In *Gundy*, although a plurality of the Supreme Court upheld the constitutionality of the statute in question against a nondelegation challenge,[94] four justices (Gorsuch, Roberts and Thomas, who dissented, and Alito, who concurred) criticized the ineffective application of the doctrine.[95] Justice Kavanaugh, who did not participate in *Gundy*, also called for replacing the intelligible principle test in an individual statement he issued in a denial of certiorari in *Paul v. United States*[96] shortly after *Gundy*.

In his dissent in *Gundy*, Gorsuch proposed replacing the intelligible principle standard with one that distinguishes between important policy decisions and decisions that fill in mere details.[97] Under this suggested standard, Congress's

---

88 U.S. Const. art. I, § 1 ("All legislative Powers herein granted shall be vested in a Congress of the United States.").

89 *See, e.g.*, *Whitman v. Am. Trucking Ass'ns*, 531 U.S. at 472 (stating that the text of Article I, § 1 vesting all legislative powers granted to Congress "permits no delegation of those powers").

90 J. W. Hampton, Jr. & Co. v. United States, 276 U.S. 394, 409 (1928) (emphasis added).

91 *See* Kristin E. Hickman, *Nondelegation as Constitutional Symbolism*, 89 Geo. Wash. L. Rev. 1079, 1081 (2021).

92 A. L. A. Schechter Poultry Corp. v. United States, 295 U.S. 495, 542 (1935); Pan. Refin. Co. v. Ryan, 293 U.S. 388, 433 (1935).

93 *See Gundy*, 139 S. Ct. at 2121.

94 *Id.*

95 *Id.* at 2131 (Alito, J., concurring) (concurring with decision but would support reconsidering the doctrine); *id.* at 2138–42 (Gorsuch, J., dissenting) (severely criticizing the intelligible principles test).

96 140 S. Ct. 342 (2019) (Kavanaugh, J., statement respecting denial of cert.).

97 Gundy, 139 S. Ct. at 2141–42 (Gorsuch, J., dissenting).

attempts to delegate important policy decisions to agencies or any other governmental body or official would be unconstitutional while delegating decisions that merely supply details to a statute passed by Congress presumably would be permissible. Soon after *Gundy* was handed down, in a case that raised the same issues, Kavanaugh agreed with the Court's denial of certiorari in light of *Gundy*, but took the opportunity to write separately that the nondelegation doctrine "may warrant further consideration in future cases."[98] Kavanaugh's proposed solution would draw directly from the major questions doctrine that is used to qualify *Chevron* and substitute that principle in the place of "intelligible principles" as the basis for the nondelegation doctrine.[99] The apparent purpose of both Gorsuch's and Kavanaugh's proposals is to curtail perceived agency activism and to restrain agency discretion.

Even in light of this judicial trend toward a less permissive nondelegation doctrine, it seems unlikely that UMC rules promulgated by the FTC would be found, categorically, to violate the nondelegation doctrine without regard to the details and context of the actual rule at issue.[100] With respect to the "major questions" analogy, the FTC's interpretation of section 6(g), endorsed by the D.C. Circuit Court of Appeals, as generally authorizing substantive competition rulemaking can hardly be said to present a "major questions doctrine" problem. The "major questions doctrine," as a limiting principle for *Chevron*, posits that courts should not read vague or minor statutory provisions to "alter the fundamental details of a regulatory scheme,"[101] or to delegate decisions relating to questions of "economic and political significance" in a "cryptic" fashion.[102]

Adjusted for use as the governing standard for the nondelegation doctrine in a rulemaking context, "major questions" would probably be best read as finding a delegation of rulemaking authority unconstitutional if it effectuates a fundamental alteration of a regulatory scheme, or has significant economic or political impact. So understood, adding competition rulemaking to the agency's toolkit, alone, cannot reasonably be said to "alter the fundamental details" of the statutory scheme of section 5. After all, the core of the FTC Act is to proscribe "unfair methods of competition" and "unfair or deceptive acts or practices," and the FTC is charged with carrying out that task. Giving the agency a supplemental means to carry out its statutory mandate is surely within the regulatory scheme that is envisioned. It would also be difficult to say that all rulemaking, in the abstract, involves issues of significant economic or political impact; it depends on the details and the context of the specific rule in question.

---

98 *Paul v. United States*, 140 S. Ct. at 342 (Kavanaugh, J., statement respecting denial of cert.).

99 *See id.*

100 *See generally* Hickman, *supra* note 91 (arguing that alternatives proposed by Gorsuch and Kavanaugh to the intelligible principle standard for the nondelegation doctrine would likely make symbolic and incremental changes only).

101 *Whitman v. Am. Trucking Ass'ns*, 531 U.S. at 468.

102 *FDA v. Brown & Williamson Tobacco Corp.*, 529 U.S. at 160.

With respect to Gorsuch's proposed replacement of the intelligible principle standard with one that focuses on drawing distinctions between important policy decisions and mere details,[103] the practical application of such a standard would be challenging since the line between making important policy decisions and filling in details is often unclear. I would argue that empowering the FTC to flesh out the standard for UMC through rulemaking, as a supplement to case-by-case adjudication, cannot be characterized as giving the agency "unbounded policy choices"[104] or as "delegation running riot"[105] that Gorsuch has found unacceptable. Thus, even if the Supreme Court were to adopt stricter limits to agency discretion following either Gorsuch's or Kavanaugh's suggested modifications to the nondelegation doctrine, the Supreme Court is unlikely to find claims of competition rulemaking authority to be categorically unconstitutional.

V. The Case for Boldness

Assuming that both statutory and constitutional bases exist for competition rulemaking, the issue of how bold or restrained the agency should be in exercising that authority is still a subject of debate. Some prefer a cautious approach, warning of potential backlash from the courts if the agency is seen as overreaching.[106] Also mentioned as a reason for restraint is the perceived need to avoid institutional conflict between the FTC and its sister agency in protecting competition in the Department of Justice, which is bound by Sherman and Clayton Act case precedents.[107] Conceivably, a cautious strategy could consist of simply taking favorable case law and "codifying" it into regulation to make enforcement easier and more efficient in similar cases in the future. Or it could involve issuing rules confined to making technical changes or modest adjustments to existing standards – such as a rule to clarify and refine the technical discount attribution test for evaluating the legality of bundled discounts.[108]

I argue, however, for bolder action. One problem with a timid approach is that it is unlikely to succeed in addressing the major market problems that have been identified and that adjudication alone has failed to resolve. As for concerns about

103 *Gundy*, 139 S. Ct. at 2141–42 (Gorsuch, J., dissenting).

104 *Id.* at 2133.

105 *Id.* at 2148.

106 *See* Ohlhausen & Rill, *supra* note 8, at 18 (recommending that the agency focus on case-by-case adjudication and engage in rulemaking only when Congress has granted "clearly-authorized, targeted rulemaking authority where appropriate").

107 *See, e.g., id.*, at 17–18.

108 *See* Cascade Health Solutions v. PeaceHealth, 515 F.3d 883, 899 (9th Cir. 2008) (analyzing and adopting the discount attribution test to determine the legality of a bundled discount); David Reichenberg & Lauren J. Stiroh, *Checking in on* PeaceHealth*: Providing Some Clearer Guidance to Bundling Sellers*, Antitrust Source 1 (Oct. 2019) (discussing and clarifying the discount attribution test). *See also* Gary A. MacDonald, Neal R. Stoll & Jessica Biggio, *The US Court of Appeals for the Ninth Circuit applies a cost-based test to attempted monopolization claim premised on multiproduct discounting (Cascade Health Solutions / PeaceHealth)*, e-Competitions September 2007, art. No. 45595.

potential judicial backlash, attempting to predict judicial reaction is somewhat unproductive. The Securities and Exchange Commission (SEC), for example, has promulgated rules to almost openly override judicial decisions, yet suffered no backlash. Indeed, even a "failed" rule in the sense that it was withdrawn and never enforced – the Cigarette Rule – is widely lauded as one of the FTC's major successes because the agency's painstaking work was evidently so well regarded that its Final Rule was adopted by Congress and preempted. There is, thus, precedent for creative rulemaking by the FTC in exceptional circumstances.

1. The Problem with Technical or Modest Refinements Only

The problem with using rules only to tinker around the edges is that it is unlikely to be adequate. Calls for the FTC to supplement adjudication with competition rulemaking pursuant to section 6(g) are largely motivated by the conviction that *ex post* enforcement of the Sherman and Clayton Acts has resulted in substantial underenforcement of the antitrust laws. In particular, there is concern that current antitrust enforcement is incapable of protecting against certain types of anticompetitive conduct or of promoting competition in some problem markets, such as those served by digital platforms.[109] Though the rubric of the principal antitrust laws is elastic and capable of more expansive coverage than current enforcement would suggest, the default rule-of-reason standard and the consumer welfare paradigm are difficult to apply for purposes of identifying exclusionary conduct or anticompetitive mergers in a modern economy, especially in digital platform markets.[110] And promulgating rules only to make technical or other minor refinements to existing antitrust doctrines would not resolve the intractable market problems that seem to elude conventional antitrust application and solutions. To succeed where traditional antitrust enforcement has failed and to open some markets to competition, bolder use of competition rulemaking may be needed.[111]

A bold approach does not necessarily entail defining, categorically, certain types of acts as per se unfair methods of competition, or otherwise generating inflexible, bright-line tests.[112] It can create rebuttable presumptions of illegality for certain competitively suspicious conduct and set forth the conditions or criteria which, if satisfied, would trigger such a presumption.[113] By reducing the burden of proof for the agency if the specified conditions or criteria exist, such a rule can have significant practical impact without invoking per se illegality treatment, which is often not ideal for resolving issues of anticompetitiveness and unfairness.

---

109 *See generally* Rogerson & Shelanski, *supra* note 1.

110 *See* Chopra & Khan, *supra* note 1, at 359.

111 *See* Wu, *supra* note 7, at 61 (noting the "potential… [of the usage] of rules to pursue the goals of antitrust… lies in opening markets long-closed to effective competition, and the consequent gains for consumers and the economy.").

112 Chopra & Khan, *supra* note 1, at 366–67 (quoting former FTC Commissioner Philip Elman, who said that rulemaking can be related to "standards, guidelines, pointers, criteria, or presumptions.").

113 Vaheesan, *supra* note 4, at 651.

For example, the issue of noncompete agreements – contract terms prohibiting employees from working for their employer's competitors after leaving the employer – has long been a troubling one.[114] As vertical restraints, they are extremely difficult to challenge under the Sherman Act. But these restrictive agreements can often raise serious fairness issues with respect to employees as their future employment prospects are limited as a result. They also have adverse competition implications for rivals of the firms imposing the noncompete agreements because those agreements restrict the rivals' potential labor pool. Thus, promulgating a rule that would ease the burden of proof for the FTC challenging a noncompete agreement as a section 5 violation would be desirable.

The rule need not and should not be a blanket, bright-line one declaring *all* noncompete agreements to be per se unlawful since some noncompete agreements can have legitimate justifications, as common law has long recognized.[115] Their usage, for example, may induce employers to provide valuable employee training, which they might be reluctant to do absent some post-employment restrictions, because of concerns that the training provided could benefit a competitor who subsequently hires the employee.[116] A noncompete clause could also be justified to ensure that an employer's trade secrets, to which an employee has access, are protected from a competitor for whom the employee may work absent any noncompete restrictions binding the employee.[117]

Finding the right balance in adjudication under the Sherman Act is difficult and time-consuming, and tends to lead to underenforcement. The FTC could supplement adjudication with the use of its various policymaking tools, including its authority to collect data, and conduct studies and hearings,[118] in order to better understand the conditions under which a noncompete agreement is most likely or least likely to have legitimate business justifications. Informed by that research and analysis, it can then better balance the competing interests and engage in rulemaking.

For example, if the information collected and analyzed confirms the common wisdom that minimum-wage, low-skill employees generally have little access to trade secrets or customer information and typically receive no expensive employer-paid training, then that could support a rule providing that noncompete agreements are per se unlawful under section 5 when they are demanded of employees below

114 *See, e.g.*, Alan B. Krueger & Eric A. Posner, *A Proposal for Protecting Low-Income Workers from Monopsony and Collusion* 7–8, 10–11 (Hamilton Project, Policy Proposal 2018-05, Feb. 2018), https://www.hamiltonproject.org/assets/files/protecting_low_income_workers_from_monopsony_collusion_krueger_posner_pp.pdf; Council of Economic Advisers Issue Brief, Labor Market Monopsony: Trends, Consequences, and Policy Responses 5–6 (Oct. 2016) [hereinafter CEA Issue Brief], https://obamawhitehouse.archives.gov/sites/default/files/page/files/20161025_monopsony_labor_mrkt_cea.pdf.

115 *See* CEA Issue Brief, *supra* note 114, at 8 (asserting that evidence of noncompete agreements required of low-income workers is an "indication of an unreasonable and likely unjustified use" because they were unlikely to be needed "to protect employers' trade secrets and investments in employee training.").

116 Krueger & Posner, *supra* note 114, at 10.

117 *Id.*

118 FTC Act, 15 U.S.C. §§ 46(b), 49, 57b-1(c).

certain wage and skill levels. Or, if the data is less conclusive, the rule could provide, in the alternative, that a noncompete clause required of employees under those conditions creates a rebuttable presumption of unreasonableness or unfairness. To the extent that such a rule is supported by reliable studies and sufficient data, it is more likely to gain a court's confidence and deference.

As another example, exclusive contracts or exclusive dealing have emerged as another problem area, especially when they are exploited by dominant digital platforms. But it is very difficult to prove that type of practice violates the Sherman Act, either as a vertical restraint or as exclusionary dominant firm conduct.[119] Drafting a rule that would create a presumption of unreasonableness and illegality in specific contexts, shown through careful studies to unfairly hinder competition, could help provide a valuable solution.

For instance, commentators have observed that, in markets served by digital platforms, practices that discourage users from multi-homing tend to reduce competition against the dominant platform.[120] Assuming that the agency has sufficient supporting data and other evidence, it could consider rules setting forth the conditions under which a dominant platform's practice of requiring or encouraging users to single-home (effectively, exclusive contracting) would be presumptively unreasonable. In other words, where the FTC's expertise and work inform the agency that, under specified conditions, certain conduct creates a risk of substantial harm, a rule might be issued to treat the conduct as presumptively unlawful when those conditions are satisfied. Such a rule could have substantial practical impact as it removes the need for the FTC to prove, in each individual instance, that the harm to competition would be more likely than not,[121] though the dominant platform would remain free to rebut that presumption.

Of course, there are many complexities involved in rulemaking in technically complicated markets, and it is not the purpose of this short chapter to propose specific rules or to prioritize areas deemed most worthy of the agency's rulemaking efforts with respect to UMC.[122] Rather, it is simply to touch on a few areas to

119 *See* Rogerson & Shelanski, *supra* note 1, at 1937–38 (discussing the difficulty of applying the rule of reason to practices, such as exclusive dealing, in digital platform markets, which tend to tip to durable monopoly).

120 *See* Giulio Federico, Fiona Scott Morton & Carl Shapiro, *Antitrust and Innovation: Welcoming and Protecting Disruption*, *in* 20 Innovation Policy and the Economy 125, 158 (Josh Lerner & Scott Stern eds., 2020) (noting that "[i]n platform markets, conduct aimed at hindering multihoming on one side of the market may be a particularly effective exclusionary strategy."); Rogerson & Shelanski, *supra* note 1, at 1938 ("It is widely recognized that any practice that requires or encourages users to single-home instead of multi-home will reduce competition."); Furman Report, *supra* note 1, at 37.

121 *See, e.g.*, Bill Baer et al., Restoring Competition in the United States: A vision for antitrust enforcement for the next administration and Congress 13, Washington Center for Equitable Growth (Nov. 2020) (advocating for legislation that would have that effect), https://equitablegrowth.org/wp-content/uploads/2020/11/111920-antitrust-report.pdf

122 Another attractive target for competition rulemaking can be found in the area of pay-for-delay reverse settlement agreements. *See generally* Hemphill, *supra* note 4. Hemphill has suggested rulemaking that would, for example adopt a presumption that when a brand-name pharmaceutical firm's payment to a generic firm is contemporaneous with a generic firm's agreement to delay entry, there is a presumption that the payment is consideration for delayed entry, and not for goods or services provided to the brand-name firm. *Id.* at 633. *See also* Chopra & Khan, *supra* note 1, at 372.

illustrate in general terms how competition rulemaking, if exercised with care, might be of use. Given the potential benefits of competition rules as an additional policy tool for the FTC, there is more to be gained from boldness than from overcaution and self-restraint.

As for the argument that competition rulemaking by the FTC could lead to undesirable divergence with the Department of Justice (DOJ) on legal standards,[123] there is a fundamental flaw with the premise that all UMC claims brought by the FTC under section 5 must be subject to the *same* legal standards as antitrust claims brought by the DOJ under the Sherman Act. Nothing in the FTC Act links UMC to the antitrust laws, except for a minor antitrust savings provision.[124] The legislative history of the Act, as previously discussed, also showed that Congress clearly intended section 5 to extend more broadly than the Sherman Act;[125] the courts' customary treatment of both laws as coextensive, therefore, was simply a judicial construct[126] that is not binding on the FTC.[127] The Supreme Court, in fact, has stated that section 5 reaches more expansively than the Sherman Act.[128]

Unfortunately, except for a brief period in the 1970s, the FTC largely acquiesced in this judicial construct. After suffering a few humiliating losses in federal courts in the early 1980s when it initiated a number of standalone section 5 cases,[129] the FTC thereafter rarely asserted claims in reliance solely on legal principles and standards outside of the Sherman Act,[130] preferring to retreat to the safe space of equating section 5 with the Sherman Act.[131] Nevertheless,

---

123 Ohlhausen & Rill, *supra* note 8, at 17–18.

124 FTC Act § 11 (codified as amended at 15 U.S.C. § 51) (stating that nothing in the FTC Act shall be "construed to alter, modify, or repeal the said antitrust Acts").

125 *See supra* notes 23–34 and accompanying text.

126 *See* Hurwitz, *supra* note 30, at 255 ("Section 5 was enacted precisely to extend to conduct outside the scope of the antitrust laws – and nothing in Section 5 references the antitrust laws. It is surely the case that current understandings of Section 5 incorporate the antitrust laws. But this is a judicial construction of the statute.").

127 *Nat'l Cable & Telecomms. Ass'n v. Brand X Internet Servs.*, 545 U.S. at 982 ("[C]ourt's prior judicial construction of a statute trumps an agency construction otherwise entitled to Chevron deference only if the prior court decision holds that its construction follows from the unambiguous terms of the statute and thus leaves no room for agency discretion.").

128 *FTC v. Ind. Fed'n of Dentists*, 476 U.S. at 454 (stating that FTC Act § 5 proscribes "not only practices that violate the Sherman Act and the other antitrust laws, but also practices that the Commission determines are against public policy for other reasons.").

129 *See infra* notes 133–135.

130 *See* Rambus, Inc. v. FTC, 522 F.3d 456, 462 (D.C. Cir. 2008) (noting that the FTC had limited its claims to conduct that would violate section 2 of the Sherman Act); Daniel Crane, *Reflections on Section 5 of the FTC Act and the FTC's Case Against* Intel, CPI ANTITRUST J. 3 (Feb. 2010 (2)) (observing that "the Commission has frequently tied itself to the Sherman Act" perhaps because it has been "shell-shocked by its treatment in the courts when it has invoked an independent Section 5"). *See also* David S. Turetsky, Jeffrey L. Kessler, A. Paul Victor, Eamon O'Kelly & Aldo A. Badini, *The US Court of Appeals for the DC Circuit overturns an FTC's ruling in the computer memory market for failing to prove unlawful monopolization (Rambus)*, E-COMPETITIONS APRIL 2008, art. No. 37369.

131 *See* Kovacic & Winerman, *supra* note 26, at 933–34 ("The Supreme Court last examined the FTC's application of Section 5 to address allegations of improper exclusion by a dominant firm in 1927. . . One would be hard-pressed to come up with a list of ten adjudicated decisions that involved the FTC's application of Section 5 in which the FTC prevailed and the case can be said to have had a notable impact, either in terms of doctrine or economic effects.").

the argument against competition rulemaking, based on the perceived need to minimize divergence in legal standards between the FTC and the DOJ, is not persuasive.

2. Addressing the Judicial Backlash Concern

One policy argument that has been made against boldness in FTC rulemaking is that an overly activist agenda by the agency might invite judicial backlash.[132] With respect to competition policy, much has been made of the fact that the Commission suffered three major losses before the circuit courts in the 1970s when it attempted to use section 5 expansively to reach conduct beyond the Sherman Act, in *Ethyl*,[133] *Boise Cascade*,[134] and *Official Airline Guides*.[135] But there is a risk of overgeneralizing from a few cases to predict judicial hostility toward any perceived agency overreach.[136] While the question of how bold or restrained any agency should be in exercising its policymaking powers does have a political dimension, and the composition of the federal judiciary, especially the Supreme Court, is a factor to be considered, it would be a mistake to overthink how courts might react. The FTC has an institutional advantage over courts in that it can "collect and aggregate information and... study market trends and industry practices over the long term and outside the context of litigation."[137] All this makes regulation by rulemaking a better choice than adjudication in certain situations. And if the agency promulgates a rule after careful study and analysis, courts may well defer to it even if the agency may appear to "overreach," as will be discussed later. At the very least, the FTC should not be so quick to assume otherwise and to exercise unnecessary self-restraint.

As a general rule, it seems improper and unwise for an agency to promulgate a rule to repudiate any Supreme Court decision with which it happens to disagree, and I am not advocating such action. However, the Supreme Court itself has recognized that even where a court has construed a statute one way, an agency's subsequent different interpretation of the same statute is still entitled to *Chevron* deference unless "the prior court decision holds that its construction follows from the unambiguous terms of the statute and thus leaves no room for agency

---

132 *See* Ohlhausen & Rill, *supra* note 8, at 2 ("The FTC has a troubling history of rulemaking overreach, one that the courts and Congress have both stepped in to limit.")

133 E.I. du Pont de Nemours & Co. v. FTC, 729 F.2d 128 (2d Cir. 1984) (known as the *Ethyl* case).

134 Boise Cascade Corp. v. FTC, 637 F.2d 573 (9th Cir. 1980).

135 Official Airline Guides v. FTC, 630 F.2d 920 (2d Cir. 1980). With respect to its consumer protection agenda, the agency's perceived overreach in that arena had led Congress to curtail some of the FTC's authority and to add burdensome, procedural requirements to UDAP rulemaking that have discouraged their use. *See supra* notes 60–66 and accompanying text.

136 *See* Thomas N. Dahdough, *The FTC and Its Critics: Just Who Are the Radicals Here?*, 20 COMPETITION: J. ANTI. & UNFAIR COMP. L. SEC. ST. B. CAL. J. 1 (2011) (providing in-depth analysis of *Ethyl, Boise Cascade, and Official Airline Guides*).

137 *See* Chopra & Khan, *supra* note 1, at 369; Hemphill, *supra* note 4, at 633.

discretion."[138] This creates space for an agency to use rulemaking creatively to lessen the potential significant impact of certain adverse court decisions, if the decision greatly hampers its ability to implement the statute as Congress intended. Two instances involving rulemaking by the SEC in response to problematic judicial decisions,[139] discussed below, provide a striking counterpoint to the argument that the FTC should tread lightly so as not to provoke an adverse Supreme Court decision.

A. *SEC "Overriding" Chiarella with Promulgation of Rule 14e-3*

In a well-known securities case, *Chiarella v. United States*, the Supreme Court held that "fraud" under section 10b of the Securities and Exchange Act (Exchange Act), the provision that governs insider trading, required a fiduciary duty between the parties to a securities transaction.[140] Without such a duty, trading using material nonpublic information could not constitute fraud and, therefore, could not violate section 10b. In a strong dissent, former Chief Justice Warren Burger would not require such a duty.[141] The potential impact of the majority decision was huge because insider trading often involves tender offers, and the purchase of the *target's* stock by a trader based on material nonpublic information concerning the tender offer obtained from an insider of the *acquiring* company. Because these traders owe no fiduciary duty to the *target* company whose stock they bought, *Chiarella* meant that many common instances of insider trading would escape the reach of section 10b. The SEC decided to partially address the *Chiarella* problem by turning to a different provision of the Exchange Act, section 14e, which bans fraud in tender offers, and to promulgate Rule 14e-3. Rule 14e-3 can best be summarized as finding a violation of section 14e if someone "trades on the basis of material nonpublic information concerning a pending offer that he knows or has reason to know has been acquired" from an insider of the offeror "*without regard to whether the trader owes a pre-existing fiduciary duty to respect the confidentiality of the information.*"[142]

In effect, the SEC passed the new rule to define "fraud" in tender offers, banned in section 14e, with*out* a requirement of fiduciary duty after the Supreme Court held in *Chiarella* that "fraud" under section 10b required such a duty. With the promulgation of Rule 14e-3, the SEC was able to ban tender offer insider trading in *Chiarella*'s situation, despite the absence of any fiduciary duty owed by the

---

138 *Nat'l Cable & Telecomms. Ass'n v. Brand X Internet Servs.*, 545 U.S. at 982.

139 Securities and Exchange Act of 1934, Rules 14e-3 and 10b-5(2).

140 Chiarella v. United States, 445 U.S. 222, 230 (1980) (finding that use of material, nonpublic information without disclosure for their own benefit "in connection with the purchase or sale of securities may operate as a fraud actionable under § 10(b)… . But such liability is premised upon a duty to disclose arising from a relationship of trust and confidence between the parties to a transaction.")

141 *Id.* at 240 (Burger, C.J., dissenting) ("[A] person who has misappropriated nonpublic information has an absolute duty to disclose that information or to refrain from trading.").

142 United States v. O'Hagan, 521 U.S. 642, 669 (1997).

trader to the target company. Though Rule 14e-3 was obviously drafted to sidestep *Chiarella* in insider trading cases involving tender offers, the Supreme Court expressly upheld its validity in *O'Hagan*, holding that Rule 14e-3 was a "'means reasonably designed to prevent' fraudulent trading on material, nonpublic information in the tender offer context."[143] The SEC's response to *Chiarella* by passing Rule 14e-3 was bold, but it successfully addressed a major practical problem in insider trading enforcement caused by the Supreme Court in *Chiarella*. Notably, the Court endorsed the rule, and there was no backlash.

B. *SEC "Overriding" Chestman on Spouses, with Rule 10b5-2*

Another example of an agency's daring adoption of a rule to effectively override a problematic court decision also involved the SEC and insider trading. In *United States v. Chestman*, in the context of an insider trading case based on the misappropriation theory, the Second Circuit Court of Appeals surprised and shocked many by declaring that "marriage does not, without more, create a fiduciary relationship."[144] Insider trading liability under the misappropriation theory requires finding that the misappropriator of the inside information owed a fiduciary duty to the source of the information.[145]

In practical terms, *Chestman* meant that so long as corporate insiders and their spouses collude in insider trading and in the story they tell, they could essentially engage in the activity with impunity. At the very least, proving liability would present major problems of proof for the government. The corporate insider would disclose material, nonpublic information to his or her spouse, but would refrain from trading himself or herself. Instead, the spouse would trade the stock, but in the spouse's individual account. Neither could be liable under the classical insider theory because the corporate insider did not trade, and the spouse, who traded, was not a classical insider.[146] Both spouses would then maintain that the information was shared in the course of routine conversation, and that the insider did not intend to generate a personal benefit, which is requisite for finding insider trading liability under the tipper/tippee theory.[147] Because the misappropriation theory of liability – the remaining theory of liability – requires the existence of a fiduciary duty owed by the misappropriator

143 *Id.* at 672–73.

144 *Chestman*, 947 F.2d at 568.

145 *Id.* at 566 ("Under [misappropriation] theory, a person violates Rule 10b-5 when he misappropriates material nonpublic information in breach of a fiduciary duty or similar relationship of trust and confidence and uses that information in a securities transaction.")

146 The spouse (who traded) also cannot be deemed a constructive or temporary insider because the nonpublic information was not entrusted to her for a business purpose that she had agreed to hold confidential.

147 Dirks v. SEC, 463 U.S. 646, 661–62 (1983) ("In determining whether a tippee is under an obligation to disclose or abstain, it is necessary to determine whether the insider's 'tip' constituted a breach of the insider's fiduciary duty.... [And,] the test [for that determination] is whether the insider personally will benefit, directly or indirectly, from his disclosure. Absent some personal gain, there has been no breach of duty to stockholders. And absent a breach by the insider, there is no derivative breach.").

to the source of the inside information, *Chestman* meant that insider trading liability involving "collaborating" spouses based on misappropriation would require proving that the trading spouse owed a duty of trust and confidence to the corporate insider spouse, *independent of the spousal relationship.*[148] Absent that proof, neither the insider nor the spouse could be found liable even where there is indisputable evidence the corporate insider had disclosed material, nonpublic information to the spouse, and the spouse then traded using that information in his or her account. *Chestman*, therefore, imposed a very high burden of proof for securities law enforcers in those insider trading cases that should normally be the easiest to establish.

The SEC responded by issuing Rule 10b5-2, which explicitly declares that "for purposes of the 'misappropriation' theory of insider trading... 'a duty of trust and confidence' exists... whenever a person receives or obtains material nonpublic information from his or her spouse...."[149] With the new rule, the SEC openly neutralized the *Chestman* problem. The fact that Rule 10b5-2 still stands, unqualified, more than two decades after it was promulgated, suggests that concerns about the court jealously guarding its authority to interpret law and would strike back against any perceived agency overreach may be exaggerated. While the lesson here is not that competition rulemaking should be used liberally to "reverse" unfavorable court decisions, these two examples serve as a reminder that there is precedent for taking bolder action in exceptional circumstances.

3. Spurring Legislative Action: The Cigarette Rule Example

But what about rules that could radically change an industry or a dominant firm's business model, or otherwise generate changes of significant economic impact? If evidence clearly shows that these types of changes are necessary to open certain markets that are now protected from competition due to distinct characteristics of those markets, should such rules be contemplated or are they a bridge too far?

For example, studies suggest that in markets where a dominant platform provider enjoys significant network effects and consumer switching costs are high, viable competition would be difficult absent rules requiring interconnection or interoperability, non-discriminatory access, or data portability from the dominant platform provider.[150] More specifically, a data-portability rule that permits users to "own" their data and freely take it with them if they switch providers would reduce the advantage of an incumbent provider (such as the dominant social media platform)

148 *Chestman*, 947 F.2d at 568.

149 Securities and Exchange Act of 1934, Rule 10b5-2(b)(3), 17 CFR § 240.10b5-2(b)(3).

150 *See, e.g.*, Rogerson & Shelanski, *supra* note 1, at 1927–36 (suggesting "light-handed" regulation in the form of interconnection/operability requirements, limits on discrimination, data portability, and line-of-business restrictions); Furman Report, *supra* note 1, at 57 (recommending "data mobility and open standards between services" requirement to overcome network effects and facilitate consumers' switching service providers).

over any actual or potential rivals. That could, in turn, encourage and facilitate competition in the market, thereby increasing consumer choice. Or a rule against "self-preferencing" could prevent a dominant firm such as Amazon from leveraging its control of its e-commerce platform into an unfair advantage over rivals in other markets that rely on its platform.

However, rules such as these could result in a restructuring of the market in a way that has significant economic and social impact. Amazon, for instance, may not exist in its current form if strict non-preferencing rules are promulgated. Ideally, these types of potentially industry-transformational regulation, if deemed necessary, should be initiated through more targeted legislation passed by Congress, not directly by agency rulemaking in reliance on the FTC Act's more general grant of authority. Moreover, such rules, if promulgated, could come close to the edge of violating the nondelegation doctrine, especially if Justices Kavanaugh's or Gorsuch's suggestions for tightening the doctrine are adopted.

My limited aim here is to consider briefly whether such rules could and should be considered if the agency's careful research and other evidence confirm that they are desirable and necessary to promote competition and consumer choice in certain markets, and Congress passes no targeted legislation. On this question, the FTC's famous Cigarette Rule – widely regarded as one of the agency's greatest success stories[151] even though the rule was never enforced and was quickly preempted by Congress[152] – may hold a valuable lesson.

The FTC's Cigarette Rule, published in 1964 (but never took effect), and its immediate tremendous impact on society and on one of the most powerful industries in the United States at that time, has become part of agency lore.[153] The proposed rule, drafted over a weekend in response to a much-anticipated surgeon general's report on the health hazards of smoking, would require all cigarette labels and advertisements to disclose that smoking may cause death from cancer, and more. And violation of the rules would constitute a UDAP under section 5.[154] The Commission then held hearings, gathered evidence, and issued a final rule, all in under six months.[155] The speed with which the Commission was able to act and the acknowledged quality of its work were no doubt aided

151 *See* Posner, *supra* note 19, at 769; Stephen Calkins, *Ninety Years and Two Days in Forty-Five Minutes*, 72 ANTITRUST L.J. 1183, 1185 (2005).

152 *See* MacLeod et al., *supra* note 63, at 943, 947–50 (discussing the history of the Cigarette Rule, including congressional reaction to it).

153 *See* Calkins, *supra* note 151, at 1185 (recounting how the Commission held hearings, gathered evidence, and succeeded in issuing a final rule, within six months, that required warnings in cigarette labeling and advertising).

154 *See* Advertising and Labeling of Cigarettes, 29 Fed. Reg. 530, 530–32 (proposed Jan. 22, 1964) (to be codified at 16 C.F.R. pt. 408) (requiring cigarette manufacturers to "disclose, clearly and prominently, in all advertising and on every pack, box, carton or other container… that cigarette smoking is dangerous to health and may cause death from cancer and other diseases.").

155 Unfair or Deceptive Advertising and Labeling of Cigarettes in Relation to the Health Hazards of Smoking, 29 Fed. Reg. 8324, 8325 (July 2, 1964) (to be codified at 16 C.F.R. pt. 408).

greatly by the fact that former Judge Richard Posner, then former Commissioner Philip Elman's assistant, was tasked with drafting the proposed rule.[156]

Given the extent to which the Cigarette Rule would have regulated one of the most important industries in the American economy then, had the rule taken effect, it was probably unsurprising that Congress immediately stepped in and took over from the FTC by passing federal legislation that mandated the same warnings and requirements contained in the final Cigarette Rule.[157] In effect, Congress adopted and "legislated" the agency's rule, created a comprehensive federal program dealing with cigarette labeling and advertising, and largely preempted that field.

One could characterize the Cigarette Rule as a "failure" in a literal sense in that it never went into effect; Congress moved expeditiously to preempt it with the Federal Cigarette Labeling and Advertising Act (FCLAA) and various other statutes subsequently passed.[158] But in a broad sense and from a policy perspective, the Cigarette Rule was a resounding success for the agency and is recognized as such even today.[159] The uniform praise for the FTC's work in that matter is well deserved because the agency's objectives were quickly and fully achieved. The agency's vision for protecting the health of consumers prevailed, and the content of the rule it prepared was adopted by Congress and codified into statutory law.

While the Cigarette Rule should not serve as license for the agency to remake any industry as it sees fit, it does show that, in exceptional circumstances, the agency should be willing to take the lead in regulation even in the face of uncertainty as to its outcome, in light of its expertise and Congress-granted mission. Ideally, complex regulations, such as those imposing interconnection and interoperability, non-discrimination, and data portability requirements, should be promulgated pursuant to more specific legislation passed by Congress than under the general UMC authority of section 5. What the Cigarette Rule has shown, however, is that if the Commission considers regulation to be substantively desirable and is more feasible than other alternatives in fulfilling its competition protection objectives with respect to specific industries, taking the initiative to conduct hearings, gather evidence, formulate proposed rules and carefully vet them is worth serious consideration. It bears remembering that Judge Richard Posner, not known as a government interventionist, has said that even

---

156 *See* Calkins, *supra* note 151, at 1186 n. 11 ("Dick Posner is probably a genius in his ability to turn out work that's first rate, and quickly. He has a great capacity to absorb masses of facts and arrange them in his brain, and out it comes. And his first drafts are like other people's last drafts, only better.") (quoting former FTC Commissioner Philip Elman in NORMAN I. SILBER, WITH ALL DELIBERATE SPEED: THE LIFE OF PHILIP ELMAN, AN ORAL HISTORY MEMOIR 342 (2004)).

157 *See* MacLeod et al., *supra* note 63, at 948 (discussing Congress's quick enactment of the Federal Cigarettes Labeling and Advertising Act after the FTC published its final Cigarette Rule).

158 *See id*, at 949–50 (discussing other federal legislation relating to the labeling and advertising of cigarette products that followed).

159 *See* Calkins, *supra* note 151, at 1185–26 (including the Cigarette Rule as one of the high points in the FTC's history); Posner, *supra* note 19 at 769.

where the "Commission's innovative efforts" have been preempted by legislation, it "deserves credit for having, as in the cigarette proceeding, precipitated" the action.[160]

VI. Conclusion

The case for competition rulemaking and for a degree of boldness on the part of the FTC is quite strong. From a legal perspective, despite its terseness and generality, section 6(g) of the FTC Act expressly authorizes the agency to "make rules and regulations for the purpose of carrying out the provisions of [the FTC Act]." *National Petroleum's* unequivocal holding that this authority includes substantive rules has been left undisturbed by subsequent legislative action, with respect to *competition* (as contrasted with UDAP) rulemaking. Furthermore, despite judicial trends toward circumscribing agency discretion and, specifically, the Supreme Court's recent *AMG* decision, the agency's broader definition of section 6(g) would likely continue to enjoy *Chevron* deference. Similarly, while the nondelegation doctrine will likely be tightened in the near future, given the current composition of the Supreme Court, it seems doubtful that competition rulemaking pursuant to section 6(g) would be categorically deemed unconstitutional under either Justice Kavanaugh's or Gorsuch's proposed alternative tests.

From a policy and strategic perspective, I disagree with the argument that the agency must tread lightly to avoid judicial backlash. Using rulemaking to make only technical adjustments or minor refinements of doctrine is unlikely to solve the major problems that seem to elude *ex post* antitrust enforcement. Predicting judicial reaction to agency "overreach" is difficult, and I argue against being overly reactive to it. Using two well-known examples of another agency (the SEC) promulgating rules that were unabashedly intended to, and did, neutralize problematic judicial interpretations of statutes, I argue there is precedent for creative rulemaking by the FTC in exceptional and appropriate circumstances. Finally, the famous Cigarette Rule, technically a "failure" in that it was withdrawn but widely recognized as a major success because it spurred needed legislation, illustrates the potential outsize benefits of pushing the limits if the agency's rulemaking is well informed by its expertise and is backed by strong data and other evidence.

---

160 Posner, *supra* note 19, at 770.

Dead-End Road: *National Petroleum Refiners Association* and FTC "Unfair Methods of Competition" Rulemaking

MAUREEN K. OHLHAUSEN AND BEN ROSSEN*
Baker Botts

Abstract

The Federal Trade Commission (FTC) has never tried to travel down the road of "unfair methods of competition" (UMC) rulemaking in the nearly fifty years since the D.C. Circuit decided National Petroleum Refiners Association v. FTC. This paper explains how that road is essentially a dead end. Part II discusses the history of the FTC's rulemaking authority and summarizes arguments in favor of UMC rules. Part III discusses National Petroleum Refiners and explains why it would be overruled using modern principles of statutory interpretation. Part IV rebuts the argument that Congress ratified the FTC's UMC rulemaking authority in Magnuson-Moss and later legislation, and Part V argues that the subsequent history of the octane rating rule at issue in National Petroleum Refiners is further evidence that the FTC lacks authority to promulgate UMC rules.

---

* Ms. Ohlhausen is Partner and Global Section Chair of the Antitrust & Competition Law Practice Group of Baker Botts LLP and former Acting Chairman and Commissioner of the U.S. Federal Trade Commission. Mr. Rossen is Special Counsel in the Antitrust & Competition Law Practice Group of Baker Botts LLP. The views are those of the authors and do not necessarily reflect the views of the firm or any client.

I. Introduction

The Federal Trade Commission (FTC) has long steered the direction of competition law by engaging in case-by-case enforcement of the FTC Act's prohibition on unfair methods of competition, interpreted as generally coterminous with the Sherman Act. Recently, some have argued that the FTC's exclusive reliance on case-by-case adjudication is too long and arduous a route and urged the Commission to take a shortcut by invoking its purported authority to promulgate unfair methods of competition (UMC) rules under section 6(g) of the Federal Trade Commission Act.[1] These critics argue that UMC rulemaking would reduce ambiguity in the law, lower the costs of enforcement, and allow increased public participation through notice-and-comment procedures.[2] They also assert that UMC rules can reach much further than the Sherman Act and regulate much broader swathes of business conduct.

Proponents of UMC rulemaking rely on *National Petroleum Refiners Association v. FTC*, a 1973 D.C. Circuit decision, which upheld the Commission's authority to issue broad legislative rules under the FTC Act.[3] They argue that *National Petroleum Refiners* provides a clear path and that Congress effectively ratified the D.C. Circuit's decision when it enacted detailed rulemaking procedures governing unfair or deceptive acts or practices (UDAP) in the Magnuson-Moss Warranty–Federal Trade Commission Improvement Act of 1975 (Magnuson-Moss). Because Magnuson-Moss did not address UMC rules, the argument goes, the Commission's authority to issue such rules was left intact, the rules are governed by the Administrative Procedure Act[4] (APA), and any FTC interpretations of UMC are entitled to *Chevron* deference. They argue that the FTC merely needs to race down a wide-open road with streamlined APA rulemaking to make sweeping changes to the competition landscape for all U.S. businesses subject to FTC oversight.

As this paper will address, the premise of this argument is fundamentally incorrect. As discussed in another paper[5] and outlined below, modern courts reject the type of permissive statutory analysis applied in *National Petroleum Refiners*. Even since that recent paper, the Supreme Court has posted additional stop signs for agencies seeking to newly assert broad powers not explicitly granted by Congress. Moreover, contemporaneous congressional reaction to *National*

---

1 Rohit Chopra & Lina M. Khan, *The Case for "Unfair Methods of Competition" Rulemaking*, 87 U. Chi. L. Rev. 357 (2020).

2 *Id.*

3 482 F.2d 672 (D.C. Cir. 1973).

4 5 U.S.C. § 553 *et seq.*

5 Maureen K. Ohlhausen & James Rill, *Pushing the Limits? A Primer on FTC Competition Rulemaking*, U.S. Chamber of Com. (Aug. 12, 2021), https://www.uschamber.com/assets/archived/images/ftc_rulemaking_white_paper_aug12.pdf.

Petroleum Refiners was not to embrace broad FTC rulemaking but rather to put in place strong guardrails on FTC UDAP rulemaking. As this paper explores, the congressional history of the particular FTC rule at issue – the octane rating rule – also points in the direction of a lack of broad UMC rulemaking, as Congress eventually adopted the rule as solely a UDAP provision with heightened restrictions on FTC rulemaking.

Thus, the road to UMC rulemaking, which the agency wisely never tried to travel down in the almost fifty years since *National Petroleum Refiners*, is essentially a dead end. If the agency tries to go that route, it will be an unfortunate detour from its clear statutory direction to engage in case-by-case enforcement of section 5.

Part II of this paper discusses the history of the FTC's rulemaking authority and summarizes the arguments in favor of UMC rules. Part III discusses *National Petroleum Refiners* and explains why it would be overruled using modern principles of statutory interpretation, while Part IV rebuts the argument that Congress ratified the FTC's UMC authority in Magnuson-Moss and later legislation. Finally, Part V argues that the subsequent history of the octane rating rule at issue in *National Petroleum Refiners* is further evidence that the FTC lacks authority to issue UMC rules.

II. Broad UMC Rulemaking Authority Contradicts the History and Evolution of the FTC's Authority

The FTC Act grants the Commission broad authority to investigate unfair methods of competition and unfair and deceptive acts or practices across much of the American economy. Rather than defining with specificity particular violations of the FTC Act, Congress granted the agency broad investigatory powers and provided for case-by-case enforcement and adjudication before an administrative tribunal with deep subject matter expertise. As originally enacted in 1914, the FTC Act empowered the Commission to prevent "unfair methods of competition" and established an elaborate adjudicative and investigative framework in sections 5 and 6 of the Act. The 1938 Wheeler-Lea amendments[6] expanded the FTC's authority to also prevent "unfair or deceptive acts or practices"

The FTC's administrative adjudicative authority under "Part 3" is central to the FTC's mission of preserving fair competition and protecting consumers,[7] as reflected by the comprehensive adjudicative framework established in section 5 of the FTC Act.[8] Section 5 authorized the Commission to prevent UMC (and later UDAP) by filing a complaint concerning the conduct at issue, holding hearings

6 Wheeler-Lea Act of 1938, ch. 49, § 3, 52 Stat. 111.

7 16 C.F.R. Part 3.

8 15 U.S.C. § 45.

before an administrative tribunal, and, if persuaded the law has been violated, issuing cease-and-desist orders that can be enforced in federal court.[9] A key feature of Part 3 adjudication is that the litigation process is overseen and ultimately decided by subject-matter experts attuned to the goals, legal frameworks, and other details of antitrust and consumer protection law, who would be well suited to resolve difficult and novel questions of law and fact.[10] To further the agency's expertise, section 6 of the FTC Act detailed various investigative powers of the Commission to collect confidential business information and conduct industry studies.

In contrast to this detailed adjudicative and investigatory framework, the original FTC Act contained only one sentence describing the agency's ability to make rules, buried rather inconspicuously among provisions authorizing investigations into foreign trade conditions and publications of reports to Congress. As originally enacted, section 6(g) provided that the FTC would have authority "[f]rom time to time [to] classify corporations and... to make rules and regulations for the purpose of carrying out the provisions of this [Act]."[11] Whereas section 5 provided a detailed administrative scheme for the enforcement of cease-and-desist orders and judicial review of agency decisions, the FTC Act fails to provide for any sanctions for violations of rules promulgated under section 6 or otherwise specify that such rules would carry the force of law.[12] This minimal delegation of power arguably conferred the right to issue procedural but not substantive rules.[13] Early legislative amendments to the FTC's authority only underscored the Commission's lack of substantive rulemaking authority. For example, statutes like the Wool Products Labeling Act[14] and the Fur Products Labeling Act[15] expressly conferred legislative rulemaking authority

---

9 Federal Trade Commission Act of 1914, 38 Stat. 719 § 5.

10 *See, e.g.*, Maureen K. Ohlhausen, *Administrative Litigation at the FTC: Effective Tool for Developing the Law or Rubber Stamp?*, 12 J. Comp. L. & Econ. 623, 624 (2016).

11 38 Stat. 722 § 6(g) (codified as amended at 15 U.S.C. § 46(g)).

12 *See* Am. Bar Ass'n, Comments of the Antitrust Law Section of the American Bar Association in Connection with the Federal Trade Commission Workshop on "Non-Competes in the Workplace: Examining Antitrust and Consumer Protection Issues" 54 (Apr. 24, 2020), https://www.americanbar.org/content/dam/aba/administrative/antitrust_law/comments/april-2020/comment-42420-ftc.pdf (asserting that "the Act['s] fail[ure] to provide any sanctions for violating any rule adopted pursuant to Section 6(g) . . . strongly suggest[s] that Congress did not intend to give the agency substantive rulemaking powers when it passed the Federal Trade Commission Act") (internal citations omitted).

13 Royce Zeisler, Chevron *Deference and the FTC: How and Why the FTC Should Use* Chevron *to Improve Antitrust Enforcement*, 2014 Colum. Bus. L. Rev. 266, 281 (2014); Thomas W. Merrill & Kathryn Tongue Watts, *Agency Rules With the Force of Law: The Original Convention*, 116 Harv. L. Rev. 467, 549 (2002).

14 Ch. 871, § 6(a), 54 Stat. 1128, 1131 (1940) (codified as amended at 15 U.S.C. § 68d(a)) (authorizing the FTC to make rules and regulations "as may be necessary and proper for administration and enforcement"). Congress gave the rules promulgated under this general rulemaking grant legislative effect through various statutory provisions. For example, section 3 provided that the introduction into commerce of any wool product that was misbranded within the meaning of the Act or of the rules or regulations promulgated by the FTC was unlawful. *Id.* § 3, 54 Stat. at 1129 (codified at 15 U.S.C. § 68h).

15 Ch. 298, § 8(b), 65 Stat. 175, 180 (1951) (codified at 15 U.S.C. § 69f(b)) (authorizing the FTC to promulgate rules and regulations "as may be necessary and proper for purposes of administration and enforcement of this Act").

to the FTC, grants of authority that would have been superfluous if Congress had already authorized such rules under section 6(g) of the FTC Act.[16]

Consistent with the understanding that Congress did not authorize substantive rulemaking, the FTC made no attempt to promulgate rules with the force of law for nearly fifty years after it was created,[17] and at various times indicated that it lacked the authority to do so.[18] Between 1914 and 1962, the FTC convened trade practice conferences to supplement some of the inefficiencies of case-by-case adjudication and identify practices that violated laws administered by the FTC.[19] The conferences gathered industry or consumer groups to identify proposed rules about a certain industry, and, after a public hearing, the FTC would issue a "trade practice conference rule."[20] Such "rules" were not considered legally binding and depended on voluntary compliance by industry.[21] In 1955, the FTC began to issue guides, which consisted of interpretive rules describing the FTC's opinion on the requirements of the FTC Act. Like trade practice conference rules, the guides did not carry the force of law.[22]

In 1962, the agency for the first time began to promulgate consumer protection trade regulation rules (TRRs), citing its authority under section 6(g).[23] Although these early TRRs plainly addressed consumer protection matters, the agency frequently described violations of the rule as both an unfair method of competition *and* an unfair or deceptive trade practice.[24] As the Commission itself has observed, "[n]early all of the rules that the Commission actually promulgated under section 6(g) were consumer protection rules."[25]

In fact, in more than a hundred years of the FTC Act, the agency has only once issued a solely competition rule. In 1967, the Commission promulgated the Men and Boys' Tailored Clothing Rule pursuant to authority under the Clayton Act,

16 Merrill & Watts, *supra* note 13, at 549.

17 *Id.* at 549–50.

18 *Nat'l Petroleum Refiners*, 482 F.2d at 693 ("[T]he agency itself did not assert the power to promulgate substantive rules until 1962 and indeed indicated intermittently before that time that it lacked such power.").

19 Merrill & Watts, *supra* note 13, at 551.

20 *Id.*

21 *Id.*

22 *Id.* at 552.

23 Perhaps because the agency recognized its limited authority in this area and the potential political ramifications from its use, FTC's initial rules were rather trivial and uncontroversial. For example, in 1963 the FTC promulgated a rule requiring sleeping bags be marked with the size of the finished product rather than the dimensions of the materials used in making the bags. 16 C.F.R. § 400 (1964). Similarly, a 1965 TRR declared that the practice of describing household electric sewing machines as "automatic," "fully automatic," or "automatic zig-zag sewing machines" violated section 5. 16 C.F.R. § 401 (1966). *See also* Merrill & Watts, *supra* note 13, at n. 443.

24 *See, e.g.*, Advance Notice of Proposed Rulemaking, Trade Regulation Rule: Advertising and Labeling as to Size of Sleeping Bags, 60 Fed. Reg. 27240 (May 23, 1995) (to be codified at 16 C.F.R. pt. 400) ("The Sleeping Bag Rule, promulgated by the Commission on October 11, 1963, declares that it is an unfair method of competition and an unfair or deceptive practice to use the 'cut size' of the materials from which a sleeping bag is made to describe the size of a sleeping bag in advertising. . . .").

25 Fed. Trade Comm'n, A Brief Overview of the Federal Trade Commission's Investigative, Law Enforcement, and Rulemaking Authority (revised, May 2021), https://www.ftc.gov/about-ftc/what-we-do/enforcement-authority.

which prohibited apparel suppliers from granting discriminatory advertising allowances that limited small retailers' ability to compete.[26] The year after the Rule was promulgated, the Supreme Court decided *FTC v. Fred Meyer, Inc.*, which recommended the Commission issue detailed guidelines concerning promotional allowances.[27] The Commission accepted this invitation the following year by publishing the so-called Fred Meyer Guides, which set out general standards for promotional allowances applicable to all industries.[28] The Fred Meyer Guides largely rendered the Tailored Clothing Rule unnecessary. It appears never to have been enforced and was subsequently repealed.[29] The rule was never subject to challenge, and, as discussed more fully below, the fact that the agency has never again attempted to promulgate a solely competition rule is rather telling that it lacks the actual authority to do so.

Soon after these developments, the FTC promulgated the octane rating rule at issue in *National Petroleum Refiners*, in which the D.C. Circuit upheld the Commission's power to promulgate substantive rules under section 6(g) of the FTC Act. Proponents of UMC rulemaking like former FTC Commissioner Rohit Chopra and current Chair Lina Khan point to *National Petroleum Refiners* as evidence that the Commission retains the power to promulgate substantive competition rules governed only by the APA and, with respect to interpretations of UMC, entitled to *Chevron* deference.[30] They argue that UMC rulemaking would deliver significant benefits by providing clear notice to market participants about what the law requires, relieving the steep expert costs and prolonged trials common to antitrust adjudications, and fostering a "transparent and participatory process" that would allow for meaningful public participation.[31]

Chopra and Khan argue that UMC rulemaking would be appropriate to regulate conduct where an extensive enforcement record already exists or where anticompetitive conduct is unlikely to be challenged by private litigants (such as noncompete clauses). In practice, however, once the Commission unlocks broad rulemaking authority, it is unlikely that the agency would limit itself to such a narrow set of circumstances.[32] Setting aside the legality of the practice, broad UMC rulemaking would distract the FTC from the main task assigned to it – case-by-case enforcement and adjudication as an expert body. Rather than

---

26 Notice of Repeal of Rule, Trade Regulation Rule: Discriminatory Practices in Men's and Boys' Tailored Clothing Industry, 59 Fed. Reg. 8527, 8528 (Feb. 23, 1994) (to be codified at 16 C.F.R. pt. 412).

27 390 U.S. 341 (1968).

28 16 C.F.R. pt. 240.

29 Notice of Repeal of Rule, , *supra* note 26. *See also* Jay B. Sykes, Cong. Rsch. Serv., LSB10635, The FTC's Competition Rulemaking Authority 1 (Aug. 12, 2021), https://crsreports.congress.gov/product/pdf/LSB/LSB10635.

30 Chopra & Khan, *supra* note 1, at 378–79.

31 *Id.*

32 Indeed, some have already called on the Commission to engage in UMC rulemaking untethered to any of the principles described by Chopra and Khan, such as a rule prohibiting all online behavioral advertising. *See* Petition for Rulemaking by Accountable Tech, 86 Fed. Reg. 73206 (Dec. 27, 2021).

applying its expertise to specific facts and complex legal issues through enforcement supported by substantial evidence, it appears that the Commission is seeking a shortcut to its desired outcome, bypassing Congress and the courts along the way.[33] Further, if it promulgates such rules through abbreviated notice-and-comment rulemaking, FTC would claim extremely broad substantive authority to directly regulate business conduct across the economy with relatively few of the procedural guardrails that Congress felt necessary for FTC's consumer protection TRRs.

With Chair Khan at the helm of the FTC, the agency has already begun to pave the way for new UMC rulemakings. For example, President Biden's Executive Order on promoting competition called on the Commission to promulgate UMC rules addressing noncompete clauses and pay-for-delay settlements, among other issues.[34] Further, as one of Chair Khan's first actions, the Commission rescinded – without replacing – its bipartisan Statement of Enforcement Principles Regarding "Unfair Methods of Competition" Under Section 5 of the FTC Act, divorcing (at least in the Commission majority's view) section 5 from prevailing antitrust law principles and leaving the business community without any current guidance as to what the Commission considers "unfair."[35] More recently, the Commission's Statement of Regulatory Priorities filed with the Office of Information and Regulatory Affairs stated that the FTC "in the coming year will consider developing both unfair-methods-of-competition rulemakings as well as rulemakings to define with specificity unfair or deceptive acts or practices."[36] As described in the following sections, this foray into UMC rulemaking is likely to take the FTC down a dead-end road.

III. The Signs are Clear: *National Petroleum Refiners* Does Not Comport With Modern Principles of Statutory Interpretation

As described above, the FTC's authority to conduct rulemaking under section 6(g) has been tested in court only once, in *National Petroleum Refiners*, where the D.C. Circuit upheld the Commission's authority to promulgate a UDAP and UMC rule requiring the disclosure of octane ratings on gasoline pumps.[37] The district

33 *See, e.g.*, Ohlhausen & Rill, *supra* note 5.

34 Exec. Order No. 14,036, 86 Fed. Reg. 36987 (July 9, 2021).

35 *See* Dissenting Statement of Commissioners Noah Joshua Phillips and Christine S. Wilson on the "Statement of the Commission on the Withdrawal of the Statement of Enforcement Principles Regarding 'Unfair Methods of Competition' Under Section 5 of the FTC Act" (July 9, 2021), https://www.ftc.gov/system/files/documents/public_statements/1591710/p210100phillipswilsondissentsec5enforcementprinciples.pdf.

36 Fed. Trade Comm'n, Statement of Regulatory Priorities 1 (Dec. 2021), https://www.reginfo.gov/public/jsp/eAgenda/StaticContent/202110/Statement_3084_FTC.pdf.

37 482 F.2d at 674.

court had ruled against the FTC, concluding that the agency lacked statutory authority to issue legislative rules under section 6(g). The D.C. Circuit panel unanimously reversed the district court on this ground and remanded for further consideration. The court rejected the argument that section 6(g) only permitted the FTC to promulgate administrative or procedural rules and instead held that the FTC could issue substantive rules applicable to the entire FTC Act, including section 5.[38] The court concluded that rulemaking would "carry out what the Congress agreed was among [the FTC's] central purposes: expedited administrative enforcement of the national policy against monopolies and unfair business practices. Under the circumstances, since Section 6(g) plainly authorizes rule-making and nothing in the statute or in its legislative history precludes its use for this purpose, the action of the [FTC] must be upheld."[39] As described in more detail below, the court's statutory interpretation and rationale for upholding such a broad grant of authority is far afield from recent Supreme Court precedent.

At the time of the decision in *National Petroleum Refiners*, section 6(g) authorized the FTC to "make rules and regulations for the purpose of carrying out the provisions of sections 41 to 46 and 47 to 58 of this title."[40] The court rejected the argument that section 6(g) only permitted the FTC to promulgate administrative and procedural rules applicable to the adjudication and enforcement powers in section 5, holding instead that the FTC could issue substantive rules defining the statutory standard of UMC or UDAP in advance of adjudicative proceedings.[41] The court disagreed that substantive rulemaking under section 6(g) would circumvent the FTC Act's adjudicatory framework in section 5 because, after promulgating rules, the FTC must still enforce them through adjudication.[42] Because section 5(b), which describes the FTC's administrative proceedings and authority to issue cease-and-desist orders, "does not use limiting language suggesting that adjudication alone is the only proper means of elaborating the statutory standard," the court concluded that rulemaking was not inconsistent with the statute.[43]

The court also rejected the contention that section 6(g) rulemaking authority was "limited to specifying the details of the Commission's nonadjudicatory, investigative and informative functions" described in the rest of section 6.[44] Instead, the court found that section 6(g) "clearly states that the Commission 'may' make rules and regulations for the purpose of carrying out the provisions

38 *Id.* at 674–78.

39 *Id.* at 693.

40 *Id.* at 676 (quoting section 6(g) of the FTC Act).

41 *Id.* at 674–78.

42 *Id.* at 675.

43 *Id.*

44 *Id.* at 676.

of Section 5"[45] and "liberally… construe[d] the term 'rules and regulations'"[46] based on "judicial precedents concerning rule-making by other agencies and the background and purpose of the Federal Trade Commission Act[.]"[47] The court claimed those precedents established "[t]he need to interpret liberally broad grants of rule-making authority like the one we construe here."[48]

After analyzing the statutory text and other agencies' rulemaking authority, the court turned to pragmatic concerns about the benefits that rulemaking provides to fulfilling the agency's mission. The court emphasized that "there is little question that the availability of substantive rule-making gives any agency an invaluable resource-saving flexibility in carrying out its task of regulating parties subject to its statutory mandate" and extolled the benefits of rulemaking over case-by-case adjudication when developing agency policy.[49] Substantive rulemaking authority would permit the FTC to carefully consider and develop ideal standards of conduct, avoid the slow development of rules through adjudication, and minimize the unfairness of a case-by-case approach that requires compliance of only the party at issue while leaving other competitors free to commit violations.[50] The court concluded that the "policy innovation" enabled by rulemaking "underscore[d] the need for increased reliance on rule-making rather than adjudication alone."[51]

In looking to the FTC Act's legislative history, the court found it "ambiguous" as to whether the FTC was limited to a prosecutorial function and reasoned that the "relationship between rule-making's probable benefits and the broad concerns evident when the FTC was created, together with the express language of section 6(g)," compelled that "any purported ambiguity of the statute be resolved in favor of the Commission's claim."[52] Further, the *National Petroleum Refiners* court was entirely unconcerned that the FTC had not asserted this authority in nearly a half-century of the agency's existence, reasoning that an agency's powers "are not lost by l[ying] dormant."[53] Nor was the court deterred by the fact that the FTC had previously taken the position that it lacked substantive rulemaking authority, finding that it was not the agency's place to define its authority and that such issues of statutory interpretation were more properly resolved by a reviewing court.[54]

---

45 *Id.* at 677.

46 *Id.* at 678.

47 *Id.*

48 *Id.* at 680.

49 *Id.* at 681–84.

50 *Id.* at 683–84.

51 *Id.* at 684.

52 *Id.* at 691.

53 *Id.* at 693–94.

54 *Id.* at 694.

The D.C. Circuit's opinion in *National Petroleum Refiners* has had an impact on the development of administrative law, but there is little question that it reads today like an anachronism. The administrative "canon" described in *National Petroleum Refiners* provides that an ambiguous grant of rulemaking authority should be construed to give agencies the broadest possible powers so that they will have flexibility in determining how to effectuate their statutory mandates.[55] Not only has the Supreme Court never explicitly adopted this approach, recent decisions strongly suggest it would decline to do so if presented the opportunity. Some scholars have gone so far as to argue that no current Supreme Court justice would approach statutory interpretation the way the D.C. Circuit did in *National Petroleum Refiners*.[56]

As discussed in another recent paper,[57] the D.C. Circuit's opinion is in clear tension with the "elephants-in-mouseholes" doctrine first described by the Supreme Court in *Whitman v. Am. Trucking Ass'ns*,[58] because it largely ignored the significance of the FTC Act's detailed adjudicative framework and instead relied on the fact that section 5(b) did not use specific limiting language that would cabin the rulemaking authority provided in section 6(g).[59] The D.C. Circuit's reasoning that Congress buried sweeping legislative rulemaking authority in a vague, ancillary provision, alongside the ability to "classify corporations," stands in direct conflict with the Supreme Court's admonition in *Whitman*.[60]

Modern courts would also look to interpret the structure of the FTC Act to "produce[] a coherent enforcement scheme."[61] For instance, in *AMG Capital Management v. FTC*, the Supreme Court struck down the FTC's use of section 13(b) to obtain equitable monetary relief, in part because the FTC Act elsewhere imposes specific limitations on the Commission's authority to obtain monetary relief. As such, the Court found it "highly unlikely that Congress would have enacted provisions expressly authorizing *conditioned* and *limited* monetary relief if the Act, via § 13(b), had already implicitly allowed the Commission to

---

55 *See* Merrill & Watts, *supra* note 13, at 492.

56 *See* Final Transcript at 295–96, Fed. Trade Comm'n, Non-Competes in the Workplace: Examining Antitrust and Consumer Protection Issues (Jan. 9, 2020), https://www.ftc.gov/system/files/documents/public_events/1556256/non-compete-workshop-transcript-full.pdf ("MR. PIERCE: So the interpretive method that was used in that case was fairly commonly used on the DC Circuit at that time. There is no Justice today, not just Gorsuch but Kagan, Breyer, there is no Justice today that would use [the reasoning of *National Petroleum Refiners*]. . . . I teach it as an illustration of something no modern court would do.").

57 *See* Ohlhausen & Rill, *supra* note 5.

58 531 U.S. 457, 468 (2001). The "elephants-in-mouseholes" doctrine provides that "Congress… does not alter the fundamental details of a regulatory scheme in vague terms or ancillary provisions – it does not, one might say, hide elephants in mouseholes." *Id.*

59 *See* Ohlhausen & Rill, *supra* note 5, at 11–12.

60 The Supreme Court applied similar reasoning in AMG Capital Management, LLC, et al. v. FTC, 593 U.S. __, 141 S. Ct. 1341, 1348 (2021) when it struck down FTC's claimed authority to obtain equitable monetary relief under section 13(b) of the FTC Act. *See* Ohlhausen & Rill, *supra* note 5, at 12. *See also* Steven A. Reed, Scott A. Stempel & Daniel S. Savrin, *The US Supreme Court holds that the FTC lacks the authority to seek equitable monetary relief in cases brought in federal court under FTC Act Section 13(b) (AMG Capital Management)*, e-Competitions April 2021, art. No. 100669.

61 *AMG*, 141 S. Ct. at 1349.

obtain that same monetary relief and more without satisfying those conditions and limitations."[1] Also in contrast to *National Petroleum Refiners*, which lauded the benefits and efficiencies of rulemaking for the agency's mission, the *AMG* court expressly rejected this mode of analysis, writing: "Our task here is not to decide whether [the FTC's] substitution of § 13(b) for the administrative procedure contained in § 5 and the consumer redress available under § 19 is desirable. Rather, it is to answer a more purely legal question" of whether Congress granted authority or not.[2] The same rationale applies to UMC rulemaking.

The unanimous *AMG* decision was no judicial detour, and the Supreme Court has routinely posted clear road signs that Congress is expected "to speak clearly when authorizing an agency to exercise powers of vast economic and political significance," as UMC rulemaking would do.[3] Since 2000, the Court has increasingly applied the "major questions doctrine" to limit the scope of congressional delegation to the administrative state in areas of major political or economic importance. For example, in *FDA v. Brown & Williamson*, the Supreme Court declined to grant *Chevron* deference to an FDA rule interpreting the Food, Drug, and Cosmetic Act as permitting the agency to regulate nicotine and cigarettes.[4] Crucial to the Court's analysis was that the FDA's rule contradicted the agency's own view of its authority dating back to 1914 while asserting jurisdiction over a significant portion of the American economy.[5] In *Utility Air Regulatory Group v. EPA*, the Court invoked the major questions doctrine to strike down EPA's greenhouse-gas emissions standards as an impermissible interpretation of the Clean Air Act, finding that "EPA's interpretation is... unreasonable because it would bring about an enormous and transformative expansion in [the] EPA's regulatory authority without clear congressional authorization."[6]

Most recently, the Supreme Court's decision striking down OSHA's COVID-19 vaccine mandate is further evidence that the lanes are closed to overbroad statutory construction. In *National Federation of Independent Business v. OSHA,* the Court narrowly construed the Occupational Health and Safety Act to find that OSHA lacked authority to impose a nationwide vaccine mandate because the statute authorizes the agency to enact only "*occupational* safety and health standards," not "broad public health measures."[7] The Court found it persuasive that the agency had never adopted a broad public health regulation in the

---

1 *Id.*

2 *Id.* at 1347.

3 *See, e.g.*, Alabama Ass'n of Realtors v. Dep't. of Health & Hum. Servs., 594 U.S. __, 141 S. Ct. 2485, 2489 (2021).

4 FDA v. Brown & Williamson Tobacco Corp., 529 U.S. 120, 159–60 (2000).

5 *Id. See also* Blake Emerson, *Administrative Answers to Major Questions: On the Democratic Legitimacy of Agency Statutory Interpretation*, 102 Minn. L. Rev. 2019 (May 2018).

6 573 U.S. 302, 324 (2014).

7 Nat'l Fed'n of Indep. Bus. v. Dep't of Lab., Occupational Safety & Health Admin., 142 S. Ct. 661, 665 (2022) (*per curiam*).

half-century of its existence, concluding that "[t]his 'lack of historical precedent,' coupled with the breadth of authority that the Secretary now claims, is a 'telling indication' that the mandate extends beyond the agency's legitimate reach."[8] The Court gave no credence to the fact that the rule would likely save lives and prevent hospitalizations, stating, "It is not our role to weigh such tradeoffs. In our system of government, that is the responsibility of those chosen by the people through the democratic processes. Although Congress has indisputably given OSHA the power to regulate occupational dangers, it has not given that agency the power to regulate public health more broadly."[9] Because broad UMC rulemaking authority under section 6(g) is similarly a question of potentially "vast economic and political significance," and would also represent a significant departure from past agency precedent, all signals suggest that the FTC's efforts to promulgate such rules would promptly be met by a flashing red light.

Finally, while *National Petroleum Refiners* lauded the benefits of rulemaking authority and emphasized its usefulness for carrying out the FTC's mission, the Supreme Court has since clarified that "[h]owever sensible (or not)" an interpretation may be, "a reviewing court's 'task is to apply the text [of the statute], not to improve upon it.'"[10] Whatever benefits rulemaking authority may confer on the FTC, they cannot justify departure from the text of the FTC Act.[11]

IV. The Road Not Taken: Congress Did Not Ratify UMC Rulemaking Authority and the FTC Did Not Assert It

Two years after the D.C. Circuit's decision in *National Petroleum Refiners*, Congress enacted the Magnuson-Moss Warranty–Federal Trade Commission Improvement Act of 1975 (Magnuson-Moss).[12] Section 202(a) of Magnuson-Moss amended the FTC Act to add a new section 18, which, for the first time, gave the FTC express authority to issue UDAP rules while imposing heightened procedural requirements for such rulemaking.[13] Congress designated Magnuson-Moss as the sole authority under which the FTC can issue trade regulation rules addressing UDAP, but the statute does not expressly address UMC rulemaking authority.[14] Instead, the statute only says that the Commission's authority to

8 *Id.* at 666 (quoting Free Enterprise Fund v. Public Co. Accounting Oversight Bd., 561 U.S. 477, 505 (2010) (cleaned up).

9 *Id.*

10 EPA v. EME Homer City Generation, L.P., 572 U.S. 489, 508–09 (2014).

11 *Id. See also, e.g., Alabama Ass'n of Realtors*, 141 S. Ct. at 2490 ("It is indisputable that the public has a strong interest in combating the spread of the COVID-19 Delta variant. But our system does not permit agencies to act unlawfully even in pursuit of desirable ends.").

12 Pub. L. No. 93-637, 88 Stat. 2183 (1975) (codified as amended in scattered sections at 15 U.S.C. § 41 *et seq.*).

13 15 U.S.C. § 57a.

14 15 U.S.C. § 57a(a)(2).

promulgate rules under section 18 "shall not affect any authority of the Commission to prescribe rules (including interpretive rules), and general statements of policy, with respect to unfair methods of competition in or affecting commerce."[15] As it currently stands, section 6(g) authorizes the FTC "(except as provided in section 57a(a)(2) of this title) to make rules and regulations for the purpose of carrying out the provisions of this subchapter."[16]

UMC rulemaking proponents argue that Magnuson-Moss effectively ratified *National Petroleum Refiners* and affirmed the Commission's authority with respect to substantive UMC rules.[17] This revisionist interpretation is incorrect. To be sure, Congress expressly ratified that case's holding with respect to UDAP rules by creating explicit rulemaking procedures, enforcement mechanisms, and remedies to address unfair and deceptive practices. But the savings provision in section 18(a)(2) that preserves "any authority" (as opposed to "the" authority) of the Commission to prescribe UMC rules reflects, at most, an agnostic view on whether FTC in fact possesses such authority. Rather, it suggests that whatever authority may exist for UMC rulemaking was unchanged by section 18 and that Congress left the question open for the courts to resolve. The FTC itself appears to have recognized this uncertainty, as evidenced by the fact that it has never even attempted to promulgate a UMC rule in the nearly fifty years following the enactment of Magnuson-Moss.[18]

Congress's ambivalence is further underscored by the express enforcement and remedial provisions in Magnuson-Moss for UDAP rule violations without any parallel scheme for UMC rules. For example, section 205(a) of Magnuson-Moss amended section 5 of the FTC Act to authorize the FTC to sue for civil penalties against a party that violates a UDAP rule.[19] Section 206(a) created a new section 19 of the FTC Act that authorizes the FTC to bring suit in federal court for equitable monetary and other relief for UDAP rule violations.[20] The fact that Congress authorized a detailed enforcement and remedial scheme for UDAP rule violations but said nothing about UMC rules strongly signals that it did not ratify the holding of *National Petroleum Refiners* for UMC rulemaking.

The legislative history of Magnuson-Moss also reflects congressional skepticism that *National Petroleum Refiners* was correctly decided. The House Report refers several times to the case, and it is apparent that Congress understood its holding.[21] The Senate bill did not contain any new provisions relating to the FTC's rulemaking

---

15 *Id.*

16 15 U.S.C. § 46(g).

17 Chopra & Khan, *supra* note 1, at 369–70.

18 Zeisler, *supra* note 13, at 282.

19 15 U.S.C. § 45(m).

20 15 U.S.C. § 57b.

21 *See* H.R. Rep. No. 93-1107 (1974), *as reprinted in* 1974 U.S.C.C.A.N. 7702.

power,[22] but the House bill, by contrast, included a proposed section 18 that eliminated section 6(g) and expressly limited the FTC's rulemaking authority to UDAP regulations.[23] Specifically, the House's proposal would have "replace[d] the existing rulemaking authority of the FTC under section 6(g) of the Act with a new section 18 which authorizes the FTC to issue rules defining with specificity the acts or practices which are unfair or deceptive and which are within the scope of section 5(a)(1) of the Federal Trade Commission Act."[24] The House bill included enhanced rulemaking procedures for UDAP rules out of concern that the APA alone provided "inadequate" procedural safeguards in light of the "potentially pervasive and deep effect of rules defining what constitutes unfair or deceptive acts or practices and the broad standards" set by the definition of UDAP.[25]

The House's version was ultimately rejected, and the final bill reflects a compromise that leaves open the question of UMC rulemaking authority without endorsing it. While Chopra and Khan suggest that *National Petroleum Refiners* remains enshrined in law because Magnuson-Moss applied only to UDAP rules,[26] congressional silence on UMC hardly endorses the Commission's authority and is not likely to persuade an appellate court today. For instance, the Supreme Court has made clear that it "does not follow... that Congress' failure to overturn a statutory precedent is reason for [a court] to adhere to it" and that it is "'impossible to assert with any degree of assurance that congressional failure to act represents' affirmative congressional approval of [a court's] statutory interpretation."[27] That is because "Congress takes no governmental action except by legislation."[28] Congressional silence merely indicates "Congress's failure to express any opinion" and offers little insight into legislative intent.[29] To rely on congressional acquiescence to a judicial interpretation, there must be "overwhelming evidence" that Congress considered and rejected the "precise issue" before the Court.[30] Although Congress considered *National Petroleum*

22 S. Rep. No. 93-1408 (1974) (Conf. Rep.), *as reprinted in* 1974 U.S.C.C.A.N. 7755, 7761 ("The Senate bill contained no provisions relating to rulemaking procedures to be followed by the Federal Trade Commission.").

23 *Id.* at 7762 ("These rules [authorized by the House bill] would have been limited to defining acts or practices which were unfair or deceptive within the meaning of section 5(a)(1) of the Act. The FTC would have been prohibited from prescribing rules with respect to unfair competitive practices."); *see also* H.R. Rep. No. 93-1107, 1974 U.S.C.C.A.N. at 7727 (section 18 "would be the exclusive substantive rulemaking authority of the FTC under the Federal Trade Commission Act. Thus, the Commission would not have rulemaking authority with respect to unfair methods of competition to the extent they are not unfair or deceptive acts or practices.").

24 H.R. Rep. No. 93-1107, 1974 U.S.C.C.A.N. at 7727.

25 *Id.*

26 Chopra & Khan, *supra* note 1, at 378.

27 Patterson v. McLean Credit Union, 491 U.S. 164, 175 n. 1 (1989) (internal citations omitted). *See also* Bob Jones Univ. v. United States, 461 U.S. 574, 600 (1983) ("Non-action by Congress is not often a useful guide" to statutory interpretation).

28 Rapanos v. United States, 547 U.S. 715, 750 (2006) (plurality opinion).

29 *Id.*

30 *Id.*

Refiners, it ultimately took no action, either affirmative or negative, on the FTC's UMC rulemaking authority. Hardly the "overwhelming evidence" required to read *National Petroleum Refiners* into the law.[31]

V. The Forgotten Journey: The History of the Octane Rating Rule Reinforces the FTC's Lack of UMC Rulemaking Authority

Those that argue that *National Petroleum Refiners* is still good law and that Congress silently endorsed UMC rulemaking have shown no interest in how the journey of the octane rating rule continued after the case and where it eventually ended. The FTC's 1971 octane rating rule declared the failure to post octane disclosures on gasoline pumps both an unfair method of competition *and* an unfair or deceptive practice. But what has remained unexplored in the debate over FTC UMC rulemaking is what happened to the rule after the D.C. Circuit's decision upheld rulemaking under section 6(g) and what that tells us about congressional and agency views on UMC authority.

The octane rating rule upheld by the D.C. Circuit never took effect and was ultimately replaced when Congress enacted the Petroleum Marketing Practices Act (PMPA), Title II of which addressed octane disclosure requirements and directed the FTC to issue new rules under the PMPA.[32] But, despite previous claims by the FTC that the rule drew on both UDAP and UMC authority, Congress declined to provide any authority beyond UDAP. While it is impossible to say whether Congress concluded that UMC rulemaking was unwise, illegal, or simply unnecessary, the PMPA – passed just two years after Magnuson-Moss – suggests that UMC rulemaking did not survive the enactment of section 18. A brief summary of the rule's meandering journey follows.

The D.C. Circuit remanded *National Petroleum Refiners* back to the district court for further consideration, limited to the adequacy of the administrative record underlying the rule. The district court, in turn, ordered the FTC to complete an environmental impact statement before attempting to put the rule into effect.[33] While the environmental impact analysis was pending, Congress began consideration of the PMPA. After its enactment, the Commission, based on an analysis of the statute and its legislative history, understood Congress to have intended the requirements of Title II of the PMPA to replace those of the original octane rating rule.[34] For example, the octane rating method specified by section 202(c)

31 *See also* Blonder-Tongue Labs., Inc. v. Univ. of Ill. Found., 402 U.S. 313, 327 n. 17, 340 n. 34 (1971) (no congressional approval of court precedent where statute was otherwise revised and provisions that would have overruled precedent "disappeared" from proposed legislation).

32 Pub. L. No. 95-297, 92 Stat. 322 (June 19, 1978).

33 44 Fed. Reg. 19160 (Mar. 30, 1979).

34 *Id.* at 19161.

of the PMPA was the same as the method that was required by the Commission's 1971 rule.[35] The FTC treated the enactment of the PMPA as effectively repealing the rule and published an announcement of the rule's repeal in the Federal Register.[36]

Section 203(a) of the PMPA gave the FTC "procedural, investigative, and enforcement powers, including the power to issue procedural rules in enforcing compliance with the requirements of [Title II] and rules prescribed pursuant to the requirements of this title."[37] The House report recounted the long history of FTC's attempts to enact an octane rating disclosure rule as well as the legal challenges the rule had faced and concluded that legislation was needed "to assure prompt and permanent enforcement of an octane posting requirement."[38] The House report further noted that the legislation should "seek to avoid wasteful repetition of much of the effort which the F.T.C. has already expended on this subject."[39]

Testimony in House subcommittee hearings centered on the question of whether the legislation should direct the FTC to enact a TRR on octane posting under expedited procedures that would be authorized by the legislation, or whether Congress should enact its own statutory requirements regarding the testing, certification, and posting of octane ratings.[40] Ultimately, Congress adopted a statutory definition of octane ratings (identical to the method adopted by the FTC in its 1971 rule) and granted the FTC rulemaking authority under the APA to update definitions and prescribe different procedures for determining fuel octane ratings.[41] Congress also specified that certain rules, such as those requiring manufacturers to display octane requirements on motor vehicles, would have heightened rulemaking procedures, such as rulemaking on the record after a hearing.[42]

Whereas the FTC's 1971 rule invoked both UDAP and UMC authority, the PMPA specifically provides that violations of the statute, or any rule promulgated under the statute, "shall be an unfair or deceptive act or practice in or affecting commerce."[43] Although section 203(d)(3) of the PMPA specifically exempts the FTC from the procedural requirements under section 18, it does not simply revert

---

35 *Id.*

36 Revocation of Trade Regulation Rule, Part 422 – Posting of Minimum Octane Numbers on Gasoline Dispensing Pumps, 43 Fed. Reg. 43022 (Sept. 22, 1978).

37 Pub. L. No. 95-297, 92 Stat. 322 (June 19, 1978).

38 H. Rep. No. 95-161, at 18 (Apr. 5, 1977).

39 *Id.*

40 *Id.* at 19.

41 PMPA § 203(c), 92 Stat. at 336.

42 *Id.* § 203(d).

43 *Id.* § 203(e), 92 Stat. at 337.

to section 6(g) or otherwise leave open a path for UMC rulemaking. The record makes clear, however, that Congress was aware of the FTC's desire to claim UMC authority in connection with the octane rating rule. When the House Committee on Interstate and Foreign Commerce in the 93rd Congress heard testimony on its version of Magnuson-Moss – which, as discussed in Part IV above, would have explicitly eliminated any FTC authority for UMC rulemaking – the FTC testified that UMC authority was necessary to regulate octane ratings, stating:

> First, the bill would appear to restrict the Commission's existing authority to promulgate rules to prohibit "unfair methods of competition." The Commission perceives no reason for curtailing its powers in this area. Admittedly, the Commission's consumer protection responsibilities are more conducive to the rulemaking process, and, for this reason, the Commission does not foresee a high level of rulemaking activity in the antitrust area. That is not to say, however, that rulemaking is not an appropriate or an effective regulatory device for antitrust enforcement. For instance, where the legality of identical, similar, or related practices of an anticompetitive nature may be addressed responsibly and more efficiently in a single proceeding than in a case-by-case adjudication, law enforcement by rulemaking would be considered more favorably.... Finally, it should be noted that some practices, such as the failure to post octane ratings involved in the *National Petroleum Refiners* case, constitute both an unfair trade practice and an unfair method of competition. These should be handled in a single proceeding in which the Commission's full authority over all activity in violation of the Act may be exercised.[44]

After Magnuson-Moss was enacted, however, neither Congress nor the FTC tried to include UMC rulemaking in the PMPA. In a written statement reflecting the FTC's views on the PMPA incorporated in the House report, the FTC described its original octane rating rule as UDAP only, stating that "[t]he Commission has for many years endorsed the idea of posting octane information on gasoline pumps... [and] promulgated a trade regulation rule which declared that the failure to post minimum octane numbers on gasoline pumps constituted an unfair and deceptive act or practice in violation of section 5 of the Federal Trade Commission Act."[45] While not dispositive, the FTC's apparent abandonment of its request for UMC authority after Magnuson-Moss, and Congress's decision to limit the PMPA exclusively to UDAP, certainly suggests that UMC did not survive *National Petroleum Refiners* and that Congress did not endorse FTC UMC rulemaking.

---

44 H. Rep. No. 93-1107, at 57, Letter from Charles A. Tobin, Secretary, Federal Trade Commission (Apr. 29, 1974) (emphasis added).

45 H. Rep. No. 95-161, at 45, Appendix II, Federal Trade Commission – Agency Views, Statement of Federal Trade Commission by Christian S. White, Asst. Director for Special Statutes (Feb. 23, 1977).

VI. Conclusion

Despite the lack of high-octane support for FTC UMC rulemaking authority, the agency appears poised to embark on a journey of broad, legislative-style competition rulemaking under section 6(g) of the FTC Act. This would be a dead end. The shortcut to rulemaking set forth in *National Petroleum Refiners* has been closed off by subsequent actions by Congress and the courts. UMC rulemaking, rather than advancing clarity and certainty about what types of conduct constitute unfair methods of competition, would very likely be viewed by the courts as an illegal left turn. It would also be a detour for the agency from its core mission of case-by-case expert adjudication of the FTC Act, which, given limited agency resources, could result in a years-long escapade that significantly detracts from overall enforcement. The FTC should instead seek to build on the considerable success it has seen in recent years with administrative adjudications, both in terms of winning on appeal and in shaping the development of antitrust law overall by creating citable precedent in key areas.

The Constitutional Revolution That Wasn't: Why the FTC Isn't a Second National Legislature

BERIN SZÓKA AND CORBIN BARTHOLD*
TechFreedom

Abstract

The Federal Trade Commission Act of 1914 did not empower the FTC to issue substantive or "legislative" rules with the force and effect of law. Reading section 6(g) to authorize such rulemakings over unfair methods of competition would broadly flout both the Act's legislative context and the Constitution's separation of powers. Had Congress delegated such a power at the time, this would have amounted to a constitutional revolution – one enacted in a short clause that, as both textual analysis and legislative history confirm, authorizes only procedural, housekeeping, or "interpretive" rules. Conventions of statutory drafting then in use, contemporary understandings of the nondelegation doctrine and the removal power, and indeed the Supreme Court's recent signals regarding nondelegation all compel a narrow reading of section 6(g). Lawmakers of the Progressive Era conferred substantive rulemaking power by specifying penalties or other sanctions for violations of rules crafted by an agency. The 1914 Act provided no such sanctions, and indeed no sanctions even for violations of the Act itself; instead, it empowered the FTC only to refer violators to federal courts for a cease-and-desist order. The Act's post-enactment history, subsequent legislative changes to it, and subsequent case law likewise do not warrant reading this section as establishing a substantive power. National Petroleum Refiners Association v. FTC (D.C. Cir. 1973) rests on outdated result- and policy-driven textual analysis. Modern courts would not uphold the FTC's authority to issue rules governing unfair methods of competition.

---

* Berin Szóka is President of TechFreedom, a nonprofit, nonpartisan technology policy think tank. He can be reached at bszoka@techfreedom.org. Corbin Barthold is Internet Policy Counsel and Director of Appellate Litigation at TechFreedom. He can be reached at cbarthold@techfreedom.org. This paper could not have been completed without the particularly tireless assistance of TechFreedom's Andy Jung and Santana Boulton.

I. Introduction

Did the Federal Trade Commission Act of 1914[1] empower the FTC to issue "substantive" or "legislative" rules with "the force and effect of law"[2] to define "unfair methods of competition" (UMC)? The Commission first claimed such power in 1962.[3] Eleven years later, the D.C. Circuit upheld that theory in *National Petroleum Refiners*.[4] Now, for the first time since that decision, the FTC has initiated UMC rulemakings, seeking public comment on two petitions.[5]

The question turns on the ambiguity of section 6(g), which provides that, among other "additional powers," the Commission "shall... have power to... [f]rom time to time classify corporations and... to make rules and regulations for the purpose of carrying out the provisions of [the Act]."[6] Agency Chair Lina Khan and former Commissioner Rohit Chopra assert that section 6(g) gives the FTC broad power to make legislative rules. They cite only *National Petroleum Refiners* and four academic articles about the case.[7] But would the question be decided the same way today? The Commission asked this question at a 2020 workshop on UMC rulemakings. Professor Richard J. Pierce, a leading scholar of administrative law,[8] called the decision "laughable" by today's standards, adding: "I teach it as an illustration of something no modern court would do."[9]

Reading section 6(g) as enabling the issuance of legislative rules is "laughable" for multiple reasons. First, such a reading broadly flouts both the Act's context

---

1 Federal Trade Commission Act, Pub. L. No. 63-203, 38 Stat. 717 (1914) [hereinafter FTC Act], https://bit.ly/3CYwaCQ.

2 U.S. Dep't of Just., Att'y Gen.'s Manual on the Admin. Procedure Act 30 n. 3 (1947) [hereinafter Attorney General Manual], http://library.law.fsu.edu/Digital-Collections/ABA-AdminProcedureArchive/1947iii.html.

3 *See* Nat'l Petroleum Refiners Ass'n. v. FTC, 482 F.2d 672, 695 n. 29 (1973) ("The Commission first announced it would enforce the prohibitions of § 5 with the assistance of substantive rules in 1962 when it amended its Rules of Practice to provide for issuance of Trade Regulation Rules, 27 Fed. Reg. 4636, 4796 (1962).").

4 *Id.*

5 *See* Petition for Rulemaking to Prohibit Exclusionary Contracts, Open Markets Institute (July 21, 2020), https://bit.ly/3F7gEGz; *see* Petition for Rulemaking to Prohibit Non-Compete Contracts, Open Markets Institute (July 21, 2020), https://bit.ly/3mcm0aX.

6 15 U.S.C. § 46(g).

7 *See* Rohit Chopra & Lina M. Khan, *The Case for "Unfair Methods of Competition" Rulemaking*, 87 U. Chi. L. Rev. 357, 378 (2020), https://bit.ly/3F9BTYk (citing Rebecca Haw, *Amicus Briefs and the Sherman Act: Why Antitrust Needs a New Deal*, 89 Tex. L. Rev. 1247, 1288–89 (2011); C. Scott Hemphill, *An Aggregate Approach to Antitrust: Using New Data and Rulemaking to Preserve Drug Competition*, 109 Colum. L. Rev. 629, 673–82 (2009); Justin Hurwitz, *Chevron and the Limits of Administrative Antitrust*, 76 U. Pitt. L. Rev. 209, 250–52 (2014); Sandeep Vaheesan, *Resurrecting 'A Comprehensive Charter of Economic Liberty': The Latent Power of the Federal Trade Commission*, 19 U. Pa. J. Bus. L. 645, 651–57 (2017)).

8 *See generally* Kenneth Culp Davis & Richard J. Pierce, Jr., Administrative Law Treatise (3rd ed., Little, Brown 1994).

9 Final Transcript at 296, Fed. Trade Comm'n, Non-Competes in the Workplace: Examining Antitrust and Consumer Protection Issues (Jan. 9, 2020), https://www.ftc.gov/system/files/documents/public_events/1556256/non-compete-workshop-transcript-full.pdf.

and the Constitution. At the time the FTC Act was passed (1914), both the nondelegation doctrine (barring Congress from handing legislative power to executive agencies) and the removal power (ensuring that the President has broad authority to remove executive-branch officers at will) were broader and more rigid than they are today. Even aside from section 6(g), the FTC Act tested these boundaries by letting the FTC enforce a broad "unfair methods" standard case by case, and by granting the FTC's commissioners "for-cause" removal protection. The half of section 6(g) at issue here, meanwhile, lies buried in a long section detailing the FTC's power simply to gather and report information in furtherance of its duties. To read section 6(g) as a grant of substantive (i.e., legislative) rulemaking authority is to assume that Congress, in a statute already at risk of bursting multiple constitutional seams, implanted, in a single vague sentence in an otherwise unrelated section, a further sweeping assault on the nondelegation doctrine. That is an untenable assumption. And as a matter of constitutional law, the proposed reading of section 6(g) *still* violates the nondelegation doctrine, a conclusion made all the clearer by the Supreme Court's recent decision in *Gundy v. United States*.[10]

Second, *National Petroleum Refiners* ignored a longstanding convention holding that Congress signals its intention that an agency may issue "legislative" or "substantive" rules with the "force and effect of law" by empowering the agency to impose some sanction upon those who violated those rules.[11] This convention holds that, absent any provision for sanctions, an agency could issue only procedural ("housekeeping") or "interpretive"[12] rules, which do no more than "advise the public of the agency's construction of the statutes and rules which it administers."[13] The FTC Act has *never* authorized sanctions for violations of the Act itself, and only with passage of the Magnuson-Moss Act of 1975 did Congress authorize civil penalties even for violations of regulations issued under the FTC Act.[14] The 1914 Act authorized a single method for applying section 5's prohibition of unfair methods of competition: the FTC would issue a cease-and-desist order, but it would be up to federal courts to enforce that order. Such enforcement involved no sanction whatsoever, merely the cessation of unlawful activity.

Further, *National Petroleum Refiners* misread the cases it cited. In each case, it was clear that the statute at issue conferred substantive rulemaking authority

10 139 S. Ct. 2116 (2019).

11 *See* Thomas W. Merrill & Kathryn Tongue Watts, *Agency Rules with the Force of Law: The Original Convention*, 116 Harv. L. Rev. 467 (2002), https://bit.ly/3D0yoSd.

12 "Interpretive rules" are "rules or statements issued by an agency to advise the public of the agency's construction of the statutes and rules which it administers." *See* Attorney General Manual, *supra* note 2, at 30 n. 3.

13 *Id.*

14 Magnuson-Moss Warranty–Federal Trade Commission Improvement Act, Pub. L. No. 93-657, 88 Stat. 2183 (1975) [hereinafter Magnuson-Moss Act]; 15 U.S.C. § 45(l).

– not only because Congress empowered the agency to sanction violations but also because of the plain text of the rulemaking provision at issue and because of other clues found in the structure of the Act. The FTC Act is just the opposite: nothing in the Act suggests that Congress intended the FTC to make substantive rules.

Third, amendments to the FTC Act enacted after *National Petroleum Refiners* are irrelevant to what Congress intended in 1914. The only relevant congressional action confirms that Congress understood an act exactly parallel to the FTC Act *not* to confer substantive rulemaking authority.

Finally, *National Petroleum Refiners* uses an obsolete form of statutory interpretation. Although it pays lip service to the text of the law, the decision in fact treats that text as an afterthought. The ruling is driven by the court's policy preferences, the supposed "broad purpose" that lies "behind" the statute, and the court's sense of what Congress "really" intended. *National Petroleum Refiners* is less a judicial decision interpreting the law than a piece of legislation (complete with legislative findings) unto itself.

In short, *National Petroleum Refiners* was wrongly decided. Section 6(g) empowers the FTC to make only procedural or interpretive rules, not legislative or substantive rules defining liability. While administrative agencies have varied in their understanding of what interpretive rules do,[15] the Administrative Conference of the United States, the official organ of the federal judiciary, has been clear: "[N]oncompliance with an interpretive rule should not form an independent basis for action in matters that determine the rights and obligations of any member of the public."[16] Thus, issuing interpretive rules regarding what is an unfair method of competition would have essentially the same effect upon regulated parties as issuing a policy statement: either way, the FTC must still police "unfair" competition case by case. And Congress and state legislatures must still be the ones that decide whether to proscribe as unlawful entire categories of methods of competition, either directly through legislation or by granting authority for the FTC (or state regulators) to make substantive rules.

II. The FTC Act in Its Historical Context

Statutory terms should be understood to "mean what they conveyed to reasonable people at the time they were written."[17] Further, "general terms as used on particular occasions," in a statute, "often carry with them implied restrictions

15 Blake Emerson & Ronald M. Levin, *Interpretive Rules in Practice*, The Regulatory Review (Oct. 30, 2019), https://bit.ly/3mhJ4VZ.

16 Administrative Conference of the United States, Agency Guidance Through Interpretive Rules 6 (2019), https://bit.ly/3F0FrfH.

17 Antonin Scalia & Bryan A. Garner, Reading Law: The Interpretation of Legal Texts 16 (Thomson/West 2012).

as to scope."[18] These are important principles here, because the Congress that passed the FTC Act in 1914 operated in a very different constitutional landscape than that which exists today.

Consider the state of two key constitutional doctrines in the early twentieth century: the nondelegation doctrine and the removal power. Both are vital to understanding why Congress crafted the FTC Act as it did – and why it is implausible in the extreme that Congress intended section 6(g) to confer the power to issue substantive rules. Simply put, when it passed the FTC Act, Congress did not bury a constitutional revolution deep in the fine print.

1. Bedrock Constitutional Principle #1: Nondelegation

Since the beginning of the Republic, it has been understood that Article I, Section 1 of the Constitution, which says that Congress alone holds "all legislative Powers," must place *some* limit on how much legislative authority Congress may hand to an executive agency. In the second half of the twentieth century, Congress would stretch that limit ever further, but in 1914 the boundaries remained firm.

The seminal statement of nondelegation is, of course, Chief Justice Marshall's declaration, in *Wayman v. Southard*, that the legislature must set the rules and policy for all "important subjects," but that it may leave to the executive the task of "fill[ing] up the details."[19] Because "nineteenth century legislators" generally "decided not to delegate broad authority to the executive branch," this statement long reigned, unchallenged and unquestioned.[20]

Although things began to change at the end of the nineteenth century with the rise of the populist movement, clear boundaries remained. The Interstate Commerce Commission, established in 1887, had no independent enforcement power, and it "lacked any power to *set* railroad rates."[21] Upholding portions of the Tariff Act of 1890 – which merely delegated certain "yes-or-no trade decisions"[22] based on findings of fact about other nations' tariff rates – the Court remained full-throated in its defense of the principle of nondelegation.[23] "That Congress cannot delegate legislative power to the President," the Court confirmed, "is a principle universally recognized as vital to the integrity and maintenance of the system of government ordained by the Constitution."[24]

---

18 Util. Air Reg. Group v. EPA, 134 S. Ct. 2427, 2451 (2014) (Breyer, J., joined by Ginsburg, Sotomayor, and Kagan, JJ., dissenting); *see also* EPIC Sys. Corp. v. Lewis, 138 S. Ct. 1612, 1631 (2018) ("[A] statute's meaning does not always 'turn solely' on the broadest imaginable 'definitions of its component words.'").

19 23 U.S. 1, 43 (1825).

20 James R. Copland, The Unelected: How an Unaccountable Elite is Governing America 24 (Encounter Books 2020).

21 *Id.* at 27.

22 *Id.*

23 Field v. Clark, 143 U.S. 649, 692 (1892).

24 *Id.*

Indeed, it remained the case that delegations of legislative power were "*never to be implied*"[25] from ambiguous statutory text.

Shortly before passage of the FTC Act, the Court, in *United States v. Grimaud* (1911), explained how the nondelegation principle applied to the distinction between an agency's ability to set its own "housekeeping" rules – rules governing its own proceedings – and an agency's ability to set substantive rules with binding effect on the public.[26] "From the beginning of the Government," *Grimaud* said, "various acts have been passed conferring upon executive officers power to make rules and regulations – not for the government of their departments, but for administering the laws which did govern. None of these statutes could confer legislative power.[27]

As *Grimaud* explained, Congress could go beyond conferring on an agency the power to make rules to "*administer*" legislatively set policies, but only if Congress set the *punishments* that would accompany the violation of such rules.[28] Congress, in other words, could give an agency the "power to fill up the details" of a legislative policy, so long as the "fine or imprisonment" or "penalties" for a violation were either "fixed by Congress" or "measured by the injury done."[29] In short, an agency had no power to set *substantive* rules unless it was doing so within a rubric of preset statutory penalties established by Congress.[30]

2. Bedrock Constitutional Principle #2: The Removal Power

The Constitution vests "the executive Power" in a single "President,"[31] who must "take Care that the Laws be faithfully executed."[32] The task of executive officers is, in Washington's words, to "assist the supreme Magistrate in discharging the duties of his trust."[33] Or, as Madison put it, "the lowest [executive] officers, the middle grade, and the highest" all "depend, as they ought, on the President."[34] The First Congress confirmed this understanding – that executive officers serve at the pleasure of the President – in what's known as the "Decision of 1789."[35]

---

25 ICC v. Railway Co. [hereinafter the *Queen and Crescent Case*], 167 U.S. 479, 494 (1897) (emphasis added). *See* Merrill & Watts, *supra* note 11, at 491 ("The *Queen and Crescent Case* suggests a nondelegation canon in the form of an 'express statement' rule: all grants of rulemaking authority confer only housekeeping powers, unless Congress expressly confers the power to make legislative rules.").

26 220 U.S. 506 (1911).

27 *Id.* at 517.

28 *Id.* at 517–18.

29 *Id.* at 517.

30 *Id.*

31 U.S. Const. art. II, § 1, cl. 1.

32 *Id.* art. II, § 3, cl. 3.

33 The Writings of George Washington 30, 334 (John C. Fitzpatrick ed., 1939).

34 1 Annals of Cong. 499 (1789) (J. Madison).

35 Saikrishna Prakash, *New Light on the Decision of 1789*, 91 Cornell L. Rev. 1021, 1066 (2006).

It passed several bills that contained no removal clause, but that discussed who would manage the papers of a removed officer.[36] The traditional view holds that Congress thereby affirmed that the Constitution empowers the President to remove officers at will.[37] As Madison explained in a letter to Jefferson, the legislators thus adopted the position "most consonant" to "the text of the Constitution" and "the requisite responsibility and harmony in the Executive Department."[38]

This is basically where things stood in 1914. *Myers v. United States* (1926), the first decision in which the Court squarely considered "whether under the Constitution the President has the exclusive power of removing executive officers,"[39] was still twelve years off. The notion that Congress could create "independent" officers with for-cause removal protections – let alone the notion that it could do so while handing those officers *legislative* power – remained uncertain and untested.

3. Putting the FTC Act in Its Proper Context

This is the constitutional background before which Congress passed the Federal Trade Commission Act of 1914. The FTC, the Act says, "shall be composed of five Commissioners," who, although "appointed by the President, by and with the advice and consent of the Senate," can be "removed by the President" only "for inefficiency, neglect of duty, or malfeasance in office."[40]

Section 5 of the Act makes a sweeping claim: it declares that "unfair methods of competition in commerce are hereby declared unlawful."[41] It then sets forth, in excruciating detail, how the Commission shall go about prosecuting such "methods."[42]

Section 6 of the Act provides the Commission with a series of ancillary powers for investigating, reporting, and publicizing the "unfair methods" barred by section 5.[43] Under section 6, the Commission may, for instance, "gather and compile information"; demand that businesses "file" with the Commission "reports or answers in writing to specific questions"; "make investigation" to ensure that adjudicatory decrees are being complied with; and "make public" "information obtained" through its investigations.[44] As with the enforcement powers in section 5, the investigatory powers in section 6 are set forth in great detail.

---

36 *Id.* at 1023 & nn. 7–9.

37 *Id.* at 1065–66.

38 Letter from James Madison to Thomas Jefferson (June 30, 1789), https://bit.ly/36BYhZd.

39 272 U.S. 52, 106 (1926).

40 FTC Act § 5, 38 Stat. at 718.

41 *Id.* at 719.

42 *Id.* at 719–21.

43 *Id.* § 6, 38 Stat. at 721–22.

44 *Id.*

Buried within section 6's detailed explanation of the Commission's investigatory powers lies section 6(g), with its single line about the Commission's power to set "rules."[45] Consider how that line sits in this image of the statutory text:

Sec. 6. That the commission shall also have power—

(a) To gather and compile information concerning, and to investigate from time to time the organization, business, conduct, practices, and management of any corporation engaged in commerce, excepting banks and common carriers subject to the Act to regulate commerce, and its relation to other corporations and to individuals, associations, and partnerships.

(b) To require, by general or special orders, corporations engaged in commerce, excepting banks, and common carriers subject to the Act to regulate commerce, or any class of them, or any of them, repectively, to file with the commission in such form as the commission may prescribe annual or special, or both annual and special, reports or answers in writing to specific questions, furnishing to the commission such information as it may require as to the organization, business, conduct, practices, management, and relation to other corporations, partnerships, and individuals of the respective corporations filing such reports or answers in writing. Such reports and answers shall be made under oath, or otherwise, as the commission may prescribe, and shall be filed with the commission within such reasonable period as the commission may prescribe, unless additional time be granted in any case by the commission.

(c) Whenever a final decree has been entered against any defendant corporation in any suit brought by the United States to prevent and restrain any violation of the antitrust Acts, to make investigation, upon its own initiative, of the manner in which the decree has been or is being carried out, and upon the application of the Attorney General it shall be its duty to make such investigation. It shall transmit to the Attorney General a report embodying its findings and recommendations as a result of any such investigation, and the report shall be made public in the discretion of the commission.

(d) Upon the direction of the President or either House of Congress to investigate and report the facts relating to any alleged violations of the antitrust Acts by any corporation.

(e) Upon the application of the Attorney General to investigate and make recommendations for the readjustment of the business of any corporation alleged to be violating the antitrust Acts in order that the corporation may thereafter maintain its organization, management, and conduct of business in accordance with law.

(f) To make public from time to time such portions of the information obtained by it hereunder, except trade secrets and names of customers, as it shall deem expedient in the public interest; and to make annual and special reports to the Congress and to submit therewith recommendations for additional legislation; and to provide for the publication of its reports and decisions in such form and manner as may be best adapted for public information and use.

(g) From time to time to classify corporations and to make rules and regulations for the purpose of carrying out the provisions of this Act.

(h) To investigate, from time to time, trade conditions in and with foreign countries where associations, combinations, or practices of manufacturers, merchants, or traders, or other conditions, may affect the foreign trade of the United States, and to report to Congress thereon, with such recommendations as it deems advisable.

45 *Id.*

Deep within this detailed section (so detailed that it clarifies how much *time* a business should have to file a report with the Commission), sitting beside a line empowering the Commission to "classify corporations" (according to whether the Commission has jurisdiction over them),[46] sits a few obscure words on making rules for "carrying out the provisions of this Act."[47]

4. If Section 6(g) Had Conferred Quasi-Legislative Power, the FTC Would Have Represented a Constitutional Revolution in 1914

In granting the Commission the power – albeit under well-defined procedures and close court supervision – to prosecute "unfair methods of competition," Congress was *already* undertaking a risky, novel, aggressive attack upon the traditional understanding of the nondelegation doctrine. Likewise, in granting the commissioners protection from being fired other than for "inefficiency, neglect of duty, or malfeasance in office," Congress was *already* undertaking a risky, novel, aggressive attack upon the traditional understanding of the removal power.

Yet to read section 6(g) as granting the Commission the power to set substantive rules defining "unfair methods of competition" is to assume that Congress was not *just* trying to *test* boundaries, but that it was on something of a kamikaze mission. After all, this reading of section 6(g) would mean that Congress wanted to hand unprecedented *legislative* power to unprecedentedly *insulated, independent* executive officers without *even the safeguards of well-defined procedures or judicial supervision*. So open-ended is the term "unfair methods of competition," in fact, that this reading would mean Congress had suddenly, in an act of startling defiance toward all governing precedent at the time, given an unaccountable mini-legislature a roving commission (so to speak) to "do justice." The Supreme Court has indeed recognized that the FTC wields remarkably broad powers, but even then, it was careful to emphasize that the FTC wields those powers only in a quasi-*judicial* role:

> [T]he Federal Trade Commission does not arrogate excessive power to itself if, in measuring a practice against the elusive but congressionally mandated standard of fairness, it, like a *court of equity*,

46 "Classification" is a key term of art in common carriage law generally and is critical to determining which corporations and services fall within the limitations imposed upon the FTC's jurisdiction by Congress. Both section 5, governing unfair and deceptive acts and practices, and section 6, governing the Commission's powers to investigate and issue reports, have always contained the same limitation: "common carriers subject to the Acts to regulate commerce" are excluded from the Commission's otherwise-general jurisdiction. 15 U.S.C. §§ 45(a)(2), 46(a). "Congress established Section 5's common-carrier exemption to avoid interagency conflict" and because "Congress did not intend the FTC to regulate common-carrier business practices." Fed. Trade Comm'n v. AT&T Mobility LLC, 883 F.3d 848, 854–55 (9th Cir. 2018). In some cases, another agency responsible for administering one of "the Acts to regulate commerce" may draw a clear line by explicitly classifying something as a non-common carrier service. *See, e.g.*, Inquiry Concerning High Speed Access to the Internet Over Cable and Other Facilities, 17 F.C.C. Rcd. 4798 ¶¶ 32–33 (2002) ("The Communications Act does not clearly indicate how cable modem service should be classified or regulated… . we herein address the classification of cable modem service for purposes of the Act."). Absent such decisions, the classification of a particular service, and thus whether it falls within the FTC's jurisdiction, may be unclear. By empowering the FTC to "classify corporations," section 6(g) allows the FTC to resolve such uncertainty not only by issuing interpretive rules that might govern future classifications, *see supra* note 12 and associated text, but also case by case ("[f]rom time to time") in enforcement actions or investigatory orders.

47 *Id.*

> considers public values beyond simply those enshrined in the letter or encompassed in the spirit of the antitrust laws.[48]

Reading section 6(g) to confer the power to make *legislative* rules assumes that Congress did this in *half* of a one-sentence *subsection* of detailed instructions about the Commission's power simply to investigate, collect, and report information. Really? Look again at the statutory text. It is utterly implausible that section 6(g) was the constitutional ticking nuclear time bomb that this reading makes it out to be.

Not surprisingly, when the Act was brought before the Court in *Humphrey's Executor v. United States* (1935), the justices did not read section 6 this way.[49] Although *Humphrey's Executor* is famous for breaking new ground concerning the removal power, the decision reads section 6 consistent with the uncontested understanding of nondelegation that reigned at the time. "The Federal Trade Commission," it says, was created "to carry into effect legislative policies *embodied in the statute* in accordance with *the legislative standard therein prescribed*, and to perform other *specified* duties as a *legislative or as a judicial aid*."[50] Consistent with this understanding of the Commission as a body that simply "fill[s] in and administer[s] the details embodied by" the "general standard" (i.e., "unfair methods of competition"), the Court understood section 6 as empowering the Commission to "mak[e] investigations and reports… for the information of Congress… in aid of the legislative power."[51] It is in *that* sense – as a maker of investigations and reports – that the Court viewed the Commission as acting as a "quasi-legislative" body.[52]

The notion that the Commission would *make substantive rules itself* is not mentioned in, or suggested by, *Humphrey's Executor*'s explicit reference to section 6. Such a power would have been revolutionary, as the Court's careful effort to describe the Commission as a mere "aid" to the other branches – a maker of *reports!* – confirms.[53] Had the justices been told that, in making their landmark ruling cabining the removal power, they were affirming the for-cause protections and overall independence of true *legislators* who had been lodged in the executive branch, they would likely have been shocked.

That is just what those justices did, concluded the D.C. Circuit, in effect, in *National Petroleum Refiners*. Yet "Statutory construction… is a holistic endeavor. A provision that may seem ambiguous in isolation is often clarified by the

48 FTC v. Sperry & Hutchinson Co., 405 U.S. 233, 244 (1972) (emphasis added).

49 295 U.S. 602 (1935).

50 *Id.* at 628 (emphasis added).

51 *Id.*

52 *Id.*

53 *Id.* ("In administering the provisions of the statute in respect of 'unfair methods of competition' – that is to say, in filling in and administering the details embodied by that general standard – the commission acts in part *quasi*-legislatively and in part *quasi*-judicially. In *making investigations and reports thereon for the information of Congress under § 6*, in aid of the legislative power, it acts as a legislative agency. Under § 7, which authorizes the commission to act as a master in chancery under rules prescribed by the court, it acts as an agency of the judiciary.") (emphasis added.).

remainder of the statutory scheme... because only one of the permissible meanings produces a substantive effect that is compatible with the rest of the law" – or, for that matter, with the Constitution.[54] Perhaps, when considered in total isolation, the term "carrying out the provisions of this Act"[55] could mean "make substantive rules about what 'unfair methods of competition' means." But when that term is considered in the context of the Constitution, the specific understanding of that charter that governed in 1914, and the rest of section 6, there can be no doubt that the term refers to internal housekeeping rules.

5. Congress Crafted the FTC Act to Respect a More Rigid Nondelegation Doctrine

National Petroleum Refiners artfully sidestepped the nondelegation doctrine, burying a brief discussion of the issue at the bottom of the decision. The author of the opinion, Judge Skelly Wright, does not mention why Senator Albert Cummins, "one of the bill's main proponents,"[56] assured his fellow Senators that the bill would not violate the nondelegation doctrine:

> Every lawyer understands that we can not delegate to a commission legislative power; that when we give to an administrative body the execution of a law of Congress we must at the same time give it a standard, a guide and rule which it is to apply to the particular case and determine whether that particular case falls under the prohibition of the law.[57]

In a footnote, the court reprints a legislative colloquy on the House floor:

> Mr. SHERLEY. If the gentleman will permit, the Federal Trade Commission differs from the Interstate Commerce Commission in that it has no affirmative power to say what shall be done in the future?
>
> Mr. STEVENS of Minnesota. Certainly.
>
> Mr. SHERLEY. In other words, it exercises in no sense a legislative function such as is exercised by the Interstate Commerce Commission?
>
> Mr. STEVENS of Minnesota. Yes, [t]he gentleman is entirely right. We desired clearly to exclude that authority from the power of the commission. We did not know as we could grant it anyway. But the time has not arrived to consider or discuss such a question.[58]

---

54 Smith v. United States, 508 U.S. 223, 233 (1993).

55 FTC Act § 6, 38 Stat. at 722.

56 *Nat'l Petroleum Refiners*, 482 F.2d at 706; Fed. Trade Comm'n, Statement of Chairman Leibowitz and Commissioner Rosch, In the Matter of Intel Corporation, Docket No. 9341, at 2 (Dec. 16, 2009), https://bit.ly/3kU9JIL.

57 51 Cong. Rec. 11,103 (1914).

58 *Nat'l Petroleum Refiners*, 482 F.2d at n. 19 (citing 51 Cong. Rec. 14,938 (1914)).

Judge Wright dismisses this exchange, like other floor comments, as "utterly unhelpful."[59] While the FTC Act's legislative history is indeed complex, the text of the Act is clear: The Commission could *allege* that a particular practice in a particular case was unfair; it could even order a company to cease and desist from that practice.[60] But ultimately, it would be the courts, not the Commission, that would decide what constituted an unfair method of competition.[61] The Commission's role would be that of a special prosecutor, not a judge – and not a legislator.

6. Reading Section 6(g) to Confer Legislative Power Violates the Nondelegation Doctrine as the Supreme Court Has Recently Signaled It Will Apply It

That an expanded reading of section 6(g) would have clearly violated the nondelegation doctrine, as that doctrine was understood *in 1914*, shows, as a matter of statutory interpretation, that that expanded reading is not the correct one. Equally important, however, is the fact that, as a matter of constitutional law, the expanded reading likely violates the nondelegation doctrine *today*. Although it is true that since 1914, Congress has passed, and the Court has blessed, broad delegations of power, the nondelegation doctrine also appears set for a revival.

Gundy v. United States (2019) is the Supreme Court's most recent statement on how much authority Congress may delegate to executive agencies.[62] *Gundy* upholds an "intelligible principle" test, under which Congress's power to delegate authority is broad indeed.[63] Only eight justices heard the case, however, and only four justices endorsed the regnant standard. In a brief concurrence, Justice Alito expressed his "support" for "reconsider[ing] th[at] approach," if and when a majority of the Court wishes to do so.[64] Justice Kavanaugh, who did not participate in *Gundy*, has expressed just such a willingness.[65] And Justice Ginsburg, one of the four justices to stand by the "intelligible principle" standard in *Gundy*, has been replaced by Justice Barrett.

Justice Gorsuch's dissent in *Gundy* – which Chief Justice Roberts and Justice Thomas joined, and which Justices Alito, Kavanaugh, and Barrett are likely to find attractive

---

59 *Id.* at 709.

60 FTC Act § 6, 38 Stat. at 719–20.

61 51 Cong. Rec. 11,104 (1914) (statement of Senator Cummins) ("We say that if you find that unfair competition exists then you must prevent it, but in order to ascertain what unfair competition is you must go to the courts and to the common sense of mankind, and there are many adjudications on the subject.").

62 139 S. Ct. 2116 (2019).

63 *See* Mistretta v. United States, 488 U.S. 361, 372 (1989) ("Applying this 'intelligible principle' test to congressional delegations, our jurisprudence has been driven by a practical understanding that, in our increasingly complex society, replete with ever-changing and more technical problems, Congress simply cannot do its job absent an ability to delegate power under broad general directives.").

64 139 S. Ct. at 2131 (concurring opinion).

65 *See* Paul v. United States, 140 S. Ct. 342 (2019) (Statement of Kavanaugh, J., respecting the denial of certiorari).

in a future case – thus warrants more attention than an average dissent. If the executive branch may make "laws," Justice Gorsuch notes, they will "not be few in number," nor "the product of widespread social consensus," nor "likely to protect minority interests," nor "apt to provide stability and fair notice."[66] Executive lawmaking also enables both the legislature and the executive to evade accountability, each branch blaming the other for the consequences of open-ended legislation implemented through detailed agency rules.[67] For these and other reasons, Justice Gorsuch urges the Court to end its "intelligible principle misadventure" and insists that "Congress, and not the Executive Branch, make the policy judgments" that are implemented through agency action.[68]

Even when the FTC applies it only case-by-case, under a rubric of congressionally set procedural rules and close judicial scrutiny, the "unfair methods of competition" standard is, post-*Gundy*, at high risk of being declared an unconstitutional over-delegation.[69] "The term 'unfair,'" after all, "is an elusive concept, often dependent upon the eye of the beholder."[70] Indeed, as Commissioner Phillips observed last year, the term "unfair methods of competition" in section 5 is "almost the exact [same] wording" as "codes of fair competition," the term struck down under the nondelegation doctrine in *A.L.A. Schechter Poultry Corp. v. United States*.[71]

So there might be a nondelegation problem with section 5 no matter what. Under an expanded reading of section 6(g), the problem simply becomes all the more acute. One could say that enacting substantive competition rules under section 6(g) would amount to double-dog-daring the Supreme Court to follow through on transforming Justice Gorsuch's *Gundy* dissent into a controlling opinion.

It is not hard to envision how, in its push to use essentially a single word, "unfair," to expand its power over markets, the economy, and the country itself, the FTC might ultimately ensure that its authority is snapped back into bounds that are *narrower* than those that exist today. A recent case involving another vague and open-ended word, "necessary," shows how this might occur.

That case, *Florida v. Becerra*, involved a law that gives the Surgeon General the authority to "make and enforce such regulations as in his judgment are necessary to prevent... the spread of communicable diseases."[72] The Centers for Disease

66 139 S. Ct. at 2135.

67 *Id.*

68 *Id.* at 2141.

69 *See* Corbin K. Barthold, *Pride Before the Fall at the FTC?*, Law & Liberty (Nov. 2, 2021), https://bit.ly/3rt3U85.

70 E.I. Du Pont De Nemours & Co. v. FTC, 729 F.2d 128, 137–38 (2d Cir. 1984).

71 295 U.S. 495, 553 (1935) (Cardozo, J., concurring). *See* Commissioner Noah Joshua Phillips Prepared Remarks, Fed. Trade Comm'n, Non-Compete Clauses in the Workplace: Examining Antitrust and Consumer Protection Issues (Jan. 9, 2020), https://bit.ly/2U7jGrv.

72 554 F. Supp. 3d 1241, 1264 (M.D. Fla. 2021). *See* 42 U.S.C. § 264(a).

Control (CDC) argued that, so long as it concluded that a measure was "necessary" to prevent even a *risk* of interstate transmission of a disease, the statute empowered it to take any such measure it deemed fit.[73] Although the district court adopted a narrower reading of the statute, it also ruled, in the alternative, that the CDC's preferred reading contained no "intelligible principle" and thus violated the nondelegation doctrine. As the court noted, the CDC's reading, if accepted, amounted to "a breathtaking, unprecedented, and acutely and singularly authoritarian claim" of authority.[74]

In a passage that (as here shortened) could easily be applied to an unchecked reading of "unfair methods of competition," the court marveled at some of the implications of the CDC's unchecked reading of "necessary to prevent the... spread of communicable diseases":

> [T]he [modern] law of the United States on non-delegation has... [enabled] an argument... about whether Congress, based on an ambiguous sentence or two in a statute, can bestow on an executive agent the power indefinitely to halt the operation of, and perhaps destroy, an entire industry or several industries or perhaps the industries of the entire nation, destroy businesses and lives dependent on industry,... or otherwise alter the course, history, prosperity, and health of the nation[.][75]

If it were pegged to the jurisprudence of the Sherman Act, starting with the consumer welfare standard, the phrase "unfair methods of competition" could not lead to the results contemplated in this passage. But if left to mean whatever the agency *says* it means, then the phrase certainly could. It would enable an independent commission – a group of "unelected, electorally unaccountable, and largely anonymous executive agents"[76] – to halt industries, destroy businesses, and otherwise alter the course of the nation. Whatever it takes to stamp out "unfairness."[77]

The FTC of late seems to be in a rush to insist that the word "unfair" should indeed mean whatever the Commission wants it to mean. That is the message sent by the agency's attempt to detach itself from the Sherman Act through its repeal of the Unfair Methods of Competition Policy Statement.[78] It is also the

---

73 *Id.* at 1278–80.

74 *Id.* at 1280.

75 *Id.* at 1286.

76 *Id.*

77 Perhaps the weak but still extant protections of property in the Fifth and Fourteenth Amendments would prevent the worst excesses. But *cf.* Kurt Vonnegut, Harrison Bergeron (1961) (in which the 211th, 212th, and 213th amendments to the Constitution enable the Handicapper General, by making all Americans equal in every respect, to ensure that there truly are no "unfair methods of competition").

78 *See* Fed. Trade Comm'n, Press Release, FTC Rescinds 2015 Policy that Limited Its Enforcement Ability Under the FTC Act (July 1, 2021), https://bit.ly/3ilp6bH.

message sent when the chair urges the agency to see itself as a "body whose work shapes the distribution of power and opportunity across our economy."[79]

The agency's section 5 power may be in peril no matter what the agency does. Nothing could force the issue faster, however, than an effort to assert broad rulemaking authority under section 6(g). Such an effort would send the agency hurtling toward conflict with the nondelegation doctrine. And if the agency insisted on sliding down that chute, it might well find itself with less power at the bottom than it had at the top.[80]

III. Before *National Petroleum Refiners*, Congress Signaled Its Intention to Confer Quasi-Legislative Powers by Specifying Sanctions

Professor Richard J. Pierce, the administrative law expert who told the FTC's 2020 workshop that the reasoning of *National Petroleum Refiners* was "laughable," has company among leading experts in administrative law in deriding the case. Columbia Law Professor Thomas Merrill and University of Washington School of Law Professor Kathryn Tongue Watts challenged Judge Wright's analysis in a 2001 article published in the *Harvard Law Review*.[81] Merrill and Watts conclude:

> The legislative history of the [FTC Act]. . . provides significant evidence that Congress did not intend to grant legislative rulemaking authority to the FTC. Judge Wright nevertheless pronounced this history to be "ambiguous" regarding the meaning of Section 6(g), and then relegated the details to an appendix for the especially diligent reader to consult. Such ambiguity, he said, was not enough to overcome "the plain language of Section 6(g)," which, "read in light of the broad, clearly agreed-upon concerns that motivated passage of the Trade Commission Act, confirms the framers' intent to allow exercise of the power claimed here." In the end, Judge Wright adopted what amounted to a new canon: unless the legislative history reveals a clear intent to the contrary, courts should resolve any uncertainty about the scope of an agency's rulemaking authority in favor of finding a delegation of the full measure of power to the agency.[82]

---

79 Memo from Chair Lina M. Khan to Commission Staff and Commissioners Regarding the Vision and Priorities for the FTC 2 (Sept. 22, 2021), https://bit.ly/3uqtBXl.

80 *See* Corbin K. Barthold, *Regulator Beware: Will FTC chairwoman Lina Khan's aggressive posture invite a judicial rebuke?* City Journal (Dec. 2, 2021), https://bit.ly/3EgRW6A.

81 *See* Merrill & Watts, *supra* note 11.

82 *Id.* at 556–57.

National Petroleum Refiners, Merrill and Watts lament "provided the roadmap for a more general erasure of the convention"[83] that had guided Congress for decades in drafting legislation:

> Starting around World War I, Congress began following a convention for indicating whether an agency had the power to promulgate legislative rules. Under this convention, the requisite textual signal was provided by the inclusion of a separate provision in the statute attaching "sanctions" to the violation of rules and regulations promulgated under a particular rulemaking grant. If the statute prescribed a sanction, then the authority to make "rules and regulations" included the authority to adopt legislative rules having the force of law. If the statute did not include a sanction, the authority to make "rules and regulations" encompassed only interpretive or procedural rules.[84]

This convention was clearly satisfied by the statute at issue in all but two of the cases cited by *National Petroleum Refiners*. Five statutes authorized monetary fines or imprisonment for violations of regulations issued thereunder.[85] Two statutes authorized the revocation of licenses or permits.[86] One of the statutes explicitly provided that an agency's rules could be substantive and binding.[87] As for the two exceptions, in one of them the court simply did not address

---

83 *Id.* at 557.

84 *Id.* at 493. Merrill & Watts continue: "The 'sanctions' took various forms. The clearest case, of course, was when Congress imposed criminal or monetary civil penalties on persons who violated an agency's regulations. On other occasions, however, the sanctions might take the form of the forfeiture or destruction of property, the revocation of licenses, or the denial of benefits. In contrast, if the statute was silent regarding the legal consequences for failure to conform to regulations, it was understood as granting the agency the power to make only housekeeping rules." *Id.* at 493–94.

85 Mourning v. Family Publications Service, Inc., 411 U.S. 356 (1973), involved the Truth in Lending Act of 1968, which imposed stiff fines and imprisonment for those who failed to disclose information required by any regulation issued under the Act. Consumer Credit Protection Act, Pub. L. No. 90-321, § 105, 82 Stat. 146, 151 (codified as amended, 15 U.S.C. § 1601 *et seq.*). In Public Service Comm'n of State of New York v. FPC, 327 F.2d 893, 897 (D.C. Cir. 1964), the appeals court upheld a regulation issued by the Federal Power Commission defining the criteria for issuing temporary certificates of authority to gas producers in emergencies. The Natural Gas Act's "General Penalties" provision authorized a daily penalty of up to $500 for violations of any regulation made by the Commission. Natural Gas Act of 1938 (NGA), Pub. L. No. 75-688, § 21(b), 52 Stat. 821, 833 (codified at 15 U.S.C. § 717 *et seq.*). In Morgan Stanley & Co. v. Securities Exch. Comm'n, 126 F.2d 325 (2d Cir. 1942), the Second Circuit upheld SEC rules involving the Public Utility Holding Company Act, Public Utility Act of 1935, Pub. L. No. 74-333, § 29, 49 Stat. 803. PUHCA authorized monetary fines up to $200,000 and imprisonment up to two years for "[a]ny person who willfully and knowingly violates any rule, regulation, restriction, condition, or order made or imposed by the Commission under authority of this Act." *Id.* The Motor Carrier Act authorized fines up to $500 for violations of the agency's regulations, Motor Carrier Act of 1935, Pub. L. No. 74-255, § 222(a), 49 Stat. 543, 564, and the Supreme Court upheld the Interstate Commerce Commission's authority to issue binding substantive rules under the Motor Carrier Act in Am. Trucking Ass'ns v. United States, 344 U.S. 298 (1953). U.S. Nat. Broadcasting Co. v. U.S., 319 U.S. 190 (1943), upheld the FCC's authority to make substantive rules under the Communications Act of 1934, Pub L. No. 73-416, which imposed stiff fines for rule violations, 47 U.S.C. § 502.

86 Communications Act of 1934 § 312(a) (revocation of broadcast licenses); Motor Carrier Act of 1935 § 212(a) (revocation of permits and licenses).

87 Natural Gas Act § 16, 52 Stat. at 830 ("For the purposes of its rules and regulations, the Commission may classify persons and matters within its jurisdiction and prescribe different requirements for different classes of persons or matters"). *See generally Service Comm'n of State of New York v. FPC.*

whether the agency had substantive rulemaking authority,[88] and, in the other, as we shall see, the Supreme Court – operating long after the convention was forgotten – left the matter far from resolved.[89]

The FTC Act of 1914, by contrast, is a clear-cut example of the convention identified by Merrill and Watts in action. Congress did not provide for sanctions for violations of regulations issued under the Act (or, indeed, even for violations of the Act itself). Under section 5, the key provision of the FTC Act, the Commission was "empowered and directed to prevent persons, partnerships, or corporations, except banks, and common carriers subject to the Acts to regulate commerce, from using unfair methods of competition in commerce."[90] Section 5 spelled out, at length, how this process was to work: the Commission would, upon "reason to believe" that someone was violating the Act, issue an order designating the matter for hearing, hold the hearing, and, if it concluded that a violation had occurred, issue a cease-and-desist order.[91] The Commission had no power to enforce its own orders or impose any sanction upon anyone who violated them, only the power to ask a federal court to enforce such orders.[92] Congress was unmistakably clear on this point: "The jurisdiction of the... court of appeals of the United States to enforce, set aside, or modify orders of the commission shall be exclusive."[93] The Act authorized the courts, not the FTC, to impose penalties, and only upon those who refused to comply with subpoenas issued by the FTC, those who made false statements to the FTC, corporations that failed to file reports ordered by the FTC, or employees of the FTC who divulged information obtained by the Commission.[94] No penalties could be imposed for violation of a cease-and-desist order.

"The failure to provide any sanction for the violation of rules adopted under section 6(g)," Merrill and Watts conclude, "along with the placement of the rulemaking grant in section 6, which conferred the FTC's investigative powers, clearly suggests that Congress intended the rulemaking grant to serve as an adjunct to the FTC's investigative duties, regarding which Congress had not given the agency the authority to act with the force of law."[95] In 1975, Congress

88 United States v. Oregon, 366 U.S. 643, 647–48 (1961). Judge Wright also relies on the Supreme Court's declaration in *SEC v. Chenery Corp.* (1947) that "[t]he function of filling in the interstices of the Act should be performed, as much as possible, through this quasi-legislative promulgation of rules to be applied in the future," *Nat'l Petroleum Refiners*, 482 F.2d at 692 (quoting SEC v. Chenery Corp., 332 U.S. 194, 202 (1947)). As Judge Wright acknowledges, however, "[t]here was no question that the SEC in *Chenery* had substantive rule-making powers." *Id.* at 683.

89 *See infra* at 12–13.

90 FTC Act § 5, 38 Stat. at 719.

91 *Id.*

92 *Id.*

93 *Id.* at 720.

94 *Id.*

95 Merrill & Watts, *supra* note 11, at 504–05.

amended the FTC Act to empower the agency to impose civil penalties upon those who violate orders of the Commission,[96] but the current section 5(l) would be irrelevant to Merrill and Watts's analysis of how the convention applied to the FTC Act even if the provision had been included in the 1914 Act: under section 5(l), sanctions apply not to violations of FTC regulations (or even to violations of the Act itself), but to violations of court orders imposed for previous violations of the Act. This is roughly akin to penalties for contempt of court,[97] and a far cry from indicating that Congress intended *regulations* issued by the Commission to have substantive effect.

1. The Rise and Fall of the Sanctions/Rulemaking Convention

Merrill and Watts trace the evolution of the convention by conducting a comprehensive survey of legislation enacted in the Progressive and New Deal eras.[98] They summarize its history:

> The convention… gradually developed around the second decade of the twentieth century as Congress created new administrative entities and considered what kind of rulemaking authority to give them. Moreover, as we shall see, the convention was never explicitly memorialized in an authoritative text, such as a statute, a legislative drafting guide, or a prominent judicial decision. It remained part of the unwritten "common law" of legislative drafting in the first half of the twentieth century. Accordingly, the only way to establish the existence of the convention is to examine a significant number of regulatory statutes and their associated legislative histories, supplemented by contemporary writings by knowledgeable participants in the legislative and administrative processes.[99]

This convention has its roots in two Supreme Court decisions: *United States v. Eaton* (1892) held that a "sufficient statutory authority should exist for declaring any act or omission a criminal offense,"[100] and suggested that if Congress "ma[de] it a crime to violate a regulation adopted by an agency," Congress "would have to speak 'distinctly' in criminalizing failures to abide by agency regulations."[101] While *Eaton* relied "on a blend of nondelegation

96 Magnuson-Moss Act, *supra* note 14, 15 U.S.C. § 45(l).

97 *Id.*

98 Merrill & Watts, *supra* note 11, at 495 n. 129 ("We began by identifying and analyzing numerous nineteenth- and early twentieth-century regulatory statutes, which we located through a variety of sources, including case law, legal articles and books about rulemaking, and by scanning the United States Code's Popular Name Table, which lists acts and the years in which they were enacted. We next identified those regulatory statutes that include facially ambiguous rulemaking grants and sought to determine whether there was any authority discussing whether these grants conferred legislative or merely housekeeping powers.").

99 Merrill & Watts, *supra* note 11, at 495.

100 144 U.S. 677, 688 (1892).

101 Merrill & Watts, *supra* note 11, at 500 (quoting *Eaton*, 144 U.S. at 688).

and lenity precepts,"[102] *United States v. Grimaud* (1911)[103] "framed its analysis exclusively in terms of whether the delegation was permissible."[104] The pertinent passage runs as follows:

> When Congress [has] legislated and indicated its will, it [can] give to those who were to act under such general provisions "power to fill up the details" by the establishment of administrative rules and regulations, the violation of which [can] be punished by fine or imprisonment fixed by Congress, or by penalties fixed by Congress or measured by the injury done.[105]

Another case we quoted in that section, the *Queen and Crescent* case, is also pertinent.[106] The Interstate Commerce Act of 1887 empowered the Interstate Commerce Commission to declare whether a given railroad rate was reasonable. At issue in the *Queen and Crescent* case was whether the Act further empowered the ICC to set future rates through rulemaking. The Court concluded that it did not. Although whether the Act granted the power was debatable, the Court explained, such grants of rulemaking power are "never to be implied."[107]

The convention ultimately fell into obscurity because it was never codified. Merrill and Watts explain:

> The most remarkable aspect of this drafting convention is that modern administrative lawyers are not aware of its existence.... In administrative law, as in other areas of American law, legal knowledge is transmitted through the study of appellate opinions. With no opinion to flag the issue, questions about the meaning of ambiguous rulemaking grants were ignored in post-World War II treatises and instructional materials devoted to administrative law. As a result, knowledge of the convention died out. When, in subsequent years, the Supreme Court occasionally encountered cases that implicated the meaning of such rulemaking grants, none of the parties alerted the Court to the existence of the convention, even if it would have been in their interests to do so – presumably because their lawyers did not know about it.[108]

---

102 *Id.*

103 220 U.S. 506 (1911).

104 Merrill & Watts, *supra* note 11, at 501.

105 220 U.S. at 517.

106 167 U.S. 479 (1897).

107 167 U.S. at 494.

108 Merrill & Watts, *supra* note 11, at 472.

Again, most of the cases cited by *National Petroleum Refiners* involved statutes that would clearly have satisfied the convention, had the court in question applied it; instead, in each case, the court came up with reasons for interpreting a grant of rulemaking authority to be substantive in nature.[109] And in inventing such specious reasons, those courts laid the groundwork for the confusion to which Judge Wright gave voice.

Merrill and Watts note only one statute that the Supreme Court has held to confer substantive rulemaking power that would not have satisfied his convention. In *National Labor Relations Board* (NLRB) *v. Wyman-Gordon Co.* (1969), the Supreme Court upheld the Board's ability to make substantive rules under the National Labor Relations Act of 1935 (NLRA).[110] Merrill and Watts call the decision "[p]erhaps the most influential judicial stimulus to use legislative rulemaking."[111] Judge Wright claimed that *Wyman-Gordon* "hinted that there may be circumstances where agency policy innovations should be made *only* in rule-making proceedings."[112] He also invoked a 1973 appellate decision in *Bell Aerospace* reaching the same conclusion.[113] But shortly after *National Petroleum Refiners*, the Supreme Court overruled *Bell Aerospace*, reaffirming that the NLRB could announce new interpretations of its statute through adjudication – *without* addressing whether the Board could issue legislative rules.[114] The NLRB returned to operating purely through adjudication for the next three decades. In 1991, the Supreme Court upheld a legislative rule promulgated by the NLRB under section 6(a) of the 1935 law.[115] This provision, declared the Court without further explanation, was "unquestionably sufficient to authorize the rule at issue."[116] Indeed, as Merrill and Watts note, that question simply was not raised at all.[117]

If those challenging the NLRB rule had bothered to raise the question, the Court might well have reached the opposite conclusion. For Merrill and Watts, the "legislative history of the NLRA substantiates [the] conclusion" that the Act

109 *See supra* notes 85–86.

110 394 U.S. 759 (1969).

111 Merrill & Watts, *supra* note 11, at 567.

112 *Nat'l Petroleum Refiners*, 482 F.2MEVd$/MEV$ at 682.

113 *Id.* at 682–84 (citing Bell Aerospace Div. of Textron, Inc. v. NLRB, 475 F.2MEVd$/MEV$ 485 (2d Cir. 1973)).

114 NLRB v. Bell Aerospace Co., 416 U.S. 267 (1974).

115 American Hosp. Ass'n v. NLRB, 499 U.S. 606, 609–10 (1991).

116 *Id.*

117 Merrill & Watts, *supra* note 11, at 570, note two reasons for this: "First, the pathbreaking opinions of Judges Wright and Friendly that had treated ambiguous rulemaking grants as presumptively authorizing legislative rules had by then been on the books for a decade or more. Second, although *Wyman-Gordon* did not expressly consider the NLRB's rulemaking powers under section 6(a), the opinions in that case, as well as the Court's treatment of the rulemaking versus adjudication issue in *Bell Aerospace*, implicitly suggested that the NLRB possessed legislative rulemaking powers. Thus, by the time the Court decided *American Hospital* in 1991, counsel for the Association no doubt concluded it was not worth the effort to challenge the NLRB's exercise of legislative rulemaking powers."

should not have been interpreted to confer substantive rulemaking power.[118] At most, a court reconsidering the NLRA would likely conclude that section 6(a) authorized rulemakings not to create liability, but to protect against it. Section 8(2), the only provision of the act to reference section 6(a)'s rulemaking powers, created a safe harbor from section 8's general provisions regarding unfair labor practices, allowing an employer to "permit[] employees to confer with him during working hours without loss of time or pay." Thus, whatever rulemaking power section 6(a) confers, the NLRA differs fundamentally from the FTC Act: only after authorizing "administrative rules" in a freestanding provision (§ 6(a)) and specifying a narrow substantive application of such rules (§ 8), does the NLRA authorize enforcement of the Act through adjudication (§ 10).[119] The FTC Act does the opposite: it bars unfair methods of competition (§ 5(a)(1)), describes the agency's adjudicatory process in exquisite detail (§ 5(b) – (f)), then briefly mentions rulemaking among many "additional powers" of the FTC (§ 6(g)).[120]

2. Applying That Convention to the FTC Act

In *United States v. George* (1913), the Supreme Court applied *Grimaud* to strike down a substantive regulation issued by the General Land Office. Each of the four statutory provisions invoked as authority for the regulation, concluded the Court, "confer[red] administrative power only" – and "indubitably so."[121] One of them bears a striking resemblance to section 6(g): "The Commissioner of the General Land Office... is authorized to enforce and carry into execution, by appropriate regulations, every part of the provisions of this Title not otherwise specially provided for."[122]

Congress's decision, the very next year, not to include any sanction for violations of the FTC Act, let alone rules issued by the FTC, thus speaks clearly about its intentions. As Merrill and Watts conclude:

> Neither Eaton nor Grimaud spoke directly to the question of how facially ambiguous rulemaking grants should be interpreted. Nevertheless, the decisions established points of reference that

---

118 "Upon consideration of different versions of the bill, one Senator made a proposal to limit the NLRB's rulemaking powers under what became section 6(a) to such '*reasonable* rules and regulations as may be necessary to carry out the provisions of this Act.' However, the proposal was rejected because, according to a Senate memorandum, 'in no case do the rules have the force of law in the sense that criminal penalties or fines accrue for their violation, and it seems sufficient that the rules prescribed must be "necessary to carry out the provisions" of the act.' The *Final Report* of the Attorney General's Committee of 1941 confirms this legislative history: it notes that the NLRB's 'power to "make, amend, and rescind such rules and regulations as may be necessary to carry out the provisions of this chapter" has been assumed to extend only to matters of procedure.'" *Id.* Merrill & Watts, *supra* note 11, at 511 (citing Attorney General's Comm. on Admin. Procedure, Administrative Procedure in Government Agencies, S. Doc. No. 77-8, at 98 n. 18 (1st Sess. 1941)) (internal citation omitted).

119 National Labor Relations Act, Pub. L. No. 74-198, §§ 6(a), 8, 10, 49 Stat. 449 (1935).

120 *See* FTC Act 15 U.S.C. § 45. Subsection references correspond to the current version of the Act, to which Congress has added subsections.

121 228 U.S. 14, 20 (1913).

122 *Id.* at 22 n. 2.

> Congress could use in signaling whether particular grants authorized rules and regulations having the force of law. If Congress specifically provided that the violation of a regulation would result in the imposition of sanctions, such as criminal penalties, then the rule would have the force of law (Grimaud). If Congress did not so provide, an agency could not enforce the rule with criminal penalties (Eaton), and it was doubtful whether it could be enforced with any type of civil sanction.[123]

National Petroleum Refiners, noted Merrill and Watts, failed to recognize a key difference in the precedents it relied on: "the rulemaking grants in those cases, unlike Section 6(g), were coupled with statutory provisions imposing sanctions for rule violations."[124] Merrill and Watts's explanation speaks for itself:

> The failure to provide any sanction for the violation of rules adopted under section 6(g) [or, indeed, even of the FTC Act itself], along with the placement of the rulemaking grant in section 6, which conferred the FTC's investigative powers, clearly suggests that Congress intended the rulemaking grant to serve as an adjunct to the FTC's investigative duties, regarding which Congress had not given the agency the authority to act with the force of law.
>
> The legislative history of the Act supports the conclusion that the FTC's rulemaking grant did not confer legislative rulemaking authority. Section 6(g)'s general rulemaking grant originated in the House Bill of 1914, which conferred only investigative powers, such as the power to require reports from corporations and to classify corporations. In contrast, the bill that passed the Senate granted adjudicative and investigative powers but included no rulemaking provision at all. When the conference committee met, the only rulemaking provision under consideration was the one included in the House bill. Under established practices for reconciling bills in conference, the committee could not have granted the FTC legislative rulemaking powers because neither bill had done so.[125]

IV. Post-Enactment History of the FTC Act

The FTC Act has been amended on several occasions. Its post-enactment legislative history does not supply any basis for reading section 6(g) to confer substantive rulemaking power.

---

123 Merrill & Watts, *supra* note 11, at 502.

124 *Id.* at 556.

125 *Id.* at 504–05.

1. Arguments from Subsequent Legislative History Are of Little Value

Chair Khan, former Commissioner Chopra, and Professor Gus Hurwitz, whose work Khan and Chopra cite, rely on congressional actions after 1914 to support their conclusion that Congress,[126] in 1914, intended to confer substantive rulemaking authority upon the FTC. Yet as the Supreme Court has declared, "the views of a subsequent Congress form a hazardous basis for inferring the intent of an earlier one."[127] This is especially so when Congress enacts new legislation touching upon earlier legislation whose precise meaning is "still to be authoritatively determined" and remains "a subject of speculation."[128] This was, and remains, the case for section 6(g) – with the Supreme Court having declined to review *National Petroleum Refiners* and with no other appellate court having ruled on the question.

Nor can we infer anything, as Hurwitz does, from a 1974 conference committee's rejection of a House proposal that appeared to suppose the existence of (and to curb) FTC rulemaking authority.[129] Such decisions to reject legislative language are inherently unreliable indicators of congressional intent. As the Supreme Court observed when addressing one such instance: "Whether Congress thought the proposal unwise... or unnecessary, we cannot tell; accordingly, no inference can properly be drawn from the failure of the Congress to act."[130] Here, that is doubly true: Congress decided (i) *not* to enact a proposal that (ii) might, or might not, have accurately reflected the actual state of the law. That lawmakers in 1974 *might* have thought that the FTC *might* have had UMC rulemaking authority does not actually tell us whether the Congress that enacted the FTC Act intended to confer such power in 1914. As Justice Scalia once put it, "[a]rguments based on subsequent legislative history, like arguments based on antecedent futurity, should not be taken seriously, not even in a footnote."[131]

2. The 1980 FTC Improvements Act Did Not Validate UMC Rulemaking

Hurwitz also discusses the FTC Improvements Act of 1980.[132] If anything, this law tells us even less about whether the FTC may make "unfair methods" rules

---

126 Chopra & Khan, *supra* note 7; Hurwitz, *supra* note 7.

127 CPSC v. GTE Sylvania, Inc., 447 U.S. 102, 117 (1980) (quoting United States v. Price, 361 U.S. 304, 313 (1960)).

128 United States v. Philadelphia Nat'l Bank, 374 U.S. 321, 348–49 (1963).

129 H.R. Rep. No. 93-1107 (1974), *reprinted in 1974* U.S.C.C.A.N. 7702, 7727.

130 *United States v. Price*, 361 U.S. at 312.

131 Sullivan v. Finkelstein, 496 U.S. 617, 632 (1990) (Scalia, J., dissenting) ("In some situations, of course, the expression of a legislator relating to a previously enacted statute may bear upon the meaning of a provision in a bill under consideration – which provision, if passed, may in turn affect judicial interpretation of the previously enacted statute, since statutes *in pari materia* should be interpreted harmoniously. Such an expression would be useful, if at all, not because it was subsequent legislative history of the earlier statute, but because it was plain old legislative history of the later one.").

132 Hurwitz, *supra* note 7, at 235–36.

than does what happened in 1974. As Hurwitz notes, the 1980 Act was passed in response to the FTC's "extensive and often controversial rulemaking" following passage of the Magnuson-Moss Act of 1975.[133] "The FTC had become the second most powerful legislature in the country," Hurwitz continues, trying to "ban all advertising directed at children as unfair,"[134] which "famously led *The Washington Post* to declare that the FTC had assumed the role as 'National Nanny.'"[135] The 1980 Act placed new restrictions on the FTC's UDAP rulemaking authority, stripped the FTC of authority to make rules for (among other things) children's advertising, and gave Congress a temporary veto on all FTC rules.

Given this background, what are the chances that the 1980 Act tacitly endorsed section 6(g) "unfair methods" rulemaking? Did Congress pass the 1980 Act simultaneously (i) to act on its white-hot rage at the FTC's overreaching UDAP rules and (ii) to implicitly endorse the notion that the FTC may embark on grand new adventures in the realm of "unfair methods" rulemaking? To ask the question is to answer it. It is illogical to conclude that Congress reined in the FTC's UDAP rulemaking authority with one hand but anointed the FTC a maker of "unfair methods" rules with the other. To further conclude, as one adopting this line of thought is obliged to do, that Congress made it *easier* to pass UMC rules than UDAP rules is downright perverse.

V. *National Petroleum Refiners* Stands on an Outmoded Policy- and Purpose-Driven Form of Statutory Interpretation

"Our duty," Judge Wright says at the outset of *National Petroleum Refiners*, "is not simply to make a policy judgment."[136] The FTC, after all, "is a creation of Congress, not a creation of judges' contemporary notions of what is wise policy."[137]

But those lines are just a feint. True, Judge Wright opens his opinion with a perfunctory examination of the FTC Act's text. Even on its own terms, the section – as Judge Wright concedes – fails to establish that the housekeeping-rules-only reading of section 6(g) is "implausible."[138] But in any event, after that desultory and inconclusive opening nod to the text has been made, the mask slips. Throughout the rest of his lengthy opinion, Judge Wright returns, again

133 *See* Hurwitz, *supra* note 7 and associated text.

134 Hurwitz, *supra* note 7, at 235. *See generally* J. Howard Beales III, Advertising to Kids and the FTC: A Regulatory Retrospective That Advises the Present (Mar. 2, 2004), https://www.ftc.gov/news-events/news/speeches/advertising-kids-ftc-regulatory-retrospective-advises-present.

135 *Id.*

136 *Nat'l Petroleum Refiners Ass'n.*, 482 F.2d at 674.

137 *Id.*

138 *Id.* at 685.

and again, to policy considerations. Over and over, he praises the "invaluable resource-saving flexibility" of rulemaking. According to Judge Wright:

- "[U]se of substantive rule-making is increasingly felt to yield significant benefits.... Increasingly, courts are recognizing that use of rule-making to make innovations in agency policy may actually be fairer to regulated parties than total reliance on case-by-case adjudication."[139]
- "[C]ontemporary considerations of practicality and fairness... certainly support the Commission's position here."[140]
- "Such benefits are especially obvious in cases involving the initiation of rules of the sort the FTC has promulgated here."[141]
- "[T]he policy innovation involved in this case underscores the need for increased reliance on rule-making rather than adjudication alone."[142]
- "[The FTC] has remained hobbled in its task by the delay inherent in repetitious, lengthy litigation .... To the extent substantive rule-making... is likely to deal with these problems... [it] should be upheld as [allowed under the FTC Act]."[143]
- "[T]he Commission will be able to proceed more expeditiously,... and... more efficiently with a mixed system of rule-making and adjudication[.]"[144]
- "[C]ourts have stressed the advantages of efficiency and expedition which inhere in reliance on rule-making instead of adjudication alone."[145]

Rulemaking, on this view, was the wave of the future, and all fashionable and enlightened judges understood as much. Why not, therefore, insert into statutes, wherever possible, the power to make substantive rules? Whether the defenseless texts could in fact bear such a reading appears, to Judge Wright, to have been a secondary concern at best.

When not engaging in his own, independent analysis of the costs and benefits of rulemaking, Judge Wright repeatedly invokes the FTC Act's amorphous "policies" and "purposes":

- "[R]ejecting the claim of rule-making power would run counter to the broad policies... that clearly motivated Congress in 1914."[146]

---

139 *Id.* at 681.

140 *Id.* at 683.

141 *Id.*

142 *Id.* at 684.

143 *Id.* at 690.

144 *Id.*

145 *Id.* at 692.

146 *Id.* at 695.

- "[T]he broad, undisputed policies which clearly motivated the framers of the [FTC] Act of 1914 would indeed be furthered by our view[.]"[147]
- "[R]ule-making is not only consistent with the original framers' broad purposes, but appears to be a particularly apt means of carrying them out."[148]
- The FTC needs rulemaking power "to do the job assigned... by Congress."[149]

Here again, Judge Wright strays from the task at hand – determining what the *text* of the FTC Act means. A judge may not appeal to a statute's "purpose" on the false cry that he is divining what the legislators "really" meant. "[N]o legislation pursues its purposes at all costs.... [I]t frustrates rather than effectuates legislative intent simplistically to assume that *whatever* furthers the statute's primary objective must be the law."[150] Once again, the missing ingredient through most of Judge Wright's long document – the only ingredient that truly matters – is the statutory text.

Judge Wright's opinion in *National Petroleum Refiners* is a museum piece. It is a fossilized specimen of an extinct species of statutory interpretation. Its usefulness, to a judge trying to understand the FTC Act today, is zero. Modern judges may not let their rulings be driven by "policy," or by statutory "purpose," or by the sense of personal satisfaction they would gain from handing down statute-expanding decrees. Courts have "no roving license" to rewrite a statute on the assumption that "Congress 'must have intended' something broader."[151] Judges are "expounders of what the law *is*," not "policymakers choosing what the law *should be*."[152]

VI. Conclusion

If the FTC issues substantive rules claiming the force and effect of law, those rules will be challenged. Once in court, the FTC will find itself in a terrible bind. The agency will try to build its case on *National Petroleum Refiners*; but that decision, the agency will quickly discover, is a pile of sand. The case reflected the assumptions of its time. Statutory interpretation has changed profoundly since 1973. Today, courts recognize that "Congress... does not alter the fundamental details of a regulatory scheme in vague terms or ancillary provisions – it does not, one might say, hide elephants in mouseholes."[153]

147 *Id.* at 686.

148 *Id.*

149 *Id.* at 697–98.

150 Rodriguez v. United States, 480 U.S. 522, 525–26 (1987).

151 Michigan v. Bay Mills Indian Cmty., 572 U.S. 782, 794 (2014).

152 *EPIC Sys. Corp.*, 138 S. Ct. at 1624.

153 Whitman v. Am. Trucking Ass'ns, Inc., 531 U.S. 457, 468 (2001).

It would be difficult to imagine a larger elephant than the power to issue legislative rules, rules that claim the force and effect of law,[154] and that can declare the practices of almost any business in America "unfair." Making such a value judgment is a job for Congress, the democratically accountable holder of all "legislative Powers" under the Constitution. It is simply unfathomable that the Congress of 1914 would have delegated this power to the FTC in so sly a fashion, without any debate over whether the Constitution permitted so sweeping a delegation – all without even imposing any sanctions for violations of the Act, let alone violations of rules issued under the Act. This would have been nothing less than a constitutional revolution.

And it would be difficult to imagine a smaller mousehole than section 6(g), an "additional power" to "classify corporations and… to make rules and regulations for the purpose of carrying out the provisions of this Act."

Had such an elephant been hiding in such a mousehole, the Supreme Court certainly would have noticed it in *Humphrey's Executor*.[155] Were the Court to confront such a creature today, it would say once again what Congress understood so clearly in 1914: Congress could not delegate such sweeping power to any regulatory agency even if it wanted to. At a minimum, the Court would expect Congress to speak clearly before it attempted to confer legislative power upon an agency.

Lawmakers in the Progressive era followed a simple convention for doing so – explicitly imposing sanctions for rule violations. That the Congress of 1914 included no such sanctions in the FTC Act tells us what lawmakers understood the text of section 6(g) to mean: that the FTC would issue no more than "housekeeping" or "interpretive" rules,[156] not rules with the force and effect of law. Congress did not, in short, create a second national legislature.[157]

---

154 Attorney General Manual, *supra* note 2, at 30 n. 3.

155 *See supra* note 49 and associated text at 6.

156 *See supra* notes 12 & 13 and associated text at 2.

157 *See* Berin Szóka & Geoffrey A. Manne, The Federal Trade Commission: Restoring Congressional Oversight of the Second National Legislature, Report 2.0 of the FTC: Technology & Reform Project 57–60 (2016), http://docs.house.gov/meetings/IF/IF17/20160524/104976/HHRG-114-IF17-Wstate-ManneG-20160524-SD004.pdf.

Policing Anticompetitive Practices and Protecting the Competitive Process through Adjudication vs. Rulemaking

HENRY C. SU[*]
Bradley Arant Boult Cummings

Abstract

This chapter examines whether the US Federal Trade Commission should be pursuing any aspect of its competition enforcement mission through substantive rulemaking. Assuming, for the sake of argument, that the agency has the requisite authority to engage in competition rulemaking, the question on the table is whether it should do so, in addition to or in lieu of case-by-case adjudication in its administrative tribunal and in the courts. In answering this question, three practical considerations loom large: (i) developing an evidentiary record to support the finding of a violation of US antitrust law, (ii) providing due process to those targeted by the agency for enforcement, and (iii) fostering alignment with the US Department of Justice's Antitrust Division and the courts in the articulation and evolution of US antitrust policy. Important lessons relating to each of these considerations can be drawn from the agency's enforcement program in the 1960s and 1970s against the spate of vertical mergers in the cement industry.

---

* Trial Lawyer and Partner

Policing Anticompetitive Practices and Protecting the Competitive Process through Adjudication vs. Rulemaking

This chapter examines whether the US Federal Trade Commission (FTC) should pursue any aspect of its competition enforcement mission through substantive rulemaking, in lieu of or in addition to case-by-case adjudication.[1] As a competition enforcement agency, the FTC is empowered by the US Congress to prevent and restrain violations of section 5 of the Federal Trade Commission Act (FTC Act), which prohibits "unfair methods of competition in or affecting commerce"[2] that may also violate the Sherman Act,[3] and violations of the Clayton Act, including section 7, which prohibits acquisitions where the effect "may be substantially to lessen competition, or to tend to create a monopoly."[4] Since its creation in 1914, the FTC has enforced the antitrust laws predominantly through adjudication, which involves issuing and proving up a complaint either in its own administrative tribunal and/or in a federal district court.[5] By contrast, the agency has only once in its history engaged in competition rulemaking – namely, a so-called trade regulation rule defining and banning discriminatory advertising allowances and services in the men's and boys' tailored clothing industry as violations of the Robinson-Patman Act (Tailored Clothing Rule).[6] The FTC apparently never enforced that rule, however, and subsequently repealed it because its intended purpose had been supplanted by the agency's issuance of the so-called Fred Meyer Guides on Robinson-Patman Act compliance for businesses not just in the tailored clothing industry, but across all industries.[7]

1 In this chapter, "FTC" refers to the agency as a whole, and "Commission" refers to the body of commissioners appointed by the President.

2 15 U.S.C. § 45(a)(1), (2). Section 5 of the FTC Act also prohibits "unfair or deceptive acts in or affecting commerce," which forms the centerpiece of the FTC's equally important consumer protection mission. Except to draw helpful contrasts, however, this chapter does not address the agency's enforcement of consumer protection laws within its jurisdiction, whether through adjudication or rulemaking (e.g., under the Magnuson-Moss Warranty–Federal Trade Commission Improvement Act of 1975, 15 U.S.C. § 57a). Unless the context otherwise makes clear, all references to "section 5" in this chapter pertain specifically to its prohibition of "unfair methods of competition."

3 15 U.S.C. §§ 1–2; FTC v. Motion Picture Advertising Serv. Co., Inc., 344 U.S. 392, 394–95 (1953) ("It is also clear that the Federal Trade Commission Act was designed . . . to condemn as 'unfair methods of competition' existing violations of [the Sherman and Clayton Acts]."); FTC v. Cement Institute, 333 U.S. 683, 693 (1948) ("The Commission has jurisdiction to declare that conduct tending to restrain trade is an unfair method of competition even though the [self-same] conduct may also violate the Sherman Act.").

4 15 U.S.C. §§ 18, 21(a).

5 15 U.S.C. §§ 21(b), 45(b), 53(b).

6 Trade Regulation Rule: Discriminatory Practices in Men's and Boys' Tailored Clothing Industry, 32 Fed. Reg. 15584 (Nov. 9, 1967) (to be codified at 16 C.F.R. pt. 412). *Cf.* 15 U.S.C. § 13. *See* Jay B. Sykes, Cong. Rsch. Serv., LSB10635, The FTC's Competition Rulemaking Authority 1 (2021) ("[T]he FTC's 1968 Men's and Boys' Tailored Clothing Rule occupies a unique place in the agency's history: it remains the only instance in which the Commission has deployed its putative authority to issue rules defining 'unfair methods of competition' (UMC) under Section 6(g) of the Federal Trade Commission Act (FTC Act)."); United Air Lines, Inc. v. Civil Aeronautics Bd., 766 F.2d 1107, 1118 (7th Cir. 1985) ("[T]he Federal Trade Commission; while active in promulgating rules to prohibit deceptive and otherwise fraudulent practices, has promulgated only one rule (and that back in 1967) to prohibit an antitrust violation. And that rule was of the simplest kind; it forbade the discriminatory provision of advertising allowances."). The Octane Rating Rule that was the subject of the D.C. Circuit's opinion in Nat'l Petroleum Refiners Ass'n v. FTC, 482 F.2d 672 (D.C. Cir. 1973), did not have anything to do with protecting competition, notwithstanding the rule's invocation of the FTC's authority over unfair methods of competition as well as unfair or deceptive acts or practices that hurt consumers. *See* Trade Regulation Rule: Posting of Minimum Octane Numbers on Gasoline Dispensing Pumps, 36 Fed. Reg. 23871 (Dec. 16, 1971) (to be codified at 16 C.F.R. pt. 422). Discussion of that rule is beyond the scope of this chapter.

7 Trade Regulation Rule: Discriminatory Practices in Men's and Boys' Tailored Clothing Industry, 59 Fed. Reg. 8527 (Feb. 23, 1994) (repealing 16 C.F.R. pt. 412). The FTC issued the Fred Meyer Guides in the aftermath of the eponymous US Supreme Court decision, FTC v. Fred Meyer, Inc., 390 U.S. 341 (1968).

This marked disparity between the use of adjudication and rulemaking in competition enforcement can be traced back to the FTC's institutional design by Congress. Even if rulemaking is part of the agency's competition enforcement toolkit, as the D.C. Circuit concluded in *National Petroleum Refiners Association v. FTC*,[8] the fact remains that Congress intended the FTC to utilize case-by-case adjudication as its principal tool for enforcing section 5's proscription of unfair methods of competition.[9] Here is what the legislative history says about Congress's intent.[10]

I. Legislative Intent Behind Section 5 Enforcement

The 1914 statute that both created the agency and defined its competition mission was an amalgam of two markedly different bills, one from the US House of Representatives and the other from the US Senate, each with a different conception of the agency and its core functions.[11] The House bill envisioned the FTC as a successor to the then extant Bureau of Corporations, charged with tracking – through a uniform system of annual reports – the organization, ownership, finances, operations, and business practices of corporations above a certain size threshold.[12] At the direction of the President, the attorney general, or either chamber of Congress, the agency could and would "investigate and report the facts relating to any alleged violations of the antitrust acts by any corporation."[13] Additionally, if, in the course of any investigation, the agency were to "obtain information concerning any unfair competition or practice in commerce not necessarily constituting a violation of law by the corporation investigated," it would report that to the President so that he or she in turn could recommend "legislation in relation to the regulation of commerce" to Congress.[14]

---

8 482 F.2d at 693. Suffice it to say, *National Petroleum Refiners* has been criticized by administrative law scholars. *See, e.g.*, Thomas W. Merrill & Kathryn Tongue Watts, *Agency Rules with the Force of Law: The Original Convention*, 116 Harv. L. Rev. 467, 556–57 (2002) (characterizing the D.C. Circuit's conclusion about the "plain language of Section 6(g)" to be contrary to the legislative history of the FTC Act, which provides "significant evidence" that Congress did not intend to grant legislative rulemaking authority to the FTC).

9 *See* H.R. Rep. No. 63-1142, at 18–19 (1914) (Conf. Rep.).

10 To be clear, the question of congressional intent, as framed here, is hence slightly different from the one answered by the D.C. Circuit in *National Petroleum Refiners*. Rather than asking whether Congress intended to give the FTC any substantive or legislative rulemaking authority, the inquiry here concerns Congress's intent with respect to the role of the FTC in competition enforcement.

11 H.R. 15613, 63d Cong. (2d Sess. 1914) (introduced by Rep. Covington on April 14, 1914); S. 4160, 63d Cong. (2d Sess. 1914) (introduced by Sen. Newlands on January 24, 1914). After the House voted out its bill on June 5, 1914, it was referred to the Senate Committee on Interstate Commerce. *See* 51 Cong. Rec. 9910, 9929 (1914). Instead of making amendments to the House bill, however, the Senate Committee substituted the text of the Senate bill. *See* 51 Cong. Rec. 11081 (remarks of Sen. Newlands); S. Rep. No. 63-597, at 1, 8 (1914). In other words, Senate Bill 4160, with a couple amendments, became the Senate version of House Bill 15613. The footnotes that follow will cite to and distinguish between the House version, the Senate version, and ultimately the Conference version of House Bill 15613 through the use of parentheticals.

12 H.R. 15613, § 9 (House version). The texts of the House, Senate, and Conference versions of House Bill 15613 are reprinted in the September 4, 1914 conference report, H.R. Rep. No. 63-1142, and compared to each other in the comparative print, S. Doc. No. 63-573 (1914).

13 H.R. 15613, § 10 (House version).

14 *Id.* § 11.

Lastly, in any suit successfully brought by the attorney general under the antitrust laws, the FTC could be tasked by the court hearing the case to "ascertain and report an appropriate form of decree" to remedy the proven violations,[15] and thereafter to investigate and report on "the manner in which the decree has been or is being carried out."[16]

With these key provisions, the House bill thus had the FTC playing only an investigative and monitoring role in competition enforcement, functioning essentially as an expert assistant to all three branches of the US government. Any alleged violations of the antitrust laws would be brought and proven by the attorney general, aided by relevant facts ascertained by the new agency. Any relief for such violations would be imposed by the courts, aided by advice and analysis from the new agency. And to the extent that new laws were needed to regulate "any unfair competition or practice in commerce," they would be recommended by the President and enacted by Congress, aided by reports prepared by the new agency. Notably, the rulemaking authority under section 6(g) of the FTC Act, interpreted by the D.C. Circuit in *National Petroleum Refiners*, originated from the House bill, as an adjunct power to the FTC's primary task of tracking and monitoring corporations: "That the commission may from time to time make rules and regulations and classifications of corporations for the purpose of carrying out the provisions of this act."[17]

In stark contrast, the Senate bill envisioned the FTC taking on an independent adjudicative role in addition to an investigative role.[18] As modified, the Senate version of the bill passed by the House included similar provisions calling for the agency to register and monitor corporate activities,[19] to investigate and report violations of antitrust law,[20] and to assist the attorney general and the courts with the crafting of and compliance with remedial decrees.[21] With respect to unfair methods of competition, however, the Senate version differed from the House version in a key respect. Instead of having the FTC investigate and report

---

15 *Id.* § 12.

16 *Id.* § 13.

17 *Id.* § 8.

18 As recounted by historians and those involved with the legislation, the impetus behind the Senate version of the bill was a change in President Woodrow Wilson's view of the role and powers of the FTC. Word had gotten to the Senate Committee on Interstate Commerce that the President was now endorsing the idea of an agency that would be able to issue restraining orders against the use of unfair methods of competition after holding a hearing and making findings, along the lines previously but unsuccessfully proposed by Representative Raymond Stevens. *See* Gerard C. Henderson, The Federal Trade Commission: A Study in Administrative Law and Procedure 26–27 (Yale University Press 1924); George Rublee, *The Original Plan and Early History of the Federal Trade Commission*, 11 Proc. Acad. Pol. Sci. N.Y.C. (Trade Ass'ns & Bus. Combinations) 114, 116−17 (1926). *See also* H.R. Rep. No. 63-533, at 2 (1914) (minority views of Rep. Stevens) ("Section 10 of H.R. 15660 declares unfair and oppressive competition to be unlawful and directs the commission to enforce the law."); 51 Cong. Rec. 6714 (Stevens introducing and referring H.R. 15660 to the House Committee on Interstate and Foreign Commerce).

19 H.R. 15613, 63d Cong. § 3(a–c) (1914) (Senate version).

20 *Id.* § 3(g).

21 *Id.* § 3(e–f).

on "any unfair competition or practice in commerce not necessarily constituting a violation of law" to the President so that he or she could recommend appropriate legislation to Congress, Congress would broadly declare "unfair competition in commerce" to be unlawful, and the FTC would be empowered to "prevent such unfair competition in commerce" through adjudication.[22] Following extensive debate, the Senate version was voted out of that chamber on August 5, 1914, but the House subsequently registered its disagreement with these amendments and asked for a conference with the Senate.[23]

The version that emerged out of the conference retained the FTC's adjudicative role with respect to unfair methods of competition, as proposed by the Senate, and discarded the alternative investigative role proposed by the House.[24] As explained in the accompanying conference report, section 5 in the conference version "declares unfair methods of competition to be unlawful and empowers the commission, after hearing, to order the discontinuance of the use of such methods."[25] It would be up to the five-member Commission, utilizing an adjudicative process, "to apply the rule enacted by Congress to particular business situations, so as to eradicate evils with the least risk of interfering with legitimate business operations."[26] The Commission's application of section 5 would necessarily proceed on a case-by-case basis because "[w]hether competition is unfair or not generally depends upon the surrounding circumstances of the particular case," and "[w]hat is harmful under certain circumstances may be beneficial under different circumstances."[27] Its orders would be "enforceable only through the courts" (specifically, the federal appellate courts), and judicial review would be "restricted to passing on questions of law."[28]

In the ensuing House debate over the conference version of the bill, Representative Harry Covington, one of the conferees representing the House, explained the

---

22 *Id.* § 5. *Cf.* H.R. 15613, § 11 (House version). As a historical note, Representative Dick Morgan unsuccessfully sought to replace section 11 of the House bill with a similar provision calling for the FTC to play an adjudicative role instead: "That when in the course of any investigation, or through any other reliable source, the commission shall obtain information that any corporation subject to the provisions of section 9 of this act, in conducting its business, is using any unfair competition or practice, the said corporation shall be cited to appear before said commission and a hearing shall be had thereon. If the commission shall find that the said corporation is or has been engaged in unfair competition or practices, it shall make an order commanding the said corporation to cease engaging in said unfair competition or practice . . . ." 51 Cong. Rec. 9061 (1914) (amendment proposed by Rep. Morgan).

23 51 Cong. Rec. 13319, 13434, 13450 (1914). In the US Congress, one way to resolve differences between the House and Senate versions of a particular bill is through a conference committee comprising of members representing each chamber, known as conferees, working together to arrive at a compromise version. *See The Legislative Process: Resolving Differences*, Congress.gov, https://www.congress.gov/legislative-process/resolving-differences (last visited May 1, 2022). If the compromise version garners support from a majority of the conferees for each chamber, it is reported out of committee in a conference report. *Id.* That was what happened here. *See* H.R. Rep. No. 63-1142.

24 H.R. 15613, 63d Cong. § 5 (1914) (Conference version); H.R. Rep. No. 63-1142, at 3–5. *See* S. Doc. No. 63-573, at 18 (showing no comparable provision to section 11 of the House version in the Conference version); 51 Cong. Rec. 14714–17.

25 H.R. Rep. No. 63-1142, at 18.

26 *Id.* at 19.

27 *Id.*

28 *Id.*

rationale for yielding to the Senate regarding the latter's provision on unfair methods of competition. As framed, section 5 did not authorize the FTC to act as an overseer of business that could "make terms with monopoly," regulate production or set prices, or "declare lawful or harmless for the future" particular ways of structuring or operating a corporation.[29] Instead, the FTC would be enforcing a rule of law declaring unfair competition to be unlawful, "so as to bring about the result pointed out by the statute" and intended by Congress.[30] Simply put:

> The function of the Federal trade commission will be to determine whether an existing method of competition is unfair, and, if it finds it to be unfair, to order the discontinuance of its use. In doing this it will exercise power of a judicial nature. Under the Constitution power to act finally in a judicial capacity can be conferred only upon a court.[31]

Like the Senate, the House voted in favor of the conference version, and Congress presented the bill to President Woodrow Wilson for his signature.[32] The FTC Act, including section 5's proscription of unfair methods of competition, thus became law on September 26, 1914.[33]

As reviewed above, the legislative history amply demonstrates that Congress intended for the FTC to enforce section 5 principally through adjudication, with review by the courts. Even if Congress left the door open for competition rulemaking with the inclusion of section 6(g), as *National Petroleum Refiners* has held,[34] the integrated structure of section 5 – Congress's handiwork – defines the agency's competition enforcement mission straightforwardly and tells the agency how best to carry it out.[35] This structure has remained essentially intact since its enactment. To wit, section 5(a)(1) sets forth the rule of law – that unfair methods of competition in or affecting commerce are declared to be unlawful.[36] Section 5(a)(2) both directs and empowers the FTC to prevent persons, partnerships, and corporations within its broad jurisdiction from using unfair methods

29 51 Cong. Rec. 14927 (remarks of Rep. Covington). *See also id.* at 14932 ("The Federal trade commission will have no power to prescribe the methods of competition to be used in future. In issuing its orders it will not be exercising power of a legislative nature.").

30 *Id.* at 14931.

31 *Id.* at 14932 (citation omitted).

32 51 Cong. Rec. 15019 (H.R. 15613 signed in the House); *id.* at 15044 (H.R. 15613 signed in the Senate); *id.* at 15190 (H.R. 15613 presented to the President for signature).

33 Federal Trade Commission Act, ch. 311, § 5, Pub. L. No. 63-203, 38 Stat. 717, 719 (1914) (codified as amended at 15 U.S.C. § 45).

34 *Nat'l Petroleum Refiners Ass'n*, 482 F.2d at 675 (concluding that section 5(b) does not contain any "limiting language suggesting that adjudication alone is the only proper means of elaborating the statutory standard").

35 *See* Everette MacIntyre, Comm'r, Fed. Trade Comm'n, Some Criteria for Applying Industry-Wide Enforcement Measures under the Robinson–Patman Act, Statement to the Indiana Continuing Legal Education Forum, University of Notre Dame 23 (Sept. 25, 1965) ("[T]he Commission should not be forgetful of the statutory scheme which places the cease and desist order at the heart of its enforcement measures.").

36 15 U.S.C. § 45(a)(1).

of competition.[37] Section 5(b) then defines the adjudicative process that the agency is to use, which involves (i) the Commission's issuance of a complaint stating the charges, grounded on a "reason to believe" and the public interest; (ii) notice and conduct of a hearing that affords the respondent an opportunity to be heard, and allows testimony and other evidence to be received; and (iii) if a violation of law is found, the issuance and service of a cease-and-desist order on the respondent and the preparation of a written record detailing the Commission's findings.[38] Section 5(c) spells out a procedure for judicial review of the Commission's order and judicial enforcement if that order is affirmed.[39]

The next three parts of this chapter discuss why adjudication should remain the FTC's principal tool in carrying out its competition enforcement mission. There are at least three major practical considerations at play. First, a finding of a violation of US antitrust law, including section 5's prohibition of unfair methods of competition, generally requires an evidentiary record that allows an assessment of the impact of the challenged agreement, conduct, or transaction in light of specific facts and circumstances about the relevant market, the nature and scope of competition in that market, and the firms competing in, and entering and exiting that market. Second, a cornerstone of the US justice system is that a person or entity targeted by a law enforcement agency is entitled to due process, which includes an evidentiary hearing in which the respondent can call witnesses in its defense, cross-examine, and present facts and arguments specific to its case. Third, the FTC's work as an independent and second competition enforcer at the federal level should foster alignment with the US Department of Justice's Antitrust Division (DOJ) and the courts in the articulation and evolution of US antitrust policy. Each of these considerations argues strongly in favor of adjudication over rulemaking.

II. Evidentiary Record for Antitrust Violations

As noted already, the FTC enforces US antitrust law through section 5 of the FTC Act and the Clayton Act. Focusing on section 5, the agency's enforcement of this statute, whether through case-by-case adjudication or substantive rulemaking, involves proving that the challenged agreement, conduct, or transaction constitutes an unfair method of competition, and perhaps a violation of section 1 or section 2 of the Sherman Act as well.[40] Such a determination is inherently fact-specific and best conducted on a case-by-case basis, as the US Supreme Court has repeatedly made clear.

---

37 *Id.* § 45(a)(2).

38 *Id.* § 45(b).

39 *Id.* § 45(c). Other incidents of the adjudicative process, including the jurisdiction of the court of appeals reviewing the Commission's order, service of the Commission's complaint and other process, modification and finality of the Commission's order, and penalties and injunctive relief for noncompliance, are set forth in other subsections.

40 *See supra* note 3.

Nearly a century ago, in *Maple Flooring Manufacturers Association v. United States*, the Court reminded readers of its antitrust opinions that:

> [E]ach case arising under the Sherman Act must be determined upon the particular facts disclosed by the record, and that the opinions in those cases must be read in the light of their facts and of a clear recognition of the essential differences in the facts of those cases, and in the facts of any new case to which the rule of earlier decisions is to be applied.[41]

In other words, "[t]he varying circumstances of each case determine the result."[42] Hewing to this approach, the Court has expressed more recently that it "prefer[s] to resolve antitrust claims on a case-by-case basis, focusing on the 'particular facts disclosed by the record.'"[43] And importantly, that analysis may change if the economic facts on which it is based should change: "Whether an antitrust violation exists necessarily depends on a careful analysis of market realities. . . . If those market realities change, so may the legal analysis."[44]

Relatedly, when evaluating the legality of restraints of trade under section 1 of the Sherman Act, the rule of reason demands "an enquiry meet for the case, looking to the circumstances, details, and logic of a restraint."[45] In assessing the reasonableness of a challenged restraint, a fact finder must take "into account a variety of factors, including specific information about the relevant business, its condition before and after the restraint was imposed, and the restraint's history, nature, and effect."[46] As the Supreme Court observed in *FTC v. Indiana Federation of Dentists*, the rule of reason applies equally to a case brought under section 5 of the FTC Act if the Commission has based its finding of an unfair method of competition on a section 1 violation.[47]

Moreover, the fact-intensive, case-specific nature of the inquiry does not materially change for section 5 cases that are *not* based on Sherman Act violations. The US Supreme Court said as much in *Pan American World Airways, Inc. v. United States*,

41 268 U.S. 563, 579 (1925).

42 United States v. E.I. du Pont de Nemours & Co., 351 U.S. 377, 395 & n. 22 (1956) (citing and quoting *Maple Flooring*, 268 U.S. at 579).

43 Eastman Kodak Co. v. Image Tech. Servs., Inc., 504 U.S. 451, 467 (1992) (quoting *Maple Flooring*, 268 U.S. at 579).

44 NCAA v. Alston, 141 S. Ct. 2141, 2158 (2021) (citing Ohio v. Am. Express Co., 138 S. Ct. 2274, 2285 (2018)) (citations omitted). *See also* Alden F. Abbott, *The US Supreme Court upholds a district court injunction finding unlawful certain sport association rules limiting the education-related benefits schools may make available to student-athletes (NCAA / Alston)*, E-COMPETITIONS JUNE 2021, art. No. 101238.

45 Cal. Dental Ass'n v. FTC, 526 U.S. 756, 781 (1999).

46 State Oil Co. v. Khan, 522 U.S. 3, 10 (1997). *See also* Victor D. Vital & Elizabeth Wirmani, *The US Supreme Court overrules 30-year old precedent and declares maximum resale price maintenance agreements should be reviewed under the rule of reason in a case against a gasoline wholesaler (State Oil / Khan)*, E-COMPETITIONS NOVEMBER 1997, art. No. 52952.

47 476 U.S. 447, 455, 459 (1986).

a case addressing the jurisdiction of the Civil Aeronautics Board (CAB) over certain antitrust problems involving air carriers, by virtue of the prohibition of "unfair methods of competition" under section 411 of the Civil Aeronautics Act of 1938.[48] Noting that section 411 was patterned after section 5 of the FTC Act, the Court looked to section 5's legislative history and case law for guidance on the scope of section 411.[49] It held that section 411, like section 5, "was designed to bolster and strengthen anti-trust enforcement," and that the words "unfair methods of competition" are to "take their meaning from the facts of each case and the impact of particular practices on competition and monopoly."[50]

Atlantic Refining Co. v. FTC provides an instructive example under section 5 of a fact-driven analysis of a business practice's impact on competition and monopoly.[51] The FTC challenged the legality of "sales-commission plans" between a gasoline distributor and a tire manufacturer, whereby the former, on a commission basis, undertakes to promote the sale of the latter's line of tires, batteries, and accessories to its network of gasoline wholesalers and retailers, who would then resell to consumers.[52] Although these plans shared relevant attributes with anticompetitive tying arrangements, the agency did not charge them as such under the Sherman Act, relying instead only on section 5.[53]

On appeal, the Supreme Court approved of the Commission's approach, and specifically its analytical focus on the "central competitive characteristic" of these plans, namely, "the utilization of economic power in one market to curtail competition in another[,] . . . bolstered by actual threats and coercive practices."[54] According to the Court, a business practice may be an unfair method of competition if it "bear[s] the characteristics of recognized antitrust violations," even if it "do[es] not assume [their] proportions."[55] The Court concluded that the Commission was warranted in finding a section 5 violation because instead of engaging in "a mechanical application of the law of tying arrangements," it had "looked to the entire record as a basis for its conclusion that the activity of Goodyear and Atlantic impaired competition at three levels of the tires, batteries and accessories industry."[56]

---

48 371 U.S. 296 (1963) (construing section 411 of the Civil Aeronautics Act of 1938, Pub. L. No. 75-706, § 411, 52 Stat. 973, 1003 (superseded in 1958 by the Federal Aviation Act)).

49 *Id.* at 303, 306–08.

50 *Id.* at 307–08.

51 381 U.S. 357 (1965).

52 *Id.* at 359–60.

53 *Id.* at 369.

54 *Id.*

55 *Id.* at 369–70.

56 *Id.* at 370. Indeed, the Court was satisfied with the robustness of the Commission's analysis and rejected the petitioners' argument that "the Commission should have made a far more extensive economic analysis of the competitive effect of the sales commission plan." *Id.* at 371.

Such a fact-specific, market-based assessment is not unlike an application of the rule of reason in cases under the Sherman Act, as lower courts have observed.[57] And in cases where the Commission has made only a cursory assessment of a challenged practice, reviewing courts have found that insufficient.[58] Also, the market realities under which a challenged practice is adopted matter greatly; for example, "[i]t is difficult to believe that a practice deemed lawful when competitive forces were producing changes in the market became 'unfair' when market conditions stabilized."[59]

The above decisions explain why the principal mode of enforcement of the US antitrust laws, including section 5 of the FTC Act, has been case-by-case adjudication. As borne out by the significant body of judicial opinions, the adjudicative process reliably produces an evidentiary record that is sufficiently fact-specific and market-based to support an informed judgment about whether there has been an antitrust law violation. By contrast, although the rulemaking process also involves fact-finding, it generally lacks the specificity afforded in individual cases, and intentionally so, since it seeks to pronounce the illegality of an agreement or practice on an industry-wide or market-wide basis. This fundamental distinction can be seen, for example, in the preamble to the procedures adopted by the FTC in 1962 for the promulgation of trade regulation rules (16 C.F.R. §§ 1.61, 1.62).[60]

One other observation deserves mention in this part, which is Congress's rationale in fashioning section 5 as a broad rule of law and leaving it to the FTC to apply the statute to specific business practices encountered in the field:

> It is impossible to frame definitions which embrace all unfair practices. There is no limit to human inventiveness in this field. Even if all known unfair practices were specifically defined and prohibited, it would be at once necessary to begin over again. If Congress were to adopt the method of definition, it would undertake an endless task. It is also practically impossible to define unfair practices so that the definition will fit business of every sort in every part of this country.[61]

---

57 *See, e.g.*, Shell Oil Co. v. FTC, 360 F.2d 470, 479 (5th Cir. 1966); Asheville Tobacco Bd. of Trade, Inc. v. FTC, 263 F.2d 502, 511 (4th Cir. 1959). *See also supra* notes 26–27 and the accompanying text regarding Congress's intent that section 5 be applied on a case-by-case, fact-specific basis akin to the rule of reason.

58 Sandura Co. v. FTC, 339 F.2d 847, 850 (6th Cir. 1964) ("[W]e here refuse to find Sandura's arrangements illegal without examining their particular effect on competition and the facts offered to justify the resulting restraint.") (a manufacturer's imposition of territorial limitations on distributors of its vinyl floor coverings).

59 E.I. du Pont de Nemours & Co. v. FTC, 729 F.2d 128, 140 (2d Cir. 1984).

60 Fed. Trade Comm'n, Procedures, Rules of Practice, and Orders, 27 Fed. Reg. 4609, 4611–12 (1962) (codified at 16 C.F.R. §§ 1.61–1.71). Trade regulation rules issued through this procedure were to "express the experience and judgment of the Commission, based on facts of which it has knowledge derived from studies, reports, investigations, hearings, and other proceedings, or within official notice, concerning the substantive requirements of the statutes which it administers." 16 C.F.R. § 1.61 (1962). At the same time, they were meant to "be nation-wide in effect, or . . . be limited to particular areas or industries or to particular product or geographic markets, as may be appropriate." *Id.* § 1.62.

61 H.R. Rep. No. 63-1142, at 19. *See, e.g.*, FTC v. Beech-Nut Packing Co., 257 U.S. 441, 453 (1922) ("Congress deemed it better to leave the subject without precise definition, and to have each case determined upon its own facts, owing to the multifarious means by which it is sought to effectuate such schemes.").

This was a keen observation in 1914, and it remains so today. Importantly, it frames a central challenge for substantive rulemaking, which is whether the FTC can practicably accomplish what Congress thought to be both futile and impracticable – namely, to define, identify, and prohibit in broad strokes business practices that constitute unfair methods of competition. Case-by-case adjudication would seem to be nimbler and more adaptive to the multitude of variants and scenarios that are likely to be observed in the marketplace.

III. Due Process for Respondents in Antitrust Enforcement

Competition enforcement through substantive rulemaking must afford those charged with violating a rule or regulation with an evidentiary hearing. For example, the procedures adopted by the FTC in 1962 for the promulgation of trade regulation rules gave respondents the right to a "fair hearing":

> Where a Trade Regulation Rule is relevant to any issue involved in an adjudicative proceeding thereafter instituted, the Commission may rely upon such rule, provided that the respondent shall have been given a fair hearing on the legality and propriety of applying the rule to the particular case.[62]

This provision underscores an inherent limitation of competition rulemaking: even if the FTC were able to articulate a rule declaring certain business practices in a particular market or industry to be unfair methods of competition in violation of section 5, there remains the matter of its enforcement against those participants that ostensibly are engaging in the outlawed practices despite the rule.[63] Any respondent charged with violating a rule would still have the right to argue why that rule cannot, does not, or should not apply *to its particular case* and to present relevant evidence in its defense. Competition rulemaking, therefore, does not obviate the need for case-by-case adjudication; on the contrary, it should anticipate that potential need and provide a procedural mechanism for that to occur, as the FTC did in its 1962 rules of practice and procedure.

Under the US justice system, a respondent's due process right to an evidentiary hearing in administrative proceedings arises whenever an agency undertakes to

62 Fed. Trade Comm'n, Procedures, Rules of Practice, and Orders, § 1.63, 27 Fed. Reg. at 4611 (codified at 16 C.F.R. § 1.63).

63 In a perfect world, a competition rule would serve to warn and deter firms from adopting the prohibited practices, in which case there would be no need for additional enforcement aside from monitoring for scofflaws. But that presupposes, as discussed in part II, a rule that is sufficiently clear and specific about what is being outlawed under section 5, and at the same time sufficiently broad to capture the range of variations and contexts that may exist across the market or industry in question. More likely than not, disputes will arise as to whether a rule can or should apply to a particular firm and/or a particular situation, thereby necessitating additional enforcement through adjudicative proceedings.

determine "adjudicative" facts, as opposed to "legislative" facts.[64] Appellate courts have adopted the following definitions of, and distinction between, adjudicative facts and legislative facts:

> Adjudicative facts are facts about the parties and their activities, businesses, and properties, usually answering the questions of who did what, where, when, how, why, with what motive or intent; adjudicative facts are roughly the kind of facts that go to a jury in a jury case. Legislative facts do not usually concern the immediate parties but are general facts which help the tribunal decide questions of law, policy, and discretion.[65]

"The determinative inquiry is whether the agency is engaged in rule-making, a legislative function which requires no hearing, or in adjudication, a judicial function which may require a hearing to resolve disputed facts."[66] "While the line dividing them may not always be a bright one, [there is] a recognized distinction in administrative law between proceedings for the purpose of promulgating policy-type rules or standards, on the one hand, and proceedings designed to adjudicate disputed facts in particular cases, on the other."[67]

Applying this framework to competition rulemaking, the Commission would adduce legislative facts that inform and support its view of the illegality of a particular practice under section 5. The resulting competition rule would reflect the Commission's statement of law and policy, emanating from the legislative mandate given to it by Congress to identify and prohibit the use of unfair methods of competition in commerce. The rule would apply generally and prospectively to all participants in a given market or industry.[68]

Should the Commission have to enforce the rule against a particular firm, however, it would have to institute an adjudicative proceeding to resolve any

---

64 Alaska Air Lines, Inc. v. Civil Aeronautics Bd., 545 F.2d 194, 200 (D.C. Cir. 1976) ("Where adjudicative, rather than legislative, facts are involved, the parties must be afforded a hearing to allow them an opportunity to meet and to present evidence."); Marshall v. Sawyer, 365 F.2d 105, 111 (9th Cir. 1966) ("Procedural due process requires that when, as a premise for administrative action, an agency of government makes a determination of adjudicative facts, one who has a sufficient interest or right at stake shall be afforded an evidentiary hearing before the agency[.]") (noting limited exceptions such as national security concerns).

65 Kenneth Culp Davis, *The Requirement of a Trial-Type Hearing*, 70 Harv. L. Rev. 193, 199 (1950). *See Alaska Air Lines*, 545 F.2d at 200 n. 11 (quoting these definitions); *Marshall*, 365 F.2d at 111 (same).

66 *Alaska Air Lines*, 545 F.2d at 200. *See also United Air Lines*, 766 F.2d at 1116 ("But an agency is not allowed to conduct what is in fact an adjudicative proceeding without giving the affected parties an opportunity for an evidentiary hearing, just by calling the proceeding informal rulemaking.").

67 United States v. Fla. East Coast Ry. Co., 410 U.S. 224, 245 (1973).

68 Ass'n of Nat'l Advertisers, Inc. v. FTC, 627 F.2d 1151, 1165 (D.C. Cir. 1979) (noting that "[a] section 18 [rulemaking] proceeding is directed to all members of an affected industry and is based on legislative fact"); *Alaska Air Lines*, 545 F.2d at 200 (noting that "the key question was whether the agency's action pertained to a class of individuals, indicating a rule-making function, or whether it focused on a particular individual, indicating an adjudicative function requiring a hearing"); Am. Airlines, Inc. v. Civil Aeronautics Bd., 359 F.2d 624, 631 (D.C. Cir. 1966) (distinguishing rulemaking, which is "general in scope and prospective in operation," from adjudication, the "substance and effect [of which] is individual in impact and condemnatory in purpose").

disputed facts specific to that respondent – for example, the nature of its business and activities, its rationale for adopting the challenged practice, and the competitive circumstances and conditions it faces as a market participant. The Commission would have to conduct an evidentiary hearing because adjudicative facts "are intrinsically the kind of facts that ordinarily ought not to be determined without giving the parties a chance to know and to meet any evidence that may be unfavorable to them."[69] A hearing also ensures that there will be a proper record of the facts presented, both for the Commission in making its findings and for an appellate court in reviewing those findings.

As this framework makes clear, a rule declaring a particular practice to be an unfair method of competition would not necessarily streamline competition enforcement for the FTC. True, the Commission would be able to rely on any legislative facts in the rulemaking record that inform and support its view of the illegality of a particular practice, and any findings that it has made in the rulemaking proceeding would not be subject to collateral attack. But a respondent would still have the right to distinguish (if it can) its situation from those facts and findings, arguing either that it has not engaged in the outlawed practice as described in the rule, or that its adoption of that practice does not have the requisite impact on competition or monopoly. Adjudicative facts thus take center stage, notwithstanding the legislative facts already established by the Commission.

Complicating things further, in competition rulemaking the line between legislative and adjudicative facts can become especially blurry, as the Seventh Circuit (in an opinion written by Judge Posner) observed in *United Air Lines, Inc. v. Civil Aeronautics Board*, which involved United's challenge to the CAB's rules prohibiting certain practices relating to computerized reservation systems owned and operated by the airlines.[70] As discussed in part II, the CAB was an agency charged with enforcing section 411 of the Civil Aeronautics Act of 1938, a statute patterned after section 5 of the FTC Act.[71] Through the competition rulemaking process, the agency had promulgated two rules: one prohibiting the airlines from biasing their own reservation systems (a form of self-preferencing) and from engaging in price discrimination, and another prohibiting the airlines from delisting information about connecting flights.[72]

United argued, among other grounds, that the rulemaking process was flawed because the CAB had denied its request for an evidentiary hearing and proceeded to adduce what are essentially adjudicative facts (e.g., whether United had market

---

69 Davis, *supra* note 65, at 199. "The parties know more about the facts concerning themselves and their activities than anyone else is likely to know, and the parties are therefore in an especially good position to rebut or explain evidence that bears upon adjudicative facts." *Id.*

70 766 F.2d 1107 (7th Cir. 1985).

71 *See Pan Am. World Airways, Inc.*, 371 U.S. at 303; Am. Airlines, Inc. v. N. Am. Airlines, Inc., 351 U.S. 79, 82 (1956).

72 *United Air Lines*, 766 F.2d at 1110.

power) to support an antitrust analysis of the prohibited practices.[73] This argument gave the court of appeals some pause, at least as to the prohibition of price discrimination:

> However, the distinction between legislative and adjudicative facts is not easy to apply, or facts such as market power and price discrimination – abstractions far removed from the simple observations of the eyewitness to a car crash – easy to classify with respect to it. In support of the conclusion that they are adjudicative facts, at least when they are contested, as they are here, and findings on them used to support a far-reaching regulation of a substantial market, we could point out that the Federal Trade Commission, while active in promulgating rules to prohibit deceptive and otherwise fraudulent practices, has promulgated only one rule (and that back in 1967) to prohibit an antitrust violation.[74]

Although the Seventh Circuit ultimately upheld the CAB's rulemaking for various reasons, it pointed to the inevitable blurring of legislative and adjudicative facts as a key reason why "[t]he use of rulemaking to enforce antitrust principles remains exceptional."[75] Notably, the court also went out of its way to say that by ruling in favor of the CAB, an agency that was "engaged full-time in the regulation of the airline industry," it was not deciding "whether the Federal Trade Commission, whose antitrust powers are not limited to a particular industry but range over much of the economy, is equally free to dispense with the conventional safeguards."[76] *United Air Lines* thus showcases the many hurdles and pitfalls associated with competition rulemaking, and the opinion – again, written by Judge Posner – merits close study in that regard.

Recognizing that substantive rulemaking may not always yield significant enforcement efficiencies, the US Supreme Court has repeatedly held that "the choice made between proceeding by general rule or by individual, ad hoc litigation is one that lies primarily in the informed discretion of the administrative agency."[77] The Court first made this point in *SEC v. Chenery Corp.*, a case involving

---

73 *Id.* at 1116 ("But a serious question remains of whether the Board gave United Air Lines all the procedural safeguards that United was entitled to."). *See also id.* at 1117 ("[T]he broader point is that United Air Lines did not have the opportunity it would have had in an antitrust trial to show that the 'market power' that it and other owners of computerized reservation systems appear to have really is trivial, and was not (could not have been) abused.").

74 *Id.* at 1118 (citing the aforementioned Tailored Clothing Rule). Interestingly, the Seventh Circuit contrasted the CAB's prohibition of price discrimination with the prohibition of biasing (self-preferencing) by characterizing the latter as "a problem of deception" rather than one of competition. *Id.* at 1113. In its view, an agency like the CAB or the FTC can promulgate a rule banning deception "on the basis of common sense and experience, without taking testimony about consumers' actual behavior," and "without finding that it is widespread or can substantially distort competition." *Id.* at 1112, 1117.

75 *Id.* at 1119.

76 *Id.* at 1121.

77 SEC v. Chenery Corp., 322 U.S. 194, 203 (1947). *Accord* NLRB v. Bell Aerospace Co., 416 U.S. 267, 292–94 (1974).

the Securities and Exchange Commission's enforcement of statutory standards under the Public Utility Holding Company Act, but its observations quoted below would apply equally well to the FTC's enforcement of section 5:

> In other words, problems may arise in a case which the administrative agency could not reasonably foresee, problems which must be solved despite the absence of a relevant general rule. Or the agency may not have had sufficient experience with a particular problem to warrant rigidifying its tentative judgment into a hard and fast rule. Or the problem may be so specialized and varying in nature as to be impossible of capture within the boundaries of a general rule. In those situations, the agency must retain power to deal with the problems on a case-to-case basis if the administrative process is to be effective. There is thus a very definite place for the case-by-case evolution of statutory standards.[78]

Suffice it to say, any of the foregoing scenarios may undercut the utility and efficiency of articulating a general competition rule that can be applied across the board to firms in a given market or industry.[79]

As discussed already, Congress astutely recognized that unfair methods of competition are not susceptible to specific definition, cataloguing, and prohibition.[80] Over time and in due course, new practices that could not be reasonably foreseen by the FTC would emerge through the limitless creativity and ingenuity of businesspeople. The agency likely would need to accumulate sufficient experience with those practices in order to form an expert judgment about their legality. And even then, varying circumstances and conditions may exist that make it difficult, if not impracticable, to fashion a general rule properly addressing all observable scenarios.

The upshot of all this is that competition rulemaking is unlikely to eliminate, or even alleviate, the oft-criticized costs and burdens of case-by-case adjudication unless the resulting rule can somehow address in advance facts and circumstances specific

---

78 *Chenery*, 322 U.S. at 202–03. For applications of *Chenery* to the FTC in the context of consumer protection enforcement, *see* FTC v. D-Link Sys., Inc., No. 3:17-cv-00039-JD, 2017 WL 4150873, at *4 (N.D. Cal. 2017) (also quoting FTC v. Sperry & Hutchinson Co., 405 U.S. 233, 244 (1972), and FTC v. Bunte Bros., Inc., 312 U.S. 349, 353 (1941), for the point that the FTC is tasked with giving meaning to "the elusive but congressionally mandated standard of fairness," which by its very nature, is "a flexible concept with evolving content"); FTC v. Wyndham Worldwide Corp., 10 F. Supp. 3d 602, 617–18 (D.N.J. 2014) (also quoting FTC v. Colgate-Palmolive Co., 380 U.S. 374, 385 (1965), for the point that "the proscriptions in [section] 5 are flexible, 'to be defined with particularity by the myriad of cases from the field of business'"), *aff'd*, 799 F.3d 236 (3d Cir. 2015). *See also* Richard G. Parker, Maryanne S. Kane, Katrina Robson, Mimi Vu & Randall W. Edwards, *The US District Court of New Jersey rules that the Federal Trade Commission can pursue claims against a company for failure to have adequate data security (Wyndham Worldwide)*, E-COMPETITIONS APRIL 2014, art. No. 73604.

79 Other commenters have raised the same concern about the utility of competition rulemaking. *See* Bernie R. Burrus & Harry Teter, *Antitrust: Rulemaking v. Adjudication in the FTC*, 54 GEO. L.J. 1106, 1119 (1966) ("The myriad of factors involved in even the simplest of antitrust matters would make any rulemaking proceeding so burdensome that it could not be justified in view of the limited scope and applicability of any resulting rule.").

80 H.R. REP. NO. 63-1142, at 19.

to individual respondents.[81] Otherwise, each respondent will request, as a matter of due process, that a trier of fact fully consider its own facts and circumstances before determining whether the rule in question can and should be applied to its challenged business practice. Indeed, an analogous point was pressed, albeit unsuccessfully, by Goodyear before the US Supreme Court in *Atlantic Refining Co. v. FTC*.[82]

As mentioned already, the Commission had determined in *Atlantic Refining* that "sales-commission plans" between a gasoline distributor and a tire manufacturer unlawfully leveraged economic power in order to coerce the former's network of wholesalers and retailers to promote the latter's line of tires, batteries, and accessories, in violation of section 5.[83] It therefore issued a cease-and-desist order banning Goodyear's entry into such plans not only with Atlantic Refining, but also "with any other marketing oil company."[84] On appeal, Goodyear argued that the order was overbroad because there was no evidence that other oil companies necessarily had the economic power that the Commission found Atlantic Refining to have possessed.[85]

Although the majority of the Court brushed aside this argument, Justice Goldberg was troubled by it, remarking in dissent that "the Commission has clearly precluded Goodyear, Firestone and B.F. Goodrich from entering into sales commission arrangements with any oil company no matter how small the company and no matter what the competitive factors involved are."[86] He wondered out loud whether a broad ban on sales-commission plans in the oil industry might have been better effectuated through rulemaking instead of case-by-case adjudication but recognized that the choice of enforcement tool was the Commission's to make.[87] Justice Goldberg observed, however, that:

> Whichever method the Commission chooses to use, . . . it seems obvious to me that the Commission must formulate a clear rational rule which is based on an adequate economic explication and takes into consideration the situation of all industry members affected by the rule.[88]

Although Goodyear's argument found only one sympathetic ear in the Court, the larger lesson of *Atlantic Refining* is that, win or lose, respondents can be expected to press this point in their defense – that a competition rule promulgated by the

---

81 *See, e.g.*, Life Music, Inc. v. Broadcast Music, Inc., 31 F.R.D. 3, 4 (S.D.N.Y. 1962) ("Trials of antitrust cases, consisting of complex legal and economic issues with voluminous records are generally protracted and expensive.") (citing a number of studies and reports).

82 381 U.S. 357.

83 *Id.* at 369–70.

84 *Id.* at 372.

85 *Id.* at 375–76.

86 *Id.* at 385–86 (Goldberg, J., dissenting).

87 *Id.* at 390.

88 *Id.* at 391.

FTC does not adequately take into consideration their particular situations.[89] Given this high likelihood, it makes more sense for the FTC to pursue case-by-case adjudication instead of rulemaking when it comes to competition enforcement.

IV. Alignment on Antitrust Law and Policy with DOJ and the Courts

As observed in part I, Congress created the FTC against the backdrop of Sherman Act enforcement by the DOJ and the courts.[90] By including section 5 in the FTC Act, Congress intended for the FTC to act as an independent and second competition enforcer, supplementing the DOJ's enforcement of the Sherman Act in the courts. In *FTC v. Cement Institute*, the Supreme Court made this exact observation – that "the Act's legislative history shows a strong congressional purpose not only to continue enforcement of the Sherman Act by the Department of Justice and the Federal District Courts, but also to supplement that enforcement through the administrative process of the new Trade Commission."[91] Accordingly, the FTC is empowered to use section 5 to challenge a practice that may also violate the Sherman Act (and hence fall under the DOJ's enforcement jurisdiction). Stated differently, the fact that a practice may violate the Sherman Act does not deprive the FTC of jurisdiction to declare it to be an unfair method of competition in violation of section 5.[92]

Additionally, *Cement Institute* confirmed that the FTC and the DOJ may bring overlapping and simultaneous enforcement proceedings against the same firms. Specifically, the DOJ had filed a civil action against the Cement Institute and numerous cement companies to enjoin their alleged violation of section 1 of the Sherman Act while appellate review of the Commission's cease-and-desist order was pending.[93] One of the cement company respondents, Marquette, in turn sought dismissal of the Commission proceeding, asserting that "it is contrary to the public interest to force respondents to defend both a Commission proceeding and a Sherman Act suit based largely on the same alleged misconduct."[94] But the Court rejected this argument as well, holding that Congress intended for the Sherman Act and the FTC Act to arm the federal government "with cumulative remedies against activity detrimental to competition."[95]

---

89 Note that *Atlantic Refining* was one of three cases that the FTC brought, seeking cease-and-desist orders to block the use of sales-commission agreements between major oil companies and tire manufacturers. *See also* FTC v. Texaco, Inc., 393 U.S. 223 (1968), *reversing* 383 F.2d 942 (D.C. Cir. 1967) (Texaco and B.F. Goodrich); Shell Oil Co. v. FTC, 360 F.2d 470 (Shell Oil and Firestone Tire & Rubber).

90 *See* S. Rep. No. 62-1326 (1913) (Cummins report); 49 Cong. Rec. 4126–32 (1913).

91 333 U.S. at 692.

92 *Id.* at 693.

93 *Id.* at 693–94.

94 *Id.* at 694.

95 *Id. Accord* New Jersey Wood Finishing Co. v. Minn. Mining & Mfg. Co., 332 F.2d 346, 352 (3d Cir. 1964), *aff'd*, 381 U.S. 311 (1965).

Implicit in *Cement Institute* is an understanding that the shared enforcement scheme contemplated by Congress envisions the DOJ and the FTC each utilizing case-by-case adjudication. Whether it is a Sherman Act complaint filed by the DOJ in a federal district court or an FTC Act complaint filed by the Commission in its own administrative tribunal, the resulting judgments are subject to review by the courts of appeals, and that mechanism of judicial review ensures a consistent and coherent development of antitrust law and policy.[96] This well-conceived scheme risks potential disruption, however, if the FTC were to pursue competition rulemaking in lieu of or in addition to case-by-case adjudication.

A principal reason is that judicial review of agency rulemaking is comparatively more deferential. Under the Administrative Procedure Act, substantive rules promulgated by the Commission through informal notice-and-comment rulemaking can be set aside only if they are determined to be "arbitrary, capricious, an abuse of discretion, or otherwise not in accordance with law."[97] In the context of this review, "[i]t is hornbook law that deference must be afforded to the expertise of an agency and the court must avoid substituting its opinion for that of the administrator."[98] Rather, "[t]he court's task is to discern whether the relevant factors were considered and whether the ultimate decision reflects reasoned decision-making."[99]

By contrast, the Commission's adjudicative decisions are subject to differing standards of review with respect to their factual and legal determinations. Section 5(c) of the FTC Act directly supplies the standard for the former – "The findings of the Commission as to the facts, if supported by evidence, shall be conclusive."[100] It is akin to a "substantial evidence" standard applicable to agency fact-finding.[101] The legal determinations, however, are subject to *de novo* review:

> The legal issues presented – that is, the identification of governing legal standards and their application to the facts found – are, by contrast, for the courts to resolve, although even in considering such issues the courts are to give some deference to the Commission's informed judgment that a particular commercial practice is to be condemned as "unfair."[102]

---

96 *See* H.R. Rep. No. 63-1142, at 19 (noting that the function of the court of appeals is to pass on questions of law).

97 5 U.S.C. § 706(2)(A); *see, e.g.*, United States v. JS & A Group, Inc., 716 F.2d 451, 453 (7th Cir. 1983) (enforcement of the Commission's trade regulation rule concerning mail-order merchandise, 16 C.F.R. § 435, which had been promulgated under section 6(g) prior to Congress's passage of rulemaking procedures under the Magnuson-Moss Warranty–Federal Trade Commission Improvement Act of 1975).

98 Nat'l Soft Drink Ass'n v. Block, 721 F.2d 1348, 1353 (D.C. Cir. 1983).

99 Prof'l Drivers Council v. Bureau of Motor Carrier Safety, 706 F.2d 1216, 1220 (D.C. Cir. 1983).

100 15 U.S.C. § 45(c).

101 *Ind. Fed'n of Dentists*, 476 U.S. at 454.

102 *Id. Accord* Impax Labs., Inc. v. FTC, 994 F.3d 484, 491 (5th Cir. 2021).

When it comes to the development of antitrust law and policy, the standard of review of the Commission's legal determinations is, of course, what matters, and the standard for rulemaking (i.e., rationality, no substitution of judgment, complete deference to agency expertise) is unabashedly more deferential than the standard for an adjudicative decision (i.e., *de novo* review, some deference). Faced with a more deferential standard of review, an appellate court is less able to ensure consistency and coherence in competition principles across the various statutes (Sherman, Clayton, and FTC Acts) if it is reviewing a product of Commission rulemaking.

A related reason why competition rulemaking would threaten to disrupt Congress's shared enforcement scheme has to do with the entangled relationship between the FTC Act and the Sherman Act. Although section 5 clearly empowers the FTC to challenge practices that do not violate the Sherman Act,[103] even rulemaking limited to "standalone" violations of section 5 (assuming that were possible) likely would still impact the DOJ's enforcement of the Sherman Act. Supreme Court case law has characterized standalone violations of section 5 as including practices that run counter to the public policy of the Sherman Act or violate its spirit.[104] Additionally, the Court has said that Sherman Act case law may be consulted for guidance in recognizing unfair methods of competition that bear the characteristics of recognized antitrust violations.[105]

The foregoing cases indicate a high likelihood that even competition rulemaking limited to standalone violations of section 5 would still implicate Sherman Act policies and principles, thereby potentially upsetting the cooperative and coordinated federal enforcement of the antitrust laws that US-based businesses rely upon and expect to see. The degree of overlap in competition enforcement work between the FTC and the DOJ is simply too great for rulemaking by one agency not to have an impact on the other agency.[106] This is why the two agencies, in general, have historically issued joint enforcement guidelines and statements.[107] And it is why the FTC should continue to look to case-by-case adjudication as the principal enforcement tool for section 5.

---

103 *Motion Picture Advertising Serv.*, 344 U.S. at 394 ("The 'unfair methods of competition', which are condemned by § 5(a) of the Act, are not confined to those that were illegal at common law or that were condemned by the Sherman Act."); *Cement Institute*, 333 U.S. at 694 ("It has long been recognized that there are many unfair methods of competition that do not assume the proportions of Sherman Act violations.").

104 *Sperry & Hutchinson Co.*, 405 U.S. at 239; FTC v. Brown Shoe Co., Inc., 384 U.S. 316, 321 (1966); Fashion Originators' Guild v. FTC, 312 U.S. 457, 463–64 (1941).

105 *Atlantic Refining*, 381 U.S. at 369–70. *See also New Jersey Wood Finishing Co.*, 332 F.2d at 351, *aff'd*, 381 U.S. 311 (1965).

106 The enforcement overlap would be limited, and the risk of disruption manageable, if the FTC were an agency with focused jurisdiction over a particular sector of commerce, like the Federal Communications Commission or the Federal Reserve.

107 *See, e.g.*, U.S. Dep't of Justice & Fed. Trade Comm'n, Horizontal Merger Guidelines (2010); Fed. Trade Comm'n & U.S. Dep't of Justice, Antitrust Guidelines for Collaborations Among Competitors (2000); U.S. Dep't of Justice & Fed. Trade Comm'n, Statements of Antitrust Enforcement Policy in Health Care (1996).

V. Vertical Mergers in the Cement Industry

This chapter closes with a look at a time when the FTC considered competition rulemaking to address an apparently growing trend towards vertical integration in the cement industry, i.e., cement companies acquiring ready-mix concrete producers, which are the largest consumers of cement. In its 1964 opinion in the matter of *Permanente Cement Company and Glacier Sand & Gravel Company*, the Commission described the problem of vertical integration in the cement industry as one of "growing importance and urgency" and as a phenomenon that has "apparently assumed industry-wide dimensions."[108] To better study and consider this problem, the Commission announced that it would institute a trade regulation rulemaking proceeding:

> Where a problem involves an entire industry made up of a large number of firms, it may uneconomical, inefficient, and inequitable to proceed exclusively on the basis of individual adjudicative proceedings. Industry-wide problems require, so far as is practicable, industry-wide solutions. We think a rule-making proceeding is particularly appropriate in dealing with such Section 7 problems as are here presented in the cement industry. Such a proceeding affords a better forum than do adjudicative proceedings against individual companies for organizing and appraising the general economic facts involving industry and market structure that are so important under Section 7.[109]

The agency's stated rationale for considering a trade regulation rule was exactly what one would expect: is the observed competition problem industry-wide in scope, and if so, is it of a nature that would lend itself an industry-wide solution through rulemaking, instead of case-by-case adjudication? Are there certain economies, efficiencies, and equities that may flow from rulemaking?

In February 1966, FTC Chairman Dixon appeared before the House Appropriations Committee to discuss the agency's appropriations for 1967.[110] Reporting on the status of various trade regulation rulemaking initiatives at the agency, he advised Congress that "[a]n industrywide inquiry into acquisitions by cement manufacturers is being conducted to enable the Commission to determine the most effective and appropriate method of obtaining compliance with the

---

108 No. 7939, 65 F.T.C. 410, 494 (1964).

109 *Id. See also* Fed. Trade Comm'n, Annual Report for the Fiscal Year Ended June 30, 1964, at 6, 22 (1964). The annual report also noted that the FTC was considering trade regulation rulemaking proceedings relating to alleged discriminatory pricing practices in the marketing of gasoline. *Id.* at 6. *See also Industries Will Get Merger Guidelines*, N.Y. Times, May 16, 1964, at 1, 19 ("Under the new program, the commission will conduct studies of the competitive situation in specific industries and, upon completion of its inquiries, issue broad rules that will indicate to business, in advance, whether or not certain types of mergers would be prosecuted by the Federal agency.").

110 *Independent Offices Appropriations for 1967: Hearing on the Federal Trade Commission Before the Subcomm. on Independent Offices of the H. Comm. on Appropriations*, 89th Cong., 2d Sess., 383–453 (1966).

antimerger law."[111] Looking ahead to the agenda for the fiscal year 1967, Chairman Dixon said that the FTC contemplated the promulgation of a trade regulation rule on some aspect of the merger problem in this industry, with a target date of June 1967.[112]

The inquiry mentioned by Chairman Dixon led to the April 1966 issuance of a report by the Bureau of Economics containing the staff's findings regarding merger activity involving the cement and ready-mix concrete industries.[113] The report concluded that "the merger of any of the larger factors [sic] in local concrete markets with a substantial cement supplier in that market would have manifest adverse effects on competitive conduct and performance."[114] With this report in hand, the FTC then proceeded to provide notice of a public hearing before the full Commission on vertical integration in the cement industry, to be held on June 6, 1966.[115] The hearing was subsequently moved to July 11, 1966, to give interested parties more time to review the staff report and to prepare to address the Commission.[116]

Instead of promulgating a trade regulation rule, as Chairman Dixon had told Congress the agency planned to do, on January 3, 1967, the Commission issued a statement of its enforcement policy with respect to vertical mergers in the cement industry.[117] Around the same time, the Commission responded to arguments by respondents that the industry-wide inquiry, conducted while their individual cases were pending, somehow prejudiced them by denying them their right to a fair hearing.[118] The Commission rejected this argument, pointing out that the statement of enforcement policy makes clear that "the issues in any proceeding instituted by the Commission will be decided on the merits on that case."[119] In other words, the FTC would continue to challenge anticompetitive mergers in this industry through case-by-case adjudication. The fact that the agency made a special effort to conduct an in-depth study of the general problem did not amount to prejudgment of any individual case:

> If the Commission's expertise has been enlarged as a result of the general inquiry conducted by it in connection with formulating the Statement of Enforcement Policy, that fact neither prejudices

111 *Id.* at 443.

112 *Id.*

113 Fed. Trade Comm'n, Bureau of Econ., Economic Report on Mergers and Vertical Integration in the Cement Industry (Apr. 1966).

114 *Id.* at 15.

115 Cement Industry: Notice of Public Hearing on Vertical Integrations, 31 Fed. Reg. 6285 (Apr. 22, 1966). Commissioner MacIntyre did not concur in the scheduling of a public hearing.

116 Vertical Integration in Cement Industry: Notice of Public Hearing, 31 Fed. Reg. 7772 (May 26, 1966).

117 Fed. Trade Comm'n, Commission Enforcement Policy with Respect to Vertical Mergers in the Cement Industry, *attached as App'x B to* Lehigh Portland Cement Co., No. 8680, 71 F.T.C. 1618, 1623 (1967).

118 *Lehigh Portland Cement*, 71 F.T.C. at 1619.

119 *Id.* at 1619, 1627.

> the respondents' rights nor constitutes any reason for dismissing these proceedings. Respondents are entitled to have their cases adjudicated by Commissioners with open minds, not empty ones.[120]

The federal courts subsequently sided with the Commission on the lack of prejudice to the respondents.[121]

A key lesson to take away from the FTC's conduct of trade regulation rulemaking proceedings relating to vertical mergers in the cement industry is that competition rulemaking may be relatively easy to consider as an exercise, but the intended deliverable may be much harder to come by. In this case, the FTC explored the possibility of promulgating a trade regulation rule but ultimately concluded that it would continue to enforce section 7 of the Clayton Act against anticompetitive mergers in this industry through case-by-case adjudication. It did not come away from this exercise empty-handed, however. The process yielded a staff report and a policy statement on enforcement – both entirely appropriate agency work products, as the Ninth Circuit held in *Ash Grove Cement Co. v. FTC.*[122] In essence, the FTC conducted a market study of the cement and downstream ready-mix concrete industries and, in so doing, bolstered its expertise as a competition enforcer in subsequent adjudications.[123] In an adjudicative proceeding, the FTC can always draw on its full experience and judgment from other cases, investigations, and studies, including proceedings that were labeled as rulemaking but did not result in the promulgation of any competition rule.

The FTC's decision to continue pursuing its merger enforcement program in the cement industry through case-by-case adjudication instead of rulemaking can be viewed as responding to the three practical considerations addressed in this chapter. First, although the agency did gain additional insights regarding the broader industry trend towards consolidation, particularly with downstream ready-mix concrete firms, case-by-case adjudication ensured that each merger challenge was adequately supported by specific factual and economic analyses (e.g., the local geographic markets impacted by the transaction). Second, as seen already, the respondents had no legitimate argument that they were being denied their right to due process. The fact that the Commission had conducted proceedings ostensibly for the purpose of rulemaking did not change the fact

---

120 *Id.* at 1621–22.

121 Ash Grove Cement Co. v. FTC, 577 F.2d 1368, 1373 (9th Cir. 1978) ("Ash Grove is mistaken both as to its allegation that the Enforcement Policy constitutes a 'rule' and as to its contention that the FTC cannot conduct investigations in the form of trade regulation rule proceedings."); Lehigh Portland Cement Co. v. FTC, 291 F. Supp. 628, 631 (E.D. Va. 1968) ("The Commission not only had the right but the duty to institute and conduct an industry-wide investigation re vertical acquisitions in the cement and ready-mix concrete industries.").

122 577 F.2d at 1376 ("We hold that the FTC's investigation of the cement industry through the medium of a trade regulation rule proceeding and its subsequent promulgation of a staff report and an industry guide were fully authorized by law.").

123 *Id.* ("Indeed, one of the purposes of industry investigations is to provide the agency with increased expertise in administering the law by exposing it to the factual background of relevant industries against which to judge individual mergers and acquisitions.").

that each merger challenge was still being decided on its own merits following an evidentiary hearing. Third, a competition rule might have led to dissonance with the DOJ's merger enforcement program, particularly with respect to vertical mergers. Instead, the Commission issued a policy statement on enforcement – essentially a precursor to the merger guidelines that the two agencies eventually would jointly issue.[124]

124 The DOJ would issue its first merger guidelines in 1968. The FTC's policy statement on enforcement came out in 1967.

Can the Federal Trade Commission Use Rulemaking to Change Antitrust Law?

RICHARD J. PIERCE, JR.*
George Washington University School of Law

Abstract

Professor Pierce begins by questioning the claim of Chair Lina Khan that the FTC has the power to use notice-and-comment rulemaking to interpret and implement section 5 of the FTC Act. He then uses four hypothetical rulemakings to explain why the FTC cannot use rulemaking to change antitrust law even if it has the power to issue substantive rules. He concludes by referring to several contexts in which Chair Khan and the other proponents of radical change in antitrust law can team up with mainstream proponents of incremental change to move antitrust law in constructive directions.

---

* Lyle T. Alverson Professor of Law, George Washington University School of Law. I am grateful to the participants in a workshop conducted by the Center for the Study of the Administrative State for providing helpful comments on an earlier version of this article.

The new chair of the Federal Trade Commission (FTC), Lina Khan, dislikes almost every characteristic of antitrust law. She disagrees with the consumer welfare maximization goal that enforcement agencies and courts have been attempting to further for almost half a century.[1] She believes that courts should instead attempt to further multiple economic and political goals that include keeping firms from becoming too large and powerful, protecting small firms from big firms, protecting employees, and creating open markets that function in accordance with a bill of rights that forbids many practices as unlawful in all circumstances.[2]

Chair Khan also dislikes the procedures that enforcement agencies and courts have been using to create and implement antitrust law for over a century. Antitrust law is based on judicial interpretations of two statutes – the Sherman Act[3] and the Clayton Act.[4] Both statutes are worded so broadly, however, that the Supreme Court has long analogized its decisions that interpret the statutes to the common law decision-making process.[5] Antitrust law evolves gradually as the Court decides each case that comes before it. Moreover, with only a few exceptions, the Court uses the "rule of reason" to decide whether a firm's conduct violates antitrust law.[6] As a result, the same conduct can be legal or illegal depending on a detailed analysis of the effects of the conduct in the circumstances in which it takes place.

There is strong evidence that both President Biden and Chair Khan's Democrat colleagues on the Commission share her views and support her efforts. Shortly after Chair Khan was confirmed, President Biden held a press conference at which he signed a lengthy Executive Order on Promoting Competition in the American Economy.[7] The order expressed his support for most of the changes in law that Chair Khan wants to make. He signed the order with Chair Khan standing behind him. He then handed her the pen that he used to sign the order. Since Chair Khan assumed the chairmanship, the FTC has issued many orders by a three-to-two vote, with the other two Democrats voting with Chair Khan on every order.[8]

---

1 Lina M. Khan, *Amazon's Antitrust Paradox*, 126 Yale L.J. 710, 716–17, 738–44 (2017).

2 *Id.* at 738–44.

3 15 U.S.C. § 1 *et seq.*

4 15 U.S.C. § 15 *et seq.*

5 *E.g.*, Leegin Creative Leather Products v. PSKS, 551 U.S. 877, 899–900 (2007). *See* Peter J. Carney & Kristen J. McAhren, *The US Supreme Court overturns its long-standing prohibition against vertical agreements between manufacturers and their dealers setting minimum resale prices (Leegin Creative)*, e-Competitions June 2007, art. No. 38050.

6 *Id.* at 885–87.

7 Exec. Order No. 14,036, 86 Fed. Reg. 36987 (July 9, 2021).

8 On September 30, 2021, FTC Commissioner Rohit Chopra resigned to become Director of the Consumer Financial Protection Board. That created a situation in which the FTC now has two Democrats and two Republicans. Unless and until the President nominates and the Senate confirms another Democrat who shares Chair Khan's views, she is unlikely to persuade a majority of her colleagues to take actions that reflect her views.

Chair Khan plans to use two means to make the changes in antitrust law that she considers to be essential. She plans to increase the circumstances in which the FTC disapproves of proposed mergers and acquisitions,[9] and she plans to use the FTC's rulemaking power to transform other aspects of antitrust law.[10] I will focus initially on her proposed use of rulemaking in this essay. Chair Khan will experience some challenges in her efforts to block the many mergers and acquisitions that she opposes, but those challenges are not nearly as formidable as the challenges that she will confront in her efforts to use rulemaking to make major changes in antitrust law in contexts other than mergers and acquisitions.

Part I of the article discusses the advantages and disadvantages of rulemaking as a potential means of reshaping antitrust law. Part II discusses the FTC's power to issue rules of various types. Part III discusses the potential for the FTC to use rulemaking to change antitrust law in four areas that Chair Khan has identified as particularly good candidates for rulemakings – creating a right to repair products, banning non-compete clauses in employment contracts, aggressively enforcing a ban on predatory pricing, and outlawing reverse payments to settle patent disputes involving prescription drugs. Part IV identifies several important changes in antitrust law that courts would be likely to embrace and that would move the law in the direction that Chair Khan prefers.

I conclude that the FTC probably lacks the power to use notice-and-comment rulemaking to implement section 5 of the FTC Act. I also conclude that, even if the FTC has that power, it cannot use that power to make most of the major changes in antitrust law that Chair Khan envisions. The FTC can use rulemaking to improve antitrust law by limiting the use of non-compete clauses in employment contracts, but the FTC can accomplish that goal more rapidly and with less legal risk by using a combination of the tools that it has long used. The FTC can also make significant incremental changes in antitrust law that courts are likely to embrace.

I. The Advantages and Disadvantages of Rulemaking

Chair Khan supports her proposed use of rulemaking to transform antitrust law with a long list of criticisms of the FTC's traditional near-exclusive reliance on adjudication to create and implement antitrust law and a long list of advantages that rulemaking could provide. Chair Khan criticizes the FTC's reliance on adjudication on the basis that it is slow and cumbersome; it does not yield the kind of clear standards that businessmen, the private bar, and agencies need;

---

9 Fed. Trade Comm'n, Statement of Chair Lina M. Khan, Commissioner Rohit Chopra, and Commissioner Rebecca Kelly Slaughter on the Withdrawal of the Vertical Merger Guidelines (Sep. 15, 2021), https://www.ftc.gov/legal-library/browse/cases-proceedings/public-statements/statement-chair-lina-m-khan-commissioner-rohit-chopra-commissioner-rebecca-kelly-slaughter.

10 Rohit Chopra & Lina M. Khan, *The Case for "Unfair Methods of Competition" Rulemaking*, 87 U. Chi. L. Rev. 357 (2020).

it undermines effective enforcement by rendering it extremely expensive and cumbersome; it calls on generalist judges to analyze and apply technical economic issues that they are not equipped to evaluate; and it relies heavily on expert witnesses who are well paid to provide testimony that favors the firms that employ them.[11] By comparison, Chair Khan praises rulemaking because it is capable of creating clear standards of conduct; it allows broader participation by members of the public in the process of shaping the law; it provides a basis for more efficient and effective enforcement of the law; it is capable of changing the law more rapidly; and it provides a much greater opportunity for agencies with expertise in economics to shape the law.[12]

Chair Khan couples her criticism of adjudication and her praise of rulemaking with harsh criticism of the rule of reason that modern courts apply to decide whether most forms of conduct violate antitrust law.[13] She praises the per se approach that courts often used in the 1960s.[14] Cases that are subject to the rule of reason require years to adjudicate; they do not yield clear standards of conduct; the rule of reason renders enforcement of antitrust law expensive and inefficient, and the rule of reason requires generalist judges to perform a function that they are not well equipped to perform. By contrast, per se rules announce clear standards of conduct; they make enforcement of antitrust law far more efficient and effective; and they call on generalist judges to perform functions that they know how to perform.

I agree with all of Chair Khan's criticisms of the adjudication process and her praise for the rulemaking process. I have made similar arguments in many contexts for decades.[15] I have even supported greater use of rulemaking by the FTC to announce standards that the agency finds to be sound interpretations of antitrust law.[16] I also share her criticisms of the rule of reason and her praise for per se rules. Those generalizations must be qualified, however, based on the well-documented limitations of both rulemaking and per se rules.

The most important limitation of both rulemaking and per se rules is their inability to capture and reflect variations in the effects of many forms of conduct on the performance of markets. A per se rule performs well in a context in which we have reason to believe that a particular type of conduct produces bad effects on the performance of markets in all or most circumstances. A per se rule produces bad results, however, if it prohibits conduct that yields net social benefits

---

11 *Id.* at 359–63.

12 *Id.* at 363–74.

13 *Id.* at 359–63.

14 Khan, *supra* note 1, at 717–22.

15 *E.g.*, Kristin E. Hickman & Richard J. Pierce, Jr., Administrative Law Treatise § 4.8 (6th ed., Wolters Kluwer 2019).

16 Richard J. Pierce, Jr., *The Rocky Relationship Between the Federal Trade Commission and Administrative Law*, 83 Geo. Wash. L. Rev. 2026, 2040–41 (2015).

in many circumstances. Many scholars believe that most of the forms of conduct that Chair Khan wants to prohibit in all circumstances create net benefits to society in many circumstances.[17] The Supreme Court relied heavily on per se rules from 1940 until 1974, with demonstrably bad results.[18] The rules often prohibited conduct that benefited society and encouraged conduct that harmed society.

Rulemaking also has other well-known disadvantages. The kinds of rules that Chair Khan wants to issue – legislative rules that have the force of law – require use of notice and comment.[19] The notice-and-comment rulemaking process is long and resource-intensive.[20] A typical notice-and-comment rulemaking takes many years to complete and requires the agency to devote significant resources to a single proceeding.[21]

Two other types of rules – interpretive rules and policy statements – lack the force of law but can be issued quickly and with only a modest commitment of agency resources.[22] Legislative rules have two other characteristics that sometimes make them more valuable than interpretative rules or policy statements. Courts sometimes confer more deference on statutory interpretations that are announced in legislative rules than in interpretative rules, and legislative rules are more difficult to change than interpretative rules.[23] The first advantage has greatly diminished, however, as the Supreme Court has reduced the power of the deference that it once conferred on legislative rules,[24] and the second advantage exists only when there is reason for concern that changes in the leadership of an agency will induce the agency to rescind a socially beneficial rule. As Neil Chilson has explained, the FTC often can use a combination of interpretative rules, policy statements, and enforcement actions to obtain results that are much better than the results it can obtain through use of legislative rules.[25]

---

17 *See, e.g.*, Herbert Hovenkamp, *Antitrust and Platform Monopoly*, 130 YALE L.J. 1952 (2021) (describing the many variables that must be considered in the process of evaluating the effects of various forms of conduct).

18 *See, e.g.*, ROBERT H. BORK, THE ANTITRUST PARADOX: A POLICY AT WAR WITH ITSELF (Basic Books 1978) (explaining and documenting the adverse effects of the antitrust decisions of the 1940s, 1950s and 1960s).

19 Hickman & Pierce, *supra* note 15, at §§ 4.3, 5.1-5.4.

20 Richard Pierce, *Rulemaking Ossification Is Real: A Response to Testing the Ossification Hypothesis*, 80 GEO. WASH. L. REV. 1493 (2012).

21 Richard Pierce, *The Administrative Conference and Empirical Research*, 83 GEO. WASH. L. REV. 1564, 1566–69 (2015).

22 Hickman & Pierce, *supra* note 15, at §§ 4.4, 4.5.

23 Aaron L. Nielson, *Sticky Regulations*, 85 U. CHI. L. REV. 85 (2018).

24 Chair Khan has identified the potential availability of *Chevron* deference for a statutory interpretation adopted through the process of issuing a legislative rule as a potential advantage of use of the notice-and-comment process to issue a legislative rule. Chopra & Khan, *supra* note 10, at 375. In the past, that might have been a good reason for an agency to prefer issuance of a legislative rule to issuance of an interpretive rule. During the last few years, however, the Supreme Court has severely qualified the strength of *Chevron* deference, thereby greatly reducing the potential advantage that an agency can get as a result of issuing a legislative rule rather than an interpretive rule. *See* Kristin E. Hickman & Mark R. Thomson, *The* Chevron*ization of* Auer, 103 MINN. L. REV. HEADNOTES 103 (2019).

25 Neil Chilson, *Old Laws and New Technology*, GEO. L. & P. L. REV. (forthcoming 2022).

Rules issued through use of the notice-and-comment process also have another important characteristic that is relevant to Chair Khan's plan. They are subject to judicial review. I consider that to be a virtue of the rulemaking process, but Chair Khan is likely to experience it primarily as a major impediment to issuance of the kinds of rules that she proposes. Courts are unlikely to uphold most of those rules.

A closely related limitation of rulemaking and per se rules is tied to the goals that Chair Khan seeks to further by announcing a new set of per se rules. She wants to replace the effort to maximize consumer welfare that courts and agencies have pursued for the past half-century with a long list of goals that the new per se rules would further.[26] Any attempt to create and announce rules that simultaneously further the goals that Chair Khan wants to pursue is certain to fail.

I use one simple pattern of facts to illustrate the inherent inconsistency of such a multiple-goal approach during the first week of my antitrust course. Suppose that a market consists of three large firms, each of which accounts for 30% of the market, and one hundred small firms, each of which accounts for 0.1% of the market. Suppose that the process of making the product that is sold in the market has evolved in ways that provide the opportunity to reduce the costs of producing the product substantially by increasing the scale at which the product is produced up to the level of production of each of the three large firms.

Now suppose that you discover that the three large firms have entered into an agreement to sell the product at a price far above their cost of production. How should antitrust law address that situation? If the goal is to maximize consumer welfare, the answer is easy. The three large firms should be punished for engaging in price fixing. If the goal is to protect the one hundred small firms from the three large firms, the answer is also easy. The three large firms should be encouraged to engage in price fixing. The resulting large price increase would protect the small firms from going out of business.

This is just one of an unlimited number of entirely realistic circumstances in which any agency that attempts to further multiple goals with antitrust law would have to make tradeoffs among goals. Chair Khan does not tell us how she would make those tradeoffs, but her discussion of economies of scale provides a powerful clue.[27] She criticizes scholars who characterize economies of scale as "objective technical demands of production and distribution." She characterizes them instead as barriers to entry that are inconsistent with her definition of a competitive market. The kinds of per se rules that Chair Khan proposes would produce good results only if you believe that it would be good to increase significantly the prices that consumers pay for many goods and services and to reduce significantly the quantity of goods and services that consumers can buy.

---

26 Khan, *supra* note 1, at 710, 716–17, 738–44.

27 *Id.* at 719–20.

The advantages and disadvantages of the rulemaking process that Chair Khan proposes will become more apparent when I describe the likely results of Chair Khan's attempt to implement her plan in four illustrative contexts in Part III of this article.

II. FTC Power to Issue Rules

An agency has the power to issue legislative rules to implement a statute only if Congress has given it that power.[28] The FTC has no power to issue rules to implement the two primary sources of antitrust law – the Sherman Act and the Clayton Act. There is a lively debate about whether the FTC has the power to implement the provision in section 5 of the FTC Act of 1914 that makes it illegal to engage in "unfair methods of competition." The FTC has never attempted to use rulemaking for that purpose, but that is the power that Chair Khan plans to use to make major changes in antitrust law.[29]

Section 5 of the FTC Act states that "[u]nfair methods of competition in or affecting commerce, and unfair or deceptive acts or practices in or affecting commerce, are hereby declared unlawful."[30] Section 5 continues by describing in detail the process of adjudication that the FTC is required to use to implement that declaration.

Section 6 of the FTC Act is titled "Additional powers of Commission."[31] It describes a wide variety of powers, most of which are powers to investigate and to gather and report data of various types. Subsection (g) of section 6 is titled: "Classification of corporations; regulations." It empowers the Commission to "classify corporations and... to make rules and regulations for the purpose of carrying out the provisions of this subchapter."

Between 1914 and 1962, the FTC, Congress, courts, and scholars were unanimous in their belief that the FTC did not have the power to issue legislative rules.[32] There was universal agreement that section 6(g) of the FTC Act gave the FTC only the power to issue procedural rules and rules that govern investigations and the process of classifying corporations. That view is consistent with the legislative history of the Act and its structure. The statute has a provision that instructs courts to enforce orders that the FTC issues in adjudications, but it does not have a provision that authorizes courts to enforce rules that the FTC issues.[33]

---

28 Hickman & Pierce, *supra* note 15, at § 4.2.

29 Chopra & Khan, *supra* note 10, at 377–79.

30 5 U.S.C. § 45(a)(1).

31 5 U.S.C. § 46.

32 Thomas W. Merrill & Kathryn Tongue Watts, *Agency Rules with the Force of Law: The Original Convention*, 116 Harv. L. Rev. 467, 506 (2002).

33 *Id.* at 504–05.

In 1962, the FTC announced for the first time that it was going to rely on section 6(g) as the basis to issue what it called trade regulation rules – rules that would have the force of law and that would prohibit specified forms of conduct.[34] The FTC's power to issue those rules was challenged in the D.C. Circuit in the context of a rule that prohibited the retail sale of gasoline without posting the octane content of the gasoline. The court upheld the rule and the power of the FTC to issue legislative rules in its 1973 decision in *National Petroleum Refiners v. FTC*.[35]

The court was not troubled by the inconsistency of the FTC's new position with the universal belief of the FTC, Congress, courts, and scholars for the first forty-eight years of the existence of the agency that it lacked that power.[36] Nor was the court troubled by the detailed description of the process of adjudicating section 5 disputes that immediately followed the sentence in section 5 that declared that "unfair or deceptive acts" and "unfair methods of competition" are unlawful. The court acknowledged that the FTC could rely on adjudication to implement section 5, as it had for sixty years, but it noted that the statute did not say that the FTC could *only* use adjudication to implement section 5.[37]

The court devoted most of its opinion to a detailed description of the advantages of the rulemaking process.[38] The court's reasoning process can be summarized as follows: An agency can do its job more effectively if it has the power to issue legislative rules, and the statute that created the FTC has a passing reference to the power to issue rules of some kind. It follows that the agency has the power to issue legislative rules even though the agency, Congress, courts, and scholars believed that it lacked that power for almost fifty years.

The method of statutory interpretation that the D.C. Circuit used in *National Petroleum Refiners* was used by several circuits in the 1970s.[39] It was never embraced by the Supreme Court, however, and no court has used it in decades.[40] I will return to discussion of the continued viability of the holding in *National Petroleum Refiners* after I discuss the congressional reaction to that decision.

After its surprising victory in *National Petroleum Refiners*, the FTC began to use its newfound rulemaking power to begin rulemakings that challenged the marketing practices that firms had long used in many markets. Congress reacted negatively to the FTC's aggressive use of its rulemaking power. Congress enacted two statutes that made it extraordinarily difficult – perhaps impossible – for the

34 *Id.* at 549–54.

35 482 F.2d 672 (D.C. Cir. 1973).

36 *Id.* at 685–86.

37 *Id.* at 677–78.

38 *Id.* at 681–83, 690–93.

39 Merrill & Watts, *supra* note 32, at 557–70.

40 *Id.* at 528–45, 570–78.

FTC to use its new power to issue legislative rules. Those statutes added fifteen procedures that the FTC was required to use in any rulemaking that it undertook to implement section 5 of the FTC Act.[41]

The FTC was able to use rulemaking to issue about a dozen legislative rules to implement section 5 of the FTC Act before Congress amended it by adding many mandatory procedures. The FTC was able to issue those rules in an average of 2.94 years each.[42] After Congress enacted the first statute that imposed some new procedural mandates in 1975, the FTC was able to issue seven more rules, but the new rulemaking procedure increased the average length of a rulemaking from 2.94 years to 5.57 years.[43] The FTC also abandoned several other rulemakings after spending an average of 8.66 years on each.[44] In 1980, Congress enacted another statute that amended the FTC Act. That statute added still more lengthy procedures that the FTC must use to complete a rulemaking to implement the FTC Act.[45] The FTC has not attempted to issue any legislative rule to implement the FTC Act since Congress amended the Act in 1980.[46]

Under Chair Khan's leadership, the FTC recently amended its rules for using the rulemaking process that Congress created in the 1975 and 1980 amendments to the FTC Act.[47] The amendments to the rules of procedure are intended to restore the viability of the process. Those changes might trim a year or two from the length of the process. The process would still take over five years to issue a single rule, however. It is unlikely that Chair Khan will try to use a process that takes at least five years to issue a single rule in her effort to implement her ambitious agenda to transform most of antitrust law.

Chair Khan is relying instead on a combination of the D.C. Circuit's opinion in *National Petroleum Refiners* and one provision of the 1975 statute that amended the FTC Act. That provision states:

> The Commission shall have no authority under this Act [the FTC Act] other than its authority under this section, to prescribe any rule with respect to unfair or deceptive acts or practices in or affecting commerce (within the meaning of section 5(a)(1)). The preceding

---

41 Jeffrey S. Lubbers, *It's Time to Remove the "Mossified" Procedures for FTC Rulemaking*, 83 Geo. Wash. L. Rev. 1979, 1982–84 (2015).

42 *Id.* at 1985–87.

43 *Id.* at 1988–89.

44 *Id.* at 1989.

45 *Id.*

46 *Id.* at 1989–90. For a contrasting perspective on the effects of the Magnuson-Moss Act, *see* Kurt Walters, *Reassessing the Mythology of Magnuson-Moss: A Call to Revive Section 18 Rulemaking at the FTC*, 16 Harv. L. & Pol'y Rev. (forthcoming 2022).

47 Fed. Trade Comm'n, Statement of Commissioner Rebecca Kelly Slaughter Joined by Chair Lina M. Khan and Commissioner Rohit Chopra Regarding the Adoption of Revised Section 18 Rulemaking Procedures (July 1, 2021), https://www.ftc.gov/legal-library/browse/cases-proceedings/public-statements/statement-commissioner-rebecca-kelly-slaughter-joined-chair-lina-m-khan-commissioner-rohit-chopra.

> sentence shall not affect any authority of the Commission to prescribe rules (including interpretive rules), and general statements of policy, with respect to unfair methods of competition in or affecting commerce.[48]

Since the "section" to which the provision refers describes the new mandatory procedures that the FTC must use in rulemakings to define an "unfair or deceptive act," the FTC is required to use those procedures when it issues a rule that defines an "unfair or deceptive act." This peculiarly worded provision raises many other questions, however. Chair Khan interprets it as an implicit legislative endorsement of the D.C. Circuit's decision in *National Petroleum Refiners* in the context of the FTC's power to use notice-and-comment rulemaking to define "unfair methods of competition." As so interpreted, the amendment would allow the FTC to use pure notice-and-comment rulemaking, unburdened by the additional procedures that Congress mandated for rulemakings to define "unfair or deceptive acts," to issue legislative rules that define "unfair methods of competition."[49] That may be a plausible interpretation of the amendment, but it is far from a necessary interpretation.

There are many reasons to question whether Congress simultaneously conditioned the FTC's power to issue rules that define "unfair or deceptive acts" in ways that had the effect of making that power nearly impossible to exercise and endorsed the FTC's power to use a less demanding procedure to issue rules that define "unfair methods of competition." First, it is difficult, if not impossible, to distinguish between an "unfair or deceptive act" and an "unfair method of competition." Most of the acts that the FTC had previously defined as "unfair or deceptive acts" also qualify as "unfair methods of competition." They prohibit firms from using particular methods to advertise or market their goods or services. Did Congress intend to authorize the FTC to use notice-and-comment rulemaking to prohibit "unfair methods of competition" that do not also qualify as "unfair or deceptive acts"? If so, what conduct that is not an "unfair or deceptive act" qualifies as an "unfair method of competition"? It is not clear that there is any conduct that qualifies as an "unfair method of competition" that does not also qualify as an "unfair or deceptive act."

Second, the reference to interpretive rules and general statements of policy in the second sentence of the provision suggests another possible interpretation of the sentence. Perhaps Congress was just trying to make it clear that it was not qualifying the FTC's power to issue interpretive rules or general statements of policy to implement section 5 by requiring the FTC to use the extraordinarily burdensome procedures that it was requiring the FTC to use when it issued legislative rules.

---

48 Pub. L. No. 93-637, § 202(a)(2).

49 Chopra & Khan, *supra* note 10, at 377–79.

That interpretation would be consistent with the general principles of administrative law and statutory interpretation that apply to other agencies. While an agency does not have the power to issue legislative rules to implement a statute unless Congress has explicitly given the agency that power, agencies need no explicit statutory authority to issue interpretive rules or general statements of policy.[50] It is hard to imagine any circumstance in which Congress would want to limit any agency's power to announce to the public its non-binding interpretations of the statutes that it implements or the policies that it intends to further when it implements the statute.

An agency can issue an interpretive rule or a policy statement without following any statutorily prescribed procedure, since rules of that type have no legally binding effect.[51] By contrast, agencies are required to use the notice-and-comment process to issue legislative rules because they have the force of law. Like all agencies, the FTC has long used the process of issuing interpretive rules and policy statements to provide the public with valuable information about the agency's non-binding statutory interpretations and the policies that it is trying to further. It would make sense for Congress to make it clear that the additional procedures that it required the FTC to use when it engages in the process of creating a legislative rule do not apply to the process of announcing its statutory interpretations or its general policies.

Chair Khan's belief that the FTC can use the notice-and-comment process to issue rules that transform antitrust law is necessarily based on her belief that the D.C. Circuit's 1973 decision in *National Petroleum Refiners* remains good law today. It also depends on the validity of her belief that Congress implicitly ratified that decision in the context of rules that define "unfair methods of competition" in the 1975 statute in which it amended the FTC Act to make it nearly impossible for the FTC to issue rules that define "unfair or deceptive acts." I am skeptical that the Supreme Court will find Chair Khan's arguments persuasive.

As Tom Merrill and Kathryn Watts have explained in detail, the method of statutory interpretation that the D.C. Circuit used in *National Petroleum Refiners* has never been embraced by the Supreme Court; it has not been used by any court in decades; and it is inconsistent with the principles of separation of powers that the Supreme Court has emphasized for decades.[52] One of the most important of those principles is that no agency has the power to take an action that has the force of law unless Congress has clearly conferred that power on the agency.

If the FTC attempts to rely on the D.C. Circuit's decision to support its effort to use rulemaking to transform antitrust law, the Supreme Court is likely to

50 Hickman & Pierce, *supra* note 15, at § 4.2.1.

51 *Id.* at §§ 4.4, 4.5.

52 Merrill & Watts, *supra* note 32, at 590–92.

reject that attempt. The Supreme Court has shown no reluctance to overrule longstanding circuit precedents that are based on long-abandoned methods of statutory interpretation. Thus, for instance, in 2019 the Supreme Court unanimously overruled a 1974 D.C. Circuit precedent with the following statement: "*National Parks'* contrary [holding] is a relic from a 'bygone era of statutory interpretation.'"[53] The Supreme Court is likely to use similar language in the process of overruling *National Petroleum Refiners*.

The Supreme Court is also likely to reject the argument that Congress implicitly ratified the D.C. Circuit's decision by including a strangely worded provision in a 1975 statute that amended the FTC Act. It seems unlikely that Congress intended to make it clear that the FTC has the power to issue legislative rules that define "unfair methods of competition" in the same statute in which it made it nearly impossible for the FTC to issue legislative rules that define "unfair or deceptive acts." Moreover, the vast bulk of the circumstantial evidence of the intent of Congress supports the contrary view. For nearly half a century, Congress repeatedly acted on the basis of its belief that the FTC lacks the power to issue legislative rules to implement the FTC Act.

The Supreme Court's 2022 decision in *NFIB v. Department of Labor*[54] adds another reason for skepticism that the Court would uphold an attempt by the FTC to make major changes in antitrust law by issuing rules that define "unfair methods of competition" as that term is used in the FTC Act. In *NFIB*, the Court applied the major questions doctrine as the basis for its holding that OSHA lacks the power to issue a rule that requires employers to require their employees to be vaccinated against Covid-19. The Court held that an agency cannot take an unprecedented action that has major economic or political consequences unless it can support its action by reference to a statute that clearly authorizes the agency to take the action.

Any FTC attempt to use rulemaking to define an "unfair method of competition" in a way that would make a major change in antitrust law would be an ideal candidate for application of the major questions doctrine. It would be unprecedented. The FTC now claims that a statute that was enacted in 1914 gives it the power to use rulemaking for this purpose even though it has never previously used the statute for that purpose. Any major change in antitrust law would qualify as an action with major economic and political consequences. Neither the original text of the FTC Act nor the strangely worded 1975 amendment to that statute would qualify as the "clear statement" of authority that the Court requires when an agency addresses a major question.

---

53 Food Marketing Institute v. Argus Leader Media, 139 S. Ct. 2356, 2364 (2019). *See* Nowell D. Bamberger, Matthew D. Slater, Alexis Collins & Vicens Elizabeth, *The US Supreme Court issues a decision limiting the circumstances under which a federal agency may be compelled to disclose the confidential information received by the agency, from a private party (Food Marketing Institute / Argus Leader Media)*, E-COMPETITIONS JUNE 2019, art. No. 91131.

54 142 S. Ct. 661 (2022).

In the following section, I will assume that the FTC has the power to issue legislative rules to define "unfair methods of competition" and explain why that power is not sufficient to enable Chair Khan to implement her ambitious agenda.

III. Four Illustrations of Potential FTC Uses of Rulemaking to Transform Antitrust Law

In this section, I will predict the likely results of potential FTC efforts to use rulemaking to transform antitrust law in four in four contexts. I will begin by discussing the FTC's suggestion that it might issue a rule that creates a right to repair products.Many companies that make and sell products, particularly high-tech products, preclude the owners of those products from repairing the products themselves or from using an independent company to repair the products. Chair Khan has identified the creation of a right to repair as a high priority in her efforts to use rulemaking to change antitrust law, and President Biden expressed his support for such an effort both in his executive order and in the press conference at which he announced that order.

I will follow that discussion with a discussion of the context in which I am most optimistic that the FTC can use rulemaking to make antitrust law more effective. I believe that the FTC can use rulemaking to make antitrust law more effective in its application to non-compete clauses in employment contracts. This is one of the changes in law that President Biden urged in his executive order on antitrust law. He signaled his strong interest in making such a change in the press conference in which he signed the executive order by describing the adverse effects of non-compete clauses on wages.

I have chosen predatory pricing as the third context in which I will discuss the FTC's efforts to use rulemaking to change antitrust law. Chair Khan has repeatedly emphasized her belief that predatory pricing is widespread and extremely damaging. She devotes scores of pages of her scholarly writing to harsh criticism of the Supreme Court's approach to predatory pricing. She is likely to place a high priority on the issuance of a rule that reflects her strong belief that antitrust law must be changed in ways that make it impossible for large firms to engage in predatory pricing.

The final context I will discuss is "reverse payments" in royalty disputes between manufacturers of prescription drugs and companies that want to make and sell generic equivalents of those drugs. Generic equivalents of brand-name drugs usually sell at prices far below the price of the brand-name drug once the initial patent on the brand-name drug expires. Manufacturers of brand-name drugs try to avoid having to compete with low-priced generic equivalents by obtaining a second patent on the drug, suing the manufacturer of the generic equivalent for allegedly infringing on that patent, and settling the infringement case by agreeing to make a large payment to the manufacturer of the generic equivalent in return for a commitment not to market the generic equivalent. Critics of reverse payment agreements argue that they are just agreements to continue to charge monopoly prices for the drugs by paying a potential manufacturer of generic equivalents not to make a competing product. President Biden included reverse payments agreements on his list of practices that he wants to eliminate, and Chair Khan has referred to reverse payments agreements as one of the leading candidates for an FTC rulemaking.

1. Creating a Right to Repair

Many manufacturers of products take a variety of steps to make it difficult or impossible for consumers to repair the products that they own or to have those products repaired by an independent service organization (ISO).[55] President Biden included the creation of a right to repair in his executive order on antitrust law.[56] In one of its first actions after Lina Khan became chair of the FTC, the agency issued a policy statement that suggested that it is seriously considering use of rulemaking to create a right to repair.[57]

The FTC has long had clear statutory authority to prohibit manufacturers from using one method of denying consumers the right to repair products that they own. The Magnuson-Moss Warranty Act prohibits manufacturers from conditioning a warranty on a consumer's use of service provided or approved by the manufacturer except in specified narrow circumstances.[58] The agency cannot use that statutory authority to create a right to repair, however, because conditioning a warranty on the use of a service provider approved by the manufacturer of a product is only one of at least nine ways in which manufacturers restrict consumers from engaging in self-repair or using repair services provided by an ISO.[59]

In its recent policy statement on the right to repair, the Commission urged the public to "submit complaints and provide other information to aid in greater enforcement of the Magnuson-Moss Warranty Act and its implementing regulations." It then stated that it will "scrutinize repair restrictions for violations of the antitrust laws." Finally, it stated:

> Third, the Commission will assess whether repair restrictions constitute unfair acts or practices, which are also prohibited by Section 5 of the Federal Trade Commission Act. In addition,

---

55 Fed. Trade Comm'n, Nixing the Fix: An FTC Report to Congress on Repair Restrictions 1–6 (May 2021) [hereinafter Report].

56 86 Fed. Reg. at 36992.

57 Fed. Trade Comm'n, Policy Statement of the Federal Trade Commission on Repair Restrictions Imposed by Manufacturers and Sellers (July 21, 2021), https://www.ftc.gov/legal-library/browse/cases-proceedings/public-statements/policy-statement-federal-trade-commission-repair-restrictions-imposed-manufacturers-sellers. *See also* Remarks of Chair Lina M. Khan Regarding the Proposed Policy Statement on Right to Repair (July 21, 2021), https://www.ftc.gov/legal-library/browse/cases-proceedings/public-statements/remarks-chair-lina-m-khan-regarding-proposed-policy-statement-right-repair.

58 15 U.S.C. § 2302.

59 Report, *supra* note 55, at 6.

> the Commission will analyze any material claims made to purchasers and users to ascertain whether there are any prohibited deceptive acts or practices, in violation of Section 5 of the Federal Trade Commission Act.

In a footnote, the Commission noted that section 5 prohibits both "unfair or deceptive acts" and "unfair methods of competition."

Those passages in the policy statement are consistent with Chair Khan's view that the FTC can use its section 5 authority to issue rules that declare that acts that do not violate the Sherman or Clayton Act are prohibited as "unfair or deceptive acts" or as "unfair methods of competition." The reference to the prohibition of "unfair or deceptive acts" in section 5 suggests that the Commission is considering use of its power to issue legislative rules that prohibit manufacturers from engaging in "unfair or deceptive acts" to create a right to repair. It is hard to take that suggestion seriously, however. The FTC has the power to issue rules to prohibit "unfair or deceptive acts" only by using procedures that are so burdensome and time-consuming that the FTC abandoned its efforts to use that authority over forty years ago.

The reference to the prohibition on "unfair methods of competition" in section 5 suggests that the Commission is considering use of notice-and-comment rulemaking unburdened by those procedures to create a right to repair. Chair Khan believes that the combination of the D.C. Circuit's decision in *National Petroleum Refiners* and a provision in a 1975 statute that amended the FTC Act gives the FTC the power to use notice-and-comment rulemaking to prohibit "unfair methods of competition" without having to use the additional procedures that Congress mandated for rulemakings to issue rules that prohibit "unfair or deceptive acts." If her view prevails in court, the FTC might be able to complete a rulemaking to create a right to repair by declaring that all manufacturers' restrictions on repair are illegal "unfair methods of competition" in only two or three years. Any such rule would have to survive judicial review, however.

The Supreme Court has never had occasion to evaluate an agency's attempt to create a right to repair because no agency has ever attempted to create such a right. The Court has addressed a closely related question, however. Can a manufacturer that has previously allowed ISOs to repair its products change its policy and practices in ways that preclude ISOs from continuing to repair the products? Kodak initially permitted ISOs to repair its photocopying machines. It then changed its policy and decided that all repairs had to be made by Kodak. It implemented the new policy by refusing to sell replacement parts to ISOs.

The ISOs filed a complaint in 1987 in which they alleged that Kodak's change in policy violated the Sherman and Clayton Antitrust Acts. Kodak filed a motion for summary judgment. The district court granted the motion, but a divided panel of a circuit court reversed. In 1992, the Supreme Court also divided in

Eastman Kodak v. Image Technical Services Inc.[60] Three justices would have upheld the grant of summary judgment.[61] Those justices expressed the view that a manufacturer can never violate antitrust law by precluding ISOs from repairing its products. The six-justice majority reversed the grant of summary judgment. They held that the plaintiffs could prevail if they can prove that the manufacturer has market power in the market for repair of its products and if the manufacturer cannot prove that its new policy has good effects.[62]

It was difficult for the ISOs to prove that the manufacturer had market power in the market for repair of its products because that depends on the cross-elasticity of demand for the products and for repair of the products. That, in turn, depends on the magnitude of the information asymmetries in the market for the products. In the absence of significant information asymmetries, a manufacturer cannot exercise market power in the market for repair of its products because any increase in the price it charges for repairs would reduce the demand for its products.

Kodak argued that its new policy allowed it to improve the quality of its products by providing it with complete and prompt feedback from repair personnel. That feedback enabled it to identify flaws that it could then correct in the process of designing and manufacturing the products. Kodak also argued that its new policy helped consumers by eliminating confusion about whether performance deficiencies were caused by flaws in the product or errors in the process of repairing the products. With its new policy in effect, consumers could hold Kodak responsible for all performance deficiencies, whether they were caused by defects in the product or errors in the process of repairing the products. The Supreme Court instructed the lower court to require the ISOs to prove that Kodak had market power in the market for repair of its products and to allow Kodak to have an opportunity to prove that its new policy yielded benefits that offset any adverse effects of its potential exercise of market power in the repair market.

After a lengthy jury trial, the ISOs prevailed. The jury found that Kodak had market power in the repair market and that Kodak had not proven that its restrictions on repair had offsetting good effects. The Ninth Circuit upheld the jury verdict.[63] The process of adjudicating the case required ten years, however. No plaintiff has been able to reach a jury in any case in which a manufacturer's restrictions on repair have been challenged as a violation of antitrust law since the Supreme Court decided *Kodak*. Moreover, the FTC has expressed its belief that no plaintiff would have any claim under *Kodak* unless the manufacturer initially allowed ISOs to repair its products and then changed its policy.[64]

---

60 504 U.S. 451 (1992).

61 *Id.* at 486.

62 *Id.* at 481–85.

63 Image Tech. Services, Inc. v. Eastman Kodak, 125 F.3d 1195 (9th Cir. 1997).

64 Report, *supra* note 55, at 14.

The time required to litigate *Kodak* and the aftermath of the case illustrate the accuracy of Khan's complaints that the adjudication process, combined with the rule of reason, reduces the effectiveness of antitrust law by making the outcome of antitrust cases depend on the results of a long and complicated decision-making process. The Supreme Court's reasoning in *Kodak* also illustrates the major disadvantage of rules and rulemaking as a means of implementing a statute, however. Rules are only effective if they prohibit a practice completely or in circumstances that are easy for an agency or a court to identify without the need for a long hearing. Rules are not capable of improving a decision-making process when the effects of a practice depend on many variations in the circumstances in which the conduct takes place.

The Supreme Court believes that restrictions on repair imposed by manufacturers of products can have both good and bad effects, depending on the circumstances in which the conduct occurs. The Court also believes that it is impossible to determine whether restrictions on repair have good or bad effects without conducting a lengthy hearing. If the Court is right, it is impossible to write a rule that will produce acceptable results.

The FTC recently submitted a report to Congress that suggests that it agrees with the Supreme Court's belief that the effects of the restrictions on the right to repair that manufacturers impose vary greatly depending on many characteristics of the circumstances in which the restrictions are imposed. The FTC identified and discussed nine ways in which manufacturers restrict their customers' ability to engage in self-repair.[65] The FTC identified and discussed four potential adverse effects of restrictions on repairs,[66] but it also identified and discussed six potential beneficial effects of restrictions on repairs.[67] The FTC seemed to agree with the Supreme Court that the adverse effects of restrictions on repair depend on whether the manufacturer has market power in the repair market,[68] and the FTC explicitly recognized that manufacturers' justifications for their restrictions "need to be scrutinized on a case-by-case basis."[69]

It is hard to imagine any version of a rule that purports to create a right to repair that a court would uphold. Even if the Supreme Court agrees with Chair Khan that the FTC has the power to create legally binding rules of conduct by declaring that a practice is illegal because it is an "unfair method of competition," the FTC would have no chance of persuading a court to uphold a rule that prohibits manufacturers from using the many methods that they now use to restrict the

65 *Id.* at 17–18.

66 *Id.* at 38–44.

67 *Id.* at 24–38.

68 *Id.* at 9.

69 *Id.* at 10.

ability to repair. Such a decision would be inconsistent with the reasoning of the Supreme Court in *Kodak*. The FTC might be able to persuade a court to uphold a rule that says that a manufacturer is prohibited from restricting consumers' ability to engage in self-repair or to use the services of an ISO if the manufacturer has market power in the repair market and it is unable to provide evidentiary support for any of the potential six justifications for its restrictions. A rule of that type would have none of the beneficial effects of a rule, however. It would not change the status quo in this area of antitrust law.

2. Banning Non-Compete Clauses

Many firms include non-compete clauses in their employment contracts. The clauses prohibit an employee from leaving their job to take a job with a competing firm. In his executive order on competition, President Biden stated his desire to ban non-compete clauses.[70] He emphasized the importance of such a ban during the press conference in which he signed the order. Chair Khan has also identified a ban on non-compete clauses as one of the goals of her plan to use rulemaking to change antitrust law.

It is easy to document the adverse effects of non-compete clauses.[71] They inflict significant harm on employees by prohibiting them from taking jobs that would improve their pay or working conditions. They significantly impair the performance of labor markets by limiting the role of competition.[72] They are responsible for a significant part of the large gap between constantly increasing labor productivity and stagnant wage levels that has existed for thirty years.[73] They have also contributed to the large disparities in income and wealth in the U.S. population that have increased dramatically in recent years.[74]

Non-compete clauses also impair the performance of markets for goods and services.[75] Small firms and startups cannot compete effectively with the large firms that now dominate many markets unless they can hire some of the experienced workers that work for the large established firms. Non-compete clauses preclude them from being able to lure those workers away from the market incumbents, thereby crippling their efforts to succeed in entering a market. Because of non-compete clauses, a new market entrant often cannot succeed

70 86 Fed. Reg. at 36992.

71 Richard J. Pierce, Jr., *The U.S. Federal Trade Commission Workshop on Noncompete Clauses*, 23 Utilities Law Review, Issue 1 (2020).

72 On Amir & Orly Lobel, *Driving Performance: A Growth Theory of Noncompete Law*, 16 Stan. Tech. L. Rev, 833, 844–68 (2013).

73 Economic Policy Institute, The Productivity–Pay Gap (2018).

74 John M. Abowd, Kevin L. McKinney & Nellie L. Zhao, *Earnings Inequality and Labor Mobility Trends in the United States: Nationally Representative Estimates from Longitudinally Linked Employer-Employee Data* (Nat'l Bureau of Econ. Rsch., Working Paper No. 23224, 2017).

75 Marshall Steinbaum, *Antitrust, the Gig Economy and Labor Market Power*, 82 L. & Cont. Prob. 45 (2019).

even if it would be able to offer a superior product or service because it cannot hire experienced workers to make the product.

Non-compete clauses have long been prohibited by antitrust law unless they are reasonable in scope and justified on the basis that they serve some beneficial purpose.[76] Courts have accepted three justifications for non-compete clauses: to protect the intellectual property rights of the employer, to protect the employer's investment in training employees, and to protect the employer from potential loss of customers as a result of solicitation of the firm's customers by the former employee.

In recent years, firms have increased their use of non-compete clauses significantly. Employers now include non-compete clauses in 30 to 50% of all employment contracts, including contracts to employ people as cooks in fast-food restaurants and to serve as janitors. In a high proportion of cases, there is no possibility that the employer could justify the clauses based on some beneficial effect.

Antitrust enforcement agencies have long ignored non-compete clauses because of their belief that state employment law was adequate to ensure that employers do not include them in contracts in circumstances in which they cannot be justified. Recent studies have found that state law is not effective for that purpose, however. Non-compete clauses are as common and as effective in states that prohibit them as they are in states that permit them.[77] Most employees lack access to the services of a lawyer who can tell the employee that the non-compete clause in their contract is illegal. As a result, the existence of an illegal non-compete clause is almost always effective in deterring an employee from leaving their job to work for a competitor.

The Supreme Court's June 21, 2021, opinion in *NCAA v. Alston*[78] provides powerful evidence that the Court would be receptive to an FTC campaign to outlaw most non-compete clauses. The justices made it clear that they unanimously support efforts to use antitrust law to improve the performance of labor markets. The Court is prepared to hold unlawful any anticompetitive practice that employers adopt as a means of artificially depressing wages. Non-compete clauses fit that characterization perfectly.

The FTC could use the notice-and-comment process to issue a legislative rule that bans non-compete clauses in a high proportion of employment contracts. As long as the rule did not apply to the few contexts in which the clauses can be justified as furthering some socially beneficial purpose, the FTC would have a good chance of being able to defend such a rule in court. The easiest way to describe the scope of a rule that bans most non-compete clauses would be

---

76 Mitchell v. Reynolds, 24 Eng. Rep. 347 (QB 1711).

77 Phillip D. Thomas, *Would California Survive the MOVE Act?: A Preemption Analysis of Employee Noncompetition Law*, 2017 U. Chi. Legal Forum 823, 826–33 (2017).

78 141 S. Ct. 2141 (2021). *See* Swathi Bojedla, *The US Supreme Court unanimously affirms that a school sports association's compensation limits for "education-related benefits" violate antitrust law (NCAA / Alston)*, e-Competitions June 2021, art. No. 102344.

to make it contingent on an employee's salary – e.g., non-compete clauses are an unfair method of competition in any employment contract applicable to any employee who earns less than X dollars per year. The FTC would have no problem defending such a rule by referring to solid empirical evidence that non-compete clauses cause a lot of harm to labor markets and to product markets and that they cannot have any beneficial effect when they are contained in employment contracts applicable to low-paid employees.

The FTC does not need to use the notice-and-comment process to accomplish that worthy goal, however. It can issue an interpretive rule in which it announces and explains why it interprets section 5 of the FTC Act to ban the inclusion of non-compete clauses in contracts to employ low-paid employees. It can couple that interpretive rule with a general statement of policy in which it announces its intention to take aggressive action against any employer who acts in a manner that is inconsistent with its interpretation of the Act. It can follow those two actions with a couple of well-chosen, high visibility enforcement actions against firms that act in ways that are inconsistent with its interpretation of the Act by including non-compete clauses in the employment contracts of low-paid employees.

That approach to the problem would be as effective as the issuance of a legislative rule, and it would have major advantages over the issuance of a legislative rule. There is no doubt that the FTC has the power to issue interpretive rules and policy statements to implement section 5 of the FTC Act. It has issued scores of interpretive rules and policy statements for many decades. The FTC can issue interpretive rules and policy statements in days, in contrast to the years required to complete a notice-and-comment rulemaking.

There is also no doubt about the FTC's authority to use adjudication to implement section 5. It has exercised that power for over a century. The enforcement actions would be easy to win, given the powerful empirical evidence that non-compete clauses cause significant harm to the performance of both labor markets and product markets and that non-compete clauses in the contracts of low-paid employees have no plausible offsetting benefits. In a matter of months, the FTC could use the combination of an interpretive rule, a policy statement, and a couple of high-visibility enforcement actions to ban non-compete clauses in the contracts of low-paid workers.

By contrast, the notice-and-comment proceeding required to issue a legislative rule would take years to complete. Once the FTC issued such a rule, it would be subjected to judicial review to determine whether the FTC has the power to issue legislative rules to implement section 5 of the FTC Act. Since the FTC has never previously attempted to exercise that power, there is a good chance that the issue would go all of the way to the Supreme Court. That would delay the effect of the rule for many years. If the FTC lost in that test of its authority, it would have wasted many years of hard work and a great deal of its scarce enforcement resources engaging in an exercise in futility.

3. Aggressive Enforcement of a Ban on Predatory Pricing

Predatory pricing is the use of below-cost prices to drive competitors out of business. President Biden did not mention predatory pricing in his executive order on competition, but Chair Khan has emphasized the need to engage in aggressive enforcement of a ban on predatory pricing in her scholarly writing.[79] Her strong desire to engage in aggressive enforcement of a prohibition against predatory pricing, combined with her strong desire to issue legislative rules to enforce section 5 of the FTC Act, suggests that she would like to issue a rule that would be a major part of an FTC effort to engage in aggressive enforcement of a ban on predatory pricing.

It would be easy for the FTC to persuade a court to uphold a rule that bans predatory pricing. Predatory pricing has long been a violation of antitrust law. The problem is the unanimous position of the justices that courts and enforcement agencies should not engage in aggressive efforts to ban predatory pricing. The justices take that position because of their belief that predatory pricing is rarely attempted and even more rarely successful, coupled with their belief that aggressive efforts to prohibit predatory pricing have the unintended adverse effects of discouraging firms from reducing the price that they charge for a good or service and encouraging firms to engage in price fixing.

The Supreme Court encouraged aggressive efforts to eliminate predatory pricing during the 1960s.[80] The results were awful.[81] When a firm angered a competitor by reducing the price it charged, the competitor often filed a complaint or threatened to file a complaint alleging that the firm was engaged in predatory pricing. The risk of being a defendant in an antitrust case that was based on a claim of predatory pricing discouraged firms from reducing the prices that they charged for goods and services. The threat to file such a complaint also led to discussions between the two firms about ways of settling their dispute. The easiest way to settle such a dispute is to agree to raise the price that the firm charges and to agree never to charge a price below the price that the competing firm charges. Those two incentives – the incentive not to reduce prices and the incentive to raise prices at the request of a competitor – are the opposite of the incentives that antitrust law usually tries to create.

In the meantime, scholars published articles that questioned whether predatory pricing could ever be used successfully to earn monopoly profits by driving competitors out of business.[82] To be successful, a predatory pricing complaint

---

79 Khan, *supra* note 1, at 722–30, 756–75, 803.

80 *E.g.*, Utah Pie Co. v. Continental Baking Co., 386 U.S. 685 (1967) (holding that three firms violated antitrust law by charging prices below their average cost, thereby reducing the plaintiff's share of the market from 66.5% to 45.3%).

81 Ward S. Bowman, *Restraint of Trade by the Supreme Court: The Utah Pie Case*, 77 Yale. L.J. 70 (1968).

82 *E.g.*, John S. McGee, *Predatory Price Cutting: The Standard Oil (N.J.) Case*, 1 J.L. & Econ. 137 (1978).

must be based on the belief that a firm that is well-capitalized can increase its profits by driving its less well-capitalized competitors out of business by charging below-cost prices and then recouping its losses and increasing its profits by charging monopoly prices. That strategy is rarely, if ever, successful, however.

The problem with any effort to engage in successful predatory pricing lies in the attempt to recoup the firm's losses once it has driven its competitors out of business. During the period in which the firm charges below-cost prices, it is certain to lose money. It can recoup its losses and come out ahead only if its attempt to charge monopoly prices does not encourage other firms to enter the market before it has completed the recoupment process. That is impossible in most circumstances.

If the firms that participate in the market in which a firm attempts to implement a predatory pricing strategy have high fixed costs, the firm that engages in predatory pricing will have to charge below-cost prices for many years before it can drive its competitors out of business. During that period, the firm will lose so much money that it would have to charge monopoly prices for many years just to recoup its losses. It would be highly unlikely to succeed in any such effort, however. The monopoly prices that the firm charged would encourage other firms to enter the market. It would be easy for firms to do so by acquiring the assets of the former competitors for a low price and using those assets to compete with the firm that engaged in the predatory pricing. That would deprive the firm of the opportunity to earn monopoly profits.

If the firms that participate in the relevant market have low fixed costs, the firm that engages in predatory pricing might be able to drive its competitors out of business quickly. A market in which firms have that kind of cost structure is also a market in which the barriers to entry are low, however. As a result, the firm that engaged in predatory pricing would attract new entrants quickly as soon as it began to charge monopoly prices, thereby making it impossible for the firm to recoup its losses.

By 1986, a majority of justices believed that the Court's prior efforts to encourage aggressive enforcement of the ban on predatory pricing were increasing prices and encouraging price fixing. They were also influenced by the scholarship that concluded that predatory pricing rarely, if ever, succeeds. Based on those beliefs, the Court issued an opinion in which it rejected a claim of predatory pricing and announced a new test that made it difficult for any plaintiff to prevail by filing a complaint based on a claim that a competitor is engaged in predatory pricing.[83] The majority stated that its decision was based on its belief that "predatory pricing schemes are rarely tried, and even more rarely successful."[84] In 1993, the Court rejected another claim based on an allegation of predatory

---

83 Matsushita v. Zenith Radio Corp., 475 U.S. 574 (1986).

84 *Id.* at 589.

pricing.[85] It repeated its belief that "predatory pricing schemes are rarely tried, and even more rarely successful,"[86] and added that "unsuccessful predation is in general a boon to consumers."[87]

In its 1993 opinion, the Court announced a new standard that made it unlikely that any plaintiff could succeed by filing a complaint that is based on predatory pricing. The Court identified two predicates for recovery in a predatory pricing case: First, a plaintiff seeking to establish competitive injury resulting from a rival's low prices must prove that "the prices complained of are below an appropriate measure of its rival's costs."[88] Second, the plaintiff must prove that the defendant had a "reasonable prospect . . . of recouping its investment in below-cost prices."[89]

Some justices dissented in 1986 and 1993, but the Court issued an opinion in 2007 that made it clear that all nine justices now embrace both the test that the Court announced in 1993 and the belief that predatory pricing is rarely attempted and even more rarely successful.[90] Over that same period, both the Department of Justice (DOJ) and the FTC came to the same conclusion. Neither agency has brought a case based on a predatory pricing theory in decades.

Chair Khan is highly critical of the Supreme Court's approach to predatory pricing.[91] She is particularly critical of the requirement that the plaintiff must prove that the defendant had a reasonable prospect of recoupment.[92] If Chair Khan wants to use rulemaking to further her goal of aggressive enforcement of a ban on predatory pricing, she will have to persuade her colleagues to issue a rule that declares that predatory pricing is an "unfair method of competition" even if a firm has no expectation that it can recoup its losses. There is no chance that the Supreme Court would uphold such a rule given the clearly articulated and strongly held unanimous views of the justices.

There is another context in which Chair Khan may be able to act in accordance with her views on predatory pricing without attempting to contradict the Supreme Court, however. There is ample support for the Supreme Court's belief that

---

85 Brooke Group Ltd. v. Brown & Williamson Tobacco Corp., 509 U.S. 209 (1993). *See* Steven J. Cernak, *The US Supreme Court establishes a test for proving the existence of predatory pricing (Brooke Group)*, e-Competitions June 1993, art. No. 98743.

86 *Id.* at 226.

87 *Id.* at 224.

88 *Id.* at 222–23.

89 *Id.* at 224–25.

90 Weyerhaeuser Co. v. Ross-Simmons Hardwood Lumber Co., 549 U.S. 312 (2007) (the plaintiff's theory was that the defendant had engaged in predatory bidding rather than predatory pricing, but the reasoning is the same in both contexts). *See* David Olsky, *The US Supreme Court clarifies that the test for predatory pricing also applies to situations of predatory bidding (Weyerhaeuser / Ross-Simmons Hardwood Lumber)*, e-Competitions February 2007, art. No. 37145.

91 Khan, *supra* note 1, at 722–30, 756–75, 803.

92 *Id.* at 730, 762–68.

predatory pricing is rarely attempted and even more rarely successful when it is used to obtain market power by driving competitors out of business. However, there is support for the belief that a firm can obtain market power by using predatory pricing to drive down the market value of its competitors' assets and then acquiring those assets at a bargain price. That is the pattern of behavior that The American Tobacco Company used between 1890 and 1906 to obtain a monopoly on the production and sale of tobacco.[93]

The FTC does not need to issue a rule to deter companies from using predatory pricing to reduce the cost of acquiring their competitors, however. It can accomplish that goal much more effectively by refusing to allow firms with market power to acquire their competitors. The FTC has much greater power to preclude firms with market power from acquiring their competitors than it does to issue rules to define unfair methods of competition. The FTC has already announced its intention to be more aggressive in that arena than it has been in the past, and its efforts to do so are well supported by a wide range of respected scholars.[94] Once firms with market power realize that they will not be allowed to acquire their competitors, they will have no incentive to engage in predatory pricing.

4. Banning Pay-for-Delay Agreements in Prescription Drug Patent Disputes

Manufacturers of prescription drugs invariably obtain a patent on the drug that allows them to charge a monopoly price for the drug for the life of the patent. Once the patent expires, a competitor can make and market a generic equivalent of the drug. A statute authorizes a single firm to market the generic equivalent for a period of six months to encourage the firm to enter the market with a generic equivalent to the brand-name drug.[95] Once a generic equivalent becomes available, the manufacturer of the brand-name drug no longer has monopoly power. It must significantly reduce the price that it charges for the brand-name drug.

Manufacturers of brand-name drugs are understandably reluctant to lose their monopoly power. They use a variety of techniques to retain their monopoly power. One technique is to file an application for a second patent that covers some aspect of the drug. When a rival firm files an application to sell the generic equivalent of the drug after the first patent expires, the manufacturer of the brand-name drug files an action in which it claims that the rival firm would be violating its second patent if it begins to make and sell the generic equivalent. The two firms then resolve the patent infringement suit by entering into an agreement in which the firm that planned to make and sell the generic equivalent

---

93 Malcolm R. Burns, *Predatory Pricing and the Acquisition Costs of Competitors*, 94 J. Pol. Econ. 266 (1986).

94 *E.g.*, Hovenkamp, *supra* note 17, at 2039–48; Steve C. Salop, *Invigorating Vertical Merger Enforcement*, 127 Yale L.J. 1962 (2018); John Kwoka, Mergers, Merger Control, and Remedies: A Retrospective Analysis of U.S. Policy (MIT Press 2015).

95 21 U.S.C. § 355(j)(5).

agrees to refrain from doing so in return for a payment from the manufacturer of the brand-name drug. The manufacturer of the brand-name drug is then able to continue to sell the drug at a monopoly price for the duration of the second patent even though no court has decided whether that patent precludes the rival firm from making and selling the generic equivalent. The contract between the two firms looks suspiciously like an agreement in which one firm agrees to refrain from competing with another firm in return for a share of the resulting monopoly profits that the other firm earns.

President Biden included in his executive order on competition a request that the FTC use its rulemaking authority to stop "unfair anticompetitive conduct or agreements in the prescription drug industries, such as agreements to delay the market entry of generic drugs or biosimilars."[96] Chair Khan has argued that the FTC should use its rulemaking power to create "clear rules by which [courts can] evaluate these agreements."[97]

The main obstacle to this effort is the reception that the FTC got from the Supreme Court when it attempted to further that goal eight years ago. In *Federal Trade Commission v. Actavis*,[98] the FTC urged the Court to adopt a set of rules applicable to pay-for-delay contracts. Notably, the FTC specifically relied on the prohibition of "unfair methods of competition" in section 5 of the FTC Act[99] – the same statutory provision that the FTC would have to rely on to persuade a court to uphold a rule that would make it easy for the FTC to prevail in challenges to reverse payment agreements. The rule that the FTC asked the Court to approve would have made it relatively easy for the FTC to prevail in its attempt to preclude firms from entering into agreements of this type by establishing a rebuttable presumption that reverse payment agreements are unfair methods of competition.[100] The justices divided with respect to their preferred approach to this class of agreements, but they unanimously rejected the rule the FTC urged them to adopt.[101] The majority adopted an approach that the FTC has not been able to use to block any pay-for-delay agreement.[102]

President Biden and Chair Khan seem to believe that the FTC can succeed in persuading the Supreme Court to adopt rules that the justices have unanimously

---

96 86 Fed. Reg. at 36992.

97 Chopra & Khan *supra* note 10, at 372.

98 570 U.S. 136 (2013). *See* Michael A. Carrier, *The US Supreme Court issues first ruling on antitrust legality of reverse-payment drug patent settlements (Actavis)*, E-COMPETITIONS JUNE 2013, art. No. 53120.

99 Brief for the Petitioner at 12, FTC v. Watson Pharmaceuticals, No. 12-416 (Jan. 22, 2013).

100 *Id.* at 15–40.

101 570 U.S. at 158–59.

102 The majority describes its complicated approach in five pages. *Id.* at 154–58. The circuit court had rejected the majority's approach on the basis that it was not administratively feasible. It concluded that it would be time consuming, complex, and uncertain. *Id.* at 153, 157. The dissenting justices would have held that any reverse payment settlement that is within the scope of a patent is immune from attack under antitrust law. *Id.* at 160–77.

rejected by using rulemaking rather than adjudication as their point of entry. That belief is unrealistic. The FTC had the opportunity to persuade the justices to accept the agency's preferred rules when it presented them, along with the studies that the FTC had completed in support of its proposed rules, in the context of the adjudication that gave rise to the Court's decision in *Actavis*. It failed to persuade a single justice to adopt its proposed rules. If the FTC uses the power that it claims to have to issue a similar rule to implement section 5 of the FTC Act, that rule will elicit the same reaction from the justices.

IV. Incremental Changes That Chair Khan Can Make

Chair Khan proposes to use notice-and-comment rulemaking to make major changes in antitrust law by declaring many practices to be "unfair methods of competition" within the meaning of that term in section 5 of the FTC Act. That raises two questions. Does the FTC have the power to use the notice-and-comment process to implement section 5? If it has that power, can it use the rulemaking process to make the major changes in antitrust law that Chair Khan proposes?

I conclude that the FTC probably lacks the power to use notice-and-comment rulemaking to implement section 5 of the FTC Act. I also conclude that, even if the FTC has that power, it cannot use it to make most of the major changes in antitrust law that Chair Khan envisions. The FTC can use rulemaking to improve antitrust law by limiting the use of non-compete clauses in employment contracts, but it can accomplish that goal more rapidly and with less legal risk by using a combination of the tools that it has long used – interpretive rules, policy statements, and adjudication.

Chair Khan cannot implement her radical agenda for change because of doubts about the power of the FTC to issue legislative rules and strong resistance from courts that long ago rejected her approach to antitrust law. There is an easy path to reform of antitrust law, however. Traditional industrial organization scholars and antitrust scholars have been urging major incremental changes in antitrust law for years. Each of those changes would move antitrust law in the direction that Chair Khan prefers. Each is well supported by studies, and each is likely to be embraced by the courts. Chair Khan should join hands with the proponents of incremental change to implement a series of changes that further both her goals and theirs.

It would be easy to change antitrust law in ways that place more emphasis on monopsony power and on the welfare of employees who are injured by widespread anticompetitive practices. It has long been illegal to enter into a no-poaching agreement with a competing employer or to include a non-compete clause in an employment contract in the absence of a strong justification for the clause.[103]

---

103 Richard Pierce, *The Federal Trade Commission Workshop on Non-Compete Clauses*, 22 UTIL. L. REV. (2020).

Yet both practices have become common. The enforcement agencies and the courts should become far more aggressive in enforcing those existing prohibitions.

Proponents of incremental change have been urging changes of this type for years.[104] They support the need for the changes with excellent scholarship that documents the severe harm that no-poaching agreements and widespread use of non-compete clauses in the contracts of low-wage employees inflict on workers. Many Republicans agree with the need for such changes. The FTC and the DOJ Antitrust Division were already moving in that direction at the end of the Trump administration.[105] The Supreme Court made clear its strong and unanimous support for use of antitrust law to improve the performance of labor markets in its 2021 opinion in *NCAA v. Alston*.[106]

The proponents of incremental change have also called for major changes in merger law and policy for years. It is easier for the FTC to make changes in the law that governs mergers and acquisitions than it is to make changes in the law that governs other types of behavior. The Hart-Scott-Rodino Act requires any firm that plans to implement a merger or acquisition above a specified size to notify the FTC and the DOJ of its plan, and then authorizes the FTC or the DOJ to challenge the legality of any planned merger or acquisition.[107] Section 7 of the Clayton Act empowers the FTC to obtain an injunction against any proposed merger or acquisition when its effect "may be substantially to lessen competition, or to tend to create a monopoly."[108]

Industrial relations scholars urge several types of changes in merger law. First, John Kwoka has documented the adverse effects of many of the mergers that the FTC or DOJ declined to oppose.[109] Those mergers created unduly concentrated markets with resulting increases in price. That problem is easy to remedy by changing the measures of market concentration in the joint horizontal merger guidelines that DOJ and FTC use to determine when a proposed merger creates the risk of an unduly concentrated market.

Many traditional scholars also urge the FTC and DOJ to put a halt to "Pacman" acquisitions, i.e., the hundreds of acquisitions of small competitors that the large platform firms have made in recent years.[110] By acquiring startups and small competitors, large platform firms eliminate the most likely sources of future

104 Eric A. Posner, *The Rise of the Labor-Antitrust Movement*, Competition Policy International (Nov. 29, 2021).

105 Pierce, *supra* note 103.

106 141 S. Ct. 2141 (2021).

107 15 U.S.C. § 18A.

108 15 U.S.C. § 18.

109 Kwoka, *supra* note 94.

110 Hovenkamp, *supra* note 17, at 2039–49.

competition. That change is also easy to make by changing the market concentration measures in the Joint FTC/DOJ horizontal merger guidelines.

Finally, many traditional scholars have long urged the FTC and DOJ to begin to challenge the vertical mergers among large firms that create a serious risk of harming the performance of markets by raising rivals' costs.[111] The FTC and DOJ can make that important change in law and policy by publishing new joint guidelines on vertical mergers. They can then defend their application of the new guidelines in court by relying on the many excellent scholarly studies that support the need for this change.

Proponents of radical change and proponents of incremental change may also be able to find common cause in identifying and prohibiting the abusive practices of some platform firms. Many traditional scholars who oppose proposals to dissolve platform firms or to subject them to price controls also believe that many of their patterns of behavior cause serious harm to the performance of markets.[112] Many agree that the courts have made it too difficult for enforcement agencies to prohibit those practices.

The Supreme Court recently divided five-to-four in its first effort to address antitrust problems created by platform firms.[113] Many traditional scholars believe that the majority erred when it combined the difficult-to-satisfy rule of reason with a duty to consider simultaneously both of the two markets in which a platform firm participates.[114] It is entirely realistic to believe that the proponents of radical change can team up with the proponents of incremental change to persuade at least one justice to join the four dissenting justices in accepting proof that a practice clearly harms one of the two markets in which the firm participates as adequate to establish a violation of antitrust law.

Some proponents of radical change in antitrust law will be tempted to resist my proposed alliance and characterize it as a suggestion that they capitulate. I can only respond with an apt cliché: don't let the perfect be the enemy of the good.

---

111 Salop, *supra* note 94, at 2021.

112 Hovenkamp, *supra* note 17.

113 Ohio v. Am. Express Co., 138 S. Ct. 2274 (2018). *See* Natalie Hayes & Carrie C. Mahan, *The US Supreme Court rejects Government antitrust challenge against anti-steering provisions of a credit-card network company (American Express)*, e-Competitions June 2018, art. No. 88732.

114 Herbert Hovenkamp, *Platform Firms and The Rule of Reason: The* American Express *Case*, 2019 Col. Bus. L. Rev. 35 (2019).

Legal Constraints on FTC Competition Rulemaking

ALDEN F. ABBOTT*
The Mercatus Center at George Mason University

Abstract

Under the Biden administration, the U.S. Federal Trade Commission (FTC) appears poised to launch an unprecedented effort to transform American antitrust policy through the promulgation of rules, rather than reliance on case-by-case adjudication, as in the past. The FTC has a long history of rulemaking, centered primarily on consumer protection. The legal basis for FTC competition rulemaking, however, is enormously weak and fraught with uncertainty, in at least five respects.

First, a constitutional principle known as the "nondelegation doctrine" suggests that the FTC may not, as a constitutional matter, possess the specific statutory delegation required to issue rules that address particular competitive practices. Second, principles of statutory construction strongly suggest that the FTC's general statutory provision dealing with rulemaking refers to procedural rules of organization, not to substantive rules bearing on competition. Third, even assuming that proposed competition rules survived these initial hurdles, principles of administrative law would pose a substantial risk that competition rules would be struck down as "arbitrary and capricious." Fourth, there is a high probability that courts would not defer to an FTC statutory construction that authorized "unfair methods of competition" rules. Fifth, any attempt by the FTC to rely on its more specific consumer protection rulemaking powers to reach anticompetitive practices would be cabined by the limited statutory scope of those powers (and the possible perception that the FTC's procedural protections are weak), and quite probably would fail.

---

* Senior Research Fellow at the Mercatus Center of George Mason University.

In sum, the cumulative weight of these legal risks indicates that the probability FTC competition rulemaking would succeed is extremely low. As such, the FTC may wish to undertake a sober assessment of the legal landscape before embarking on a competition rulemaking adventure that almost certainly would be destined for failure. The Commission could better promote consumer welfare by applying its limited resources to antitrust enforcement rather than competition rulemaking.

I. Introduction

The U.S. Federal Trade Commission (FTC) is a venerable American institution. In over a century of existence, it has been a policy leader in developing American thinking about and in enforcing antitrust and consumer protection law.[1] Pursuant to several specific statutory mandates, it has also promulgated a substantial number of consumer protection rules, dealing with a wide variety of practices. It has almost never, however, enacted substantive rules seeking to regulate specified forms of business conduct that affect competition in the marketplace.

In 2021, however, the prospects for FTC competition rulemaking changed dramatically. A new Biden administration FTC chair, Lina Khan, publicly emphasized that the Commission should undertake "unfair methods of competition" (UMC) rulemakings. In December 2021, the FTC issued a "Statement of Regulatory Priorities" (SRP) stating that "the Commission in the coming year will consider developing both unfair-methods-of competition [UMC] rulemakings as well as rulemakings to define with specificity unfair or deceptive acts or practices [UDAP]."[2] The SRP also summarized the status of FTC rules and guides that are subject to periodic review.

With regard to UDAP rules, the SRP highlighted for consideration "rules that allow the agency to recover redress for consumers who have been defrauded and seek penalties for firms that engage in data abuses." The SRP also explained that "the abuses stemming from surveillance-based business models are particularly alarming," and thus the FTC would consider a possible rulemaking focused on "curbing lax security practices, limiting intrusive surveillance, and ensuring that algorithmic decision-making does not result in unlawful discrimination."

---

1 The term "antitrust law" (typically termed "competition law" overseas) is generally deemed to encompass those statutes directed at preventing anticompetitive private business behavior. The terms "antitrust law" and "competition law" are used interchangeably in this essay. More broadly, the term "competition policy" is often used to refer to those legal principles and policies aimed generally at enhancing competition within an economy (such as through regulatory reform).

2 Fed. Trade Comm'n, Statement of Regulatory Priorities 2 (Dec. 10, 2021) (citations omitted), https://www.reginfo.gov/public/jsp/eAgenda/StaticContent/202110/Statement_3084_FTC.pdf [hereinafter SRP].

With respect to UMC rules, the FTC painted with a broad brush, and referenced President Biden's July 2021 Executive Order on Competition:

> Over the coming year, the Commission will also explore whether rules defining certain "unfair methods of competition" prohibited by section 5 of the FTC Act would promote competition and provide greater clarity to the market. A recent Executive Order encouraged the Commission to consider competition rulemakings relating to non-compete clauses, surveillance, the right to repair, pay-for-delay pharmaceutical agreements, unfair competition in online marketplaces, occupational licensing, real-estate listing and brokerage, and industry-specific practices that substantially inhibit competition. The Commission will explore the benefits and costs of these and other competition rulemaking ideas.
>
> Recently, the Commission published in the Federal Register a "Request for Public Comment Regarding Contract Terms that May Harm Fair Competition," which included for reference two public petitions for competition rulemaking the Commission has received. One of those petitions was to curtail the use of non-compete clauses, and the other was to limit exclusionary contracting by dominant firms, but the Commission also solicited additional examples of unfair terms. Members of the public filed thousands of comments, which the Commission's staff are carefully reviewing.[3]

In short, significant FTC competition-related rulemaking initiatives are to be expected in 2022. The prospect that those initiatives will yield binding rules that survive legal scrutiny is, however, vanishingly small.

This essay will explore legal doctrines that seriously constrain the FTC's ability to enact competition rules.[4] After summarizing the FTC's authority to engage in rulemaking, it will turn to five major legal impediments to successful competition rulemaking that the FTC must confront. Each of these impediments creates substantial competition rulemaking legal risks for the Commission. Considered collectively, these impediments point to an extremely low likelihood of competition rulemaking success. Accordingly, the FTC should reconsider its bold competition rulemaking agenda and focus instead on devoting those rulemaking resources to other initiatives within its purview, including competition enforcement actions and

---

3 *Id.* at 2 (citations omitted).

4 The views expressed herein are solely attributable to the author, and do not necessarily represent the views of the Mercatus Center at George Mason University. The author served as general counsel of the Federal Trade Commission from 2018 to 2021. This essay builds in part upon arguments previously outlined in Alden F. Abbott, *FTC Competition Regulation: A Cost-Benefit Appraisal*, Mercatus Center Policy Brief (June 2021), https://www.mercatus.org/system/files/abbott_-_policy_brief_-_ftc_competition_regulation_a_cost-benefit_appraisal_-_v1_2.pdf; and Alden F. Abbott & Andrew Mercado, *FTC Rulemaking on Noncompete Agreements*, Mercatus Center Policy Brief (Sept. 2021), https://www.mercatus.org/system/files/abbott_and_mercado_-_policy_brief_-_a_critical_appraisal_of_ftc_rulemaking_procedures_for_noncompete_agreements_-_v1.pdf.

policy studies. Such a reset of FTC priorities would likely yield a far better allocation of scarce governmental resources to initiatives that benefit consumers and avoid the imposition of unwarranted costs on private actors and the competitive process.

II. Discussion

1. FTC Rulemaking: An Overview

The Federal Trade Commission is an independent federal agency created pursuant to the Federal Trade Commission Act of 1914. The FTC's mission is to protect consumers and promote competition.[5] It does this primarily through enforcement actions,[6] directed at practices that violate section 5 of the FTC's Act's prohibitions on "unfair methods of competition" and "unfair or deceptive acts or practices." While the FTC has also promulgated binding rules and non-binding enforcement guides[7] throughout the course of its history, its principal means for advancing its mission has been enforcement, not regulation. As the FTC explains:

> The basic statute enforced by the FTC, Section 5(a) of the FTC Act, empowers the agency to investigate and prevent unfair methods of competition, and unfair or deceptive acts or practices affecting commerce. This creates the Agency's two primary missions: protecting competition and protecting consumers. The statute gives the FTC authority to seek relief for consumers, including injunctions and restitution, and in some instances to seek civil penalties from wrongdoers. The FTC has the ability to implement trade regulation rules defining with specificity acts or practices that are unfair or deceptive and the Commission can publish reports and make legislative recommendations to Congress about issues affecting the economy. The Commission enforces various antitrust laws under Section 5(a) of the FTC Act as well as the Clayton Act. The FTC monitors all its orders to ensure compliance.[8]

---

5 For an official overview of FTC history, *see* Fed. Trade Comm'n, Our History, https://www.ftc.gov/about-ftc/our-history (last visited Jan. 5, 2022).

6 In addition, the FTC periodically holds public hearings and workshops on policy questions related to competition and consumer protection. It also occasionally engages in "advocacy" efforts that recommend state governments weigh competition and consumer welfare in considering particular laws and regulations. Discussion of these policy initiatives is beyond the scope of this essay.

7 Enforcement guides have been directed to particular practices that have given rise to consumer protection abuses. In issuing particular guides, the FTC has consistently stated that "[t]he Guides are administrative interpretations of the law intended to help advertisers comply with the Federal Trade Commission Act; they are not binding law themselves. In any law enforcement action challenging the allegedly deceptive use of testimonials or endorsements, the Commission would have the burden of proving that the challenged conduct violates the FTC Act." Fed. Trade Comm'n, FTC Publishes Final Guides Governing Endorsements, Testimonials (Oct. 5, 2009), https://www.ftc.gov/news-events/press-releases/2009/10/ftc-publishes-final-guides-governing-endorsements-testimonials.

8 Fed. Trade Comm'n, What the FTC Does, https://www.ftc.gov/news-events/media-resources/what-ftc-does (last visited Jan. 5, 2022). FTC rules are regularly subject to review: "The FTC conducts regular reviews of all its rules and guides on a rotating basis to make sure they are up-to-date, effective, and not overly burdensome. The agency has been doing these reviews since 1992, and has eliminated dozens of rules and modified many others to keep pace with changes in the marketplace." *Id.*

FTC rules may be divided into three categories: section 6(g) rules, section 18 rules, and rules promulgated pursuant to statutes other than the FTC Act.

A. *Section 6(g) Rules*

Section 6(g)[9] of the original Federal Trade Commission Act ("section 6(g)") is a very short provision that empowers the FTC to "classify corporations" and also authorizes the Commission "to make rules and regulations for the purpose of carrying out the provisions of this subchapter [embodying the statutory authorities bestowed on the FTC[10]]." Section 6(g) is a very tiny part of section 6 of the FTC Act, which delineates FTC powers to conduct investigations, issue reports, make criminal referrals to the Justice Department, cooperate with foreign enforcers, and expend funds for meetings with foreign officials and law enforcement groups. Section 6(g) primarily has been used by the Commission to enact procedural rules governing investigations and internal processes, not substantive rules dealing with business conduct. Substantive section 6(g) rulemaking largely lay dormant during the FTC's first half-century. After promulgating a few minor substantive rules before 1962, however, the FTC issued a variety of rules over the next decade, focused on consumer protection, not competition. Only one rule, dealing with price discrimination in men's and boys' tailored clothing,[11] dealt solely with an unfair method of competition. That 1968 rule apparently was never enforced, and it was rescinded in 1994.[12]

Section 6(g) substantive rules today are subject to the informal rulemaking requirements of section 553 of the Administrative Procedure Act (APA),[13] which apply to the vast majority of federal agency rulemaking proceedings. Informal rulemaking is fairly straightforward:

> The informal rulemaking process defined by the APA consists of four main steps. First, Congress must pass legislation that either creates an administrative agency or gives guidance or directives to an existing agency. The legislation forms the basis for the rules, which should be geared towards achieving the goals identified by Congress.
>
> The second step is twofold: the agency must draft a proposed rule and publish notice of the proposed rule.

---

9 15 U.S.C. § 46(g).

10 15 U.S.C. Chapter 2, Subchapter I: Federal Trade Commission, 15 U.S.C. §§ 41–58, as amended.

11 Trade Regulation Rule: Discriminatory Practices in Men's and Boys' Tailored Clothing Industry, 16 C.F.R. 412 (1968).

12 Trade Regulation Rule: Discriminatory Practices in Men's and Boys' Tailored Clothing Industry, 59 Fed. Reg. 8527 (1994) (notice of repeal of rule); Trade Regulation Rule: Discriminatory Practices in Men's and Boys' Tailored Clothing Industry, 58 Fed. Reg. 35907 (1993) (notice of proposed rulemaking).

13 5 U.S.C. § 553 *et seq.*

> The third step, known as the comment period, begins when the proposed rule is published and continues for at least 30 days. During this time, members of the public may comment on the proposed rule.
>
> The fourth step, codification of the final rule, takes place once all periods for public comment ha[ve] passed and the agency has made any final revisions to the rule. Most rules have an "effective date" set far enough into the future to allow affected parties to bring themselves into compliance.[14]

In 1971, the FTC enacted a section 6(g) rule stating that it was both an "unfair method of competition" and an "unfair act or practice" for refiners or others who sell to gasoline retailers "to fail to disclose clearly and conspicuously in a permanent manner on the pumps the minimum octane number or numbers of the motor gasoline being dispensed." In 1973, in the *National Petroleum Refiners* case,[15] the U.S. Court of Appeals for the District of Columbia Circuit upheld the FTC's authority to promulgate this and other binding substantive rules. The court rejected the argument that section 6(g) authorized only nonsubstantive regulations regarding the FTC's nonadjudicatory, investigative, and informative functions, spelled out elsewhere in section 6. Notably, however, the FTC has not enacted any 6(g) competition rules in the nearly fifty years since the *National Petroleum Refiners* case was decided.

B. *Section 18 Rules*

In 1975, Congress granted the FTC specific consumer protection rulemaking authority (authorizing enactment of trade regulation rules dealing with unfair or deceptive acts or practices) through section 202 of the Magnuson-Moss Warranty Act, which added section 18 to the Federal Trade Commission Act ("section 18"). Section 18 imposes hearing-type requirements that are not found in APA informal rulemakings. As the FTC explains:

> Under Section 18 of the FTC Act, 15 U.S.C. Sec. 57a, the Commission is authorized to prescribe "rules which define with specificity acts or practices which are unfair or deceptive acts or practices in or affecting commerce" within the meaning of Section 5(a)(1) of the Act. Among other things, the statute requires that Commission rulemaking proceedings provide an opportunity for informal hearings at which interested parties are accorded limited rights of cross-examination. Before commencing a rulemaking proceeding, the Commission must have reason to believe that the practices to be addressed by the rulemaking are "prevalent." 15 U.S.C. Sec. 57a(b)(3).

---

14 Informal Agency Rulemaking, Justia (last reviewed Apr. 2018), https://www.justia.com/administrative-law/rulemaking-writing-agency-regulations/informal-rulemaking.

15 Nat'l Petroleum Refiners Ass'n v. FTC, 482 F.2d 672 (D.C. Cir. 1973).

> Once the Commission has promulgated a trade regulation rule, anyone who violates the rule "with actual knowledge or knowledge fairly implied on the basis of objective circumstances that such act is unfair or deceptive and is prohibited by such rule" is liable for civil penalties for each violation.[16]

Section 18 consumer protection rulemakings impose adjudicatory-type hearings and other specific requirements on the FTC, unlike more flexible section 6(g) APA informal rulemakings. However, as noted above, the FTC can obtain civil penalties for knowing violation of Magnuson-Moss rules, something it cannot do if 6(g) rules are violated. Since 1975, the FTC has promulgated only seven Magnuson-Moss rules, reflecting the "slow and cumbersome" nature of those rulemakings, according to some scholarly critics. The FTC has nevertheless issued a wide variety of substantive consumer protection rules in recent decades under various special statutes directed at specific consumer protection problems identified by Congress.[17]

C. *Non-FTC Act Rules*

Over the years, Congress has passed a variety of statutes empowering the FTC to address particularized problems, through FTC enforcement and rulemaking initiatives, as appropriate. There are 82 such statutes currently in force.[18] Fifty-eight deal solely with consumer protection matters, eight address both competition and consumer protection questions, and only sixteen deal solely with competition matters.

FTC rules adopted pursuant to the many specialized consumer protection statutes ("special consumer protection statutes," most of which were adopted in recent decades) largely obviated the need for and displaced section 6(g) consumer protection rulemaking initiatives of the 1960s. Laws such as the Children's Online Privacy Protection Act (directing the FTC to promulgate rules controlling online websites' collection of children's personal information),[19] the CAN-SPAM Act (directing the FTC to issue rules requiring the labeling of sexually explicit commercial emails as such and establishing the criteria for determining the primary purpose of a commercial email),[20] and the Economic Growth, Regulatory Relief,

---

16 Fed. Trade Comm'n, A Brief Overview of the Federal Trade Commission's Investigative, Law Enforcement, and Rulemaking Authority (revised, May 2021), https://www.ftc.gov/about-ftc/what-we-do/enforcement-authority (last visited Jan. 28, 2022).

17 *Id.*

18 *See* Fed. Trade Comm'n, Legal Library: Statutes, https://www.ftc.gov/enforcement/statutes (last visited Jan. 6, 2022). For a description of specific FTC rules and guides, *see* Fed. Trade Comm'n, Legal Library: Rules, https://www.ftc.gov/enforcement/rules/rules-and-guides (last visited Jan. 6, 2022).

19 Fed. Trade Comm'n, Children's Online Privacy Protection Act, https://www.ftc.gov/enforcement/statutes/childrens-online-privacy-protection-act (last visited Jan. 7, 2022).

20 Fed. Trade Comm'n, Controlling the Assault of Non-Solicited Pornography and Marketing Act of 2003 (CAN-SPAM Act), https://www.ftc.gov/enforcement/statutes/controlling-assault-non-solicited-pornography-marketing-act-2003-can-spam-act (last visited Jan. 7, 2022).

and Consumer Protection Act (directing the FTC to issue a rule implementing the Act's military credit monitoring provisions),[21] among many others, convey congressional instructions that precisely delineate the path the FTC should follow in developing rules to address defined problems.

The specialized competition laws ("special competition statutes") involve such targeted substantive and procedural topics as, for example, fisheries conservation and management,[22] litigation settlements between patented and generic drug makers,[23] research and production joint ventures,[24] outer continental shelf oil and gas leases,[25] export trade associations,[26] and international antitrust cooperation.[27] Any FTC rules enacted under those laws inevitably are closely tied to and limited by the specific grant of congressional authority.

Only one of the competition-related statutory grants, the Hart-Scott-Rodino Act of 1976 (HSR),[28] involves rulemaking that is highly significant to antitrust enforcement across the board. HSR establishes very detailed thresholds that determine whether any proposed merger must be notified to the FTC and Department of Justice (DOJ) prior to consummation. Accordingly, it is both of economy-wide significance and quite specific. HSR also authorizes FTC regulations to implement the detailed guidance found in the statute. Those rules, which were first promulgated in the 1970s and have been tweaked over time, directly carry out the statutory mandate and yield finely honed guidance to the private sector (similar to the detailed guidance that non-antitrust primarily regulatory agencies typically provide). In marked contrast to HSR, the section 6(g) reference to rulemaking is an extremely short and general provision that provides no framework to guide the development of possible substantive competition rules.

---

21 Fed. Trade Comm'n, Economic Growth, Regulatory Relief, and Consumer Protection Act, https://www.ftc.gov/enforcement/statutes/economic-growth-regulatory-relief-consumer-protection-act (last visited Jan. 7, 2022).

22 Fed. Trade Comm'n, Magnuson-Stevens Fishery Conservation and Management Act, as amended by the Consolidated Appropriations Act of 2004, https://www.ftc.gov/enforcement/statutes/magnuson-stevens-fishery-conservation-management-act-amended-consolidated (last visited Jan. 4, 2022).

23 Fed. Trade Comm'n, Medicare Prescription Drug, Improvement, and Modernization Act of 2003, https://www.ftc.gov/enforcement/statutes/medicare-prescription-drug-improvement-and-modernization-act-2003 (last visited Jan. 6, 2022).

24 Fed. Trade Comm'n, National Cooperative Research and Production Act of 1993, https://www.ftc.gov/enforcement/statutes/national-cooperative-research-and-production-act-1993 (last visited Jan. 6, 2022).

25 Fed. Trade Comm'n, Outer Continental Shelf Lands Act Amendments of 1978, https://www.ftc.gov/enforcement/statutes/outer-continental-shelf-lands-act-amendments-1978 (last visited Jan. 6, 2022).

26 Fed. Trade Comm'n, Webb-Pomerene Act, https://www.ftc.gov/enforcement/statutes/webb-pomerene-act (last visited Jan. 6, 2022).

27 Fed. Trade Comm'n, International Antitrust Enforcement Assistance Act of 1994, https://www.ftc.gov/enforcement/statutes/international-antitrust-enforcement-assistance-act-1994 (last visited Jan. 6, 2022).

28 15 U.S.C. § 18a. *See generally* Fed. Trade Comm'n, Hart-Scott-Rodino Antitrust Improvements Act of 1976, https://www.ftc.gov/enforcement/statutes/hart-scott-rodino-antitrust-improvements-act-1976 (last visited Jan. 6, 2022). For detailed links to the administration of HSR (including informal guidance) and the rules implementing it, *see* Fed. Trade Comm'n, Premerger Notification Program, https://www.ftc.gov/enforcement/premerger-notification-program (last visited Jan. 6, 2022).

2. Legal Impediments to FTC Competition Rulemaking

In order to promulgate new FTC competition rules falling outside the ambit of specialized statutes, the FTC would have to rely primarily on section 6(g). Such rulemaking endeavors would face at least five legal doctrinal obstacles.

- First, the "nondelegation doctrine" suggests that, under section 6(g), Congress did not confer on the FTC the specific statutory authority required to issue rules that address particular competitive practices.
- Second, principles of statutory construction strongly indicate that the FTC's general statutory provision dealing with rulemaking refers to procedural rules of organization, not substantive rules bearing on competition.
- Third, even assuming that proposed competition rules survived these initial hurdles, principles of administrative law would raise the risk that competition rules would be struck down as "arbitrary and capricious."
- Fourth, there is a substantial possibility that courts would not defer to the FTC's construction through rulemaking of its "unfair methods of competition" as authorizing the condemnation of specific competitive practices.
- Fifth, any attempt by the FTC to rely on its more specific section 18 rulemaking powers to reach anticompetitive practices would be cabined by the limited statutory scope of those powers.

Considering these obstacles collectively, it is exceptionally unlikely that FTC competition rules will survive legal challenge.

A. *The Nondelegation Doctrine Could Deny the FTC "Unfair Methods of Competition" Rulemaking Authority*

A core United States constitutional principle is the separation of powers, which confers the power to legislate on Congress, to execute the laws on the executive branch, and to interpret the laws on the judicial branch. Article I, Section 1 of the Constitution, which states that Congress alone holds "all legislative Powers,"[29] necessarily constrains the amount of legislative authority Congress may confer on the other branches of the federal government. Limitations on congressional delegation of such authority are embodied in the "nondelegation doctrine." According to the Supreme Court, for a delegation to pass legal muster, Congress must "lay down by legislative act an intelligible principle to which the person or body authorized to [act] is directed to conform."[30]

---

29 U.S. Const., art. I, § 1 ("All legislative Powers herein granted shall be vested in a Congress of the United States, which shall consist of a Senate and House of Representatives.").

30 J. W. Hampton, Jr. & Co. v. United States, 276 U.S. 394, 409 (1928).

Two eminent constitutional law scholars have concisely described the general contours of the doctrine and limitations on its application:

> For most of American history, judges and commentators have assumed that Congress cannot "delegate" legislative authority and the Supreme Court has located this rule in Article I, Section 1.... Individual Justices have opined that the nondelegation doctrine ought to be treated as a serious limitation on Congress's authority....
>
> [Nevertheless,] [w]hile the principle of nondelegation persists, the Supreme Court has allowed a lot of delegation, so long as Congress includes intelligible principles to guide discretion....
>
> Particularly since the New Deal, Congress often legislates in open-ended terms that give substantial authority to executive branch officials and judges. Since 1935, almost all the Justices on the Supreme Court have either applied the nondelegation doctrine leniently, to allow large-scale delegations accompanied by vague limiting principles... or have said the doctrine of unconstitutional delegation is not readily enforceable by the courts....
>
> The Court, however, sometimes gives effect to the values undergirding the nondelegation principle through narrow interpretations of statutory delegations. For example, the Supreme Court has overruled agency rules adopted pursuant to congressional delegations, on the ground that the agency is advancing a big change in policy. "We expect Congress to speak clearly if it wishes to assign to an agency decisions of vast 'economic and political significance.'" *Utility Air Regulatory Group v. EPA* (2014) (plurality opinion) (quoting FDA v. *Brown & Williamson Tobacco Corp.* (2000)); *see also King v. Burwell* (2015).[31]

In short, the nondelegation doctrine has continued to receive lip service as a constitutional limiting principle. Although it seldom has been applied directly to strike down regulatory schemes, it has sometimes led the Supreme Court to narrowly construe the scope of a statutory delegation to strike down sweeping agency actions without invoking the doctrine.

There are recent signs, nevertheless, that the Supreme Court may be willing to apply the nondelegation doctrine directly in an appropriate case. In 2019, in *Gundy*

---

31 William N. Eskridge, Jr. & Neomi Rao, *Article I, Section 1: General Principles*, Interactive Constitution, https://constitutioncenter.org/interactive-constitution/interpretation/article-i/clauses/749 (last visited Jan. 7, 2022). Eskridge is John A. Garver Professor of Jurisprudence at Yale Law School and Rao, a former professor of law at the Scalia Law School, is a federal judge on the U.S. Court of Appeals for the District of Columbia Circuit. Former Columbia Law School Professor (and current Harvard Law School Dean) similarly has stated that "the [Supreme] Court has long enforced the nondelegation doctrine by narrowly construing statutes that otherwise risk conferring unconstitutionally excessive agency discretion." John F. Manning, *The Nondelegation Doctrine as a Canon of Avoidance*, 2000 Sup. Ct. Rev. 223 (2000) (citation omitted).

v. United States,[32] Justices Gorsuch, Roberts, and Thomas, in dissent, argued that a statutory delegation to the U.S. attorney general to issue certain regulations involved "unbounded policy choices" and was illegitimate. Although Justice Alito did not join the dissent, he stated in his *Gundy* concurrence that he would support reconsideration of the nondelegation doctrine in a future case. Justice Kavanaugh, who had not participated in the case, subsequently stated in another matter that Justice Gorsuch's "scholarly analysis of the Constitution's nondelegation doctrine in his *Gundy* dissent may warrant further consideration in future cases."[33] As such, it appears that at least five Supreme Court justices – a majority – may be inclined to strike down a rule on nondelegation grounds if and when a good factual vehicle presents itself.[34]

This state of affairs would present a serious nondelegation doctrine challenge to the FTC's successful promulgation of section 6(g) "unfair methods of competition" rules.

First, the term "unfair method of competition" in section 5(a) of the FTC Act is very general and open-ended in nature and has not been further cabined through subsequent legislation. In marked contrast, the special competition and consumer protection laws previously described contain very precise and narrow legislative directives that clearly express "an intelligible principle" to support delegation. To be sure, the term "unfair and deceptive acts and practices" that informs section 18 rulemaking endeavors may be less narrowly defined than the language found in the special statutes. Nevertheless, as previously stated, section 18 (unlike section 6(g)) provides a detailed statutory roadmap to guide rulemaking. Moreover, "unfairness" has been defined precisely by Congress in section 5(n) of the FTC Act.[35] In addition, "deception," which has a longstanding common law history, has also been described in detail in an FTC policy statement.[36] Thus, section 18 rulemakings also reasonably can be viewed as being guided by an "intelligible principle" that would have been ascertainable at the time that section 18 was enacted. Confronted with these glaring differences in kind, the Supreme Court could well conclude that, unlike the case of other substantive FTC rules, the "intelligible principle" requirement for delegation has not been met with respect to "unfair method of competition" rules.

---

32 139 S. Ct. 2116 (2019).

33 Paul v. United States, 140 S. Ct. 342 (2019) (Kavanaugh, J., concurring).

34 It appears unlikely that Justices Breyer, Kagan, and Sotomayor would be similarly inclined. The position of Justice Barrett on nondelegation issues is not yet known. As a law professor, she opined that "the notoriously lax 'intelligible principle' test reflects the Court's conclusion that the decision of how to carry out routine social and economic policy belongs almost entirely to Congress." Amy Coney Barrett, *Suspension and Delegation*, 99 CORNELL L. REV. 251, 318 (2014).

35 *See* discussion of section 5(n) in Section II.E. of this essay, *infra.*

36 Fed. Trade Comm'n, FTC Policy Statement on Deception (Oct. 14, 1983), https://www.ftc.gov/system/files/documents/public_statements/410531/831014deceptionstmt.pdf. That Policy Statement, based on a detailed synthesis of well-established FTC precedents, explains that for deception to be present: (i) there must be a representation, omission or practice that is likely to mislead the consumer; (ii) viewed from the perspective of a consumer acting reasonably in the circumstances; (iii) that is material (meaning consumer is likely).

Second, in 2021, in *AMG Capital Management*,[37] a unanimous Supreme Court held that Congress's grant of injunctive power to the FTC in section 13(b) of the FTC Act did not include the power to obtain monetary relief for harm to consumers. During the oral argument for that case, Justice Kavanaugh stated:

> [W]ith good intentions the agency [the FTC] pushes the envelope and stretches the statutory language to do the good or prevent the bad. The problem is [this] results in a transfer of power from Congress to the Executive Branch on whether to exercise this authority.[38]

As former FTC Chair Maureen Ohlhausen and former Assistant Attorney General for Antitrust James Rill have stated, "[t]he same concerns [noted by Justice Kavanaugh] apply with even greater force to FTC competition rulemaking, which casts the FTC in a legislative role under a highly vague grant of statutory authority."[39]

Third, as current FTC Commissioner Noah Phillips has pointed out,[40] the Supreme Court might well take note that in the well-known *Schechter Poultry* case,[41] the Supreme Court applied the nondelegation doctrine to strike down the National Industrial Recovery Act (NIRA), which authorized the president to approve "codes of fair competition," a term similar to "unfair methods of competition."[42] Courts may be expected to take note of the fact that a voting member of the FTC seriously doubts its authority to engage in competition rulemaking on nondelegation grounds.

Taken together, these considerations indicate there is a non-insignificant risk that a Supreme Court majority would hold that the nondelegation doctrine applies to section 6(g) rules directed at "unfair methods of competition."

---

37 AMG Capital Management, LLC, et al. v. FTC, No. 19-508, slip op. (Apr. 22, 2021), 593 U.S. ____ (2021). *See* Steven A. Reed, Scott A. Stempel & Daniel S. Savrin, *The US Supreme Court holds that the FTC lacks the authority to seek equitable monetary relief in cases brought in federal court under FTC Act Section 13(b) (AMG Capital Management)*, e-Competitions April 2021, art. No. 100669.

38 S. Ct. (No. 19-508), Transcript of Oral Argument at 53, https://www.supremecourt.gov/oral_arguments/argument_transcripts/2020/19-508_3f14.pdf.

39 Maureen K. Ohlhausen & James Rill, *Pushing the Limits? A Primer on FTC Competition Rulemaking*, U.S. Chamber of Com. 16 (Aug. 12, 2021), https://www.uschamber.com/assets/archived/images/ftc_rulemaking_white_paper_aug12.pdf.

40 Prepared Remarks of Commissioner Noah Joshua Phillips, Non-Compete Clauses in the Workplace: Examining Antitrust and Consumer Protection Issues 6–7 (Jan. 9, 2020), https://www.ftc.gov/system/files/documents/public_statements/1561697/phillips_-_remarks_at_ftc_nca_workshop_1-9-20.pdf.

41 A. L. A. Schechter Poultry Corp. v. United States, 295 U.S. 495 (1935).

42 As Commissioner Phillips explained, although the *Schechter* court distinguished NIRA from the FTC Act, "the key distinction that saved the FTC was its *adjudicative* process, in which the Commission, acting as 'a quasi judicial body', determines what are unfair methods of competition 'in particular instances, upon evidence, in light of particular competitive conditions' via a process of formal complaint, fair notice and hearing, and findings supported by evidence – all subject to judicial review. That is different from rulemaking. Non-delegation concerns may also be exacerbated by other factors here, including the lack of clarity in the rulemaking authority." Phillips, *supra* note 40, at 6–7 (citing *Schechter Poultry Corp.*, 295 U.S. at 531–34).

B. *Principles of Statutory Construction Constrain Section 6(g) Rulemaking*

Even assuming that the Supreme Court agreed that Congress could have constitutionally delegated "unfair methods of competition" rulemaking authority to the FTC, a serious question remains whether section 6(g) of the FTC Act represents a permissible statutory vehicle to implement such a delegation. There are strong reasons to believe that it does not.

First, in a recent set of public comments filed with the FTC, the Antitrust Section of the American Bar Association notes:

> [T]he Commission's [6(g)] rulemaking authority is buried within an enumerated list of investigative powers, such as the power to require reports from corporations and partnerships, for example. Furthermore, the [FTC] Act fails to provide any sanctions for violating any rule adopted pursuant to Section 6(g). These two features strongly suggest that Congress did not intend to give the agency substantive rulemaking powers when it passed the Federal Trade Commission Act.[43]

Rephrased, this argument suggests that the structure of the Federal Trade Commission Act indicates that the rulemaking referenced in section 6(g) is best understood as an aid to FTC processes and investigations, not a source of substantive policymaking. Although the *National Petroleum Refiners* decision rejected such a reading, that ruling came at a time of significant judicial deference to federal agency activism and may be dated. Furthermore, the Antitrust Section of the American Bar Association continues: "Given that Magnuson-Moss was enacted to address concerns raised by *National Petroleum Refiners* and similar cases, it's hard to see Section 6(g), with its vague and broad language, as providing a firm footing for informal antitrust rulemaking by the Commission."[44]

Second, the Supreme Court's April 2021 decision in *AMG Capital Management v. FTC* further bolsters the statutory structure argument that section 6(g) does not authorize substantive rulemaking. In *AMG*, the Court unanimously held that section 13(b) of the Federal Trade Commission Act, which empowers the FTC to seek a "permanent injunction" to restrain a violation of the Act, does not authorize the FTC to seek monetary relief from wrongdoers. The Court's opinion rejected the FTC's argument that the term "permanent injunction" had historically been understood to include monetary relief. The court noted that

43 American Bar Association Antitrust Law Section, Comments of the Antitrust Law Section of the American Bar Association in Connection with the Federal Trade Commission Workshop on "Non-Competes in the Workplace: Examining Antitrust and Consumer Protection Issues" 54, Apr. 24, 2020 [hereinafter ABA FTC Comments], https://www.americanbar.org/content/dam/aba/administrative/antitrust_law/comments/april-2020/comment-42420-ftc.pdf.

44 *Id.* at 57.

the injunctive language was "buried" in a lengthy provision that focuses on injunctive, not monetary relief (note that the term "rules" is similarly "buried" within 6(g) language dealing with unrelated issues). The court also pointed to the structure of the Federal Trade Commission Act, with detailed and specific monetary relief provisions found in sections 5(l) and 19, as "confirm[ing] the conclusion" that section 13(b) does not grant monetary relief. By analogy, a court could point to Congress's detailed enumeration of substantive rulemaking provisions in section 18 (a mere two years after *National Petroleum Refiners*) as cutting against the claim that section 6(g) can also be invoked to support substantive rulemaking. Finally, the Supreme Court in *AMG* flatly rejected a number of relatively recent appeals court decisions that upheld section 13(b) monetary relief authority. It follows that the FTC cannot confidently rely on judicial precedent (stemming from one arguably dated court decision, *National Petroleum Refiners*) to uphold its competition rulemaking authority.

Further supporting this analysis of *AMG*'s relevance in limiting section 6(g) rulemaking is the Supreme Court's "elephants in mouseholes" doctrine. First enunciated in 2001 in *Whitman v. American Trucking*, this doctrine stresses that "Congress... does not alter the fundamental details of a regulatory scheme in vague terms or ancillary provisions – it does not, one might say, hide elephants in mouseholes."[45] Finding unprecedented sweeping regulatory authority in a very short phrase buried within a longer statutory provision centered on procedures would seem to fit the "elephant in a mousehole" characterization perfectly.[46]

Third, the FTC may obtain statutory civil penalties for section 18 violations,[47] and may obtain sanctions for violations of the special consumer protection and competition statutes described above. In contrast, the FTC possesses no statutory authority to obtain remedies for violations of section 6(g) rules, strongly supporting the understanding that Congress did not authorize the FTC to promulgate substantive rules under section 6(g).[48]

---

45 Whitman v. Am. Trucking Ass'ns, 531 U.S. 457, 468 (2001).

46 As former FTC Chair Ohlhausen and former Assistant Attorney General for Antitrust Rill point out, "[t]he FTC's claim of broad substantive [section 6(g) unfair methods of competition] rulemaking authority based on the absence of limiting language and a vague, ancillary provision authorizing rulemaking alongside the ability to 'classify corporations' stands in conflict with the Court's admonition in *Whitman*." Ohlhausen & Rill, *supra* note 39, at 11.

47 *Id.* at 13–14.

48 *See* Thomas W. Merrill & Kathryn Tongue Watts, *Agency Rules with the Force of Law: The Original Convention*, 116 Harv. L. Rev. 467, 504–05 (2002) ("The failure to provide any sanction for the violation of rules adopted under section 6(g), along with the placement of the rulemaking grant in section 6, which conferred the FTC's investigative powers, clearly suggests that Congress intended the rulemaking grant to serve as an adjunct to the FTC's investigative duties, regarding which Congress had not given the agency the authority to act with the force of law."). In a similar vein, citing these authors, the American Bar Association contends that the facts that "the Commission's rulemaking authority is buried within an enumerated list of investigative powers... [and] the [FTC] Act fails to provide any sanctions for violating any rule adopted pursuant to Section 6(g)... strongly suggest that Congress did not intend to give the agency substantive rulemaking powers when it passed the Federal Trade Commission Act." ABA FTC Comments, *supra* note 43, at 54.

In short, even if the nondelegation doctrine does not constrain it, the FTC faces a substantial risk that the Supreme Court would hold that section 6(g) does not convey substantive rulemaking powers upon the Commission.

C. *The APA "Arbitrary and Capricious" Standard Would Threaten Individual Competition Rules*

The FTC also faces litigation risks from the APA requirements applicable to informal rulemaking.[49] Even if nondelegation and section 6(g) substantive rulemaking hurdles were surmounted, individual rules would face a significant risk of being struck down as "arbitrary and capricious."

Courts can overturn informal agency rules found to be "arbitrary, capricious, an abuse of discretion, or otherwise not in accordance with law."[50] The "arbitrary or capricious" test is met if a court determines that a rule's underlying factual assertions are unreasonable. In order to avoid a finding of unreasonableness, the FTC would have to provide a sufficient basis to justify a determination that a particular practice barred by rule is inevitably anticompetitive. Doing so might prove difficult, because it would be in tension with the traditional "rule of reason" analysis of antitrust litigation, which evaluates particular practices on a fact-specific, case-by-case basis. If a reviewing court were to find that the FTC rulemaking record did not sufficiently take into account potential procompetitive manifestations of a condemned practice, for example, it might decide that the rule is arbitrary and strike it down. (The existence of prior antitrust rule of reason case law decisions upholding particular examples of the conduct condemned by a rule could bolster a judicial finding that the rule is unreasonable.) This risk would appear to be not insubstantial, particularly given the lack of a preexisting competition rulemaking tradition that could help guide rulemaking review by the courts. A somewhat related substantial litigation risk could arise from the claim that a novel FTC construction of "unfair methods of competition" through rulemaking would violate due process of law, to the extent that it were to "fall[] substantially outside the norms of established antitrust jurisprudence."[51]

D. *The Courts Would Probably Fail to Defer to FTC Rulemaking Interpretations of "Unfair Methods of Competition"*

FTC's "unfair methods of competition" rules could be struck down even if nondelegation doctrine, substantive section 6(g) authority, and APA hurdles were met. Specifically, courts could choose not to defer to FTC constructions

49 For an overview of APA review of agency actions, *see* Jared P. Cole, Cong. Rsch. Serv., R44699, An Introduction to Judicial Review of Federal Agency Action (Dec. 2016).

50 5 U.S.C. § 706(2)(A).

51 Justin (Gus) Hurwitz, *Chevron and the Limits of Administrative Antitrust*, 76 U. Pitt. L. Rev. 209, 267 (2014).

of the term "unfair methods of competition," and thereby invalidate rules that were based on such constructions.

The FTC might be expected to argue that courts should defer to its construction of "unfair methods of competition" in rulemakings, in light of "*Chevron* deference," the doctrine that "instructs that when reviewing certain agency interpretations of statutes, courts should defer to the agency's construction if the statute is ambiguous and the agency's construction is reasonable."[52] Specifically, *Chevron* entails a two-part test, in which the reviewing court (i) first asks "Congress has directly spoken to the precise question at issue," in which case the court merely applies the law and the agency's interpretation is not an issue. But (ii) "if the statute is silent or ambiguous with respect to the specific issue," the court will defer to the agency's interpretation if it "is based on a permissible construction of the statute."[53] The Supreme Court has held "that administrative implementation of a particular statutory provision qualifies for *Chevron* deference when it appears that Congress delegated authority to the agency generally to make rules carrying the force of law, and that the agency interpretation claiming deference was promulgated in the exercise of that authority."[54]

The probability appears poor that the Supreme Court would grant *Chevron* deference to agency "unfair methods of competition" interpretations in FTC rulemakings, for four principal reasons.

First, *Chevron* deference increasingly has been disfavored and limited by "textualist" judges and scholars,[55] who emphasize that statutory interpretation is the core role of the judiciary, not of the other two branches of the federal government. Two Supreme Court justices (Justices Thomas and Gorsuch) have expressed broad and seemingly fundamental concerns about the *Chevron* framework, while several others (including Justices Kavanaugh, Alito, Roberts, and Breyer) have raised questions about the breadth of its applications or supported not applying it in certain situations.[56]

Second, even without overruling *Chevron*, the Supreme Court already has shown a willingness not to apply the doctrine or to limit its scope in a variety of circumstances:

> In recent high-profile cases involving agencies' interpretations of statutes, the Supreme Court either has ignored *Chevron* altogether,

52 Valerie C. Brannon & Jared P. Cole, Cong. Rsch. Serv., LSB10204, Deference and its Discontents: Will the Supreme Court Overrule *Chevron*? 1 (Oct. 11, 2018), https://sgp.fas.org/crs/misc/LSB10204.pdf. *See generally* Valerie C. Brannon & Jared P. Cole, Cong. Rsch. Serv., R44954, *Chevron* Deference: A Primer (Sept. 19, 2017), https://sgp.fas.org/crs/misc/R44954.pdf; Joseph Postell & Paul Larkin Jr., *Not Above the Law: Ending the Misguided Chevron–Auer Deference Regime*, Heritage Foundation Legal (Sept. 7, 2018), https://www.heritage.org/courts/report/not-above-the-law-ending-the-misguided-chevron-auer-deference-regime. The doctrine draws its name from the Supreme Court's decision in Chevron U.S.A., Inc. v. NRDC, 467 U.S. 837 (1984).

53 *Chevron*, 467 U.S. at 842–43.

54 United States v. Mead Corp., 533 U.S. 218, 226–27 (2001).

55 For example, Postell & Larkin, *supra* note 52, at 2, argue that "[t]he most fundamental threat that judicial deference poses to constitutionalism is its inconsistency with the judicial power itself."

56 *See, e.g.*, R. Randall Kelso, *Justifying the Supreme Court's Standards of Review*, 52 St. Mary's L. J. 973 (2021); Brannon & Cole, Deference and its Discontents, *supra* note 52.

> as in *King v. Burwell* (a decision upholding the constitutionality of the Affordable Care Act) or has substituted its own reading for that of the agency in spite of *Chevron's* application, as in *Michigan v. EPA* (a decision invalidating an Environmental Protection Agency regulation for mercury emissions from power plants).
>
> This judicial sidestepping of deference has been ongoing for years. In 2000, for example, the Court decided *FDA v. Brown & Williamson Tobacco Corp.*, a case involving the FDA's interpretation of the federal Food, Drug, and Cosmetic Act. The Court did not defer to the FDA but construed the statute itself, concluding that the FDA's regulation of tobacco products was unauthorized. Moreover, in a separate line of cases, the Court has whittled away the scope of agency interpretations that qualify for *Chevron* deference in the first place.[57]

Notably, the Supreme Court has avoided applying agency regulatory interpretations to various "major questions" of great "economic and political significance" (such as, for example, disputes involving the Affordable Care Act and the application of food and drug law to tobacco products) – either by determining from the start not to apply *Chevron* or by finding *Chevron* applies but electing nevertheless to reject agency statutory constructions.[58]

Given this background, the Supreme Court could readily determine that whether a broad array of hitherto unregulated commercial practices should be newly regulated on grounds of "unfairness" poses a "major question" for Congress that is beyond the scope of the FTC's authority, rendering *Chevron* inapplicable.[59]

Third, the Supreme Court's willingness to accept FTC interpretations of "unfair methods of competition" developed in section 6(g) rulemakings would be substantially undermined by the FTC's July 1, 2021, rescission of the 2015 FTC policy statement construing that term ("UMC Policy Statement").[60] As I have stressed:

> The bipartisan UMC Policy Statement has originally been supported by all three Democratic commissioners, including then-Chairwoman Edith Ramirez. The policy statement generally respected and promoted the rule of law by emphasizing that, in applying the facially broad "unfair methods of competition" (UMC) language, the FTC would be guided by the well-established

---

57 Postell & Larkin, *supra* note 52, at 5 (citations omitted).

58 Brannon & Cole, *Chevron* Deference: A Primer, *supra* note 52, at 9–10.

59 The Supreme Court might well find support based on its decision in FDA v. Brown & Williamson Tobacco Corp., 529 U.S. 120 (2000), in which the Court held that Congress had not authorized the FDA to regulate tobacco products and therefore invalidated the agency's regulations. The Court could also refer to the "elephants in mouseholes" doctrine of *Whitman v. American Trucking*, discussed above, to bolster the case that it would be inappropriate to defer to the FTC's construction of section 6(g) as authorizing competition rules.

60 Fed. Trade Comm'n, Statement of Enforcement Principles Regarding "Unfair Methods of Competition" Under Section 5 of the FTC Act (Aug. 13, 2015), https://www.ftc.gov/system/files/documents/public_statements/735201/150813section5enforcement.pdf.

> principles of the antitrust rule of reason (including considering any associated cognizable efficiencies and business justifications) and the consumer welfare standard. The FTC also explained that it would not apply "standalone" Section 5 theories to conduct that would violate the Sherman or Clayton Acts.
>
> In short, the UMC Policy Statement sent a strong signal that the commission would apply UMC in a manner fully consistent with accepted and well-understood antitrust policy principles. As in the past, the vast bulk of FTC Section 5 prosecutions would be brought against conduct that violated the core antitrust laws. Standalone Section 5 cases would be directed solely at those few practices that harmed consumer welfare and competition, but somehow fell into a narrow crack in the basic antitrust statutes (such as, perhaps, "invitations to collude" that lack plausible efficiency justifications). Although the UMC Statement did not answer all questions regarding what specific practices would justify standalone UMC challenges, it substantially limited business uncertainty by bringing Section 5 within the boundaries of settled antitrust doctrine.
>
> The FTC's announcement of the UMC Policy Statement rescission unhelpfully proclaimed that "the time is right for the Commission to rethink its approach and to recommit to its mandate to police unfair methods of competition even if they are outside the ambit of the Sherman or Clayton Acts." As a dissenting statement by Commissioner Christine S. Wilson warned, consumers would be harmed by the commission's decision to prioritize other unnamed interests. And as Commissioner Noah Joshua Phillips stressed in his dissent, the end result would be reduced guidance and greater uncertainty.[61]

The elimination of a consensus FTC understanding establishing consistent principles cabining the term "unfair methods of competition," combined with a sharp partisan split on interpretation of the term, would severely undermine the credibility of the FTC in seeking to defend rule-specific applications of that term before reviewing courts. Such a loss of credibility could be manifested in a refusal to even consider according *Chevron* deference to the Commission.

Fourth, the fact that FTC competition rules would implicate interpretations of antitrust law – a body of law that has developed through case law (not rules) and that is also enforced by the Justice Department – would further bolster the policy case for denying the FTC *Chevron* deference. As I have explained:

> [Competition rules] would raise serious economic policy questions. The inherent inflexibility of rule-based norms is ill suited to deal

61 Alden Abbott, *FTC Antitrust Enforcement and the Rule of Law*, TRUTH ON THE MARKET (Aug. 9, 2021) https://truthonthemarket.com/2021/08/09/ftc-antitrust-enforcement-and-the-rule-of-law.

> with dynamic evolving market conditions, compared with matter-specific antitrust litigation that flexibly applies the latest economic thinking to particular circumstances. As such, rules would be expected to generate far higher error costs than traditional litigation. In addition, FTC application of normative competition rules that the DOJ could not employ would lead to potential costly inconsistencies in antitrust enforcement, an affront to the rule of law. Any alleged special advantages of competition rules over traditional litigation (such as reduced delay in acting against competitive harm or clarification of the elements of a particular anticompetitive practice) would be highly questionable at best and not comparable in magnitude to far more certain rule-related costs.[62]

Such considerations would solidify the conclusion that FTC competition rules implicate "major questions" of antitrust policy and interagency jurisdiction that should be left to Congress, and are outside the purview of the FTC's interpretive authority.[63]

To be sure, it cannot be stated with certainty that the FTC would be denied *Chevron* deference by any reviewing federal court. A number of scholars have contended that the FTC should be granted *Chevron* deference if it engages in substantive competition rulemaking.[64] Moreover, "[a]lthough the Supreme Court applies *Chevron* inconsistently, the courts of appeals appear to be more deferential in their application of the doctrine."[65] Nevertheless, with respect to the Supreme Court, the scholarship that contends *Chevron* should apply does not adequately come to grips with the four considerations strongly counseling against its application that are summarized above. Accordingly, should the applicability of section 6(g) to competition rulemaking come before the Supreme Court (and this author believes that the Court would eventually agree to review this question, given its great importance), it appears highly probable that the Court would deny the FTC *Chevron* deference.[66]

---

62 Abbott, *supra* note 4, at 9 (citation omitted). Similar points are made by Ohlhausen & Rill, *supra* note 39, at 16–18.

63 These considerations, as well as the considerations highlighted in the third point, also heighten nondelegation doctrine concerns that Congress would not have sought to confer upon the FTC broad and ill-defined competition rulemaking authority.

64 *See* Rohit Chopra & Lina M. Khan, *The Case for "Unfair Methods of Competition" Rulemaking*, 87 U. Chi. L. Rev. 357, 377 (2020); Christian Carlson, *Antitrusting the Federal Trade Commission: Why Courts Should Defer to Federal Trade Commission Antitrust Decision Making*, 12 DePaul Bus. & Com. L. J. 361 (2014); Hurwitz, *supra* note 51; Royce Zeisler, Chevron *Deference and the FTC: How and Why the FTC Should Use* Chevron *to Improve Antitrust Enforcement*, 2014 Colum. Bus. L. Rev. 266 (2014).

65 Postell & Larkin, *supra* note 52, at 6.

66 The one Supreme Court decision where the FTC argued for *Chevron* deference supports this conclusion. In Cal. Dental Ass'n v. FTC, 526 U.S. 756, 765–69 (1999), the FTC argued it should be granted deference to its interpretation that the FTC Act applies to a nonprofit association, California Dental. The Court applied its own statutory construction in finding that the FTC Act indeed granted the Commission jurisdiction over California Dental and declined to invoke *Chevron* and defer to the Commission's interpretation. (On the substantive question presented in this matter, the FTC did not assert *Chevron* deference for its interpretation of section 5 of the FTC Act.)

E. ***Section 18 of the FTC Act Has Only a Limited Role (and, Quite Possibly, No Role) to Play in Promulgating Competition Rules***

Given the substantial legal risks that confront section 6(g) rulemaking, the FTC might turn to section 18 ("unfair or deceptive acts or practices") as a possible vehicle for the promulgation of new competition rules. The scope of possible application of section 18 to competition questions is, however, quite limited at best. Furthermore, section 18 may confront its own problems, in light of a recent change in section 18 procedures instituted by a narrow 3-2 majority of the Commission.

i. Deception

The FTC is unlikely to use deception as the basis for rules dealing with harm to competition. The FTC Policy Statement on Deception, embodied in a long letter submitted to Congress in 1983, concludes that:

> The Commission will find an act or practice deceptive if there is a misrepresentation, omission, or other practice, that misleads the consumer acting reasonably in the circumstances, to the consumer's detriment. The Commission will not generally require extrinsic evidence concerning the representations understood by reasonable consumers or the materiality of a challenged claim, but in some instances extrinsic evidence will be necessary.[67]

This Policy Statement, though not subsequently formalized through a congressional enactment, has been relied upon by the FTC as authoritative guidance for nearly forty years, and has enjoyed quasi-legislative status and respect. The focus on a "misrepresentation, omission, or other practice" that misleads consumers, is naturally directed to concerns about harm directly imposed on consumers by a business practice. It does not, however, fit naturally into concerns about business behavior that harms the process of competition. As such, a "deception" theory would not appear to be a good vehicle for a competition rule.

ii. Unfairness

The term "unfair act or practice" might appear at first glance to refer to practices that unfairly harm competition, and therefore may be well suited for a section 18 "unfairness" rulemaking.[68] Nevertheless, in a section 18 rulemaking based on unfairness, the FTC must be mindful of the statutory definition of an "unfair act or practice" set forth in section 5(n) of the FTC Act:

> The Commission shall have no authority… to declare unlawful an act or practice on the grounds that such act or practice is unfair unless

---

67 FTC Policy Statement on Deception, *supra* note 36, at 6. The Statement cites and discusses a large number of FTC cases that bear on this definition.

68 The following discussion of potential competition-related section 18 unfairness rulemakings draws upon Abbott & Mercado, *supra* note 4.

> the act or practice causes or is likely to cause substantial injury to consumers which is not reasonably avoidable by consumers themselves and not outweighed by countervailing benefits to consumers or to competition. In determining whether an act or practice is unfair, the Commission may consider established public policies as evidence to be considered with all other evidence. Such public policy considerations may not serve as a primary basis for such determination.[69]

Section 5(n) codifies the meaning of unfair acts or practices, and thereby bounds the FTC's application of rulemakings covering such conduct. In particular, section 5(n) creates a well-defined implicit cost-benefit framework for determining whether acts or practices may be characterized as unfair. First, the conduct must not be "unfair" in some abstract sense; rather, it must impose measurable harm on consumers who acted reasonably. Second, such harm must be greater than any countervailing benefits to competition or consumers – in short, the conduct must on net be harmful, that is, it must fail a cost-benefit test.

In certain respects, a draft section 18 competition rule that met this cost-benefit requirement would stand a better chance of passing legal muster than a section 6(g) rule. Specifically, it would be less likely to be viewed as an unconstitutional delegation, given the precise congressionally prescribed standard for determining unfairness. It would also qualify as a substantive rule, since section 18 facially deals with substantive rulemaking, unlike section 6(g). The section 18 rule would also be subject to special statutory due process protections that could obviate the "arbitrary and capricious" problem of APA rulemaking (but those protections may be put at risk by actions of current FTC leadership, as explained below).

The biggest problem in devising a defensible section 18 rule, however, would be the need to show that it satisfied the required section 5(n) cost-benefit paradigm. The FTC would have to show actual consumer injury stemming from a condemned type of conduct; it would have to explore plausible claims advanced of countervailing benefits to consumers or the competitive process; and it would have to demonstrate convincingly that the conduct's benefits were less weighty than the harms. Jumping through these hoops successfully could prove very difficult.

To take a not unrealistic example, consider a possible section 18 rule that forbade certain types of "noncompete agreements," under which an employer requires that employees agree not to seek future employment with a competitor.[70] A rulemaking directed at harmful noncompete agreements would proceed by characterizing specific noncompete clauses as unfair acts. Consistent with the language of

---

69 15 U.S.C. § 45(n).

70 The FTC noted in its December 2021 Statement of Regulatory Priorities that it would give serious consideration to a "competition rulemaking[] relating to non-compete clauses." SRP, *supra* note 2, at 2. Given the substantial risks that attend section 6(g) competition rulemakings, the FTC might well consider whether such a rulemaking would better fit under its section 18 authority to promulgate "unfair acts or practices" rules.

section 5(n), the FTC would be required to account for the benefits of noncompete clauses for consumers and the competitive process, which include reduced cost or better quality for companies. Although some evidence shows that wages are lower with the presence of noncompete agreements, this evidence is not universal, and there may well be company-level procompetitive and proconsumer benefits stemming from noncompete agreements that outweigh the effect of lower wages.[71]

From the protection of intellectual property rights (for example, the preservation of trade secrets and sensitive proprietary information) to the investment in human capital (specialized employment training which might benefit "free-riding" competitors), businesses may have a multitude of justifications for their use of noncompete agreements. Even if workers face lower wages when subject to noncompete agreements, these workers may gain specialized skills that are job specific, and subsequent specialization increases worker productivity in a particular job that may not apply to other positions.

In light of these far-reaching benefits, a broad rule banning noncompete agreements outright would most likely not pass judicial review, given its incompatibility with the text of section 5(n). Banning noncompete agreements for all workers ignores any benefits to companies, workers, or competition, and only accounts for the costs associated with harm to workers. In short, statutorily mandated calculations would most likely fail to show universal and irredeemable net costs of noncompete agreements. At best, a very limited rule that sought to improve marketplace information about noncompete requirements without banning such requirements might have a realistic possibility of being upheld.[72]

More generally, the specific case of a broad ban on noncompete agreements illustrates the risks that the FTC would run in seeking to ban a broad array of "nonstandard contracts," which the law and economics literature demonstrates often engender substantial efficiencies and counter market failure.[73] Crafting section 18 rules that preserve such welfare-enhancing effects may frequently prove unworkable, and may engender serious error costs (calling into doubt cost-benefit balancing calculations). This could in turn routinely lead appeals courts to hold that the FTC's section 5(n) cost-benefit test had not been met in reviewing individual section 5(n) competition rules.

Even worse for the FTC, reviewing courts might not even reach the point of reviewing the specifics of individual "unfair acts or practices" competition rules. The Supreme Court could plausibly hold (and, if my analysis is correct, likely

71 *See* Abbott & Mercado, *supra* note 4, at 2–4.

72 A narrow rule that required employers to proffer noncompete agreement terms prior to the signature of a contract might pass legal muster. It could be seen as allowing companies the benefits of noncompetes while at the same time protecting workers by putting them on notice so that they might consider alternative employment opportunities before accepting an offer. Abbott & Mercado, *supra* note 4, at 8–10, discuss the legal basis for such a "limited informational rule" (which could draw upon the example of a 2018 Massachusetts state law).

73 *See generally, e.g.*, Alan J. Meese, *Market Failure and Non-Standard Contracting: How the Ghost of Perfect Competition Still Haunts Antitrust,* 1 J. Comp. L. & Econ. 21 (2005).

would hold) that section 18 should not be read to apply to competition issues. Such an interpretation could follow naturally from the understanding that Congress clearly designed section 18 to authorize consumer protection rules, and that this section has been applied solely to consumer protection questions for nearly half a century. A newfound and unprecedented FTC finding that section 18 implicates competition issues would smack of a jurisprudentially disfavored attempt to fit an "elephant in a mousehole." Moreover, it appears illogical that Congress would have contemplated the FTC setting rules that affect antitrust, in light of antitrust's public policy significance as a case enforcement regime (not a rulemaking regime) shared by the FTC and DOJ. Specific legislative language authorizing FTC competition-related rulemaking would have been required, but was never enacted, let alone debated in Congress. Taken together, these considerations would strongly support a Supreme Court holding that *Chevron* is inapplicable to FTC section 18 competition rulemaking interpretations (whether on "major question" grounds or on the basis that "Section 18 clearly does not extend" to competition). Faced with construing section 18's language itself, the Supreme Court likely would hold that competition rulemaking is unauthorized, considering the unprecedented nature and risks to antitrust jurisprudence of competition rules.

iii. Section 18 and Due Process

There is yet one more consideration that clouds the outlook for section 18 competition rules, in the unlikely event that the FTC would be able to overcome the serious legal obstacles previously addressed. Specifically, the Commission majority's July 2021 decision (by a 3-2 vote) to "streamline" section 18 procedures by revising its rules of practice[74] has been criticized by the two dissenting commissioners (Noah Phillips and Christine Wilson) as an affront to due process:

> The majority asserts that the revisions to Section 18 procedures are designed to "streamline" rulemaking and reduce "red tape." (To be clear, the red tape in question helps avoid the ill-advised application of red tape to American businesses.) What the changes – adopted without public input – in fact do is fast-track regulation at the expense of public input, objectivity, and a full evidentiary record. We see no need for bulldozing procedural safeguards in our Section 18 rulemaking Rules of Practice and are concerned in particular that the reforms undercut the independence of those charged with conducting evidentiary hearings, limit valuable input from the public, and reverse decades of practice regarding agency transparency.[75]

---

74 Fed. Trade Comm'n, Press Release, FTC Votes to Update Rulemaking Procedures, Sets Stage for Stronger Deterrence of Corporate Misconduct (July 1, 2021), https://www.ftc.gov/news-events/press-releases/2021/07/ftc-votes-update-rulemaking-procedures-sets-stage-stronger.

75 Dissenting Statement of Commissioners Christine S. Wilson and Noah Joshua Phillips Regarding the Commission Statement on the Adoption of Revised Section 18 Rulemaking Procedures 3 (July 9, 2021) (citation omitted), https://www.ftc.gov/system/files/documents/public_statements/1591702/p210100_wilson-phillips_joint_statement_-_rules_of_practice.pdf.

Specifically, the dissenters assert, citing specifics, that the revised section 18 procedures would detract from the independence of the FTC's presiding officer overseeing rulemaking (in particular, by stripping the officer of significant control over the hearing process); and would finalize the list of disputed factual issues with more limited public input (enabling the Commission to more easily ignore contradictory views by omitting disputed issues). The dissenters also single out as troublesome the FTC's failure to seek public comment before making these procedural revisions. In sum, according to the dissenters:

> The revisions to our Rules of Practice adopted by the majority last Thursday, without public input, undermine the goals of participation and transparency that Congress sought to advance when it enacted and amended Section 18. These changes will facilitate more rules, but not better ones. These changes will also provide additional opportunities for legal challenges in federal court, given that new rules will be formulated pursuant to an agenda-driven process that limits public input and facilitates a biased evidentiary record.[76]

The dissenters' specific warning that the revised section 18 procedures could be legally challenged in federal court casts a further shadow on all future section 18 substantive rulemakings, whether based on traditional consumer protection concerns or on novel competition concerns. Even if courts were reluctant to strike down the revisions on due process grounds (a question that is far from clear), the existence of rulemaking procedures that appeared unfairly to "stack the deck" in the Commission's favor would further color the thinking of judges, as they decided whether to uphold particular rules or to find that rulemaking authority existed in the first place. Judges would find it easier to reject arguments supporting novel FTC competition rulemaking powers if they perceived the FTC to be weak on due process, if not a rogue agency.

F. *All Relevant Legal Considerations Indicate that FTC Competition Rulemaking Initiatives Would Almost Certainly Fail*

Assessing the likelihood that federal courts (and, in particular, the Supreme Court) will uphold the FTC's competition rulemaking authority is more art than science. Nevertheless, as already discussed, multiple legal factors all point to the ultimate failure of FTC competition rulemaking initiatives.[77]

The specific sources of legal threats to competition rulemaking reinforce each other. The nondelegation doctrine, reflecting the constitutional separation of powers, casts substantial doubt on whether Congress has granted the FTC power

76 *Id.* at 6.

77 This conclusion assumes, of course, that Congress does not enact specific legislation authorizing FTC competition rulemaking.

to enact "legislative" rules under section 6(g). Principles of statutory construction that point to the procedural nature of section 6(g) rulemaking underscore the lack of a substantive delegation of authority to the FTC. Recent "*Chevron* doctrine" limitations that collectively point to a refusal to defer to FTC statutory constructions further enhance nondelegation doctrine and statutory interpretations that reject FTC authority to issue substantive rules. Administrative law "arbitrary and capricious" limitations circumscribing "unfair methods of competition" findings also argue against deference to FTC rule formulations. Finally, section 18 efforts to justify competition rules based on "unfair acts or practices" principles would confront section 5(n) cost-benefit limitations, as well as statutory interpretation and due process concerns. In short, "the whole is more than the sum of the parts," and complementary legal concerns aggregated together create a monumental legal obstacle to FTC competition rulemaking, one which would be almost impossible to overcome.

A final observation strongly supporting this conclusion is warranted. Simply put, FTC competition rulemaking runs counter to the U.S. jurisprudential zeitgeist. The Supreme Court's recent unanimous repudiation of FTC injunctive monetary relief authority in the *AMG Capital Management* case clearly evinced a concern that the Commission had strayed beyond its long-understood enforcement boundaries, based on the structure of the FTC Act. The Court's opinion emphasized that the FTC should not be deemed to enjoy powers not readily inferable from structural statutory limitations. It also stressed that any significant expansion of the FTC's traditional powers must flow from new congressional grants of authority, not from novel agency interpretations that dramatically expand the FTC's enforcement reach. In so doing, the opinion imposed a major limit on FTC remediation of a clear "bread and butter" violation of FTC law (*AMG* involved monetary relief for plainly harmful deception). It logically follows by analogy that the Court would be even less inclined to authorize a novel and dramatic agency innovation, competition rulemaking, falling well outside the traditional ambit of substantive FTC regulatory activity.[78]

III. Conclusion

The current FTC leadership may be expected (at least initially) to proceed with competition rulemaking efforts, given Chair Khan's strong support for this initiative. Rulemaking, of course, requires the gathering of evidence and the taking of testimony. Moreover, new competition rules imposing limitations on

---

78 On January 24, 2022, the Supreme Court agreed to review the question "[w]hether Congress impliedly stripped federal district courts of jurisdiction over constitutional challenges to the Federal Trade Commission's structure, procedures, and existence by granting the courts of appeals jurisdiction to 'affirm, enforce, modify, or set aside' the Commission's cease-and-desist orders." Axon Enterprise, Inc. v. Federal Trade Commission, *cert. granted* (U.S. Jan. 24, 2022) (No. 21-86), https://www.supremecourt.gov/qp/21-00086qp.pdf. Although it is not directly on point, Axon may reflect continuing Supreme Court concerns that the FTC may be exceeding the scope of its statutory authority in bringing certain enforcement actions – a concern that would apply "in spades" (a fortiori in legal parlance) to a novel form of rulemaking.

specified business practices or industry sectors would likely be appealed to U.S. courts of appeal. Eventually, one would expect the Supreme Court to step in to review the legal status of a particular competition rule and, most likely, the legality of FTC competition rulemaking itself. All of this would entail a substantial commitment of scarce public and private resources and take a considerable amount of time – the current FTC leadership likely would be long gone before a final legal resolution by the Supreme Court. Yet the end result would be in all likelihood a ruling that the FTC lacked substantive competition rulemaking authority. In short, the FTC rulemaking saga would almost surely entail pure waste, to the detriment of consumer welfare, producer welfare, and sound government.

This conclusion, based on legal analysis, is competition policy-neutral. Proposing rules that are doomed to legal failure is in no one's interest, whether one believes that new FTC competition rules would advance sound public policy (as does Chair Khan) or believes instead that they would reduce economic welfare (as I do).[79]

It is, of course, possible that FTC leadership, contemplating this likely scenario, will "wise up" and pull the proverbial regulatory plug before too much time has elapsed and too many resources have been squandered. The opportunity cost of continuing along the regulatory path is high. Instead of being wasted, resources that would have been dedicated to rulemaking can focus instead on high value-added cases and seminal competition research (something in which the FTC excels).[80] It is to be hoped that the FTC's leadership will come to this realization and end its pursuit of competition rulemaking.

---

79 I recently argued that the pursuit of competition rules (i) likely would fail as a legal matter and waste resources; (ii) would generate large error costs and penalize economically efficient business behavior; and (iii) could create or enhance barriers to entry and raise less connected rivals' costs, harming consumers and economic efficiency. Alden Abbott, *FTC Statement of Regulatory Priorities: Storm Clouds Are Looming*, Truth on the Market (Dec. 15, 2021), https://truthonthemarket.com/2021/12/15/ftc-statement-of-regulatory-priorities-storm-clouds-are-looming.

80 *See* Fed. Trade Comm'n, Policy, https://www.ftc.gov/policy (last visited Jan. 18, 2022).

Pushing the Limits? A Primer on FTC Competition Rulemaking

MAUREEN K. OHLHAUSEN AND JAMES F. RILL*
Baker Botts

Abstract

Congress granted the Federal Trade Commission investigative and information-gathering powers and an administrative adjudication process to prosecute "unfair methods of competition." The FTC cannot, however, act as a legislature with broad authority to expand or alter the laws that Congress has tasked it with enforcing. Recent proposals for aggressive unfair methods of competition rulemaking, predicated on section 6(g) of the FTC Act, would have the effect of claiming a quasi-legislative power for the Commission based on a thin statutory reed authorizing "rules and regulations for the purpose of carrying out the provisions of" that Act. This would distract the agency from its core mission of case-by-case expert application of the FTC Act through administrative adjudication. It would also be inconsistent with the explicit grants of rulemaking authority that Congress has given the FTC throughout its history and run afoul of the congressional and constitutional "guardrails" that cabin the Commission's authority.

* Ms. Ohlhausen is Partner and Global Section Chair of the Antitrust & Competition Law Practice Group of Baker Botts LLP and former Acting Chairman and Commissioner of the U.S. Federal Trade Commission. Mr. Rill is Senior Counsel in the Antitrust & Competition Law Practice Group of Baker Botts LLP and former Assistant Attorney General of the U.S. Department of Justice Antitrust Division. The authors' analysis and views found within this paper are their own based on their expert experience as former competition enforcers, not necessarily the views of Baker Botts LLP or its clients.

I. Introduction

Since its founding in 1914, the Federal Trade Commission (FTC) has held a unique and multifaceted role in the U.S. administrative state and the economy. It possesses powerful investigative and information-gathering powers, including through compulsory process; a multilayered administrative adjudication process to prosecute "unfair methods of competition" (and later, "unfair and deceptive acts and practices" as well); and an important role in educating and informing the business community and the public.[1] What the FTC cannot be, however, is a legislature with broad authority to expand, contract, or alter the laws that Congress has tasked it with enforcing.

Recent proposals for aggressive unfair methods of competition (UMC) rulemaking, predicated on section 6(g) of the FTC Act, would have the effect of claiming just this sort of quasi-legislative power for the Commission based on a thin statutory reed authorizing "rules and regulations for the purpose of carrying out the provisions of" that Act.[2] This usurpation of power would distract the agency from its core mission of case-by-case expert application of the FTC Act through administrative adjudication. It would also be inconsistent with the explicit grants of rulemaking authority that Congress has given the FTC throughout its history and run afoul of the congressional and constitutional "guardrails" that cabin the Commission's authority.

- *The FTC has a troubling history of* ***rulemaking overreach****, one that the courts and Congress have both stepped in to limit*
- *Congress has explicitly provided for informal* ***APA notice-and-comment rulemaking through specific statutes****, such as the Children's Online Privacy Protection and Telemarketing and Consumer Fraud and Abuse Prevention Acts*
- *Congress, however, has* ***not explicitly*** *granted informal rulemaking authority to the FTC relating to its broad section 5 authority*
- *Rather, Congress provided the FTC explicit rulemaking authority for unfair and deceptive acts and practices through specific* ***"Magnuson-Moss" procedures***
- *Congress has made no such grant for unfair methods of competition rulemaking, instead empowering FTC to undertake* ***case-by-case administrative adjudication*** *of competition cases to shape the law*
- *Although the FTC and DOJ cooperate on the issuance of* ***voluntary guidance*** *to the business community (such as the Merger Guidelines), unlike rules, such guidance is* ***not legally binding***

---

1 Fed. Trade Comm'n, About the FTC, https://www.ftc.gov/about-ftc; Marc Winerman, *The Origins of the FTC: Concentration, Cooperation, Control, and Competition*, 71 Antitrust L.J. 1, 97 (2003) ("[T]hen, as now, the agency combined formal powers to investigate (those emphasized in the House debate), formal powers to prosecute (those emphasized in the Senate debate), and informal authority to educate and work with business to facilitate compliance with the law (those emphasized by [President] Wilson).").

2 15 U.S.C. § 46(g).

II. FTC's Unique Role as an Administrative Adjudicator

1. FTC's Original Purpose: Applying Administrative Expertise on a Case-by-Case Basis

The FTC's Part III adjudication authority is central to its mission of preserving fair competition in the U.S. economy. To challenge an alleged "unfair method of competition" under that process, the Commission first votes on the filing of a complaint regarding the conduct at issue. Assuming the matter is not settled immediately under a consent order, a walled-off group of FTC attorneys then takes on a prosecutorial role as "complaint counsel," going through a litigation process very much resembling a federal lawsuit culminating in a bench trial. Complaint counsel and respondents go through the discovery process, make pretrial evidentiary motions or motions for summary decision, and ultimately argue at a trial-like hearing before an administrative law judge (ALJ), presenting fact and expert witness testimony, along with documentary and other evidence. Whatever the decision of the ALJ, either complaint counsel or the respondent have the opportunity to appeal to the full Commission, which reviews both the factual and legal determinations of the ALJ *de novo*.[3]

Although the procedural protections of administrative adjudication are similar (likely by design) to those in federal court, one notable distinction is the fact that the litigation process is overseen, and ultimate decisions made, by subject-matter experts attuned to the goals, legal frameworks, and other details of antitrust and consumer protection law, the two mission areas of the FTC. The commissioners themselves are often veteran antitrust practitioners, each counseled by a team of specialized attorney-advisors. Given the sometimes highly technical nature of antitrust analysis, particularly when complex econometrics are involved, the benefit of this expertise should not be underestimated. As capable as generalist federal judges may be, by their own admission, they sometimes "d[o] not try th[ese] case[s] very well."[4] Utilizing both trial court and appeals court jurists who are steeped in the nuances of antitrust has the benefit of eliminating a considerable learning curve, increasing the likelihood of "getting it right" in the first instance.

Consistent with these benefits, the FTC has enjoyed considerable success in recent years with its administrative adjudications, both in terms of winning on appeal and in shaping the development of antitrust law overall (not simply a separate

---

3 Although this process sometimes places an administrative defendant in the somewhat awkward position of arguing its innocence before the same panel that approved the complaint initiating the prosecution in the first place, the evidentiary standard is considerably higher for sustaining a liability finding (or reversing a finding of no liability), requiring a preponderance of evidence (more likely than not) standard as opposed to a mere "reason to believe" that a violation may have occurred to issue a complaint. Fed. Trade Comm'n, A Brief Overview of the Federal Trade Commission's Investigative, Law Enforcement, and Rulemaking Authority § II.A. (revised, May 2021), https://www.ftc.gov/about-ftc/what-we-do/enforcement-authority.

4 *In re* Nexium (Esomeprazole) Antitrust Litig., 309 F.R.D. 107, 110 (D. Mass. 2015). *See also* Jeffrey May, *The US District Court for the District of Massachusetts rejects a request for a new trial to challenge a pay-for-delay agreement (Nexium)*, e-Competitions July 2015, art. No. 75199.

category of UMC law) by creating citable precedent in key areas.[5] These successes include challenges to hospital mergers in *Evanston Northwestern Healthcare* and *ProMedica Health System*, in which the FTC secured a conduct remedy and divestiture, respectively.[6] FTC won an important administrative victory in *North Carolina Board of Dental Examiners*, upheld at the Supreme Court, establishing limits on the state action defense and anticompetitive actions by state licensing boards.[7] The FTC's decision in *McWane*, upheld by the Eleventh Circuit, has become an oft-cited example in exclusive dealing cases.[8] And the FTC has won major victories in challenging already-consummated acquisitions in administrative adjudication, such as in *Chicago Bridge & Iron Co.* and *Polypore International.*[9]

2. FTC's Shift from Administrative Process to Federal Court

Despite this enviable administrative record, the FTC has – until very recently – turned increasingly to federal court for its enforcement actions. The FTC Act does allow for the FTC to seek preliminary injunctions in federal district court before proceeding in its internal administrative actions, a useful tool for putting pending mergers on hold and other instances when the status quo cannot be easily restored.[10] The same statute allows, "in proper cases" and with "proper proof," courts to grant the FTC a "permanent injunction."[11] Until the Supreme Court put a stop to this practice in May 2021, the FTC used this provision to seek monetary relief, including disgorgement of allegedly ill-gotten gains, a remedy that would otherwise require going through administrative adjudication and meeting other strict requirements, including time limits (filing of a complaint within three years and filing of a request in federal court for monetary redress within a year after a cease-and-desist order) and a finding of objectively "dishonest or fraudulent" conduct.[12]

Likely due to the relative ease of this process and the allure of money in a much wider array of cases, FTC's enforcement actions began to be weighted more and more heavily towards federal court and away from administrative adjudication. This shift was accelerated by the FTC's 2012 decision to jettison its own policy

5 *See* Maureen K. Ohlhausen, *Administrative Litigation at the FTC: Effective Tool for Developing the Law or Rubber Stamp?*, 12 J. Comp. L. & Econ. *623 (2016)*.

6 ProMedica Health Sys. v. FTC, 749 F.3d 559 (6th Cir. 2014), *cert. denied*, 575 U.S. 996 (2015); *In re* Evanston Nw. Healthcare Corp., 2008 FTC LEXIS 62 (2008).

7 N.C. State Bd. of Dental Exam'rs v. FTC, 574 U.S. 494 (2015). *See also* Christopher Sagers, *The US Supreme Court decides on whether nominally public body must show "active supervision" by the state government to enjoy antitrust immunity (North Carolina State Board of Dental Examiners)*, e-Competitions February 2015, art. No. 72018.

8 McWane, Inc. v. FTC, 783 F.3d 814 (11th Cir. 2015), *cert. denied*, 577 U.S. 1216 (2016). *See also* Helen Cho Eckert & David R. Garcia, *The US Court of Appeals for the 11th Circuit holds that a rebate program requiring exclusivity from distributors was unlawful maintenance of monopoly power (McWane)*, e-Competitions April 2015, art. No. 72658.

9 Chi. Bridge & Iron Co. N.V. v. FTC, 534 F.3d 410 (5th Cir. 2008); Polypore Int'l, Inc. v. FTC, 686 F.3d 1208 (11th Cir. 2012), *cert. denied*, 570 U.S. 917 (2013).

10 15 U.S.C. § 53(b).

11 *Id.* § 53(b)(2).

12 15 U.S.C. § 57b(a)(2).

statement on the use of disgorgement, which was followed, predictably, by a large increase in the number of "permanent injunctions" pursued in federal court.[13] As the Supreme Court noted while striking down in May 2021 the FTC's expansive interpretation of what could be included in a "permanent injunction," the FTC brought as many federal antitrust suits seeking disgorgement in the four years after this change as the two decades preceding it, with "dozens" of cases filed every year.[14] As described below in greater detail, the Court found that the FTC's pursuit of disgorgement under the category of "permanent injunction" simply stretched the statutory language beyond its breaking point, particularly given the availability of similar remedies to FTC after obtaining a cease-and-desist order through its usual administrative procedures.[15]

With this judicial course correction, now would be an ideal time for the FTC to begin a return to its roots with increased use of its administrative adjudication process to seek relief against antitrust violators and develop antitrust law, which other enforcers may also utilize. However, as a result of its July 1, 2021, open meeting and the recently issued Executive Order 14036,[16] the FTC appears to be headed for another misadventure in response to calls to claim authority for broad, legislative-style "unfair methods of competition" rulemaking out of section 6(g) of the FTC Act.[17]

III. FTC's Rulemaking Authority Was Meant to Complement Its Case-by-Case Adjudicatory Authority, Not Supplant It

1. FTC Administrative and Rulemaking Processes: A Comparison

A. *Informal Notice-and-Comment Rulemaking*

Informal rulemaking refers to the basic Administrative Procedure Act (APA) requirements in 5 U.S.C. § 553, which include adequate public notice of the proposed rule and a meaningful opportunity to comment on the proposed rule

13 *See* Maureen K. Ohlhausen, Dollars, Doctrine, and Damage Control: How Disgorgement Affects the FTC's Antitrust Mission 7 (Apr. 20, 2016), https://www.ftc.gov/system/files/documents/public_statements/945623/160420dollarsdoctrinespeech.pdf.

14 AMG Cap. Mgmt. LLC v. FTC, 141 S. Ct. 1341, 1346–47 (2021). *See also* Jarod Bona, *The US Supreme Court rules that the FTC is unauthorized to seek monetary damages in antitrust cases (AMG Capital Management)*, e-Competitions April 2021, art. No. 103294.

15 *Id.* at 1348–49.

16 Exec. Order No. 14,036, 86 Fed. Reg. 36987 (July 9, 2021).

17 *See, e.g.*, Rohit Chopra & Lina M. Khan, *The Case for "Unfair Methods of Competition" Rulemaking*, 87 U. Chi. L. Rev. 357, 371 (2020) (arguing that "[r]ulemaking would advance clarity and certainty about what types of conduct constitute – or do not constitute – an 'unfair method of competition'"). The Commission recently took a significant and misguided step towards this goal by rescinding – without replacing – its bipartisan Statement of Enforcement Principles Regarding "Unfair Methods of Competition" Under Section 5 of the FTC Act, divorcing (at least in the Commission majority's view) section 5 from prevailing antitrust law principles and leaving the business community without any current guidance as to what the Commission considers "unfair." *See* Dissenting Statement of Commissioners Noah Joshua Phillips and Christine S. Wilson on the "Statement of the Commission on the Withdrawal of the Statement of Enforcement Principles Regarding 'Unfair Methods of Competition' Under Section 5 of the FTC Act" (July 9, 2021), https://www.ftc.gov/system/files/documents/public_statements/1591710/p210100phillipswilsondissentsec5enforcementprinciples.pdf.

(hence "notice-and-comment" rulemaking). These requirements function as a "default" process for rulemaking when Congress does not specify a more stringent standard and set a "minimum degree of public participation the agency must permit."[18] As discussed below, however, Congress *has* specified a more stringent rulemaking standard for FTC's consumer protection rulemaking under the Magnuson-Moss Warranty–Federal Trade Commission Improvement Act of 1975.[19] Nevertheless, Congress has directed the FTC on several occasions to use informal notice-and-comment rulemaking through statutes that provide the agency detailed guidance on rulemaking topics and goals and that specifically exempt it from the additional burdens of Magnuson-Moss rulemaking. Some examples of such statutes include the Telephone Disclosure and Dispute Resolution Act of 1992, the Children's Online Privacy Protection Act of 1998, and the Telemarketing and Consumer Fraud and Abuse Prevention Act.[20]

Under the APA, the notice requirement of informal rulemaking is meant to "afford[] interested parties a reasonable opportunity to participate in the rulemaking process."[21] This is generally achieved by a notice of proposed rulemaking (NPRM) published in the *Federal Register*.[22] There is an exemption to the notice requirement for some rules, such as interpretative rules and general statements of policy, or under a narrowly construed good cause exception.[23] An NPRM must include:

(1) the time, place, and nature of public rulemaking proceedings;

(2) reference to the legal authority under which the rule is proposed; and

(3) either the terms or substance of the proposed rule or a description of the subjects and issues involved.[24]

The comment requirement focuses on giving the public an opportunity to participate in the rulemaking process. This participation can consist of the "submission of written data, views, or arguments with or without opportunity for oral presentation."[25] After considering the points presented from such participation, the agency must "incorporate in the rules adopted a concise general

---

18 Todd Garvey, Cong. Rsch. Serv., R41546, A Brief Overview of Rulemaking and Judicial Review 2 (Mar. 27, 2017), https://crsreports.congress.gov/product/pdf/R/R41546.

19 Magnuson-Moss Warranty–Federal Trade Commission Improvement Act, Pub. L. No. 93-637, 88 Stat. 2183, 2193 (1975) (codified as amended at 15 U.S.C. §§ 45–46, 49–50, 52, 56, 57a–c, 58, 2301–12).

20 *See* Jeffrey S. Lubbers, *It's Time to Remove the "Mossified" Procedures for FTC Rulemaking*, 83 Geo. Wash. L. Rev. 1979, 1989, 1991–92 (2015).

21 Forester v. Consumer Prod. Safety Comm'n, 559 F.2d 774, 787 (D.C. Cir. 1977).

22 5 U.S.C. § 553(b). Publication in the *Federal Register* is not required when the "persons subject thereto are named and either personally served or otherwise have actual notice thereof in accordance with law." *Id.*

23 *Id.* § 553(b)(A) – (B). *See also* Mack Trucks, Inc. v. EPA, 682 F.3d 87 (D.C. Cir. 2012) (holding the good cause exception is to be narrowly construed).

24 5 U.S.C. § 553(b)(1) – (3).

25 *Id.* § 553(c).

statement of their basis and purpose."[26] The statement of basis and purpose is often a major element of the rulemaking record and serves to provide the public with the agency's basic justification for the final rule. This is not to say that all comments must be addressed in the final rule, but the agency is required to consider "significant comments" that would affect the final rule.[27] The final rule can differ from the proposed rule, but it is generally required to be a reasonably foreseeable "logical outgrowth" of the originally proposed rule.

After the agency has completed the comment process, the final rule and general statement of the basis and purpose must be published thirty days before the rule's effective date.[28] Following the final rule, there is a statutorily mandated right to petition for the issuance, amendment, or repeal of the rule.[29] Informal rulemaking can be completed in a few months, but more substantive rules may take a year or more.[30]

B. *Hybrid and Magnuson-Moss Rulemaking*

Hybrid rulemaking refers to congressionally specified rulemaking procedures that impose additional requirements beyond those of informal rulemaking but stop short of the full requirements of formal rulemaking. Hybrid rulemaking was popular in the 1970s following the initial shift towards informal rulemaking but became less common over time.

The FTC's Magnuson-Moss rulemaking is perhaps the most frequently cited example of hybrid rulemaking. In 1975, the Magnuson-Moss Warranty–Federal Trade Commission Improvement Act authorized the FTC to promulgate legislative rules under section 18 of the FTC Act.[31] Such rules are called trade regulation rules (TRRs), "which define with specificity acts or practices which are unfair or deceptive acts or practices in or affecting commerce" and may "include requirements prescribed for the purpose of preventing [unfair or deceptive] acts or practices."[32] Despite a flurry of activity following its inception, Magnuson-Moss rulemaking has been dormant for nearly forty years, with the procedures used only for updates to existing TRRs.[33]

---

26 *Id.*

27 *See, e.g.*, Am. Mining Cong. v. EPA, 965 F.2d 759, 771 (9th Cir. 1992) (significant comments "raise relevant points and which, if adopted, would require a change in the agency's proposed rule.").

28 5 U.S.C. § 553(d).

29 *Id.* § 553(e).

30 Pre-Magnuson-Moss rules at the FTC took an average of about 3 years, and more recent rules under the APA process averaged 287 days. Lubbers, *supra* note 20, at 1997–98.

31 *See, e.g.*, Fed. Trade Comm'n, *supra* note 3.

32 Magnuson-Moss Warranty–Federal Trade Commission Improvement Act, 15 U.S.C. § 57a(a)(1)(B).

33 *See, e.g.*, Timothy J. Muris, *Rules Without Reason: The Case of the FTC*, 6 Regulation 20 (1982) (noting that of the first nineteen rulemaking proceedings – all of which started before the end of 1978 – only five resulted in final rule as of 1982, and most of those had been remanded or overturned).

Magnuson-Moss rulemaking imposes additional procedural requirements beyond the standard notice-and-comment procedures under the APA, but fewer than formal rulemaking[34] – resulting in a "hybrid" rulemaking process.[35] Additional Magnuson-Moss rulemaking requirements begin with an advance NPRM before the standard notice of proposed rulemaking, published in the *Federal Register* and submitted to congressional committees.[36] Going beyond APA requirements, the notice of proposed rulemaking must state "with particularity the text of the rule, including any alternatives, which the Commission proposes to promulgate, and the reason for the proposed rule."[37] Throughout the Magnuson-Moss rulemaking process, the FTC must make a public record of its meetings and communications with relevant parties.[38]

Magnuson-Moss rulemaking also requires an informal hearing, if requested, with numerous procedural requirements, including cross-examination by interested parties.[39] Following such a hearing, the hearing officer must prepare a staff report and recommendation, which is published in the *Federal Register*, seeking comments for at least sixty days.[40]

Further, the FTC must prepare a regulatory analysis of the final rule and a statement of basis and purpose to accompany the final rule. The statement of basis and purpose must include:

> (A) a statement as to the prevalence of the acts or practices treated by the rule;
>
> (B) a statement as to the manner and context in which such acts or practices are unfair or deceptive; and
>
> (C) a statement as to the economic effect of the rule, taking into account the effect on small business and consumers.[41]

The final regulatory analysis must include:

> (A) a concise statement of the need for, and the objectives of, the final rule;
>
> (B) a description of any alternatives to the final rule which were considered by the Commission;

---

34 Formal rulemaking is required to be fully "on the record" with strict procedures observed, 5 U.S.C. §§ 556–57, and is very infrequently used.

35 *Compare* 5 U.S.C. § 553, *with* 15 U.S.C. § 57a. *See also, e.g.*, Admin. Conference of the U.S., Recommendation No. 79-1–Hybrid Rulemaking Procedures of the Federal Trade Commission (June 1979), https://www.acus.gov/recommendation/hybrid-rulemaking-procedures-federal-trade-commission.

36 15 U.S.C. §§ 57a(b)(2)(A), 57a(b)(2)(C).

37 *Id.* § 57a(b)(1).

38 *See, e.g., id.* §§ 57a(i), 57a(j).

39 *See, e.g., id.* § 57(c).

40 *See, e.g., id.* § 57(c)(1)(B).

41 *Id.* § 57a(d)(1).

(C) an analysis of the projected benefits and any adverse economic effects and any other effects of the final rule;

(D) an explanation of the reasons for the determination of the Commission that the final rule will attain its objectives in a manner consistent with applicable law and the reasons the particular alternative was chosen; and

(E) a summary of any significant issues raised by the comments submitted during the public comment period in response to the preliminary regulatory analysis, and a summary of the assessment by the Commission of such issues.[42]

Ultimately, the lengthy and complicated process of promulgating rules through Magnuson-Moss rulemaking fell out of favor. Only seven rules and nine amendments have been issued under Magnuson-Moss rulemaking.[43] Those rules each took, on average, over five years to issue.[44] In contrast, when the FTC has been authorized to promulgate rules under notice-and-comment APA procedures, the process averages under a year to complete.[45] The Commission, over the objection of Commissioners Wilson and Phillips, recently trimmed its own procedural rules for Magnuson-Moss rulemaking to eliminate requirements for an internal staff report and neutral appointment of a presiding officer, giving the majority commissioners more direct control over the shape of rulemaking hearings.[46] While these changes could result in faster Magnuson-Moss rulemaking than in the past, they also remove safeguards that were originally adopted in response to valid concerns over bias, public input, and accountability for the Commission.[47]

C. *The Role of Targeted Informal and Magnuson-Moss Rulemaking in the FTC's Mission*

Although the processes for promulgating statute-specific rules under informal notice-and-comment rulemaking and Magnuson-Moss rulemaking are quite different, they share one essential characteristic: the fact that Congress has made a clear grant of authority to the FTC, with either particular procedures for rulemaking spelled out in detail (in the case of Magnuson-Moss) or detailed guidance on rulemaking topics and goals in the case of targeted notice-and-comment. In both cases, the Congressional delegation of power to FTC is

42 *Id.* § 57b-3(b)(2).

43 Lubbers, *supra* note 20, at 1997.

44 *Id.* at 1997–98 ("[I]t took the agency 5.57 years, on average, to issue the seven rules it managed to issue using these formalized procedures.").

45 *Id.*

46 Dissenting Statement of Commissioners Christine S. Wilson and Noah Joshua Phillips Regarding the Commission Statement on the Adoption of Revised Section 18 Rulemaking Procedures 5 (July 9, 2021), https://www.ftc.gov/system/files/documents/public_statements/1591702/p210100_wilsonphillips_joint_statement_-_rules_of_practice.pdf.

47 *Id.* at 4–5.

well-defined, either in terms of the substantive scope of the proposed rule or the procedural path that must be taken to provide the rule with force of law. Put differently, the Commission either has greater discretion with regard to the substantive content of a rule or has greater freedom in implementing it through quicker and less burdensome procedures – but not both. This dichotomy reflects Congress's prerogative to prioritize speed over flexibility, or vice versa, without simply handing over its legislative duties to an independent agency.

The fact that Congress has chosen to maintain the Magnuson-Moss rulemaking framework despite its procedural burdens strongly indicates that Congress views those strictures as important safeguards against hasty or reactionary rulemaking by FTC on broad matters of substance. Despite several decades in which to consider loosening these rulemaking requirements, Congress has chosen to leave them in place as a check on FTC's authority.

On the other side of the equation, Congress clearly knows how to lay out a specific path for rulemaking and give FTC greater rein to follow it with simplified procedures when it deems particular subject matter to be in need of expedited rulemaking treatment, as with the Children's Online Privacy Protection Act[48] and similar statutes. The fact that the rulemaking authorizations from these statutes do not simply "default" to informal notice-and-comment, but explicitly exempt the process from Magnuson-Moss procedures,[49] lends additional weight to the conclusion that Congress views the constraints of Magnuson-Moss as important institutional safeguards against overzealous regulation by the FTC.

2. Broad "Unfair Methods of Competition" Rulemaking Is Inconsistent with FTC's Mission

In sharp contrast with these well-defined grants of power, broad legislative-style rulemaking against unfair methods of competition under section 6(g) of the FTC Act would be bounded neither by meticulous procedural requirements nor by a specific congressional mandate. Instead, the purpose of such rules could only be to expand the scope of liability currently recognized by the courts by attempting to create new bright-line conduct or merger-related prohibitions, loosen substantive liability standards, or lower burdens of proof for the Commission as antitrust plaintiff.[50] In the case of bright-line conduct prohibitions, the result will be rules frozen in time and unresponsive to rapidly changing industry dynamics. Unlike case-by-case adjudication, which benefits from the continued evolution of economic and industrial learning, substantive unfair methods of competition rulemaking would rely on static and potentially inaccurate views of how markets function.

---

48 Children's Online Privacy Protection Act of 1998, Pub. L. 105-277 (codified at 15 U.S.C. §§ 6501–06).

49 *See, e.g.*, 15 U.S.C. § 6502(b)(1) (directing that "the Commission shall promulgate under section 553 of title 5," the statute governing informal notice-and-comment rulemaking, regulations regarding child online privacy).

50 *See* Chopra & Khan, *supra* note 17, at 372–74 (suggesting the possibility of UMC rulemaking to condemn "pay-for-delay" settlements and employment non-compete agreements).

Any such misguided rules would then require additional rulemaking or an act of Congress to correct, undermining the flexibility of future FTC adjudications.

As described below, broad rulemaking of this sort would also be very likely to encounter stiff resistance in the courts due to its tenuous statutory basis and the myriad constitutional and institutional problems it creates. But even aside from the issue of legality, such a move would be a major distraction from FTC's core mission as an expert case-by-case adjudicator of competition issues. Rather than applying its expertise to specific facts and complex legal issues through administrative adjudication and influencing the development of antitrust law through hard-earned victories supported by substantial evidence, it would be far too tempting for the Commission to simply regulate its way to the desired outcome, bypassing all neutral arbiters along the way. And by seeking to promulgate such rules through abbreviated notice-and-comment rulemaking, FTC would be claiming extremely broad substantive authority to directly regulate business conduct across the economy with relatively few of the procedural protections that Congress felt necessary for FTC's trade regulation rules in the consumer protection context. This approach risks not only a diversion of scarce agency resources from meaningful adjudication opportunities, but also potentially a loss of public legitimacy for the Commission should it try to exempt itself from these important rulemaking safeguards.

IV. FTC Lacks Authority to Promulgate Legislative-Style Competition Rules

The FTC has historically been hesitant to exercise UMC rulemaking authority under section 6(g) of the FTC Act, which simply states that the FTC shall have power "[f]rom time to time [to] classify corporations and... to make rules and regulations for the purpose of carrying out the provisions" of the FTC Act.[51] Current proponents of UMC rulemaking argue for a broad interpretation of this clause allowing for legally binding rulemaking on any issue, including antitrust, subject to FTC's jurisdiction. But the FTC's past reticence to exercise such sweeping powers is not a result of mere timidity; rather, it is likely due to the existence of significant and unresolved questions regarding the FTC's UMC rulemaking authority from a statutory and constitutional perspective.

1. Absence of Statutory Authority

The FTC's authority to conduct rulemaking under section 6(g) has been tested in court only once, in *National Petroleum Refiners Association v. FTC* (also known as the "Octane Rating" case).[52] In that case, the FTC had attempted to

51 15 U.S.C. § 46(g).

52 Nat'l Petroleum Refiners Ass'n v. FTC, 482 F.2d 672 (D.C. Cir. 1973).

promulgate a rule defining the failure to post octane rating numbers on gasoline pumps at service stations as "an unfair method of competition and an unfair or deceptive act or practice."[53] The D.C. Circuit found that section 6(g) did confer such authority, but Congress responded two years later with the Magnuson-Moss Warranty – Federal Trade Commission Improvement Act of 1975. The Magnuson-Moss Act created a new, far more complex rulemaking scheme that applied to FTC's consumer protection rules only, expressly excluding rulemaking on unfair methods of competition from its grant of authority.[54] The statute's provision that unfair methods of competition rulemaking is unaffected by the legislation manifests strong congressional design that such rules would be governed not by Magnuson-Moss but by the FTC Act itself.[55] Proponents of UMC rulemaking argue that Magnuson-Moss left FTC's competition rulemaking authority intact and entitled to *Chevron* deference,[56] but as has been pointed out by many commentators over the decades, that would be highly incongruous given that *National Petroleum Refiners* dealt with *both* UMC and UDAP authority under section 6(g).[57] Yet Congress's reaction was to provide specific UDAP rulemaking authority and expressly take no position on UMC rulemaking. As further evidenced by the fact that the FTC has never even attempted to promulgate a UMC rule in the years following the enactment of Magnuson-Moss,[58] the Act is best read as declining to endorse the FTC's UMC rulemaking authority and instead leaving the question open for future consideration by the courts.

Turning to the terms of the FTC Act, modern statutory interpretation takes a far different approach than the court in *National Petroleum Refiners*, which discounted the significance of section 5's enumeration of adjudication as the means for restraining UMC and UDAP, reasoning that section 5(b) did not use limiting language and that section 6(g) provides a source of substantive

53 *Id.* at 674.

54 15 U.S.C. § 57a(a)(2).

55 *Id.* ("The Commission shall have no authority under this subchapter, other than its authority under this section, to prescribe any rule with respect to unfair or deceptive acts or practices in or affecting commerce... The preceding sentence shall not affect any authority of the Commission to prescribe rules... with respect to unfair methods of competition in or affecting commerce."). The reference to "any authority" of the FTC to engage in UMC rulemaking – as opposed to "the authority" – reflects Congress's agnostic view on whether the FTC possesses any such authority. It simply means that whatever authority exists for UMC rulemaking, these other provisions do not affect it, and Congress left the question open for the courts to resolve.

56 *See* Chopra & Khan, *supra* note 17, at 375–79 (arguing that FTC has UMC rulemaking authority through section 6(g) and that such rules would be entitled to *Chevron* deference); Chevron USA, Inc. v. Nat. Res. Def. Council, Inc., 467 U.S. 837 (1984).

57 *See, e.g.*, Am. Bar Ass'n, Comments of the Antitrust Law Section of the American Bar Association in Connection with the Federal Trade Commission Workshop on "Non-Competes in the Workplace: Examining Antitrust and Consumer Protection Issues" 57 (Apr. 24, 2020), https://www.americanbar.org/content/dam/aba/administrative/antitrust_law/comments/april-2020/comment-42420-ftc.pdf ("And given that Magnuson-Moss was enacted to address concerns raised by *National Petroleum Refiners* and similar cases, it's hard to see Section 6(g), with its vague and broad language, as providing a firm footing for informal antitrust rulemaking by the Commission.").

58 Royce Zeisler, Chevron *Deference and the FTC: How and Why the FTC Should Use* Chevron *to Improve Antitrust Enforcement*, 2014 Colum. Bus. L. Rev. 266, 282 (2014).

rulemaking authority.[59] This approach is in clear tension with the "elephants-in-mouseholes" doctrine developed by the Supreme Court in recent years. "Congress... does not alter the fundamental details of a regulatory scheme in vague terms or ancillary provisions – it does not, one might say, hide elephants in mouseholes."[60] The FTC's recent claim of broad substantive UMC rulemaking authority based on the absence of limiting language and a vague, ancillary provision authorizing rulemaking alongside the ability to "classify corporations" stands in conflict with the Court's admonition in *Whitman*. The Court in *AMG* recently applied similar principles in the context of the FTC's authority under the FTC Act:

> But to read those words as allowing what they do not say, namely, as allowing the Commission to dispense with administrative proceedings to obtain monetary relief as well, is to read the words as going well beyond the provision's subject matter. In light of the historical importance of administrative proceedings, that reading would allow a small statutory tail to wag a very large dog.[61]

The "dog" here, substantive UMC rulemaking authority, is at least as large as the canine in *AMG*, for it carries the authority to declare large swaths of conduct illegal under the antitrust laws in a way that would dramatically affect business in the U.S. economy. The Court in *AMG* also looked to "the structure of the Act" and emphasized that it should be read to "produce[] a coherent enforcement scheme."[62] Applying the principles enunciated in *Whitman* and *AMG*, section 5 is best read as specifying the sole means of UMC enforcement (adjudication), and section 6(g) is best understood as permitting the FTC to specify how it will carry out its adjudicative, investigative, and informative functions. Thus, section 6(g) grants ministerial, not legislative, rulemaking authority. In *AMG*, the Court emphasized "the historical importance of administrative proceedings" and declined to give the FTC a shortcut to desirable outcomes in federal court.[63] Similarly, granting broad UMC rulemaking authority to the FTC would permit it to circumvent the FTC Act's defining feature of case-by-case adjudications.

Notably, this reading of the FTC Act would accord with how the FTC viewed its authority until 1962, a fact that the D.C. Circuit found insignificant, but that later doctrine would weigh heavily.[64] In *AMG*, for example, the Supreme Court stated that "[i]n construing § 13(b), it is helpful to understand how the Commission's

---

59 *Nat'l Petroleum Refiners Ass'n*, 482 F.2d at 675–76.

60 Whitman v. Am. Trucking Ass'ns, 531 U.S. 457, 468 (2001).

61 *AMG*, 141 S. Ct. at 1348 (2021); *see also id.* at 1349 (using the "elephants-in-mouseholes" doctrine to explain that FTC's "broad reading" of section 13(b) "could not have been Congress' intent"). *See also* Bona, *supra* note 14.

62 *AMG*, 141 S. Ct. at 1348–49.

63 *Id.* at 1348.

64 *Nat'l Petroleum Refiners*, 482 F.2d at 693–94.

authority (and its interpretation of that authority) has evolved over time."[65] Courts should consider an agency's "past approach" toward its interpretation of a statute, and an agency's longstanding view that it lacks the authority to take a certain action is a "rather telling" clue that the agency's newfound claim to such authority is incorrect.[66] Conversely, even widespread judicial acceptance of an interpretation of an agency's authority does not necessarily mean the construction of the statute is correct.[67] In *AMG*, the Court gave little weight to the FTC's argument that "the courts of appeals have, until recently, consistently accepted its interpretation."[68] It also rejected the FTC's argument that "Congress has in effect twice ratified that interpretation in subsequent amendments to the Act."[69] "Congress' acquiescence to a settled judicial interpretation can suggest adoption of that interpretation"; however, "when Congress has not comprehensively revised a statutory scheme but has made only isolated amendments... it is impossible to assert with any degree of assurance that congressional failure to act represents affirmative congressional approval of a court's statutory interpretation."[70] Because the amendments did not address the scope of section 13(b), they did not convince the Court in *AMG* that Congress had acquiesced in the lower courts' interpretation.[71]

The court in *National Petroleum Refiners* also lauded the benefits of rulemaking authority and emphasized that the ability to promulgate rules would allow the FTC to carry out the purpose of the Act.[72] But the Supreme Court has emphasized that "however sensible (or not)" an interpretation may be, "a reviewing court's task is to apply the text of the statute, not to improve upon it."[73] "[P]ractical difficulties... do not justify departure from [a statute's] plain text."[74] Whatever benefits UMC rulemaking authority may confer on the FTC, they cannot justify departure from the text of the FTC Act.

---

65 *AMG*, 141 S. Ct. at 1345–46.

66 Loving v. IRS, 742 F.3d 1013, 1021 (D.C. Cir. 2014) ("In light of the text, history, structure, and context of the statute, it becomes apparent that the IRS never before adopted its current interpretation for a reason: It is incorrect."); *see* Fin. Plan. Ass'n v. SEC, 482 F.3d 481, 490 (D.C. Cir. 2007) ("[A]n additional weakness exists in the SEC's interpretation: It flouts six decades of consistent SEC understanding of its authority under [the statute]."). *See also* Util. Air Regul. Grp. v. EPA, 573 U.S. 302, 324 (2014) (noting that courts are properly "skeptic[al]" when "an agency claims to discover in a long-extant statute an unheralded power" to issue major regulations); Bankamerica Corp. v. United States, 462 U.S. 122, 131 (1983) ("[J]ust as established practice may shed light on the extent of power conveyed by general statutory language, so the want of assertion of power by those who presumably would be alert to exercise it, is equally significant in determining whether such power was actually conferred."); cf. Printz v. United States, 521 U.S. 898, 905 (1997) (reasoning that if an asserted government power were "highly attractive" but nevertheless went long unused, "we would have reason to believe that the power was thought not to exist").

67 *AMG*, 141 S. Ct. at 1351. *See also* Bona, *supra* note 14.

68 *AMG*, 141 S. Ct. at 1351 (noting 8-2 circuit split).

69 *Id.*

70 *Id.* (cleaned up).

71 *Id.*

72 *Nat'l Petroleum Refiners Ass'n*, 482 F.2d at 681–91.

73 EPA v. EME Homer City Generation, L.P., 572 U.S. 489, 508–09 (2014) (cleaned up).

74 *Id.* at 509.

In sum, even *Chevron* requires the agency to rely on a "permissible construction" of the statute,[75] and it is doubtful that the current Supreme Court would see a broad assertion of substantive antitrust rulemaking as "permissible" under the vague language of section 6(g).

Additionally, because the FTC Act fails to provide for any sanctions for violations of rules promulgated pursuant to section 6, this seems to indicate that Congress never intended to give the FTC substantive rulemaking authority at all.[76] Even scholars who believe section 6(g) confers competition rulemaking authority have noted this ambiguity and have pointed out that while the FTC Act may technically confer rulemaking authority, the Act does not specify that those rules would be binding.[77] Importantly, the FTC is the only entity with authority to enforce the FTC Act's prohibition on unfair methods of competition.[78] It would therefore be very odd for Congress to grant the FTC sole UMC rulemaking authority, yet not arm the agency (or anyone else) with the means to enforce violations of those rules. By contrast, Congress clearly provided the FTC in Magnuson-Moss the authority to initiate civil actions for UDAP rule violations. Section 205(a) of Magnuson-Moss[79] amended section 5 of the FTC Act to permit the FTC to commence a civil action to recover a civil penalty against a party that knowingly violates a UDAP rule,[80] and section 206(a) of Magnuson-Moss[81] created a section 19 of the FTC Act that authorizes the FTC to commence a civil action against a party that violates a UDAP rule.[82] Notably, Magnuson-Moss did not authorize civil actions by the FTC for UMC rule violations. The creation of an enforcement scheme for violations of UDAP rules and the lack of any such scheme for UMC rules strongly signals that Congress did not ratify the holding of *National Petroleum Refiners* for UMC rulemaking.

Further, both the FTC's arguments in *AMG* and the prospect of UMC rulemaking reflect a turn away from the FTC's traditional role as an influencer in the antitrust arena through its expert case-by-case adjudications, instead taking a "shortcut" to results in federal court or through broad rulemaking. The Supreme Court clearly

75 *Chevron*, 467 U.S. at 843.

76 Am. Bar Ass'n, *supra*, note 57, at 54 (asserting that the Act's "fail[ure] to provide any sanctions for violating any rule adopted pursuant to Section 6(g)... strongly suggest[s] that Congress did not intend to give the agency substantive rulemaking powers when it passed the Federal Trade Commission Act") (internal citations omitted).

77 Rebecca Haw, *Amicus Briefs and the Sherman Act: Why Antitrust Needs a New Deal*, 89 Tex. L. Rev. 1247, 1288 (2011) ("But Congress's delegation of rulemaking authority to the FTC was ambiguous in scope, allowing it to 'make such rules and regulations' but not specifying whether those rules would be binding.") (quoting Dominique Custos, *The Rulemaking Power of Independent Regulatory Agencies*, 54 Am. J. Comp. L. 615, 619 & n. 22 (2006)).

78 *See, e.g.*, Holloway v. Bristol-Myers Corp., 485 F.2d 986 (D.C. Cir. 1973).

79 Codified at 15 U.S.C. § 45(m).

80 15 U.S.C. § 45(m)(1)(A).

81 Codified at 15 U.S.C. § 57b.

82 15 U.S.C. § 57b(a)(1). These provisions also granted the FTC authority to initiate civil actions for certain violations of cease-and-desist orders respecting UDAP. 15 U.S.C. §§ 45(m)(1)(B), 57b(a)(2).

noted "the historical importance of [FTC's] administrative proceedings" in *AMG*, tracing the history of FTC's enforcement methods;[83] observed that the Commission "has been authorized to enforce the [FTC] Act through its own administrative proceedings" since its creation in 1914;[84] and stated that the Act includes special allowances of authority when the FTC uses its administrative process to impose "cease and desist orders."[85] While any challenge to future FTC competition rulemaking would be primarily focused on the specific text of the statute at issue, the Court has indicated that (at least where such language is ambiguous) its interpretation may be colored by the historic importance of the FTC administrative process and ways that the challenged authority deviates from that norm.

Some advocates for UMC rulemaking suggest that the widely accepted Merger Guidelines issued jointly by the FTC and the Department of Justice (DOJ) can serve as a model for such rules.[86] But there is a fundamental difference between nonbinding guidelines drafted to provide transparency to the public about the standards used in antitrust enforcement and rules promulgated with the force of law. The Horizontal Merger Guidelines were accepted as persuasive – rather than binding – authority after many federal courts had the opportunity to evaluate them, judge their consistency with the antitrust laws the agencies are tasked with enforcing, and apply their principles to the facts of numerous merger cases in conjunction with other evidence of competitive effects. An "unfair method of competition" rule would short-circuit that process because it would immediately have the force and effect of law, creating immediate liability for conduct that otherwise would have been subject to detailed, case-specific factual and economic analysis.

2. Constitutional Vulnerabilities

Compounding the shifting statutory sands underneath FTC's claimed authority for UMC rulemaking is the fact that the potential breadth of such rules and lack of clear guidance in section 6(g) itself leads to the distinct possibility that any such rule promulgated under section 6 runs afoul of the constitutional nondelegation doctrine.

The nondelegation doctrine requires Congress to provide "an intelligible principle" to assist the agency to which it has delegated legislative discretion.[87] Although long considered moribund, the doctrine was recently addressed by

---

83 *AMG*, 141 S. Ct. at 1348. *See also* Bona, *supra* note 14.

84 *AMG*, 141 S. Ct. at 1346.

85 *Id.* at 1349.

86 *See* Chopra & Khan, *supra* note 17, at 367 ("While they were not promulgated as agency rules, certain elements of the merger guidelines eventually came to serve as rules once courts adopted them. The merger guidelines stipulate the analytical framework that the agencies rely on to enforce the merger law. Agency rulemaking could do the same for 'unfair methods of competition.'").

87 J. W. Hampton, Jr., & Co. v. United States, 276 U.S. 394, 409 (1928).

the U.S. Supreme Court in *Gundy v. United States*,[88] underscoring that limits to Congress's ability to transfer unfettered legislative-like powers to federal agencies remain relevant. Although the statute in that case was ruled permissible by a plurality of justices, a majority of the Court's current members expressed concerns that the Court has long been too quick to reject nondelegation arguments, arguing for stricter controls in this area. In a concurrence, Justice Alito lamented that the Court has "uniformly rejected nondelegation arguments and has upheld provisions that authorized agencies to adopt important rules pursuant to extraordinarily capacious standards,"[89] while Justices Gorsuch, Roberts, and Thomas dissented, decrying the "unbounded policy choices"[90] Congress had bestowed, stating that it "is delegation running riot" to "hand off to the nation's chief prosecutor the power to write his own criminal code."[91]

The *Gundy* dissent cited to *A. L. A. Schechter Poultry Corp. v. United States*,[92] where the Supreme Court struck down Congress's delegation of authority based on language very similar to section 5 of the FTC Act. *Schechter Poultry* examined whether the authority that Congress granted to the President under the National Industrial Recovery Act (NIRA) violated the nondelegation clause. The offending NIRA provision gave the President authority to approve "codes of fair competition,"[93] which comes uncomfortably close to the FTC Act's "unfair methods of competition" grant of authority. Notably, *Schechter Poultry* expressly differentiated NIRA from the FTC Act based on distinctions that do not apply in the rulemaking context. Specifically, the Court stated that despite the similar delegation of authority, unlike NIRA, actions under the FTC Act are subject to an adjudicative process. The Court observed that the Commission serves as "a quasi judicial body" and assesses what constitutes unfair methods of competition "in particular instances, upon evidence, in the light of particular competitive conditions."[94] That essential distinction disappears in the case of rulemaking, where the Commission acts in a quasi-legislative role and promulgates rules of broad application.

Although Justice Kavanaugh did not participate in the *Gundy* ruling because he was not on the Court when the case was argued, he suggested shortly after *Gundy* that he too was interested in revisiting the Court's nondelegation jurisprudence, stating that "Justice Gorsuch's thoughtful *Gundy* opinion raised

88 Gundy v. United States, 139 S. Ct. 2116 (2019).

89 *Id.* at 2130–31.

90 *Id.* at 2133.

91 *Id.* at 2148.

92 A. L. A. Schechter Poultry Corp. v. United States, 295 U.S. 495 (1935).

93 *Id.* at 521–22 (citing National Industrial Recovery Act § 3).

94 *Id.* at 532–34.

important points that may warrant further consideration in future cases."[95] Further, Justice Kavanaugh recently highlighted the need to maintain the separation of powers demanded by the Constitution, suggesting a majority of the current Court may be inclined to strike down as excessively broad and amorphous a claim of rulemaking authority over "unfair methods of competition."

During the oral argument for *AMG Capital Management v. FTC*, discussed above, Justice Kavanaugh made comments implying a strong reticence to allow an expansive interpretation of the FTC's authority: "[W]ith good intentions, the agency pushes the envelope and stretches the statutory language to do the good or prevent the bad. The problem is [this] results in a transfer of power from Congress to the Executive Branch to decide whether to exercise this [] authority."[96] The same concerns apply with even greater force to FTC competition rulemaking, which casts the FTC directly in a legislative role under a highly vague grant of statutory authority.

It appears that the nondelegation doctrine may be poised for a revival and may play a significant role in the Supreme Court's evaluation of expansive attempts by the Biden administration to exercise legislative-type authority without explicit congressional authorization. This would create a challenging backdrop for the FTC to attempt aggressive new UMC rulemaking.

V. Antitrust Rulemaking by FTC Is Likely to Lead to Inefficient Outcomes and Institutional Conflicts

Aside from these significant statutory and constitutional issues raising doubts as to the legality of competition rulemaking by the FTC, there are also a number of policy and institutional factors counseling against broad, legislative-style antitrust rulemaking.

1. Legislative Rulemaking on Competition Issues Runs Contrary to the Purpose of Antitrust Law

The core of U.S. antitrust law is based on broadly drafted statutes that, at least for violations outside the criminal conspiracy context, leave determinations of likely anticompetitive effects, procompetitive justifications, and ultimate liability up to fact finders charged with highly detailed, case-specific determinations. Indeed, it is inherent in the "rule of reason" – the default legal framework for any antitrust claim not falling within the "red zone" of per se prohibited conduct – that the inquiry is deeply rooted in the history, effects, and context of each

95 Paul v. United States, 140 S. Ct. 342, 342 (2019) (Kavanaugh, J., statement regarding denial of certiorari).

96 Transcript of Oral Argument at 53, AMG Cap. Mgmt., LLC v. FTC, 141 S. Ct. 1341 (2021) (No. 19-508). *See also* Bona, *supra* note 14.

particular industry and practice being challenged. Although no fact finder is infallible, this requirement for highly fact-bound analysis helps to ensure that each case's outcome has a high likelihood of preserving or increasing consumer welfare. As detailed above, the FTC's administrative process is in some ways the pinnacle of this model, combining the concept of detailed case-specific factual inquiry with administrative law judges focused entirely on competition and consumer protection issues. On appeal, an ALJ's determinations are evaluated first by another panel of typically seasoned, well-advised antitrust experts – the Commission itself – and the final determinations of the Commission are entitled to significant deference should they be challenged in the courts of appeal.

Legislative rulemaking would replace this quintessential fact-based process with one-size-fits-all bright-line rules. Competition rules would function as per se-like prohibitions but based on notice-and-comment procedures rather than the broad and longstanding legal and economic consensus usually required for per se condemnation under the Sherman Act. Past experience with similar regulatory regimes should give reason for pause here: the Interstate Commerce Commission, for example, failed to efficiently regulate the railroad industry before being abolished with bipartisan consensus in 1996, costing consumers, by some estimates, as much as several billion (in today's) dollars per year in lost competitive benefits.[97] As FTC Commissioner Christine Wilson observes, regulatory rules "frequently stifle innovation, raise prices, and lower output and quality without producing concomitant health, safety, and other benefits for consumers."[98] By sacrificing the precision of case-by-case adjudication, rulemaking advocates are also losing one of the best tools we have to account for "market dynamics, new sources of competition, and consumer preferences."[99]

2. Potential for Institutional Conflict with DOJ

In addition to these substantive concerns, UMC rulemaking by FTC would also create institutional conflicts between the FTC and DOJ and lead to divergence between the legal standards applicable to the FTC Act, on the one hand, and the Sherman and Clayton Acts, on the other. At present, courts have interpreted the FTC Act to be generally coextensive with the prohibitions on unlawful mergers and anticompetitive conduct under the Sherman and Clayton Acts, with the limited exception of invitations to collude. But because

---

97 Christine S. Wilson & Keith Klovers, *The Growing Nostalgia for Past Regulatory Misadventures and the Risk of Repeating Those Mistakes with Big Tech*, 8 J. Antitrust Enf't 10, 13 (2020) (citing Brookings Institution study showing annual consumer harm of at least $500 million in the late 1960s, or around $4 billion per year adjusted for inflation).

98 Christine S. Wilson, Antitrust on the Antiques Roadshow: Appraising U.S. Antitrust Laws in a Modern Economy, Address Before the NetChoice "Defining the Digital Market" Event 11 (Apr. 27, 2021), https://www.ftc.gov/system/files/documents/public_statements/1589480/wilson-netchoice-keynote.pdf.

99 *Id.* at 12.

the FTC alone has the authority to enforce the FTC Act, and rulemaking by FTC would be limited to interpretations of that Act (and could not directly affect or repeal case law interpreting the Sherman and Clayton Acts), it would create two separate standards of liability. Given that the FTC and DOJ historically have divided enforcement between the agencies based on the industry at issue, this could result in different rules of conduct depending on the industry involved.[100] Types of conduct that have the *potential* for anticompetitive effects under certain circumstances but generally pass a rule-of-reason analysis could nonetheless be banned outright if the industry is subject to FTC oversight. Dissonance between the two federal enforcement agencies would be even more difficult for companies not falling firmly within either agency's purview; those entities would lack certainty as to which guidelines to follow: rule-of-reason precedent or FTC rules. In a further whipsaw, the agencies have of late opened competing investigations of the same conduct by the same company, which leads to additional legal dissonance and burden on the subject of the investigation. It could also create an uneven playing field between competitors who are overseen by different agencies, such as common carriers or banks (overseen solely by DOJ due to exemptions in the FTC Act) and non-common carrier communication providers or non-bank financial institutions, who may be subject to FTC oversight.

These institutional conflicts highlight a risk to the FTC from pursuing aggressive legislative-style rulemaking of triggering rebukes from Congress, much like the passage of the Magnuson-Moss Act after FTC's last rulemaking spree in decades past. For example, the One Agency Act, introduced in 2021 by Senator Lee,[101] would abolish the FTC's antitrust enforcement authority and consolidate its competition-related resources and cases with the DOJ Antitrust Division, citing "the risk of different industries receiving different antitrust enforcement" and the principle that "antitrust enforcement shouldn't hinge on a coin toss."[102] The One Agency Act is just the latest salvo by critics of the FTC in Congress; the Standard Merger and Acquisition Reviews Through Equal Rules Act, or SMARTER Act, has been a perennial threat to FTC's merger review authority for the last several years, passing in the House of Representatives several times over the past decade. Reintroduced most recently in October 2020,[103] the SMARTER Act would strip the FTC of its ability to adjudicate merger cases through its administrative process, forcing the Commission to litigate all mergers

---

100 *See* Maureen K. Ohlhausen, *Section 5 of the FTC Act: Principles of Navigation*, 2 J. Antitrust Enf't 1, 14 (2014) ("Of even greater concern, such use of UMC subjects businesses engaged in the same conduct to different liability standards based solely on the agency to which an investigation happens to be cleared. This could transform the FTC and DOJ's informal clearance procedures from a matter of administrative efficiency to a deciding factor for liability for certain conduct.").

101 One Agency Act, S. 633, 117th Cong. (2021).

102 Mike Lee, *One Agency for Antitrust*, Wall St. J., Nov. 17, 2020, https://www.wsj.com/articles/one-agency-for-antitrust-11605653810?fbclid=IwAR2uA1q6Z27XleHsL3Z0JB_gE2qKQvAia2KyhucRqbj2WgkFNAZBeTYY2v0.

103 Standard Merger and Acquisition Reviews Through Equal Rules Act of 2020, S. 4876, 116th Cong. (2020).

in federal court as the DOJ currently does.[104] The prospect of legislative UMC rulemaking would only serve to widen the disparity in standards applied by the FTC and DOJ, and thus add even more fuel to the fire of calls for reform of the FTC's authority in this area.

Following its rebuke at the Supreme Court in the *AMG* case, now is the time for the FTC to focus on its core, case-by-case administrative mission, taking full advantage of its unique adjudicative expertise, while also using its clearly authorized, targeted rulemaking authority where appropriate. Broad UMC rulemaking, however, would be an aggressive step in the wrong direction – away from FTC's core mission and towards a no-man's-land far afield from FTC's governing statutes.

104 Press Release, Sens. Lee Tillis Grassley Introduce SMARTER Antitrust Reform (Oct. 27, 2020), https://www.lee.senate.gov/public/index.cfm/2020/10/sens-lee-tillis-grassley-introduce-smarter-antirust-reform.

Regulatory Rents: An Agency-Cost Analysis of the FTC Rulemaking Initiative

JONATHAN M. BARNETT*
University of Southern California

Abstract

The Federal Trade Commission's initiative to use rulemaking powers to target "unfair methods of competition" under the FTC Act is part of a broader package of dramatic recent changes in antitrust enforcement policy and practice by FTC leadership. These changes, which have rejected the consumer-welfare standard and rule-of-reason balancing tests, represent a strategic effort to bypass the rigorous standards of federal antitrust case law and qualify for the deference generally accorded agency rulemaking by federal courts. Principal-agent analysis suggests that these changes, by detaching antitrust enforcement from antitrust case law and substituting regulatory discretion for structured guidelines, raise a significant risk that the agency will undertake actions that depart from its statutory mandate by targeting practices that do not pose any credible threat of competitive harm.

---

* Torrey H. Webb Professor of Law, Gould School of Law, University of Southern California. Comments are welcome at jbarnett@law.usc.edu.

I. Introduction

It has long been recognized that administrative agencies are exposed to capture by firms in the industries that they regulate.[1] Regulated firms are repeat players that often have lobbying resources to secure favorable treatment while individual regulators may have incentives to accrue goodwill among regulated firms to secure favorable employment positions after public service. Capture generally leads regulators to underenforce relative to their statutory mandate. Less attention has been paid, however, to the risk that regulators may overenforce relative to their statutory mandate. This may occur due to ideological commitments that override rule-of-law commitments or reputational incentives to secure "headline" monetary judgments or other dramatic remedies, which accrue goodwill for the agency in securing funding from the legislature and for individual regulators in securing other positions in public service or the private sector.[2] This scenario can be called regulatory *self*-capture.

Both the regulatory capture and self-capture scenarios can be analyzed within a principal-agent framework, which has been widely applied in the corporate governance literature to analyze the relationship between shareholders and managers. I apply this framework to assess the extent to which the proposed rulemaking initiative by the Federal Trade Commission (FTC), in which the agency seeks to pursue "unfair methods of competition" (UMC) outside the traditional avenue of case-by-case adjudication, increases agency-cost risks by facilitating enforcement actions against practices that do not pose any credible threat of competitive harm.

These concerns over regulatory self-capture are grounded in a sequence of actions and statements by FTC leadership[3] leading up to the announcement of the UMC rulemaking initiative in December 2021.[4] Those policy changes decoupled UMC enforcement from well-established case-law understandings of the Sherman and Clayton Acts, rejected the consumer welfare standard as a guiding enforcement principle, and adopted an unusually expansive understanding of the breadth of discretion accorded the agency to enforce section 5 of the FTC Act. Moreover, the agency has declined to provide any substitute definition of

1 For the classic treatment, *see* George J. Stigler, *The Theory of Economic Regulation*, 2 Bell J. Econ. & Mgmt. Sci. 3 (1971).

2 On the reputational incentives that drive prosecutors to seek to maximize financial awards, *see* Margaret H. Lemos & Max Minzner, *For-Profit Public Enforcement*, 127 Harv. L. Rev. 854, 856–57 (2014).

3 "FTC leadership" refers to the chair and the majority commissioners, given that almost all actions described in this contribution were publicly opposed by the minority commissioners. At the time of this writing, the composition of the Commission is as follows, with party affiliation designated as "D" (Democrat) or "R" (Republican) in parentheses: Chair Lina M. Khan (D); Commissioner Rebecca Kelly Slaughter (D); Commissioner Noah Joshua Phillips (R); Commissioner Christine S. Wilson (R). Until October 12, 2021, Rohit Chopra (D) served as a commissioner.

4 Fed. Trade Comm'n, Statement of Regulatory Priorities (Dec. 10, 2021), https://www.reginfo.gov/public/jsp/eAgenda/StaticContent/202110/Statement_3084_FTC.pdf [hereinafter FTC 2021].

UMC, leaving prosecutorial discretion largely unbounded by any constraining principle. Together these policy steps confer unprecedented authority to intervene in market transactions on the basis of an open-ended definition of "unfair" business practices. This conflation of lawmaking and law enforcement in an administrative entity raises significant concerns that regulators will take enforcement actions that do not conform to the agency's targeted statutory mandate to preserve competitive markets.

This chapter is organized as follows. In Section II, I apply the principal-agent framework to the antitrust context. In Section III, I describe recent policy changes by FTC leadership that expand the agency's ability to target purported UMC practices through litigation or rulemaking. In Section IV, I provide a strategic account of the agency's rulemaking initiative and related policy changes and apply the principal-agent model to assess the extent to which this policy shift is likely to increase agency-cost risks. A brief conclusion follows.

II. The Principal-Agent Model in the Antitrust Context

In this section, I apply a principal-agent model to the regulatory institutions mandated to enforce the federal antitrust laws. This exercise suggests that antitrust enforcement by regulatory authorities poses high agency-cost risks due to the inherent difficulty in anticipating and specifying business practices that have a "net" anticompetitive effect. Accordingly, it is expected that antitrust law designed in the public interest would favor high evidentiary standards and robust judicial scrutiny to minimize the risk that the regulator will deviate from its statutory mandate.

1. The Principal-Agent Model

The principal-agent model is a widely applied tool for evaluating any relationship in which a principal delegates authority to an agent to execute a particular action or set of actions. The classic example is the relationship between shareholders in a public corporation and the managers that run the corporation on a day-to-day basis,[5] but it can be applied more broadly. In business, governmental, and other organizations, principals delegate authority to agents for a variety of reasons that make it more efficient for the principal to retain the agent to perform a particular action or set of actions.

Following the principal-agent model, any potential efficiencies that arise as a result of any such delegation of authority must be offset against potential inefficiencies that arise as a result of failure by the agent to act in conformity with the principal's instructions. This may arise due to a variety of factors, including self-enrichment, shirking, or incompletely specified instructions.

5 For the classic source, *see* Michael C. Jensen & William H. Meckling, *Theory of the Firm: Managerial Behavior, Agency Costs and Ownership Structure*, 3 J. Fin. Econ. 305 (1976).

The principal's ability to deter deviations by the agent is inherently limited by transaction costs that limit the principal's ability to draft perfectly specified instructions to govern the agent's behavior or to perfectly monitor the agent's conformity to those instructions.

This framework can be applied to evaluate the relationship between the legislature, construed as the principal, and a regulator, construed as the agent. Just as dispersed shareholders in a public corporation accrue efficiency gains by delegating operational authority to managers, the members of the legislature (who are in turn agents of the voters) accrue efficiency gains by delegating implementation of a statute to the regulator. As the corporate governance literature recognizes, shareholders also incur a cost when delegating power to managers. Given the inability to specify managers' behavior in all circumstances or to monitor managers' behavior continuously, shareholders are exposed to the risk that managers will take actions that benefit themselves at the expense of the shareholders. Much of corporate law reflects an attempt to institute safeguards to align the interests of managers with shareholders, but without unduly impinging upon the managers' freedom of action, which would undercut the efficiency gains that arise from delegating authority to the managers in the first place.

The same logic applies in the political context. When establishing an administrative agency, legislators (and, by extension, the public represented by legislators) enjoy efficiency gains by empowering specialized regulators to implement the relevant statute. Yet this gain comes at a price. Regulators may deviate from the intent behind the statute in a manner that benefits themselves at the expense of the principal. Even setting aside outright corruption, regulators can benefit from deviations that satisfy their ideological preferences, preference for leisure, or pursuit of favorable positions in the private or public sector. This can lead to both under- and overenforcement relative to statutory intent. Much of administrative law is designed to minimize these deviations through various mechanisms, such as requiring that regulators provide notice and opportunity for public comment, undertake cost-benefit or other objective analysis of proposed regulations, make timely disclosures to the public, and provide parties targeted by regulatory action with a meaningful opportunity to challenge such action. At the same time, excessive safeguards would risk eliminating the efficiency gains that arise from delegating implementation to the regulator in the first place.

2. Using Legal Standards and Process to Minimize Agency Costs

While the principal-agent model anticipates that the agent will attempt to pursue its own interests at the expense of the principal, this risk varies in severity in different principal-agent relationships. In particular, this risk will tend to be higher as the principal's instructions decrease in specificity, which creates a "specification gap" that enables the agent to act in a manner that favors its interests over the principal. This relationship is reversed when the principal provides the agent with more specified instructions and is able to monitor compliance with those instructions.

The level of specification is not entirely a function of the investments made by the principal; rather, certain types of instructions are subject to an inherent "specification limit." That limit will vary depending on the type of action that is being specified. By way of illustration, the motor vehicle code can specify with precision the obligation to drive a motor vehicle up to a certain maximum speed. However, the motor vehicle code cannot specify with precision the obligation to drive a motor vehicle "responsibly," the interpretation of which can vary depending on particular circumstances. In general, rule-like obligations will tend to be situated at the higher end of the specification continuum, which gives rise to lower agency costs, while standard-like obligations will tend to be situated at the lower end of the specification continuum, which gives rise to higher agency costs.

The relationship between obligation type, specification costs, and agency-cost risks is important in the regulatory context because legislatures can use this relationship to manage the tradeoff between regulatory independence, which enhances the efficiency gains from delegating authority, and constraints on regulatory action, which limit the efficiency costs from delegating authority. In the case of legal obligations that have more rule-like characteristics and can be specified at a lower cost, those constraints can be relaxed; whereas the opposite policy should be followed in the case of legal obligations that have more standard-like characteristics and therefore exhibit higher specification costs. Constraints on regulatory action can be calibrated both through evidentiary standards and the mechanisms through which regulatory action is subject to external scrutiny and review.

In the antitrust context, these principles recommend that constraints on regulatory action should probably be high in most cases. That is because antitrust statutes mostly exhibit standard-like characteristics: there is no feasible objective definition of "restraints of trade" (section 1 of the Sherman Act), "monopolization" or "attempted monopolization" (section 2 of the Sherman Act) or "unfair methods of competition" (section 5 of the FTC Act),[6] in each case as distinguished from the large set of business practices that pose no material risk of competitive harm. Everything else being equal, a legislature that delegated authority to a regulator to implement these standard-like legal obligations but sought to minimize agency costs would constrain regulatory independence given the difficulty of drafting highly specified legislative instructions. In practice, this has been accomplished in antitrust law through judicial development of

6 For the statutory sources, *see* 15 U.S.C. §§ 1, 2, 45(a).

the various forms of rule-of-reason analysis, which anchor the identification of most antitrust violations in an evidence-intensive framework that balances benefits and harms to competition,[7] subjecting a regulatory agency's assertions to review by a disinterested party in a forum in which the defendant is entitled to the highest levels of due process. As I will show, FTC leadership has taken steps designed to remove or mitigate these constraints on the agency's scope of action and minimize its exposure to external scrutiny.

3. Summing Up

This discussion has applied the agency-cost framework to derive general principles that a publicly minded legislature would be expected to follow in designing the constraints – specifically, the evidentiary standard and review mechanism – under which a regulator operates when implementing a particular statute. In the antitrust context, it is expected that those constraints – both substantive and procedural – would tend to be significant since most offenses under the antitrust statutes have a standard-like quality, which implies that the "instructions" delivered to the agent will not be well specified. The UMC offenses targeted in the FTC Act have an especially strong standard-like quality, in light of statutory language that refers to "unfair methods of competition," a phrase that lacks any well-developed interpretation in regulatory guidance or case-law interpretation. Hence, an efficient institutional design would seek to minimize agency-cost risks, without unduly restricting the agency's enforcement capacities, by adopting a reasonably high evidentiary burden and requiring that the regulator demonstrate to an independent decision-maker that it has met this burden in any particular enforcement action.

III. Regulatory Shift at the FTC

The FTC's rulemaking initiative is part of a broader package of procedural and substantive changes that have been undertaken by FTC leadership since the start of the Biden administration in January 2021. In this section, I describe how the significant changes made by FTC leadership to certain long-standing enforcement principles and procedures work together with the agency's initiative to expand the use of its purported rulemaking powers concerning UMC under section 5 of the FTC Act.

1. Legal Roadblocks to Populist Antitrust

The FTC's rulemaking initiative did not emerge in a vacuum. It reflects support across large swaths of the political spectrum, as reflected in the 2020 report issued by the majority members of the U.S. House of Representatives Committee

7 On the rule of reason, *see* Herbert Hovenkamp, *The Rule of Reason*, 70 Fla L. Rev. 81 (2018).

on the Judiciary,[8] proposed legislation at the federal and state levels, and litigation by federal and state enforcers, for expansive application of the antitrust laws to target reportedly excessive concentration levels and anticompetitive practices in markets dominated by leading technology companies. Populist arguments in favor of dramatic structural remedies against digital platforms often pay little attention to well-established antitrust principles that require in most cases a showing of actual or likely competitive harm to support such remedies. This generally requires a specific definition of the relevant market followed by a fact-intensive demonstration that the defendant exerts market power and uses such power for anticompetitive purposes. Policymakers who seek to constrain digital platforms through antitrust litigation but cannot show market power and competitive harm might face a legal dead end since, outside cases involving horizontal collusion, courts generally insist on these evidentiary predicates. This is illustrated by the FTC's ongoing suit against Meta Platforms (Facebook's parent company), which was initially dismissed in June 2021 due to the agency's failure to provide evidence showing that it would be able to demonstrate with a reasonable likelihood that the defendant had market power.[9]

There are potential detours around this judicial roadblock through legislative or regulatory action. Congress may intervene by enacting legislation that obligates courts to issue certain remedies against digital platforms and other companies that exceed certain size thresholds or prohibits certain practices that are deemed inherently to pose a high risk of anticompetitive harm.[10] This same objective may be achieved by federal antitrust agencies that deploy rulemaking powers to issue regulations to the same effect, provided that the governing statute grants such powers to the agency.

There are two critical differences between legislative and regulatory detours around the case law's evidentiary predicates for bringing a cause of action under the antitrust statutes. The first difference favors regulatory action; the second favors legislative action.

Legislative action usually has high transaction costs and, as a result, often has a low likelihood of enactment. Legislative action involves a deliberative process that requires assembling support from elected representatives who may have only somewhat overlapping policy preferences. This may either block legislative action or result in a statute that is heavily modified to secure sufficient support. By contrast, regulatory action does not require gaining support through the

---

8 Subcommittee on Antitrust, Commercial and Administrative Law of the Committee on the Judiciary, Majority Staff Report and Recommendations, Investigation of Competition in Digital Markets (2020), https://judiciary.house.gov/uploadedfiles/competition_in_digital_markets.pdf?utm_campaign=4493-519 [hereinafter Subcommittee Report].

9 Cat Zakrzewski & Rachel Lerman, *Court says FTC hasn't provided evidence Facebook is a monopoly, dismisses lawsuit*, Wash. Post, June 28, 2021, https://www.washingtonpost.com/technology/2021/06/28/ftc-facebook-antitrust-complaint-dismissed.

10 On legislation of this type that has been proposed, *see* Jay B. Sykes, Cong. Rsch. Serv., R46875, The Big Tech Antitrust Bills (Aug. 13, 2021), https://sgp.fas.org/crs/misc/R46875.pdf.

voting process and, in certain cases, may be executed without the delays associated with extensive public deliberation. Nonetheless, the costs and delays associated with notice-and-comment and other process requirements under federal administrative law can be considerable and, as discussed subsequently,[11] it is not clear that rulemaking is always faster or less costly compared to adjudication.

Second, the legal scope of legislative action is far broader than the legal scope of administrative action by a particular agency. While the scope of legislative action at the federal level is only constrained by constitutional limitations, the scope of administrative action is limited to the specific powers delegated to the agency by statute and is therefore exposed to legal challenges that the agency has acted beyond its statutory mandate. Illustrating this risk, the Supreme Court in *AMG Capital Management, LLC v. FTC*, a 2021 decision, narrowly construed the FTC's statutory powers to seek injunctive relief under section 13(b) of the FTC Act,[12] holding that those powers did not clearly specify, and therefore did not encompass, the FTC's historical practice of seeking monetary disgorgement remedies under that provision.[13]

2. The Regulatory Shift

In 2021, FTC leadership took actions that depart from the incremental process through which antitrust law, both through case law and regulatory guidelines, has generally developed. In short order, FTC leadership abrogated long-standing enforcement principles and policies, often without providing meaningful opportunities for public comment as has been the agency's settled practice, especially when making major changes in agency policy.[14] In particular, FTC leadership withdrew certain foundational guidelines of antitrust enforcement but declined to issue new guidelines, leaving regulatory discretion substantially unconstrained by any clearly stated decision-making framework.

The agency's swift expansion of the scope of its regulatory powers and blanket dismissal of decades of federal antitrust case law and agency guidelines run counter to the view that administrative action is a practically expedient exception to Congress's constitutional monopoly on lawmaking powers and, as reflected in the procedural requirements of the Administrative Procedure Act (APA),[15] should

---

11 *See infra* note 66 and accompanying discussion.

12 15 U.S.C. § 57(a).

13 AMG Capital Management, LLC, et al. v. FTC, No. 19-508, slip op. (Apr. 22, 2021), 593 U.S. ____ (2021). *See* Steven A. Reed, Scott A. Stempel & Daniel S. Savrin, *The US Supreme Court holds that the FTC lacks the authority to seek equitable monetary relief in cases brought in federal court under FTC Act Section 13(b) (AMG Capital Management)*, e-Competitions April 2021, art. No. 100669.

14 Dissenting Statement of Commissioners Noah Joshua Phillips and Christine S. Wilson on the "Statement of the Commission on the Withdrawal of the Statement of Enforcement Principles Regarding 'Unfair Methods of Competition' Under Section 5 of the FTC Act" 1 (July 9, 2021), https://www.ftc.gov/system/files/documents/public_statements/1591710/p210100phillipswilsondissentsec5enforcementprinciples.pdf (noting that the Commission withdrew the 2015 Statement "with next to no notice or public input").

15 60 Stat 237 (1946) (codified as amended in various sections of Title 5).

therefore be used in a manner that makes a special effort to preserve due process, notice, and transparency principles.[16] In particular, this form of regulatory unilateralism pays no heed to the concerns over administrative overreach expressed by the Supreme Court in several recent decisions. This includes not only *AMG Capital Management*, as discussed immediately above, but also *National Federation of Independent Business et al. v. Department of Labor, et al.*, a 2022 decision in which the Court struck down a vaccine mandate issued by the Occupational Safety and Health Administration, on grounds of lack of specific statutory authority.[17] In a 2016 decision that upheld a statutory provision that immunizes certain decisions by a U.S. patent office tribunal from judicial appeal, these same concerns were expressed in a dissenting opinion by Justices Gorsuch and Sotomayor, who stated that the Court's decision "carries us another step down the road of ceding core judicial powers to agency officials and leaving the disposition of private rights and liberties to bureaucratic mercy."[18] Continuing to show concern over these issues, the Court in January 2022 granted certiorari in *Axon Enterprise, Inc. v. FTC*, a pending case that raises the question of whether a defendant in an FTC administrative litigation can bring a declaratory judgment action in federal court to contest the constitutionality of the agency's internal litigation process.

Table 1 lists chronologically certain actions and statements by FTC leadership since January 2021 that culminated in the announced rulemaking initiative at the end of the year. For the sake of brevity, the table omits changes specific to the merger review process.

Table 1. Significant Changes in FTC Antitrust Policy (2021)

Date	Action or Statement	Expands Agency Powers?	Dissenting Commissioners
Mar. 25, 2021	Forms new rulemaking group	Yes	N/a
July 1, 2021	Withdrawal of Statement of Enforcement Principles	Yes	Phillips, Wilson
July 1, 2021	Issues "omnibus" enforcement resolutions	Yes	Phillips, Wilson
July 1, 2021	Modifies Rules of Practice	Yes	Phillips, Wilson
Sept. 15, 2021	Withdrawal of Vertical Merger Guidelines	Yes	Phillips, Wilson
Dec. 10, 2021	Announces intention to expand UMC rulemaking activities	Yes	Phillips, Wilson

Note: Commissioner is deemed to dissent if commissioner votes against the action or, in the absence of a vote, makes an official public statement expressing disagreement with the relevant action.

16 On this view, *see* PETER H. SCHUCK, FOUNDATIONS OF ADMINISTRATIVE LAW 53 (Foundation Press 1994); Evan J. Criddle, *When Delegation Begets Domination: Due Process of Administrative Lawmaking*, 46 GA. L. REV. 117, 121–24 (2011). For extensive related discussion, *see* PHILIP HAMBURGER, IS ADMINISTRATIVE LAW UNLAWFUL? (University of Chicago Press 2014).

17 Nat'l Fed'n of Indep. Bus. v. Dep't of Lab., Occupational Safety & Health Admin., 595 U. S. __, 142 S. Ct. 661 (2022).

18 Thryv, Inc. v. Click-to-Call Technologies, LP, 140 S. Ct. 1367, 1378 (2020) (Gorsuch, J., dissenting).

3. July 1, 2021: The "New" FTC Emerges

The agency's policy changes seek to minimize constraints on its freedom to undertake enforcement actions under applicable antitrust statutes, comprised by the Sherman Act, the Clayton Act, and the FTC Act. Out of all the recent changes made by FTC leadership, the most significant is almost certainly the statement on July 1, 2021 (the July 2021 Statement) announcing the withdrawal of the FTC's 2015 statement concerning the principles that guide the agency's actions against UMC under section 5 of the FTC Act (the 2015 Statement).[19] FTC leadership announced the policy change only one week prior to voting on and adopting it,[20] which is the minimum required by law[21] but inconsistent with historical practice concerning such a significant change in agency policy.

The July 2021 statement, from which two commissioners dissented, has two important elements that undermine foundational elements of modern antitrust law and practice. These changes were accompanied by significant modifications to the agency's Rules of Practice and sweeping "omnibus" resolutions authorizing investigations into substantial portions of the U.S. economy. Together these steps led up to the rulemaking initiative announced in December 2021.

First, the July 2021 Statement rejected the consumer welfare standard that remains the bedrock principle behind the federal courts' application of the antitrust statutes and has occupied that position at least since the late 1970s.[22] The July 2021 Statement also rejected the applicability in section 5 enforcement actions of the rule of reason, which has been a core element of antitrust jurisprudence since at least the Supreme Court's 1911 decision in *U.S. v. Standard Oil*.[23] Removing these two foundational principles eliminates the two most significant constraints on prosecutorial discretion in taking action against alleged UMC.

These policy changes substantially expand the scope of the FTC's enforcement powers and, by lowering its evidentiary burden, enhance the agency's ability to prevail in internal administrative proceedings or litigation in federal court. Under

---

19 Statement of Chair Lina M. Khan, Joined by Commissioner Rohit Chopra and Commissioner Rebecca Kelly Slaughter on the Withdrawal of the Statement of Enforcement Principles Regarding "Unfair Methods of Competition" Under Section 5 of the FTC Act (July 1, 2021), https:/www.ftc.gov/system/files/documents/public_statements/1591498/final_statement_of_chair_khan_joined_by_rc_and_rks_on_section_5_0.pdf [hereinafter Statement of Chair July 2021]. For the 2015 Statement, *see* Fed. Trade Comm'n, Statement of Enforcement Principles Regarding "Unfair Methods of Competition" Under Section 5 of the FTC Act (Aug. 13, 2015), https:/www.ftc.gov/system/files/documents/public_statements/735201/150813section5enforcement.pdf [hereinafter FTC 2015].

20 Dissenting Remarks of Commissioner Noah Joshua Phillips Regarding the Commission's Withdrawal of the Section 5 Policy Statement (July 1, 2021), https://www.ftc.gov/legal-library/browse/cases-proceedings/public-statements/dissenting-remarks-commissioner-noah-joshua-phillips-regarding-commissions-withdrawal-section-5-0.

21 5 U.S.C. § 552b(e)(1).

22 *See, e.g.*, National Collegiate Athletic Ass'n v. Board of Regents of Univ. of Okla., 468 U.S. 85, 107 (1984) (citing Reiter v. Sonotone Corp., 442 U.S. 330, 344 (1979) (characterizing the Sherman Act as a "consumer welfare prescription")).

23 221 U.S. 1, 61–62 (1911).

the consumer welfare standard, a plaintiff must generally show that a challenged practice actually has, or is likely to have, a substantial adverse effect on competition, as distinguished from an adverse effect solely on a particular competitor. Applying this principle to the section 5 context, former FTC Chair Leibowitz had stated that the FTC should only bring standalone section 5 actions in "cases where there is clear harm to the competitive process and to consumers."[24] Under the rule of reason, a plaintiff must further show that any adverse competitive effect outweighs countervailing efficiencies reasonably attributable to the challenged practice, which is necessary to avoid erroneously prohibiting a practice that is "on net" procompetitive.[25]

Second, the July 2021 Statement substantially expanded the set of practices that could be deemed UMC by the agency in undertaking enforcement action. The 2015 Statement had reiterated a long-held understanding that the FTC, even when bringing standalone section 5 cases against alleged UMC, would be "guided by" the consumer welfare principle and rule-of-reason standard that the case law had developed under the Sherman and Clayton Acts.[26] The rationale behind this nuanced approach was threefold: to avoid divergent treatment of business practices across the various antitrust laws, to take advantage of the decades of learning embodied in antitrust case law, and to recognize the limited additional latitude provided to the FTC under section 5 as a "gap-filler" to address certain practices that raise competition concerns but are not clearly captured by the Sherman or Clayton Acts.[27] In contrast, the July 2021 statement held that UMC encompassed a broader set of "unfair" business practices that could not be targeted under other antitrust statutes, with the explicit aim of decoupling section 5 from Sherman Act case law.[28] Additionally, FTC leadership expressed the view that Congress "chose to leave it to the Commission to determine which practices fell into the category of 'unfair methods of competition.'"[29] The July 2021's expansive interpretation of the agency's section 5 enforcement powers would seem to be precisely the type of strained statutory reading that the Supreme Court had unanimously rejected less than three months earlier when it had rejected the agency's position that its injunctive powers under the

---

24 *Oversight of the Federal Trade Commission Bureau of Competition and the Department of Justice Antitrust Division: Hearing Before the H. Comm. on the Judiciary*, 111th Cong., at 13 (2010).

25 *See* Hovenkamp, *supra* note 7.

26 FTC 2015, *supra* note 19.

27 Former Commissioner Ohlhausen raises the important point that the "gap-filler" justification may no longer be especially applicable since the scope of the Sherman Act has expanded significantly under case-law interpretations since 1914, the year in which the FTC Act was enacted. It may therefore be reasonable to view section 5 as being largely "coextensive" with the Sherman and Clayton Acts, with a possible exception for invitations to collude and certain exchanges of sensitive information among competitors. *See* Section 5: Principles of Navigation, Remarks of Maureen K. Ohlhausen, Commissioner, Federal Trade Commission, U.S. Chamber of Commerce, Washington, D.C., at 16 (July 25, 2013), http://www.ftc.gov/sites/default/files/documents/public_statements/section-5-principles-navigation/130725section5speech.pdf.

28 Statement of Chair July 2021, *supra* note 19.

29 *Id.* at 3.

FTC Act encompassed disgorgement remedies despite the absence of any specific statutory language to that effect.[30]

On the same day that FTC leadership abandoned the consumer welfare standard and the rule of reason as guiding principles in pursuing UMC, it also adopted resolutions that enable individual commissioners to authorize the use of "compulsory process" (such as the use of subpoenas) in support of investigations into possible UMC violations in large industry sectors, including technology companies, digital platforms, health care, and pharmaceuticals.[31] This departs from historical practice at the agency, which had required consideration by the full Commission to initiate the use of compulsory process in support of an investigation (although approval by an individual commissioner was sufficient to approve subsequent subpoena requests within the context of the same investigation), supplemented by the issuance of a resolution explaining the purpose and scope of the investigation.[32] By discarding these procedural safeguards, the omnibus resolutions reduce transaction costs but increase the risk that the agency could use its investigative powers in a manner that departs from legislative intent, since the use of those powers only requires approval by a single commissioner, apparently without any requirement to provide a publicly available explanation for granting such approval.

4. Summing Up

The FTC's rejection of the consumer welfare standard for section 5 purposes enables the agency to take action against purported UMC that stand outside the reasonably understood purview of the antitrust laws and the agency's mandate to preserve competitive markets. The rejection of the rule of reason and its balancing-test methodology implies that the agency is willfully assuming the risk of false-positive enforcement errors by potentially prohibiting practices that make consumers better off. Moreover, given the failure to adopt new principles and methodologies to guide enforcement action, section 5 has effectively been converted into a legislative blank check to target practices deemed to be "unfair" by regulatory fiat. While FTC leadership stated in its July 2021 Statement that, even in the absence of clearly defined enforcement principles, "the Commission will exercise responsibly its prosecutorial discretion... consistent with legal precedent,"[33] these changes enable regulators to take enforcement actions that appear to be subject to few constraints other

---

30 *AMG Capital Management*, 593 U.S.

31 Statement of Commissioner Rebecca Kelly Slaughter Joined by Chair Lina Khan and Commissioner Rohit Chopra Regarding the Adoption of Revised Section 18 Rulemaking Practices (July 1, 2021), https://www.ftc.gov/legal-library/browse/cases-proceedings/public-statements/statement-commissioner-rebecca-kelly-slaughter-joined-chair-lina-m-khan-commissioner-rohit-chopra.

32 Debbie Feinstein, C. Scott Lent, Matthew Tabas & Samantha Shulman, *FTC Open Meeting Announces Expansion of FTC's Antitrust Enforcement Focus*, Arnold & Porter (July 8, 2021), https://www.arnoldporter.com/en/perspectives/publications/2021/07/ftc-open-meeting-announces-expansion.

33 Statement of Chair July 2021, *supra* note 19, at 7.

than the commissioners' subjective determination of what constitutes an "unfair" business practice and equally subjective determination of what constitutes a "responsible" exercise of prosecutorial discretion. It is hard to see how this "just trust us" approach reflects a meaningful commitment to minimize the agency-cost risks that are inherent to any delegation of enforcement power by legislators to regulators.

IV. Assessing the Agency Costs of the FTC Rulemaking Initiative

This section comprises two components. First, I provide an account of the strategic objectives reflected in the FTC's rulemaking initiative and accompanying policy changes during the preceding twelve-month period. Second, I assess the extent to which the proposed rulemaking initiative is likely to give rise to agency costs in the form of regulatory capture or self-capture, with a focus placed on the latter contingency.

1. A Strategic Account of the Rulemaking Initiative

The policy changes undertaken by FTC leadership reflect a strategic effort to bolster the agency's regulatory authority by adopting a generous interpretation of section 5 that expands the set of practices that can be deemed a UMC while concurrently dismissing the rule of reason's demanding balancing-test methodology. Yet even these significant policy shifts do not provide a secure detour around the roadblock posed by case law's commitment to the consumer welfare standard and, outside the limited set of "per se" illegal practice, the rule of reason, in interpreting and applying the antitrust laws. Any particular cause of action brought by the agency under its broad interpretation of section 5 may not survive a challenge in court, which may adhere to case law that tends to treat even standalone section 5 claims using the standards that would apply to similar claims under the Sherman or Clayton Acts. When the agency has sought to bring standalone section 5 claims that venture substantially beyond the contours set forth in case law under the Sherman or Clayton Acts, the courts have not been persuaded that this conformed to rational legislative design.[34] A federal court explained its concerns on this point: "[S]ome workable standard must exist for what is or is not to be considered an unfair method of competition under § 5. Otherwise, companies subject to FTC prosecution would be the victims of 'uncertain guesswork rather than workable rules of law.'"[35] Recognizing the

34 *See, e.g.*, FTC v. Abbott Labs, 853 F. Supp. 526, 535–36 (D.D.C. 1994); Boise Cascade Corp. v. FTC, 637 F.2d 573, 577–82 (9th Cir. 1980); E.I. du Pont de Nemours & Co. v. FTC, 729 F.2d 128, 136–40 (2d Cir. 1984); Official Airlines Guides, Inc v. FTC, 630 F.2d 920, 927–28 (2d Cir. 1980). *But see* FTC v. Sperry & Hutchinson Co., 405 U.S. 233, 244 (1972) (holding that the FTC can take into account "public values beyond simply those enshrined in the letter or encompassed in the spirit of the antitrust laws").

35 *Abbott Labs*, 853 F. Supp. at 535–36 (quoting E. I. du Pont de Nemours & Co. v. FTC, 729 F.2d 128 at 139 (2d Cir. 1984)).

agency-cost risks inherent to the delegation of regulatory power, another court had observed that an expansive understanding of section 5 might lead to enforcement actions that reflect "social, political, or personal reasons" rather than an objective assessment of competitive harm.[36]

The failures of past UMC litigations to pass muster under judicial review might explain why FTC leadership seeks to shift at least some section 5 enforcement from adjudication to rulemaking, which, for reasons explained below, would likely enable the agency to operate under a relaxed level of judicial scrutiny.

In March 2021, the agency announced the formation of a rulemaking group to "streamline" the rulemaking process.[37] In December 2021, the agency published its Annual Regulatory Plan for 2022, in which it stated its intentions to expand its UMC-related rulemaking activity, in part on the ground that a case-by-case adjudicative approach had resulted in a "hyper-concentrated economy."[38] In announcing its rulemaking initiative, the agency specifically explained that the shift to enforcement through rulemaking was motivated in part by the Court's decision in *AMG Capital Management* (which, as noted previously, had rejected the agency's view that its explicit authority under the FTC Act to seek injunctive relief implicitly encompassed the authority to seek monetary disgorgement).[39] However, *AMG Capital Management* does not necessarily preclude the agency from making a rule prohibiting certain practices as UMC (so long as the agency in fact has such statutory authority), providing for monetary damages, and then enforcing the rule against entities that are deemed to have engaged in such practices. According to views expressed previously by FTC Chair Khan and former Commissioner Chopra,[40] the agency purportedly has UMC rulemaking authority under section 6(g) of the FTC Act, which generally refers to the power "to make rules or regulations for the purpose of carrying out the provisions of" the FTC Act.[41] Given the scope of this contribution, I note that this interpretation of the statute has been contested by other commentators (who observe that the

---

36 *Official Airlines Guides*, 630 F.2d at 927.

37 Fed. Trade Comm'n, Acting Chairwoman Slaughter Announces New Rulemaking Group (Mar. 25, 2021), https://www.ftc.gov/news-events/news/press-releases/2021/03/ftc-acting-chairwoman-slaughter-announces-new-rulemaking-group.

38 FTC 2021, *supra* note 4, at 1.

39 *AMG Capital Management*, 593 U.S.

40 Rohit Chopra & Lina M. Khan, *The Case for "Unfair Methods of Competition" Rulemaking*, 87 U. Chi. L. Rev. 357, 375–79 (2020).

41 15 U.S.C. § 46(g). FTC leadership relies as well on Nat'l Petroleum Refiners Ass'n v. FTC, 482 F.2d 672, 698 (D.C. Cir. 1973) ("We hold that under the terms of its governing statute… and under Section 6(g)… in particular, the Federal Trade Commission is authorized to promulgate rules defining the meaning of the statutory standards of the illegality the Commission is empowered to prevent."). However, as observed by Maureen Ohlhausen and James Rill, the decision appears to have been qualified by the enactment of the Magnuson-Moss Warranty Act in 1975 (*see* Maureen K. Ohlhausen & James Rill, *Pushing the Limits? A Primer on FTC Competition Rulemaking*, U.S. Chamber of Com. 10–11 (Aug. 12, 2021), https://www.uschamber.com/assets/archived/images/ftc_rulemaking_white_paper_aug12.pdf), which provides extensive notice-and-comment and related procedures for formulating rules concerning specified "unfair or deceptive acts or practices" (*see* 15 U.S.C. § 57a(1)(A)). Moreover, the statute appears to take an agnostic position concerning any potential rulemaking authority the FTC may retain concerning UMC, *see* 15 U.S.C. § 57(a)

statute *does* specifically provide for rulemaking authority concerning "unfair or deceptive acts or practices" or UDAP and therefore gives rise to a negative implication that Congress did not specifically authorize the use of such rulemaking authority concerning UMC),[42] without addressing whether this interpretation is persuasive as a matter of statutory construction.

Enforcement through rulemaking rather than litigation achieves three key strategic objectives. First, rulemaking allows the agency to set "the rules of the game," which compares favorably with the inherently unpredictable outcome of an enforcement litigation (exacerbated in the antitrust context by the demanding pleading standards in a cause of action governed by the rule of reason). Second, rulemaking can be used to prohibit certain practices on a per se basis, relieving the agency in future enforcement actions from any probative burden other than showing that the defendant had engaged in the prohibited practice. This would detour around the strong presumption in federal antitrust case law against using rules of per se illegality except in the case of conduct that is "manifestly anticompetitive."[43] Third, so long as a court agreed that the agency had such rulemaking authority under the FTC Act, any rule adopted by the agency under such authority would then likely enjoy the deference accorded to regulatory interpretations of ambiguous statutes under the *Chevron* doctrine.[44] Importantly, *Chevron* deference applies so long as the agency has "a reasonable interpretation of the statute – not necessarily the only possible interpretation, nor even the interpretation deemed most reasonable by the courts."[45] By using section 6(g) rulemaking as an alternative mechanism for section 5 enforcement (and including sufficiently formal rulemaking procedures that courts often demand to grant *Chevron* deference[46]), the agency increases the likelihood that it will defeat legal challenges to any UMC-targeted rule it promulgates under such authority or any action it subsequently takes to enforce such a rule against specific business practices.

---

(2) (stating that the Commission's authority to prescribe rules concerning "unfair or deceptive acts or practices… shall not affect *any* authority of the Commission to prescribe rules… with respect to unfair methods of competition") (emphasis added). The use of the article "any" rather than "the" suggests an affirmative drafting choice not to resolve this question.

42 *See, e.g.*, Aurelien Portuese, American Precautionary Antitrust: Unrestrained FTC Rulemaking Authority, Information Technology & Innovation Foundation (Jan. 31, 2022), https://itif.org/publications/2022/01/31/american-precautionary-antitrust-unrestrained-ftc-rulemaking-authority; Ohlhausen & Rill, *supra* note 41, at 10–14.

43 Continental TV, Inc, v. GTE Sylvania, Inc., 433 U.S. 36, 49–50 (1977).

44 Chevron U.S.A., Inc, v. Natural Resources Defense Council, Inc., 467 U.S. 837 (1983). On this point specifically, *see* U.S. v. Mead Corp., 533 U.S. 221, 226–27 (2001) (holding that "[a]dministrative implementation of a particular statutory provision qualifies for *Chevron* deference when it appears that Congress delegated authority to the agency generally to make rules carrying the force of law, and that the agency interpretation claiming deference was promulgated by the exercise of [real] authority"). There is one potentially important qualification: as discussed subsequently, *see infra* notes 74–75, the Supreme Court's 2015 decision in Michigan v. Environmental Protection Agency, 576 U.S. __ (2015), suggests that, in certain contexts, *Chevron* deference might not apply if a court determines that agency rulemaking was not supported by a sufficient cost-benefit analysis.

45 Entergy Corp. v. Riverkeeper, Inc., 556 U.S. 208, 218 (2009).

46 Christensen v. Harris County, 529 U.S. 576, 587 (2000) (suggesting that *Chevron* deference is appropriate when an agency reaches a legally binding interpretation through formal procedures, such as notice-and-comment rulemaking).

It is now possible to appreciate the three-party strategy undertaken by FTC leadership to substantially expand its regulatory powers without seeking any specific legislative mandate. First, FTC leadership jettisoned established principles that had largely aligned standalone section 5 causes of action with the case law, and demanding evidentiary standards, that govern analogous causes of action under the Sherman and Clayton Acts. Second, FTC leadership declined to specify a substitute set of enforcement principles but rather took the view that the agency enjoys broad discretion to identify UMC for purposes of section 5. Third, FTC leadership indicated an intention to shift some UMC enforcement activity from litigation to rulemaking under its expansive interpretation of section 6(g) of the FTC Act. If that interpretation is upheld, then any UMC rules promulgated by the FTC may qualify for the deferential treatment federal courts typically accord agency rulemaking. In the aggregate, this three-step strategy would expand the set of practices that can be pursued as a UMC, empower the agency to prescribe rules that prohibit specified practices as per se antitrust violations, and deploy the "umbrella" of *Chevron* deference to shield from legal challenge any exercise of this rulemaking authority.

2. The Agency Costs of UMC Rulemaking

For purposes of the following discussion, I will set aside whether FTC leadership's expansive understanding of section 5 of the FTC Act and the rulemaking powers granted under section 6(g) of the FTC Act would survive judicial scrutiny, either as a matter of statutory or constitutional interpretation (both being far from theoretical questions given the concerns about administrative overreach expressed by the Court in several recent decisions[47]). Rather, I will discuss the extent to which this policy shift is likely to exacerbate agency-cost risks through regulatory deviations from statutory intent and, specifically, through overenforcement relative to the agency's targeted mission to preserve competitive markets. Following the analytical framework developed in Section II, it would be expected that antitrust enforcers would operate under significant constraints on regulatory independence and a high level of judicial scrutiny since the governing statute sets forth legal obligations that are difficult to specify fully, which inherently gives rise to agency-cost risks when enforcement powers are delegated by the legislature to a regulatory entity. These expectations are largely confirmed by the historical development of antitrust case law and agency guidelines, which has developed a rigorous framework for evaluating enforcement actions under the Sherman and Clayton Acts, and the consensus view that had anchored application of section 5 of the FTC Act in that same framework. Recent policy changes by FTC leadership remove these constraints on regulatory action and select an implementation mechanism – rulemaking rather than litigation – that is likely to qualify for a low level of judicial scrutiny. Given the standard-like language of section 5 of the

47 *See supra* note 17.

FTC Act, these changes restore the agency-cost risks that courts and agencies had sought to minimize by refinement over several decades of a nuanced and evidence-based framework to guide regulatory action and judicial review. Having largely rejected this analytical toolset, FTC leadership offers no assurance against regulatory departures from its statutory mandate other than a precatory statement that the agency will use its largely unbounded discretion "responsibly."[48]

These agency-cost concerns are not merely theoretical. As Commissioner Wilson has noted, the agency's previous significant attempt to expand substantially exercise of its rulemaking authority, following enactment of the Magnuson-Mass Warranty Act in 1975,[49] elicited a public outcry that resulted in legislative intervention (the Federal Trade Commission Improvements Act of 1980[50]) that "stripped [the FTC] of funding, stripped [the FTC] of legal authorities, and required [the FTC] to institute new and substantial rulemaking steps to foster public trust."[51] There are four reasons that support a significant risk that the agency is heading again in the same direction (although, in the current political climate, a similar legislative counterreaction seems unlikely at present).

A. *Rulemaking by Fiat*

UMC are defined in the FTC Act using vague language, and there is no well-developed body of case law or regulatory guidance that has specifically refined that definition. As a matter of historical practice, courts and the agency (for example, in the 2015 Statement[52]) had sought to address this "specification gap" by anchoring section 5 in the rich body of case law under the Sherman and Clayton Acts, which provides a well-structured framework for assessing the potential competitive gains and harms attributable to certain business practices. The agency's policy shift untethers UMC from that body of case law and, in doing so, restores the specification gap in the statutory language. Following the analytical framework presented in Section II, this linguistic vacuum restores a high level of agency-cost risk since the vague statutory language provides regulators with opportunities to depart from imperfectly specified, standard-like instructions from the legislature. That risk is compounded by the fact that FTC leadership has declined to provide any substitute guidelines to structure future UMC enforcement, other than asserting that the statute provides regulators with "responsibly" exercised discretion to make that determination.[53] This effectively

48 *See supra* note 33.

49 Pub. L. No. 93-637 (codified at 15 U.S.C. § 57a).

50 Pub. L. No. 96-252, 94 Stat. 374.

51 Dissenting Statement of Commissioner Christine S. Wilson Regarding the Open Commission Meeting 5 (July 1, 2021), https://www.ftc.gov/legal-library/browse/cases-proceedings/public-statements/dissenting-statement-commissioner-christine-s-wilson-0.

52 FTC 2015, *supra* note 19.

53 *See supra* note 34.

substitutes regulatory preferences for enforcement principles that had been grounded in a well-developed body of legal and economic principles to guide regulatory action, judicial review, and market expectations.

Confirming these concerns, FTC leadership has already taken actions and made statements suggesting that it seeks to use the agency's enforcement powers to pursue policy objectives that are not clearly encompassed by, and in some cases would appear to be inconsistent with, its statutory mandate to preserve market competition.

In July 2021, the FTC approved a modification to its "Rules of Practice" that omitted the following language from the description of the FTC's Bureau of Competition: "The Bureau's work aims to preserve the free market system and assure the unfettered operation of the forces of supply and demand."[54] In a memo distributed to FTC staff in September 2021, the FTC chair advanced the view that the agency's mission lies in targeting generalized harms that impact workers and independent businesses, rather than only consumers.[55] More specifically, the memo expressed the view that the agency's work "shapes the distribution of power and opportunity,"[56] which suggests that the agency's mission encompasses redistributive objectives rather than, as has long been understood, preserving conditions in which competitive forces determine market outcomes (while other bodies of law, especially the tax system, may be used for redistributive purposes through the legislative process). In a draft strategic plan released in October 2021, the agency's mission statement is described as preserving "fair competition" for the "benefit of the public," which differs from the last such plan through the use of the qualifier, "fair," in conjunction with "competition" and making reference to the "public" rather than consumers specifically as the beneficiaries of the agency's actions.[57] Additionally, the new strategic plan omits language that had appeared in the last such plan stating that the agency would seek to accomplish its mission "without unduly burdening legitimate business activity"[58] (an omission that most likely reflects the agency's dismissal of rule-of-reason balancing analysis). In the merger review process, at least one commissioner and several practitioners have observed that agency staff has been

54 Dissenting Statement of Commissioners Christine S. Wilson and Noah Joshua Phillips Regarding the Commission Statement on the Adoption of Revised Section 18 Rulemaking Procedures 1 (July 9, 2021), https://www.ftc.gov/legal-library/browse/cases-proceedings/public-statements/dissenting-statement-commissioners-christine-s-wilson-noah-joshua-phillips-regarding-commission.

55 Memo from Chair Lina M. Khan to Commission Staff and Commissioners Regarding the Vision and Priorities for the FTC (Sept. 22, 2021), https://www.ftc.gov/legal-library/browse/cases-proceedings/public-statements/memo-chair-lina-m-khan-commission-staff-commissioners-regarding-vision-priorities-ftc [hereinafter Memorandum].

56 *Id.* at 2.

57 For the draft 2021 plan, *see* Fed. Trade Comm'n, Strategic Plan for Fiscal Years 2022–2026 (Oct. 2021), https://www.regulations.gov/document/FTC-2021-0061-0001. For the earlier plan, *see* Fed. Trade Comm'n, Strategic Plan for Fiscal Years 2014 to 2018 (Apr. 2014), https://www.ftc.gov/system/files/documents/reports/2014-2018-strategic-plan/spfy14-fy18.pdf.

58 *See* Fed. Trade Comm'n, Strategic Plan for Fiscal Years 2014 to 2018, *supra* note 57 at 3.

using its investigatory powers to seek information from merging parties on matters that do not have a plausible relationship to competitive harm as that concept is generally understood in federal case law and agency guidelines.[59] Any such practice would arguably constitute an abuse of regulatory power since it implies that the agency is gathering proprietary information that, in the event of a legal challenge by the transacting parties, could not be the basis for a legally defensible case against the transaction being investigated.

B. *Rulemaking Without Scrutiny*

The FTC chair has called for taking steps to "democratize" the agency.[60] In the rulemaking context, however, the agency has taken actions that point in the opposite direction. In July 2021, the FTC made preemptive changes to its "Rules of Practice." While these changes relate to the agency's rulemaking powers concerning UDAP under section 18 of the FTC Act, it raises concerns that any attempted rulemaking concerning UMC under section 6(g) of the FTC Act would be accompanied by similar procedural changes to limit external and internal comment and review. The changes to the Rules of Practice indicate an intent to dilute due process protections, and to limit opportunities for outside parties and even internal specialized staff to provide input, in the rulemaking process. In particular, the revisions substitute the FTC chair for the administrative law judge as the "presiding officer" in any UDAP rulemaking procedure,[61] which provides the chair with authority to run the rulemaking hearing process.[62] This is an inherently conflicted arrangement since the chair would be supervising a hearing process concerning a rule that the chair had likely initiated or supported. Additionally, the revisions eliminate the standard practice in UDAP rulemaking of issuing a staff report that provides an objective analysis of the rulemaking record and recommendations on the final rule,[63] which similarly limits the opportunity for public comment or internal review. While streamlining the rulemaking process could in general reflect a sensible interest in reducing bureaucratic delays, it is hard to fathom any credible argument for adopting specific changes that create a conflict of interest and deprive the Commission of the benefits of an objective analysis of proposed rules.

---

59 Commissioner Christine S. Wilson, Governing is Hard: Antitrust Enforcement in the First Year of the Biden Administration, Remarks for the Mercatus Antitrust Forum: One Year of Biden Antitrust 22 (Jan. 26, 2022), https://www.ftc.gov/news-events/news/speeches/governing-hard-antitrust-enforcement-first-year-biden-administration; Bryan Koenig, *'Nontraditional Questions' Appearing in FTC Merger Probes*, Law360 (Sept. 24, 2021), https://www.law360.com/articles/1425218.

60 Memorandum, *supra* note 555, at 2.

61 15 U.S.C. § 57(a)(1)(B); 16 CFR Subpart B.

62 Statement of the Commission Regarding the Adoption of Revised Section 18 Rulemaking Procedures (July 9, 2021), https://www.ftc.gov/legal-library/browse/cases-proceedings/public-statements/statement-commission-regarding-adoption-revised-section-18-rulemaking-procedures.

63 *Id.*

C. *Rulemaking Promotes Arbitrary Treatment and Facilitates Regulatory Capture*

Advocates of UMC rulemaking (including members of current FTC leadership) argue that, as compared to governance by adjudication, governance by rulemaking would deliver more uniform and therefore "fairer" enforcement outcomes.[64] For two reasons, precisely the opposite outcome may result. First, insofar as FTC leadership has explicitly advocated detaching the agency's UMC rulemaking and enforcement from federal antitrust case law under the Sherman and Clayton Acts,[65] it *intentionally* seeks to create a lack of uniformity in the treatment of different firms or industries, based arbitrarily on the agency (FTC or Department of Justice) that happens to be the regulating entity. Second, the rulemaking process is more prone than litigation to regulatory capture that results in disparate treatment of certain industries or even individual firms. Federal judges serve life terms, whereas FTC commissioners have limited terms and inherent motivations to accrue goodwill for purposes of securing post-employment positions in the public or private sector. Moreover, well-resourced interest groups can more easily influence the rulemaking process through lobbying, participating in the notice-and-comment process, or initiating litigation to challenge a proposed rule. Even after a rule has been issued, impacted firms may be able to influence application of the rule, either by lobbying for modifications or, more typically, seeking waivers or "clearance" through mechanisms such as business review letters. There is no comparable opportunity for exerting continuing influence in the litigation process, which is typically a "one-off" event (aside from appellate decisions that have precedential or persuasive authority in future litigations).

D. *Rulemaking Increases Total Governance and Compliance Costs*

Advocates of UMC rulemaking argue that it will avoid the high costs of antitrust litigation.[66] While it is true that these costs are significant, this observation does not support a persuasive case for rulemaking over adjudication without considering the *total* additional governance and compliance costs associated with the rulemaking process. Those costs are substantial and could easily exceed the costs generated by an adjudicative regime.

Administrative rulemaking is far from a costless exercise, at the point of both issuance and implementation. The regulator must incur costs to comply with the internal review, notice-and-comment, and other procedures required under

---

64 *See, e.g.*, Chopra & Khan, *supra* note 40, at 359–63.

65 Statement of Chair July 2021, *supra* note 19, at 5–6.

66 Chopra & Khan, *supra* note 40, at 361–62.

the APA[67] and, if necessary, to defend the proposed rule against any legal challenges. While antitrust litigation necessitates paying economic experts,[68] this is also often true of administrative rulemaking. Federal regulations[69] and an executive order[70] require that agencies execute an analysis of the economic effects of any regulation that imposes significant costs on the economy.[71] The executive order requires a weighing of costs and benefits, including consideration of regulatory alternatives,[72] that resembles the rule-of-reason standard that FTC leadership has dismissed as being inapplicable to UMC enforcement under the agency's standalone section 5 authority.[73] These regulatory practices are consistent with the Supreme Court's 2015 decision in *Michigan v. EPA*,[74] which suggests that, even when *Chevron* deference applies, some form of cost-benefit analysis may still be necessary to pass judicial muster in the case of a legal challenge under APA requirements and principles.[75]

There are two additional cost categories. First, after issuance of a rule, regulators must incur additional costs in enforcing the rule, issuing interpretations, modifying the rule and granting waivers, or defending legally challenged applications of the rule. This is standard practice in any administrative agency. For example, the accumulated body of rules, regulations, no-action letters, and guidance issued by the Securities and Exchange Commission under its authorizing statutes are so voluminous that only a specialized practitioner can master it. Second, the private sector must incur compliance costs. Regulated firms and industries bear substantial costs under a rulemaking regime, including lobbying costs at the time the rule is formulated and, more significantly, ongoing costs to monitor and implement compliance, to seek agency interpretations or waivers, and to challenge certain applications of the rule. While estimates of private-sector compliance costs vary across industries, total costs incurred to comply with federal regulations amount to hundreds of billions of dollars each year.[76]

---

67 *See supra* note 15 and accompanying discussion.

68 Chopra & Khan, *supra* note 40, at 361.

69 2 U.S.C. § 1532. The regulation applies to any proposed regulation that would result in the expenditure by the public or private sector of $100 million or more.

70 Exec. Order No. 12,866, 58 Fed. Reg. 51, 735 (Sept. 30, 1993), as amended by Executive Order 13563, 76 Fed. Reg. 3821 (Jan. 21, 2011) [hereinafter Executive Order].

71 Cary Coglianese, *Empirical Analysis and Administrative Law*, 2002 U. Ill. L. Rev. 1111, 1119–20 (2002).

72 Executive Order, *supra* note 70, at § 1(b). The order states that, "where appropriate and permitted by law, each agency may consider . . . values that are difficult or impossible to quantify, including equity, human dignity, fairness, and distributive impacts," *see id.*, at § 1(c).

73 Statement of Chair July 2021, *supra* note 19.

74 Michigan v. Environmental Protection Agency, 576 U.S. __ (2015).

75 On this point, *see* Eugene Scalia, *Concluding Thoughts on Cost-Benefit Analysis and the Public's Impact on Rulemaking*, Regulatory Review (Sept. 27, 2017), https://www.theregreview.org/2017/09/27/scalia-public-impact-rulemaking; Valerie C. Brannon & Jared P. Cole, Cong. Rsch. Serv., R44954, *Chevron* Deference: A Primer 21 (Sept. 19, 2017), https://crsreports.congress.gov/product/pdf/R/R44954/3.

76 Coglianese, *supra* note 71, at 1112.

Taking into account the rulemaking, enforcement, and compliance costs incurred by the public and private sectors, the *total* costs generated through a rulemaking regime could easily exceed, and possibly by a significant margin, the total costs imposed by an adjudicative regime that relies on enforcement through periodic litigation against selected firms. These costs are indirectly borne by taxpayers, who fund the agency, and consumers, who purchase the regulated firms' products and services. Critically, these are the constituencies – in fact, the *ultimate* principals – on behalf of which the FTC is the statutorily designated agent.

E. *Summing Up*

The substantive and procedural elements of the FTC's rulemaking initiative raise significant concern that this initiative, together with the larger set of policy changes of which it is a part, will expand regulatory intervention in a manner that results in overenforcement outcomes relative to the agency's statutory mission to preserve competitive markets. Building on the policy shifts undertaken by the agency starting in July 2021 (in particular, the dismissal of the consumer-welfare principle and rule-of-reason standard), this initiative seeks to target a broadly defined set of UMC through preemptive rulemaking, which (if upheld by courts as a legitimate exercise of statutory authority) would likely enjoy a deferential standard of judicial review. This represents a fundamental shift in the objectives and scope of the agency's regulatory activities, which would shift from periodic intervention through litigation to correct well-evidenced competitive harms to continuous intervention through rulemaking to preempt potential competitive harms or to promote a loosely defined set of social goals that may lack any plausible relationship to competitive markets.

V. Conclusion

Any delegation of power from legislators to regulators raises the prospect that the agent will deviate from the principal's instructions as expressed in the governing statute, resulting in regulatory capture in the form of underenforcement or, as is currently more relevant, self-capture in the form of overenforcement. The FTC's rulemaking initiative and associated substantive and procedural changes represent a strategic effort by the agent to remove constraints that were designed to align its actions with the interests of the principal and appropriately reflected the standard-like quality of the antitrust statutes. These changes provide a license for the agency to undertake enforcement actions that venture beyond its targeted mandate to deter practices that pose a credible threat to competitive markets. Through the shift from adjudication to rulemaking, it appears that FTC leadership seeks to put in place a legal regime of per se antitrust violations in which regulators can intervene in market transactions absent evidence of competitive harm, while being substantially shielded from legal challenge as a result of judicial deference for agency action. Making these dramatic changes in the agency's scope of action departs from decades of historical practice at the federal antitrust agencies, is not clearly supported by statutory language and intent, and, without legislative action, is inconsistent with a meaningful commitment to the rule of law.

Case-by-Case Rules! Old Statutes and New Tech at the FTC

Neil Chilson*
Stand Together

Abstract

The Federal Trade Commission's 100+ year history has been punctuated only very occasionally by new statutes. Most of the FTC's actions are under the provision of statutes that are more than a century old. Its work has focused on enforcement actions rather than rulemaking, in part because Congress and internal norms have constrained the agency.

Yet the FTC has increasingly engaged with technologies that are often merely years old. It has created workable oversight frameworks even for new technologies while continuing to bring enforcement actions in the most egregious situations. The FTC can do this because its governing statutes set forth timeless, outcome-based principles, and the agency and courts have applied those principles in specific cases with specific facts. Both features have helped the agency avoid many of the flaws of rulemaking and have created an environment more conducive to the production of "soft law."

Unfortunately, the FTC's capabilities have most painfully lagged the tech industry when it issues rulemakings. For example, rules implementing the Children's Online Privacy Protection Act (COPPA) have lagged technology developments.

In short, the FTC is, out of necessity, more capable than many agencies of constructing the kinds of soft law frameworks that are necessary to govern fast-changing technologies. This history suggests that the FTC should lean into its strength: case-by-case enforcement. New resources should be directed at enforcement, guidance, and consumer and business education rather than detailed rulemakings. Congress should likewise provide clarity around the agency's enforcement authority and procedural measures, rather than granting it broad rulemaking authority.

---

* Senior Research Fellow for Technology and Innovation at Stand Together. Former acting Chief Technologist and Attorney Advisor to acting Chairman Maureen K. Ohlhausen at the Federal Trade Commission.

I. Introduction

The Federal Trade Commission (FTC)'s 100+ year history has been punctuated only very occasionally by new statutes. Most of the FTC's actions are under the provision of statutes that are more than a century old. In the meantime, the Commission has increasingly engaged with technologies that are often merely years old.

What is the effect of this temporal mismatch between statutes and the technology to which it is being applied? Many have said it means that the agency is inevitably behind; they use this gap to call for more financial resources and personnel, new statutes, and new rulemakings at the agency.

But the relationship between the old, authorizing statutes and the new, fast-moving tech is more complex. The oldest statutes have proven flexible and adaptable, and the FTC – with guidance from the courts – has created workable oversight frameworks even for new technologies while continuing to bring enforcement actions in the most egregious situations. In short, the FTC is, out of necessity, more capable than many agencies of constructing the kinds of soft law frameworks that are necessary to govern fast-changing technologies.

The FTC can do this because its governing statutes set forth key, outcome-based principles. The core operational language of the authorizing statutes is very high level and outcome based. This makes such statutes relatively timeless. Furthermore, the statutes have been interpreted by courts through application to actual factual matters – an approach that keeps the principles grounded in their ultimate purposes of protecting consumers and the competitive process. Both features have helped the agency avoid many of the flaws of rulemaking and have created an environment more conducive to the production of "soft law."

Indeed, where the FTC has most painfully lagged the tech industry has been where it issues rulemakings. For example, rules implementing the Children's Online Privacy Protection Act (COPPA) continue to be out of date.

This suggests that the FTC should lean into its strength: case-by-case enforcement. New resources and energy should be directed at enforcement, guidance, and consumer and business education rather than detailed rulemakings. Congress should likewise provide clarity around the agency's enforcement authority and procedural measures, rather than granting it broad rulemaking authority.

This paper first lays out the fundamental issue with government regulation of technology: the pacing problem. Then we turn to the FTC's existing statutory authority. Next, we evaluate how the agency has used that existing authority to govern emerging technology, finding that two features of the FTC regulatory approach give it increased flexibility and help ameliorate the pacing problem. Finally, we look at recent developments in the FTC that appear to be moving away from the very features that have helped the FTC stay relevant throughout decades of technological change, and then offer some warnings.

II. The Pacing Problem

One way to describe the question we are asking is how well the FTC deals with the "pacing problem," and if there is a difference in its effectiveness based on its different modes of regulation.

The pacing problem is the commonly used term for the challenge of government regulation "keeping up" with fast-moving technology. This problem has been described and decried in the academic literate studying the impact of technology on society. A commonly used definition is by bioethicist Wendall Wallach: "[T]he gap between the introduction of a new technology and the establishment of laws, regulations, and oversight mechanisms for shaping its safe development."[1]

That definition suggests two fundamental variables determining the pacing problem. First is the speed at which new technology is invented, implemented, and commercialized. The second variable is the speed at which laws, regulations and oversight mechanisms are developed, enacted, and effective.

The trends in these variables suggest that the pacing problem is worsening. While there is some debate about the rate of fundamental innovation,[2] many new applications of existing technologies are developed, commercialized, and adopted across society faster than ever.

Some examples of technology adoption in the United States are instructive. It took thirty-nine years for the telephone to go from ten to forty percent adoption. The computer moved between those two points in nearly fifteen years, and the internet just under five years. American consumers adopted the smartphone even more rapidly, with smartphones expanding from ten to forty percent of users in the United States in three years. Between 2006 and 2012, smartphones grew from six percent of total mobile phone sales to nearly two-thirds of all U.S. mobile phone sales.[3] Likewise, social media went from ten percent to forty percent of the U.S. population in about three and a half years.[4]

These examples demonstrate the increasing pace of new technologies entering the marketplace, exacerbating the pacing problem.

Meanwhile, government institutions have also become more sclerotic, unable to pass legislation or regulation at the required speed. The United States federal legislative process has become dysfunctional, unable to pass substantive legislation

---

1 Wendell Wallach, A Dangerous Master: How to Keep Technology From Slipping Beyond Our Control 72 (Basic Books 2015).

2 *See, e.g.*, Tyler Cowen, The Great Stagnation: How America Ate All the Low-Hanging Fruit of Modern History, Got Sick, and Will (Eventually) Feel Better (Dutton 2017).

3 Michael DeGusta, *Are Smartphones Spreading Faster than Any Technology in Human History?*, MIT Tech. Rev., May 9, 2019, https://www.technologyreview.com/2012/05/09/186160/are-smart-phones-spreading-faster-than-any-technology-in-human-history.

4 https://www.pewresearch.org/internet/fact-sheet/social-media.

to govern technology. State legislatures have been more active, but this has generated a wide confusion or overlapping laws for certain types of technology such as information and communications technology (ICT). Thierer et al. list four challenges for government: bureaucratic deficiencies that slow government action; overlapping, conflicting governance structures; coordination problems created by new technologies that cross the jurisdiction of many agencies; and limited ability to gather and process the knowledge necessary to create well-formed regulation.[5]

Some would solve the pacing problem by restricting the pace of innovation and commercialization.[6] Indeed, many who bemoan the pacing problem have a precautionary approach to new technology. The "precautionary principle" is the idea that new technologies or new applications should be vetted by a regulator or other accountable body before being offered to the public. As Cass Sunstein has described it, "the animating idea is that regulators should take steps to protect against potential harms, even if causal chains are unclear and even if we do not know that those harms will come to fruition."[7]

To those who support a precautionary principle, it is critical that government has the capacity, ability, authority, and opportunity to vet new technologies. Many scholars of technology governance also refer to the Collingridge dilemma, the idea that due to the slow pace of government, a new technology with unforeseeable social downsides is inextricably embedded into society before government can act.[8]

It may be that the pacing problem is intractable because of the last fact on Thierer et al.'s list: F. A. Hayek's "knowledge problem." Local actors always have more knowledge about the problems in a system. This knowledge is dispersed, tacit, impossible to aggregate, and often even contradictory. Sometimes it is only generated or made explicit in the process of trying to solve the problem. This all means that a centralized decision-maker – such as a government regulator – cannot gather all the information necessary to make the best decisions to address the problems.

In another way, the very framing of the pacing problem misunderstands the nature of innovation. It views innovation as a linear process of forward motion and wonders how to slow the forward motion or increase the forward motion of government to keep pace. But innovation is a non-linear discovery process of many individual actors exploring the possibilities that are adjacent to our current technologies.[9] In this process, innovators seek out how to apply the existing tech

5 Ryan Hagemann, Jennifer Huddleston Skees & Adam Thierer, *Soft Law for Hard Problems: The Governance of Emerging Technologies in an Uncertain Future*, 17 Colo. Tech. L.J. 37 (2018), https://papers.ssrn.com/sol3/papers.cfm?abstract_id=3118539.

6 Adam Thierer, *Problems with Precautionary Principle-Minded Tech Regulation & a Federal Robotics Commission*, Medium (Sept. 22, 2014), https://medium.com/tech-liberation/problems-with-precautionary-principle-minded-tech-regulation-a-federal-robotics-commission-c71f6f20d8bd.

7 Cass Sunstein, Laws of Fear: Beyond the Precautionary Principle (Cambridge University Press 2005).

8 Adam Thierer, *The Pacing Problem, the Collingridge Dilemma & Technological Determinism*, Tech Liberation Front (Aug. 16, 2018), https://techliberation.com/2018/08/16/the-pacing-problem-the-collingridge-dilemma-technological-determinism/.

9 Steven Johnson, Where Good Ideas Come From: The Natural History of Innovation (Riverhead Books 2010).

to create new tech or solve new problems. This non-linear process is affected by the regulatory environment. Regulation can eliminate entirely certain adjacent possibles (and perhaps create others). Thus, innovation is not something you can simply throttle back on, ensuring society will be ready for the innovation when it does eventually get here. Regulation does not just change the pace of technological innovation. It also changes the path of technology, unpredictably shaping what innovation can even be considered or contemplated.

How well is the FTC dealing with the pacing problem? One might assume that a 100-year-old agency with statutes that are predominantly from the early 20th century would be among the very worst in keeping up with new technology and would suffer mightily from the pacing problem. But the FTC's unique history and somewhat constrained legal authority has counterintuitively made it uniquely successful at keeping pace with technology. Next, we look at that legal authority.

III. The FTC's Legal Authority

1. Authorizing Statutes

The Commission has enforcement or administrative responsibilities under more than seventy statutes.[10] But nearly all its cases are brought under its primary statutes, the Federal Trade Commission Act and the Clayton Act. (Where Congress has granted additional authority to the agency, it often does so by saying that a violation of a specific statute is also considered a violation of the FTC Act.)

A. *FTC Act Section 5*

Section 5 of the FTC Act declares unlawful "unfair or deceptive acts or practices" (UDAP) and "unfair methods of competition" (UMC).[11] UDAP reflect the agency's consumer protection mission and UMC the agency's competition mission. There is little additional detail in the statute, which was enacted in 1914 to prohibit UMC and amended in 1923 to also prohibit UDAP.

The meaning of UMC and UDAP prohibitions have been fleshed out, at times controversially, during the FTC's 100-year history of applying them. The FTC's UMC authority has gained detail by reference to other competition laws (most prominently the Sherman Act) and through litigation applying those laws. There remains a lively debate over whether and by how much Section 5 is broader than other antitrust laws and whether the FTC can create rules based on Section 5 UMC authority.[12] But the scope of the law is relatively well understood, particularly when compared to the brief and amorphous language of the statute.

10 Fed. Trade Comm'n, Legal Library: Statutes, https://www.ftc.gov/enforcement/statutes.

11 15 U.S.C. § 45(a)(1).

12 Section 5: Principles of Navigation, Remarks of Maureen K. Ohlhausen, Commissioner, Federal Trade Commission, U.S. Chamber of Commerce, Washington, D.C., at 16 (July 25, 2013), http://www.ftc.gov/sites/default/files/documents/public_statements/section-5-principles-navigation/130725section5speech.pdf.

Likewise, UDAP have been fleshed out over time, although the frameworks developed most rapidly in response to a crisis. Following a controversial period of aggressive UDAP rulemaking in the late 1970s, Congress clipped the agency's wings, even temporarily defunding the agency for a short period. Chagrined, new FTC leadership rapidly developed guidance to constrain and clarify the FTC's authority under the broad UDAP statutory language. Specifically, the FTC adopted two policy statements: the Unfairness Statement and the Deception Statement.[13]

In each of these statements, the FTC derived from past cases key factors that comprised an unfair or deceptive act or practice. For example, the agency acknowledged in the Unfairness Statement that its application of unfairness was uncertain, and that "this uncertainty has been honestly troublesome for some businesses and some members of the legal profession."[14] To provide clarity, the agency highlighted the core of unfairness as a finding of substantial, unavoidable consumer harm not outweighed by benefits to consumers or competition. Since the adoption of the Unfairness Statement, establishing these three factors has been the cornerstone of FTC unfairness complaints. Indeed, in 1994 Congress adopted these three key elements of consumer injury from the Unfairness Statements as statutory limits on the agency's actions.[15] The Deception Statement likewise distilled past cases of deception, establishing a deceptive act as being characterized by a statement, omission, or practice that is likely to mislead a consumer acting reasonably in the circumstances, and where that statement, omission or practice is material to the consumer's decision-making.

The frameworks established in these statements have been applied hundreds of times, building up a body of examples in advertising claims, financial practices, marketing practices, and privacy and data security, among others.

B. *Clayton Act*

The Clayton Act, passed in 1914 – before the FTC existed – charges the FTC "with preventing and eliminating unlawful tying contracts, corporate mergers and acquisitions, and interlocking directorates."[16] The law has been amended, including by the Robinson-Patman Act (which authorizes the Commission to prevent certain discriminatory pricing and product promotion practices) and the Hart-Scott-Rodino Act (which, among other things, establishes procedures under which merging

---

13 Fed. Trade Comm'n, Commission Statement of Policy on the Scope of the Consumer Unfairness Jurisdiction (Dec. 17, 1980) (appended to *Int'l Harvester Co.*, 104 F.T.C. 949, 1070 (1984)), https://www.ftc.gov/legal-library/browse/ftc-policy-statement-unfairness [hereinafter "Unfairness Statement"]; *see also* 15 U.S.C. § 45(n) (2018) (test for unfairness). Letter from James C. Miller III, Chairman, Fed. Trade Comm'n, to Rep. John D. Dingell, Chairman, H. Comm. on Energy & Commerce (Oct. 14, 1983), https://www.ftc.gov/system/files/documents/public_statements/410531/831014deceptionstmt.pdf [hereinafter "Deception Statement"].

14 Unfairness Statement at 1.

15 15 U.S.C. § 45(n).

16 https://www.ftc.gov/enforcement/statutes/clayton-act.

companies must notify the Commission).[17] Like Section 5, this broadly and somewhat circularly defined law (anticompetitive and unlawful tying arrangements are those that "substantially lessen competition or tend to create a monopoly," for example) has been developed through repeated court application to specific facts.

C. *Others*

Congress has entrusted the FTC with the enforcement or administration of more than seventy other, more specialized laws. These include the Children's Online Privacy Protection Act, CAN-SPAM Act, Telemarketing Sales Rule, Identity Theft Act, Fair Credit Reporting Act, Equal Credit Opportunity Act, and many more. Most of these laws, which tend to focus on the FTC's consumer protection role, are much more specific in application and narrower in scope than Section 5 and the Clayton Act. Many are constructed so that a violation of their provisions is also a violation of some portion of Section 5 as well.

2. Enforcement

The FTC's primary effect on the marketplace is through enforcement of the statutes (given substance through case law and policy statements) above. As such, the Commission enforces laws and statutes intended to protect consumers and encourage competition in the market. When a majority of FTC commissioners have reason to believe that a company has violated consumer protection or competition laws, it can issue a complaint against the firm and pursue action in federal court or through its own in-house administrative law judge. The firm may then settle with the FTC. (Frequently, FTC staff negotiate and settle with the firm prior to a Commission vote on the complaint, and the complaint and settlement are presented as a package to the FTC commissioners.) If the firm chooses to contest the FTC complaint, an administrative law judge reviews the issue and makes a recommendation for the parties. After the administrative judge's decision, either party can appeal to the full Commission, and from there to a federal appellate court. If a business violates an existing FTC order or consent agreement, the agency must file with a federal district court to enforce the order. The FTC can also petition a federal district court to grant an injunction against firms that violate their orders or continue to engage in unfair or deceptive business practices.

The FTC can issue subpoenas for witnesses and evidence to support its investigations. The agency can also use its Section 6(b) authority to require a business to report specific information to the Commission. The FTC can share the information it gathers and obtains with other government agencies, including law enforcement authorities. Businesses that intend to merge or acquire another firm must also submit to FTC review, if the size of the transactions warrants government scrutiny and the FTC regulates the industry of the merging firms.

---

17 Pub. L. No. 74-692, 49 Stat. 1526, codified at 15 U.S.C. §§ 13, 13b, and 21a.

In 2020, the FTC obtained twelve merger consent orders, filed nine cases to block mergers, triggered eleven abandoned transactions, took three non-merger enforcement actions, and brought a civil penalty action.[18] On the consumer protection side, the FTC filed eighty-two enforcement actions and obtained twenty-three administrative orders; sixty-six redress, disgorgement, or permanent injunction orders; and five civil penalty orders.[19]

3. Rulemaking

From the very beginning, Congress's design for the FTC was that its primary effect be through enforcement actions. Over the past century, that design has been implemented through a focus on case-by-case enforcement actions. But Congress has granted the FTC some rulemaking authority.

The Administrative Procedure Act (APA) governs the rulemaking proceedings of most independent agencies. Controversially, the FTC in the late 1960s asserted and exercised APA rulemaking authority under FTC Act Section 6(g), a provision arguably intended for setting internal procedures.[20] Congress weighed in on that controversy by adopting specific, non-APA rulemaking requirements for the FTC in 1975, "piggybacking" these changes on a bill addressing deceptive warranties.[21] After the KidVid controversy in the late 1970s (where the FTC faced heavy criticism for broad regulatory rulemakings affecting a wide range of business practices, including advertising to children), Congress added more onerous procedural requirements to the FTC's rulemaking under Magnuson-Moss Act. Others in this volume have provided a more in-depth survey of this history.

The FTC can use the Magnuson-Moss process to create legislative rules regarding deceptive and unfair business practices. However, when the FTC engages in Magnuson-Moss rulemaking, it must follow a specific set of guidelines to enact and enforce its rules. To legitimize rules under the Magnuson-Moss process, the agency must hold public hearings to allow other groups and individuals to comment on and present evidence pertaining to the proposed rules. The FTC must also notify Congress of its rulemaking proposals, conduct studies to determine if other "regulatory alternatives" exist, and show that its rulemaking pertains to the activity it wants to regulate. The FTC must also create and maintain a rulemaking record that contains all the information from public hearings, relevant evidence, and

---

18 Fed. Trade Comm'n, Annual Highlights 2022, https://www.ftc.gov/reports/annual-highlights-2020/stats-data-2020.

19 *Id.*

20 15 U.S.C. § 46(g). *See* Richard A. Wegman, *Cigarettes and Health: A Legal Analysis*, 51 Cornell L. Rev. 678, 740 n. 280 (1966) (describing contemporaneous arguments for and against FTC APA rulemaking authority under Section 6(g), 15 U.S.C. § 46).

21 Pub. L. No. 93-637, 88 Stat. 2183 (1975); *see* Kurt Walters, *Reassessing the Mythology of Magnuson-Moss: A Call to Revive Section 18 Rulemaking at the FTC*, 16 Harv. L. & Pol'y Rev. (2022, forthcoming), at 12, https://ssrn.com/abstract=3875970 or http://dx.doi.org/10.2139/ssrn.3875970 (describing the process by which Magnuson-Moss was adopted).

a statement explaining the basis and purpose of the proposed rule.[22] These requirements make it difficult for the FTC to complete Magnuson-Moss rulemaking in an efficient and timely manner.[23] Examples of rules adopted under the Magnuson-Moss process include rules about warranties, ophthalmic practice, labeling and advertising of home insulation, vocational schools, credit practices, used motor vehicle trading, and funeral industry practices.[24] Reflecting the burdensome nature of Magnuson-Moss, no new rulemaking has been initiated under the process since 1980 (although some existing rules have been amended).[25]

Though the FTC lacks general APA rulemaking, Congress has occasionally authorized the agency to implement specific statutes in certain targeted areas using APA procedures. Examples include the Children's Online Privacy Protection Act, the Fair Credit Reporting Act, and the Telemarketing and Consumer Fraud and Abuse Prevention Act.

Whether under the Magnuson-Moss process or the APA, past FTC rulemakings have been almost entirely under the Commission's UDAP authority.[26] But new FTC Chair Lina Khan has argued that the agency can and should use rulemakings to implement its preferred policies in the competition area.[27] Such antitrust rules would be economy-wide, presumably. There are credible arguments that the agency lacks the legal authority to do such wide-ranging rulemakings under the existing statute.[28] We need not resolve that debate here; it is enough to note that the FTC may soon pursue such rulemakings.

4. Hearings, Workshops, Reports, and Other "Soft Law"

The FTC has many activities that are neither enforcement nor rulemaking. For example, the FTC holds workshops to explore new issues. Other actions the FTC can take include warning letters (sometimes private but often public), speeches and press releases by agency leadership, and consumer and business education.

---

22 15 U.S.C. § 57a: Unfair or deceptive acts or practices rulemaking proceedings.

23 *See generally*, Jeffrey S. Lubbers, *It's Time to Remove the "Mossified" Procedures for FTC Rulemaking*, 83 Geo. Wash. L. Rev. 1979, 1980 (2015).

24 *Id.* at 1985.

25 *Id.* at 1989.

26 I say "almost" because the Commission did not always clearly delineate between its consumer protection and competition authorities until the late 1970s/early 1980s. Still, the existing rules adopted by the agency are relatively easy to classify as consumer protection rules. *See* Fed. Trade Comm'n, A Brief Overview of the Federal Trade Commission's Investigative, Law Enforcement, and Rulemaking Authority (revised, May 2021), https://www.ftc.gov/about-ftc/mission/enforcement-authority ("Nearly all of the rules that the Commission actually promulgated under Section 6(g) were consumer protection rules.")

27 Rohit Chopra & Lina M. Khan, *The Case for "Unfair Methods of Competition" Rulemaking*, 87 U. Chi. L. Rev. 357 (2020).

28 Maureen K. Ohlhausen & James Rill, *Pushing the Limits? A primer on FTC competition rulemaking*, U.S. Chamber of Com. (Aug. 12, 2021), https://www.uschamber.com/assets/archived/images/ftc_rulemaking_white_paper_aug12.pdf; Richard J. Pierce, Jr, *Can the Federal Trade Commission Use Rulemaking to Change Antitrust Law?* (GW Law Faculty Publications & Other Works 1561, 2021), https://scholarship.law.gwu.edu/faculty_publications/1561.

One of the key intellectual efforts in which the FTC engages is issuing reports. Such reports summarize and analyze information it has gathered through workshops, investigations, 6(b) requests, and other means. These reports, while not legally binding, can be quite influential. For example, the FTC's 2012 *Protecting Consumer Privacy in an Era of Rapid Change: Recommendations for Businesses and Policymakers* provided guidance for businesses on best practices in the handling of data and set forth the basic framing of FTC privacy investigations for the next decade.[29]

IV. Evaluating How the FTC Handles the Pacing Problem

Having provided the basic background on the pacing problem and the FTC's existing authority, how does that existing authority enable the FTC to deal with changes in technology? The FTC's case-by-case approach has proven adaptable over time, enabling the FTC to address consumer protection and competition concerns across a wide range of new industries and new technologies over time.

1. The FTC's Case-by-Case Enforcement Enables It to Adapt to Changing Circumstances

The FTC's enforcement-focused approach offers certain advantages when dealing with changed circumstances, including adapting to the potential harms of new technology. Enforcement actions – whether enforcing statutes or regulations – are necessarily case-by-case. The FTC must investigate and pursue legal action against a defendant, either in administrative proceedings or in federal court.

A. *Rules Versus Enforcement*

In U.S. federal agencies, the default regulatory tool is rulemaking. Indeed, the FTC is somewhat unique among independent agencies in having only limited rulemaking authority.

One can think of government interventions into society along a single dimension of "level of specificity of government mandate." On the high-specificity end of the spectrum are highly detailed or prescriptive agency requirements. On the low-specificity end of the spectrum is the general application of common law principles. Let's look at two points along this spectrum: agency rulemakings and agency case-by-case enforcement.

29 Fed. Trade Comm'n, Protecting Consumer Privacy in an Era of Rapid Change: Recommendations for Businesses and Policymakers (2012), https://www.ftc.gov/sites/default/files/documents/reports/federal-trade-commission-report-protecting-consumer-privacy-era-rapid-change-recommendations/120326privacyreport.pdf.

i. Rulemaking

While agency rules could, in theory, be quite general and simple, they tend toward complicated and detailed because rulemaking is a delegation from Congress. Given that, any high-level, non-specific requirements that can be detailed could be and tend to be done by Congress.

Rules have benefits. A clear statement of government demands can help private parties comply by specifically indicating the line between legal and illegal behavior. Such bright-line rules are also easier to enforce because enforcers can more simply establish violations. The clarity provided by such rules promotes the "rule of law" by preventing arbitrary and even potentially biased application of the law to individuals.

But rules also have at least four different weaknesses.[30]

The knowledge problem. Rulemaking requires predicting the path of future technology and society, and regulators do not have all the necessary information to make optimal decisions ahead of time. This knowledge problem – as F. A. Hayek called it – is the result of several challenges. First, knowledge is often dispersed widely across an industry and its stakeholders. Second, much important knowledge is tacit, meaning it cannot be extracted or captured *even by the local users* who apply that knowledge. Third and perhaps most obviously, rules apply to future events and regulators do not have complete knowledge about the future. This lack of knowledge about the future matters because, presumably, the rules will be in effect for some time. Finally, knowledge contained in complex systems is often irreducible, meaning it is embedded in the connections between the pieces of the system. Sometimes this means that different parts of the system hold conflicting views that generate useful results through the interactions of these conflicting beliefs. This type of information cannot be averaged or summed without losing some information.

The pacing problem. The pacing problem – discussed above – is exacerbated by rulemaking. Rules take time to establish, in part because of the difficulty of gathering useful knowledge about the technologies to be regulated, but also because of procedural and bureaucratic time costs necessitated by representative government.

Expert agencies can often move faster than legislatures, lessening the pacing problem as compared to the one Congress faces. But even so, the rules they generate often trail the technology they regulate.

As rules grow outdated, the "clarity" rationale for rulemaking weakens. A rule that was clear to stakeholders on the day of its adoption may in five years be so vague as to be worse than a general, relatively timeless principle (such as "don't deceive consumers.")

---

30 Cass Sunstein, *Problems with Rules*, 83 Cal. L. Rev. 953 (1995); Caryn Devins, Roger Koppl, Stuart Kauffman & Teppo Felin, *Against Design*, 47 Ariz. St. L.J. 609 (2015).

The Procrustean problem. Rules are inevitably established using the frame of the technologies and industries dominant at the time of their adoption. Disruptive business models that do not fit into the current regulatory boxes will face significant regulatory risks in such circumstances.[31] Some have called this the "Procrustean problem" of regulation after the ancient Greek myth in which a rogue blacksmith stretches or amputates human visitors to fit his iron guest bed.[32] Regulators need to fit and classify companies according to regulatory categories, and this naturally benefits incumbent business models while disadvantaging novel and experimental approaches. This creates a status quo bias. The mismatch between existing regulation and a new business model can mean that innovative ways of accomplishing certain goals may be legally risky to pursue, not because they are dangerous or harmful, but because they were not contemplated when the regulation was developed. And most rules and statutes do not have a natural expiration or automatic process by which they fade out in application as they mismatch the new technology. Statutes or rules, once put in place, tend to remain.

At best, innovators facing the Procrustean problem will have to educate regulators and potentially pursue regulatory changes. At worst, innovators will be warned off by their lawyers and investors, will choose to pursue less legally uncertain endeavors, and the agency will not even know the chilling effect its rules are having.

There is an interesting implication here: a heavily Procrustean set of rules that stifle change can "solve" the pacing problem by slowing or stopping innovation. Yet note that this effect is not the result of a conscious or thoughtful approach to protecting the public interest by comparing new technologies to old technologies, but instead always favors the technology and business models of the past.

Regulatory capture. Regulatory capture is a problem that all agencies face.[33] However, agencies that heavily use rulemaking, particularly in a narrow sector, have a higher risk of regulatory capture. Whereas an FTC case focuses on one particular party, rulemakings directly affect operations across an entire industry. This heightens the incentive for industry players to lobby and influence an agency even when they themselves are not under investigation.

In particular, incumbent industry representatives will often help relieve a rulemaking agencies' knowledge problem and pacing problem by offering information about the industry relevant to a proposed rulemaking. This can ease the burden of regulators but can also exacerbate the Procrustean problem, embedding the incumbent industry structure into the very regulatory language and thus discouraging and blocking disruptive challengers whose models do not fit into the existing regulatory categories.

---

31 Neil Chilson, *Does Big Tech Need Its Own Regulator?, in* Report on the Digital Economy (Global Antitrust Institute 2020), https://gaidigitalreport.com/2020/08/25/does-big-tech-need-its-own-regulator.

32 Maureen K. Ohlhausen, *The Procrustean Problem With Prescriptive Regulation*, 23 CommLaw Conspectus 1 (2014) https://www.ftc.gov/system/files/documents/public_statements/606381/141222commlaw.pdf.

33 Chilson *supra* note 31.

When can rulemaking work? Agency rulemaking can be the better approach in some circumstances. Rules work best when Congress lacks detailed expertise but has provided a solid framework in a relatively slow-changing industry. In such situations, the knowledge problem is lessened because the factual landscape is well known. The pacing problem is lessened because change is slow and predictable. Rules are also most credible where there is a wide consensus on what problem is being solved and how to solve it.

ii. Case-by-Case Enforcement

Case-by-case enforcement of generally applicable principles can address some of the weaknesses of rulemaking, although it has some of its own weaknesses.

Case-by-case enforcement reduces the knowledge problem for several reasons.[34] First, it reduces the amount of relevant information that the regulator must gather. Far less knowledge is necessary to adjudicate a specific dispute or fact pattern involving just a few parties than to design standing rules for an entire industry for years or potentially decades. Second, most of the relevant information will be available to the party or parties to the case or investigation. The agency need not survey an entire industry plus all affected stakeholders to have a reasonable chance of addressing the problem in front of it. Similarly, if the agency makes a mistake in a single case or even a series of cases, every defendant has a shot of convincing the independent decision-maker that their situation is different from previous cases and that the court should find differently. Whereas mistakes in legislation or regulation are difficult to correct in an expeditious manner.

Judging harm on a case-by-case basis reduces the pacing problem. Investigations and enforcement actions, where legality is judged by the outcomes and specifically by the harms incurred, reduce the pacing problem. The categories of harms that best justify government intervention do not change rapidly. Addressing unjust financial, health, safety and other concrete harms has been the goal of legal regimes back to ancient times. These harms remain a primary motivation of the FTC's mission, although the means through which such harms can arise has changed significantly. Thus, the FTC's expertise in evaluating, on a case-by-case basis, harm to consumers and to competition helps it keep pace with changing technology. As I wrote while at the Commission:

> As an enforcement agency, the FTC focuses on outcomes: we are experts at identifying acts and practices that cause harms to consumers and competition. Interactions with customers and with competitors are part of the practices of every company, in every industry. The FTC does not micromanage these practices. Instead, we evaluate the conduct of companies to see if they live up to the promises they made to consumers. We also assess whether

34 Neil Chilson, *How the FTC keeps up on technology*, Tech@FTC (Jan. 4, 2018), https://www.ftc.gov/news-events/blogs/techftc/2018/01/how-ftc-keeps-technology.

> companies engage in other acts and practices that cause harm to consumers and competition. Harms to consumers and harms to competition often follow similar patterns across the economy. Therefore, each time we encounter a new industry or technology, we start with tried-and-true tools and applicable knowledge.[35]

If specific technological, economic, or business model expertise is needed, the agency can hire case-specific experts to guide investigations and litigation. This flexibility also helps the agency keep up with new technology. A rulemaking agency will constantly fight to bring and keep top talent from the industry it is regulating; it will often have to settle for general expertise. An enforcement agency, on the other hand, can hire for a specific case the top-tier experts in the space. Using this model, the FTC, for example, has been able to successfully enforce the law in fields as varied as aerospace to video gaming.[36]

Case-by-case reduces the Procrustean problem. Case-by-case decision-making reduces the Procrustean problem. Rather than design a single regulatory "bed" that every industry participant is fitted to, a case-by-case approach looks at what has worked in the past but can consider the unique situation before it, as well. The strictures evolve over time, adapting to new technologies. It is not so much that everyone gets a custom bed, but the bed can be adjusted when need be. For example, the FTC has applied its deception and unfairness authority to bring hundreds of privacy and data security-related consumer protection enforcement actions despite widely divergent fact patterns.[37]

Just as important as the ability of the law to adapt to new circumstances is the ability for outdated law to fade. Case-by-case law focuses on actual, existing current problems, not theoretical or future problems. This focus means that useless case law usually fades out of lack of use or is expressly eroded by court decisions over time.[38]

Rather than wait until someone is hurt and can sue, it might seem better to pass a law ahead of time to prevent potential harms. This makes sense when Congress understands the future path of a technology well and when the harms are likely to be widespread, catastrophic, and irreversible. But in most cases, even experts do not understand the future of a technology very well, let alone legislators. While detailed legislation may prevent some harms, it can also prevent beneficial uses and will likely miss other causes of harms. In these cases, it is better to prohibit or restrict certain kinds of harms, and then address new technologies or business practices as they inflict those harms.

---

35 *Id.*

36 *Id.* (listing forty-seven high-tech industries where the FTC has acted.)

37 Fed. Trade Comm'n, Federal Trade Commission 2020 Privacy and Data Security Update (2020), https://www.ftc.gov/system/files/documents/reports/federal-trade-commission-2020-privacy-data-security-update/20210524_privacy_and_data_security_annual_update.pdf.

38 Neil Chilson, *Why Joe Biden and Donald Trump are both wrong about Section 230*, Protocol (Nov. 13, 2020), https://www.protocol.com/biden-trump-section-230-repeal.

Case-by-case is harder to capture. Case-by-case approaches apply general principles across a wide range of parties and even industries. The Federal Trade Commission, for example, has general jurisdiction across the economy, with a few notable exceptions. Because it governs a wide range of industries, no specific industry is likely to form a large enough portion of the FTC's work to be able to influence the overall direction of the FTC's investigations or enforcement actions. In addition, widely varying industries will have widely varying and often competing interests.

Some case-by-case structures have the additional benefit of being broadly decentralized across many different decision-makers. Common law torts, for example, are the product of decisions by thousands of judges over hundreds of years. A special interest might win a single case but cannot easily distort the overall case law because of its decentralized nature and its focus on specific conflicts rather than entire industries.

B. *Example: The FTC's Privacy and Data Security Enforcement*

The U.S. lacks general privacy or data security statutes, although it has many sector-specific laws, some of which have been mentioned above. Despite the lack of general statutes, the FTC has brought more than 130 spam and spyware cases, approximately 80 general privacy cases, and 80 data security cases in the past twenty years.[39] The Commission has brought many of these cases under its general Section 5 deception and unfairness authority. Those statutory terms of "unfairness" and "deception" are defined in general terms ahead of time but are specifically applied in the context of privacy and data security on a case-by-case basis. As Daniel Solove and Woodrow Hartzog have described it, "through a common law-like process, the FTC's actions have developed into a rich jurisprudence that is effectively the law of the land for businesses that deal in personal information."[40]

Those concepts are further fleshed out by FTC "soft law" in guidance and reports. Many of the concepts described in such guidance resemble terms defined in various types of privacy legislation. For example, the FTC discusses what is sensitive personal information in reports, consumer and business education, and case complaints.[41] The FTC's descriptions are inductive and common-law-like, looking back to past specific cases to provide guidance for future decision-making. For example, in any specific case, the FTC may determine whether certain information is sensitive or not. The effect of assembling a definition over dozens or hundreds of cases is one of discovering what the term means rather than imposing it.[42]

---

39 Fed. Trade Comm'n, Privacy and Data Security Update, *supra* note 37.

40 Daniel J. Solove & Woodrow Hartzog, *The FTC and the New Common Law of Privacy*, 114 Colum. L. Rev. 583, 589 (2014).

41 Fed. Trade Comm'n, Protecting Consumer Privacy in an Era of Rapid Change, *supra* note 29, at 1–6.

42 Neil Chilson, *Seeing (Platforms) Like a State: Digital Legibility and Lessons for Platform Governance*, 29 Cath. U. J. L. & Tech 31 (2021), https://scholarship.law.edu/jlt/vol29/iss2/4.

2. The FTC's Environment Better Supports Soft Law Approaches

A. *Soft Law Mitigates the Pacing Problem*

Because of the increasing speed of technological innovation and the slowing of government responses, soft law is replacing hard law as the primary mechanism to govern new technologies. Hard law is legislation or common law decisions established and enforced by government. The FTC's statutes, rulemakings, and case-by-case enforcement judgements or settlements are hard law. They are legally binding on the parties involved.

In contrast, Arizona State University Law Professor Gary Marchant and his colleagues describe soft law as frameworks that "set forth substantive expectations but are not directly enforceable by government, and include approaches such as professional guidelines, private standards, codes of conduct, and best practices."[43] Adam Thierer, Jennifer Huddleston, and Ryan Hagemann provide a useful taxonomy of soft law, identifying three specific types of soft law: "(1) 'soft criteria'; (2) multistakeholder efforts; and (3) consultations, jawboning and agency threats."[44]

Compared to hard law, soft law is more agile, flexible, and easier to adapt because it avoids the procedural and legal requirements of hard law. Questions of legal authority, geographic jurisdiction, and conflict of mandatory laws are not issues for soft law, which can span jurisdictions and offer multiple overlapping solutions. In addition, soft law generally encourages collaborations between stakeholders rather than adversarial proceedings that typify hard law.[45]

B. *The FTC Environment Supports Development of Soft Law*

More so than most independent agencies, the FTC's environment fosters the development of soft law. The FTC facilitates the use of all three of the above-mentioned types of soft law. The FTC frequently deploys *soft criteria* by issuing reports, business and consumer guidance, blog posts, speeches, and other types of non-binding guidance.[46] Some of these reports are outcomes of *multistakeholder efforts*; for example, the 2012 Privacy Report mentioned earlier was the result of a series of roundtables, consultation with the Department of Commerce, and

---

43 Gary Marchant, *"Soft Law" Governance of Artificial Intelligence*, AI Pulse (Jan. 25, 2019), https://aipulse.org/soft-law-governance-of-artificial-intelligence.

44 Hagemann, Huddleston Skees & Thierer, *supra* note 5, at 46.

45 John Villasenor, *Soft law as complement to AI regulation*, Brookings (July 31, 2020), https://www.brookings.edu/research/soft-law-as-a-complement-to-ai-regulation; W. Wallach & G. Marchant, *Toward the Agile and Comprehensive International Governance of AI and Robotics* [point of view], 107 Proceedings of the IEEE 505 (2019), doi: 10.1109/JPROC.2019.2899422; Carlos Ignacio Gutierrez & Gary E. Marchant, A Global Perspective of Soft Law Programs for the Governance of Artificial Intelligence (May 27, 2021), https://ssrn.com/abstract=3855171 or http://dx.doi.org/10.2139/ssrn.3855171.

46 *See, e.g.*, Fed. Trade Comm'n, Business Guidance, https://www.ftc.gov/business-guidance.

a draft preliminary report that received more than 450 public comments.[47] And the FTC has also engaged in jawboning and agency threats to shape industry practices.[48]

Many agencies use such techniques. Yet the FTC is uniquely supportive of soft law, for two reasons. First, the Commission's limited rulemaking authority means that it does not leap to rulemaking when it identifies a problem. At most agencies, rulemaking is the first approach to solving problems, often crowding out other, perhaps better approaches, including soft law approaches. But the FTC, before it can successfully apply its enforcement authority to a new area, usually needs to demonstrate that the concerning behavior rises to the level of the general UDAP or UMC problems. The agency lays this groundwork through soft law, including workshops, reports, warning letters, and business and consumer guidance. Courts agree that these efforts do not create binding law, but they do signal to market participants the FTC's likely disposition toward various behaviors. Such signals also provoke feedback from industry, helping the agency to iteratively refine its approach in a specific area.

Second, the FTC's enforcement approach serves as a backstop for private sector soft law. The FTC's deception and unfairness authority lend credibility and legitimization to industry soft law efforts. Industry groups and consortiums often seek to form codes of conduct and industry best practices. Occasionally certification bodies privately enforce such standards through contracts and fines, but typically such standards are voluntary and carry few penalties for violation. However, if a company harms consumers by breaking promises it made in the context of self-regulation or volunteer industry best practices, the FTC can bring a deception enforcement action. This despite never having mandated or even weighed in on the best practices involved. Similarly, industry-established best practices or standards can inform the FTC's own investigations. For example, the FTC has looked to well-established industry standards as evidence of whether a specific data security practice by a company was an unfair act or practice.[49]

3. Where the FTC Has Failed to Keep Pace and Why

The FTC's case-by-case enforcement of its UDAP and UMC authority, informed by a wide range of soft law tools, has proven adaptable to a wide range of technologies, business models, and consumer harms. However, some parts of the agency's work have been less successful at adaptation and have, as a result, become ossified and mismatched to the real world.

---

47 Fed. Trade Comm'n, Protecting Consumer Privacy in an Era of Rapid Change: *supra* note 29.

48 *See, e.g.*, Fed. Trade Comm'n, Press Release, FTC Staff Reminds Influencers and Brands to Clearly Disclose Relationships (Apr. 19, 2017), https://www.ftc.gov/news-events/news/press-releases/2017/04/ftc-staff-reminds-influencers-brands-clearly-disclose-relationship.

49 Statement of the Federal Trade Commission, *FTC v. LifeLock* (Dec. 17, 2015) ("In short, the existence of a PCI DSS certification is an important consideration in, but by no means the end of, our analysis of reasonable security.").

One such area involves the Children's Online Privacy Protection Act. A pending rule review and the largest ever COPPA settlement (with YouTube) provide an interesting opportunity to explore the inflexibility of rules compared to case-by-case enforcement.

A. *COPPA Rule Review*

COPPA applies to operators of websites or online services that are directed to children under thirteen years old, or where such operators have actual knowledge that they are collecting personal information online from an under thirteen-year-old.[50] In broad strokes, the law requires covered operators "that collect personal information from children under the age of 13 to provide notice to parents and obtain verifiable parental consent before collecting, using, or disclosing personal information from these children."[51]

> The FTC's COPPA rules went into effect in 2000. The Commission typically reviews rules, including COPPA, every ten years. In 2010 the Commission initiated a COPPA rule review that finally resulted in rule changes in 2013. Yet only six years later, the Commission concluded that the rules were already aging poorly and in July 2019 began another rule review. According to the request for comment that initiated the review, "[T]he Commission is conducting its ten-year review early because of questions that have arisen about the Rule's application to the educational technology sector, to voice-enabled connected devices, and to general audience platforms that host third-party child-directed content."[52] FTC Chairman Joe Simons noted that "[i]n light of rapid technological changes that impact the online children's marketplace, we must ensure COPPA remains effective…"[53]

Indeed, since 2013 technology used by children has evolved significantly. Educational technology became a critical part of children's lives as COVID drove months and even years of remote learning. Biometric unlocking of mobile devices is common today but was rare in 2013. Children today commonly use mobile app functions that rely on facial detection and recognition technology.

Most prominently, home internet of things (IoT) devices – particularly voice-activated devices – took off after the adoption of the 2013 changes.[54] The

---

50 16 C.F.R. § 312.

51 Fed. Trade Comm'n, Press Release, FTC Seeks Comments on Children's Online Privacy Protection Act Rule: FTC to host workshop on COPPA in October as part of initiative (July 25, 2019), https://www.ftc.gov/news-events/news/press-releases/2019/07/ftc-seeks-comments-childrens-online-privacy-protection-act-rule.

52 Fed. Trade Comm'n, Request for Public Comment on the Federal Trade Commission's Implementation of the Children's Online Privacy Protection Rule, 84 Fed. Reg. 35842 (July 25, 2019), https://www.regulations.gov/document/FTC-2019-0054-0001.

53 FTC Press release *supra* note 51.

54 For example, the first Amazon Echo device was released in 2014. Brandon Vigliarolo, *Amazon Alexa: Cheat Sheet*, TechRepublic, (Sept. 24, 2020), https://www.techrepublic.com/article/amazon-alexa-the-smart-persons-guide/.

popularity of these devices meant COPPA was sufficiently out of step with the rise of voice-activated assistants that in 2017 FTC staff issued an enforcement policy statement. The statement clarified how the agency would enforce COPPA against certain operators of voice-activated devices.[55] Noting that recording children's voices, even temporarily, triggered COPPA, but recognizing the significant value of using voice as an input (particularly for children), the Commission determined it would not bring enforcement actions against companies that, without parental verifiable consent but under certain conditions, collect children's voices. The request for comment asked whether the FTC should incorporate this enforcement policy statement into the rule.

Commenters on the 2019 request for comment also raised long-standing concerns that COPPA had not effectively protected children's privacy, and yet it diminished the incentive to create useful websites, apps, and other online tools for children.[56] One party, representing approximately 5,000 small business app developers, noted that "[t]he COPPA Rule's burdensome compliance costs have resulted in many children-directed app and software developers closing down their businesses or deciding to target a general audience."[57] Small developers of content for children have also testified directly about the ambiguity of the rules and the disincentives they create.[58]

Overall, the docket drew the largest outpouring of public comments the FTC has ever encountered. More than 118,000 comments have been submitted – most concerned with the effects of the YouTube settlement discussed below. Yet, nearly three years since the initiation of the rule review, no changes have been adopted.

COPPA does have one feature that has helped it keep up with new technologies to some extent. The law authorizes the FTC to approve new parental consent mechanisms, and companies that use these approved mechanisms receive a safe harbor from FTC enforcement of COPPA violations. The FTC has approved six such safe harbors, enabling companies to comply with the law even though Congress could not contemplate all the various ways that notice and consent might be conveyed.[59]

---

55 Fed. Trade Comm'n, Enforcement Policy Statement Regarding the Applicability of the COPPA Rule to the Collection and Use of Voice Recordings (2017), https://www.ftc.gov/legal-library/browse/federal-trade-commission-enforcement-policy-statement-regarding-applicability-childrens-online.

56 *See* Comments of ACT – The App Association (Dec. 11, 2019), https://www.regulations.gov/document/FTC-2019-0054-116872.

57 *Id.*

58 Statement of Harry Jho, CEO & Co-Founder of Sockeye Media LLC and Co-Creator of Mother Goose Club, Transcript of FTC Workshop on The Future of the COPPA Rule, Panel 4: Uses and Misuses of Persistent Identifiers 49 (Oct. 7, 2019), https://www.ftc.gov/system/files/documents/public_events/1535372/transcript_of_coppa_workshop_part_2_1.pdf (stating that independent content creators have been driven by COPPA from the market for creating meaningful content for preschool children).

59 Sarah L. Bruno, et al., *COPPA safe harbors: a new course for industry self-regulatory groups*, ReedSmith (Jan. 24, 2022), https://www.reedsmith.com/en/perspectives/2022/01/coppa-safe-harbors-a-new-course.

B. *YouTube Consent Order*

The FTC's enforcement actions are case-by-case and non-prescriptive. But those actions are typically resolved with detailed and prescriptive settlement orders that set out what the company must do going forward. Such orders are at least as prescriptive as a rulemaking would be, and often even more so. The Commission's privacy and data security settlements provide good examples. For example, the FTC notes that its privacy settlements have required, among other things, "implementation of comprehensive privacy and security programs, biennial assessments by independent experts, monetary redress to consumers, disgorgement of ill-gotten gains, deletion of illegally-obtained consumer information, and providing transparency and choice mechanisms to consumers."[60]

Despite their detail, consent orders are less ossifying than legislation or regulation, primarily because they are limited in scope. They are generally targeted to specific practices by individual companies and do not affect other practices or other companies. In addition, they are typically negotiated with the target company. Each of these factors reduces the knowledge problem. The limited scope to one company also reduces the Procrustean problem to just one company – although, if the FTC adopts the same provisions across major players in a space, the effect on incumbents can be Procrustean. Still, unlike regulation, disruptive challengers need not worry that their business models do not match a consent order's provisions – because those provisions only constrain the incumbent.

But consent orders are still prescriptive and by default are twenty years long. In fast-moving industries, such mandatory practices may be irrelevant in a year, let alone decades. Thus, the pacing problem remains in the FTC's consent order practices, at least as applied to individual companies. The FTC does have some measures to address this. First, companies subject to consent orders can petition to have the order modified. This is not a speedy process, but it is faster than changing an entire regulation. Second, the FTC can learn from the effects of one consent order to modify how it deals with similar future situations.

Typically, one might expect that consent orders would not be particularly rife with regulatory capture. Given that the negotiations are typically only between the FTC and the defendant, and the rules typically only apply to defendants, there is little opportunity for the defendant to disadvantage competitors in the negotiation. Indeed, given their length and narrow scope, consent orders tend to disadvantage the defendant relative to the competition.

However, there are some exceptions that are worth highlighting. Sometimes, competitors will encourage the FTC to impose specific provisions on a competing defendant in a consent order. This is nearly the ideal regulatory situation for a competitor: the opportunity to have government place rules on a competitor

---

60 Fed. Trade Comm'n, Privacy and Data Security Update, *supra* note 37, at 1.

that do not even apply to the petitioner. When this occurs, it generally happens during the public comment period for consent orders that the FTC employs for administrative litigation.

i. YouTube Settlement

We have one recent example of the FTC, together with a tech platform, using a settlement to restructure an entire ecosystem in a way that imposes costs on others while simplifying the platform's compliance costs.

On September 4, 2019, the Federal Trade Commission announced sweeping regulatory changes to the operation of one of the internet's most popular websites. This website has 2 billion monthly active users and features content from more than 50 million individual creators, most of whom are small businesses or individuals. Many of the creators affected earn money using the website, and stand to lose, in aggregate, millions of dollars from these regulatory changes; some will need to restructure their business model. The changes also subject content creators to increased risk of stiff fines. Yet these significant regulatory changes were never put before a legislature; none of the content creators or users of the website were privy to the rationale or design of the regulation; and there was no public process for comment. Instead, the new regulation was confidentially negotiated between the website company and agency staff and put into place by a court.

The FTC's settlement with YouTube over COPPA violations has staked out a new and consequential region on the continuum between hard law and soft law. FTC settlements have long been praised by those who value the soft law benefits of such an approach: (i) flexibility to deal with case-by-case specific problems, particularly in fast-changing industries; (ii) limited need to set industry-wide rules in place; (iii) the ability to shape future behavior through a kind of common law. Such settlements have also long been criticized by those who emphasize the difference between them and hard law: (i) a creation of regulatory ambiguity; (ii) lack of process that considers the interests of the full range of stakeholders; (iii) a "rulemaking" environment with a power differential between the negotiating parties; (iv) an agency ability to accumulate incremental changes to the law that in total can be quite significant.

The YouTube settlement may be the hardest soft law ever generated through the FTC's settlement process. It differs from previous settlements in at least four ways. First, the scale of the effect. This has two components: the large number of third-party individuals affected and the significant size of that effect. Previous settlements (such as Equifax or Facebook) have been with platforms with large numbers of consumers involved, but the direct effect on those consumers was much smaller. The YouTube settlement directly compels action by, and raises regulatory risk for, millions of individuals not party to the settlement.

Second, and related to the first, it is clear from the complaint that the FTC intended the settlement to address non-compliant behavior by non-settling parties

– namely, content creators. Typically, the FTC would bring legal actions against non-compliant parties where the parties would be able to argue their case, but the YouTube settlement will eliminate many non-compliant content creators while making those that remain easier to sue.

Third, the YouTube settlement differs from other settlements because it signals significant changes to the FTC's interpretation of a statute, in this case COPPA. The FTC has authority to change the regulations implementing COPPA and has previously done so, but in APA-compliant rulemakings rather than settlements.

Fourth, the YouTube settlement differs from some other significant settlements in that the Commission used a process that did not provide any opportunity for public comment on the settlement; many other settlements have had a public comment period. (As discussed above, the FTC sought comments on the COPPA rule in July 2019 and extended the comment period after announcing the YouTube settlement; that comment period is now closed and the matter is pending at the agency.)

This hardened soft law raises many questions. Due process and administrative law concerns about the FTC's settlement process have been somewhat overblown in the past – but are harder to ignore in this case. Does this represent a new template for FTC enforcement against platforms? How should the FTC adjust the COPPA rule considering the settlement and the massive feedback from content creators? And the implications of this settlement stretch beyond FTC. It offers lessons about the effects of imposing liability on a platform for hosting non-compliant third-party content – a lesson that will be increasingly relevant as the battle over Section 230 rages.

FTC settlements have always been hard law for the settling company and soft law for everyone else. The YouTube settlement uniquely demonstrates the possibility of getting a rulemaking-like result for many parties through an FTC settlement.

V. Lessons for the Current FTC

The FTC's history of its use of rulemaking and case-by-case adjudications and the various advantages and disadvantages of each approach suggest some paths forward for the current FTC.

1. Embrace Enforcement in Fast-Moving Areas

Enforcement can be abused. Enforcers can be overtly or covertly politically motivated. They can focus on collecting scalps rather than improving the situation for consumers and competitors. Overly aggressive enforcement can chill innovation by signaling – through a process that excludes many stakeholders – an agency's disapproval of a new technology or business model. It can also be inefficient, piecemeal, and whack-a-mole, where the same bad behaviors keep continuously popping up in new places.

But in fast-moving industries or quickly evolving issues, the negative effects of poorly focused and politically motivated enforcement are likely less harmful than the Procrustean effects of even well-intentioned prescriptive regulation. A bad enforcement decision can be ignored or reversed much more easily than a bad regulatory framework. An enforcement-forward approach leaves room for the disruptor to try something new and unforeseen. It is fundamentally a more permissionless environment than are regulatory approaches.

The FTC has deep expertise in building and bringing administrative and federal cases. It should double down on this expertise. And Congress should provide more resources to the agency to expand on this expertise.

As it expands this expertise, the agency should be cautious about being overly prescriptive in settlements, especially in ways that impact third parties not involved in the cases. The YouTube settlement is unusual, and the FTC should seek to keep it that way.

2. Embrace Soft Law

For the many reasons discussed above, soft law will be the primary way by which future technology will be governed. The FTC has decades of experience in facilitating soft law developments and should lean into this capability. The FTC could expand this work by adding staff to the Office of Policy and Planning, which usually coordinates the creation of workshops and often authors the subsequent reports. It could also seek to bring cases against companies who fail to uphold their public promises to maintain certain industry standards or certifications, thereby lending credibility to private soft law efforts.

3. Use Rulemaking Judiciously

It seems the current FTC leadership is eager to shift the FTC away from its core enforcement and soft law competencies toward a more regulatory approach. Chair Lina Khan has called for broad rulemakings, outside even the specific areas to which Congress has explicitly given the agency APA rulemaking authority. For example, she has called for the agency to create competition rules. Such rules would presumably establish certain business practices, currently evaluated under the "rule of reason" in current antitrust law as per se violations of Section 5's prohibition on unfair methods of competition.[61]

Expanding FTC rulemaking is a bad idea for three reasons. First, and most importantly, for the reasons discussed at length above, rulemakings will ultimately

61 Chopra & Khan, *supra* note 27.

undermine the agency's ability to keep up with technology. Nothing about the FTC makes it immune from the knowledge problem, the pacing problem, the Procrustean problem, and the problem of regulatory capture. Because the FTC's jurisdiction is so broad, the knowledge problem and the pacing problem are worse for the FTC than for most agencies.

Second, the FTC has little practical experience in broad rulemakings. The rulemakings the FTC has done have been targeted in the harms addressed and the practices involved. A Section 5 competition rulemaking would presumably cover a wide swath of the economy and apply across many industries. Legally sustainable rulemakings that affect broad swaths of the economy and across many industries would be difficult, expensive, and time-consuming even for agencies with significant rulemaking experience and resources.

Finally, rulemaking absent an express delegation of authority from Congress raises a host of serious legal issues. Others have written on this at length.[62]

In one way, rulemakings (rather than rules) could be productive. If Chair Khan initiates rulemakings, but they fail to produce rules due to delay or lack of time before a change in administration, the intermediate outputs from those proceedings could form the basis of soft law.

VI. Conclusion

The Federal "Technology" Commission, as some have referred to it, has been surprisingly successful at adapting its regulatory tools to meet many of the goals of consumer protection and competition law in new industries. Part of this success has been a side effect of Congress punishing the agency for extra-statutory rulemaking. By limiting the FTC's rulemaking authority, Congress has left room for a more flexible, more adaptable case-by-case, common-law-like process to evolve. Case-by-case is not a flawless approach to legal constraints on companies, but it has kept the FTC up-to-date and able to deal with new developments in technology. The FTC should continue to focus on its enforcement capabilities and continue to foster soft law developments that will help it keep up with technology over the next 100 years.

62 Sean Heather, Sr., Why the FTC is Powerless When it Comes to Competition Rulemaking, U.S. CHAMBER OF COM. (Aug. 12, 2021), https://www.uschamber.com/technology/why-the-ftc-powerless-when-it-comes-competition-rulemaking; Lawrence J. Spiwak, *A Change in Direction for the Federal Trade Commission?* 22 FEDERALIST SOC'Y REV. 304 (Nov. 29, 2021), https://fedsoc.org/commentary/publications/a-change-in-direction-for-the-federal-trade-commission.

Privacy Rulemaking at the FTC

James C. Cooper*
Antonin Scalia Law School, George Mason University

Abstract

The FTC was early to recognize that the ease with which online firms could collect and share consumer information would make privacy a core consumer protection issue. The FTC skillfully has used case-by-case enforcement under its section 5 authority to address privacy concerns for nearly twenty-five years, yet there are some potentially important limitations to this approach, which are likely to dilute the FTC's ability to optimally deter harmful data practices. Recently, the FTC has expressed interest in its organic rulemaking power, dropping serious hints that it is prepared to pursue rules under its dual authorities to prevent "unfair and deceptive acts or practices" (UDAP) and "unfair methods of competition" (UMC). But before the FTC discards its enforcement-based approach to privacy, it is important to consider the opportunity costs. While a rule banning certain conduct provides legal clarity and the ability to pursue monetary remedies, it comes at the cost of flexibility. This chapter explores these tradeoffs and the legal boundaries of possible privacy rulemaking paths. If history provides any guide for potentially fertile rulemaking areas, a few candidates emerge, including notice-and-consent requirements for certain types of sensitive surveillance, and requirements about the form of privacy disclosures. Rules that go beyond these areas would have to rely on information collected in the rulemaking process and a more expansive view of the FTC's unfairness authority. Given its shaky legal grounds and the tenuous link between privacy practices and anticompetitive conduct, UMC rulemaking seems a particularly bad path for the FTC to take.

---

* Professor of Law and Director, Program on Economics & Privacy, Antonin Scalia Law School, George Mason University.

I. Introduction

The Federal Trade Commission (FTC), in many ways, has become the nation's leading privacy regulator by accident. As the Internet began to burgeon, the FTC was early to recognize that the ease with which online firms could collect and share consumer information would make privacy a core consumer protection issue.[1] Well aware of section 5's limitations in addressing some of its central privacy concerns, the FTC in 2000 asked Congress to pass privacy legislation that would give it the ability to craft privacy rules.[2] More than two decades later, the FTC is still waiting for Congress to act, but the Commission has not sat idly by: in the meantime, it has employed its century-old statute, which broadly prohibits "unfair or deceptive acts or practices" and "unfair methods of competition," in service of consumer privacy.[3] Since its first privacy case in 1999,[4] the FTC has sued countless firms, alleging that their privacy practices violated the FTC Act. Importantly, all of these cases have settled, meaning that no court has ever weighed in on the application of section 5 to privacy issues.[5]

---

1 Fed. Trade Comm'n, Privacy Online: A Report to Congress 41 (June 1998) [hereinafter "1998 Privacy Report"], https://www.ftc.gov/sites/default/files/documents/reports/privacy-online-report-congress/priv-23a.pdf ("While American businesses have always collected some information from consumers in order to facilitate transactions, the Internet allows for the efficient, inexpensive collection of a vast amount of information. It is the prevalence, ease, and relative low cost of such information collection that distinguishes the online environment from more traditional means of commerce and information collection and thus raises consumer concerns."). *Id.* at 40

2 Fed. Trade Comm'n, Privacy Online: Fair Information Practices in the Electronic Marketplace: A Report to Congress 33 (May 2000 [hereinafter "2000 Privacy Report"]), https://www.ftc.gov/sites/default/files/documents/reports/privacy-online-fair-information-practices-electronic-marketplace-federal-trade-commission-report/privacy2000.pdf (noting that "the Commission lacks authority to require firms to adopt information practice policies or to abide by the fair information practice principles on their Web sites, or portions of their Web sites, not directed to children," and urging Congress to pass legislation to set adequate protection of consumer privacy online and give rulemaking authority to an "implementing agency"). *Id.* at 34. During the early 2000s, the FTC moved away from calls for privacy legislation, instead favoring a self-regulatory approach bolstered by FTC enforcement of deception and harmful practices. *See* Timothy J. Muris, Protecting Consumers' Privacy: 2002 and Beyond, Remarks at the 2001 Privacy Conference (Oct. 4, 2001), https://www.ftc.gov/news-events/news/speeches/protecting-consumers-privacy-2002-beyond; *Behavioral Advertising Before the Sen. Comm. on Commerce, Sci., and Transp.*, 110th Cong. 1 (July 9, 2008) (statement of Lydia Parnes, Director of the Bureau of Consumer Protection, Fed. Trade Comm'n), https://www.ftc.gov/news-events/press-releases/2008/07/ftc-testifies-behavioral-advertising. However, beginning in 2009 the FTC has continued to ask Congress to pass privacy legislation that would give the FTC rulemaking authority under the Administrative Procedure Act. *See* Fed. Trade Comm'n, Protecting Consumer Privacy in an Era of Rapid Change: Recommendations for Businesses and Policymakers (Mar. 2012), https://www.ftc.gov/sites/default/files/documents/reports/federal-trade-commission-report-protecting-consumer-privacy-era-rapid-change-recommendations/120326privacyreport.pdf; *Legislative Hearing on H.R. 2221, the Data Accountability and Protection Act, and H.R. 1319, the Informed P2P User Act, Before the H.R. Comm. on Energy & Commerce*, 111th Cong. 12, 17 (2009) (statement of Eileen Harrington, Acting Director of the Bureau of Consumer Protection, FTC), https://www.ftc.gov/sites/default/files/documents/public_statements/prepared-statement-federal-trade-commission-legislative-hearing-h.r.2221-data-accountability-and-protection-act-and-h.r.1319-informed-p2p-user-act/p064504peertopeertestimony.pdf.

3 15 U.S.C. § 45(a).

4 *In re* Geocities, 127 F.T.C. 94 (1999).

5 This chapter addresses only the FTC's privacy enforcement actions, which generally revolve around the collection or use of consumer information in ways contrary to the defendants' promises or otherwise harmful to consumers. The FTC also has a vibrant program addressing data security, which typically involves firms failing to adhere to their promises to secure consumer data, or to otherwise take adequate precautions to secure consumer data, that they have collected legitimately (e.g., through sales or the provision of healthcare services). The FTC has litigated three data security cases: LabMD, Inc. v. FTC, 894 F.3d 1221 (11th Cir.

There can be no doubt that the FTC skillfully has used enforcement under its section 5 authority to address privacy concerns over the past two decades, yet there are some potentially important limitations to this approach. Perhaps most significant, the FTC lacks the ability to obtain monetary remedies to back up its privacy enforcement. But this is not the fault of the recent decision in *AMG Capital Management, LLC v. FTC*;[6] the type of harm typically associated with suspect privacy practices has never fit neatly into any of the pockets of remedial authority found in the FTC Act. Second, the decision of the Commission to challenge one firm's privacy practice does not automatically bar others from engaging in the same practice: the FTC must prove (or have a credible threat to prove) the elements of deception[7] or unfairness[8] in each case. What is more, deception – the FTC's preferred theory in privacy cases – allows only informational remedies; it cannot be used to prescribe or proscribe certain data practices. Although the Commission's enforcement decisions may constitute a quasi-common law, sketching a border between permitted and proscribed data practices, given the contextual nuance of each case, and the fact that no court has yet to bless the FTC's legal theories applied to privacy, it does so imperfectly at best.

The upshot of these limitations is likely a dilution of the FTC's ability to optimally deter harmful data practices.[9] First, the inability to secure monetary remedies that track consumer harm means that the FTC cannot force firms to internalize the external costs of their business practices, a necessary condition for optimal deterrence. Second, to the extent that the series of complaints and consents that make up the FTC's quasi-common law of privacy leaves uncertainty about the line between legal and illegal behavior, businesses may forego socially optimal behavior for fear of running afoul of the FTC Act.[10]

2018) (vacating the FTC's order as unreasonably vague); FTC v. Wyndham Worldwide Corp., 799 F.3d 236 (3d Cir. 2015) (upholding the FTC's power to proscribe "unreasonable" data security practices under its unfairness authority); FTC v. D-Link Sys., Inc., 2017 WL 4150873 (N.D. Cal. Sept. 19, 2017) (dismissing the FTC's unfairness claim due to a failure to allege a likelihood of substantial injury).

6 AMG Capital Management, LLC v. FTC, 593 U.S. __, 141 S. Ct. 1341, 1344, 1347-49 (2021) *See also* Jarod Bona, *The US Supreme Court rules that the FTC is unauthorized to seek monetary damages in antitrust cases (AMG Capital Management)*, E-COMPETITIONS APRIL 2021, art. No. 103294.

7 To make out a deception claim, the FTC must show a material misrepresentation is likely to deceive a significant minority of reasonable consumers. *See* 1983 FTC Policy Statement on Deception, https://www.ftc.gov/legal-library/browse/ftc-policy-statement-deception.

8 To make out an unfairness claim, the FTC must show that an act or practice caused, or was likely to cause, substantial consumer injury that was unavoidable and not outweighed by countervailing benefits to consumers or competition. *See* 1980 FTC Policy Statement on Unfairness, https://www.ftc.gov/legal-library/browse/ftc-policy-statement-unfairness.

9 Optimal deterrence occurs when firms perfectly internalize the external harm they cause so that they have incentives to engage in conduct only if it creates net benefits for society. *See* James C. Cooper & Bruce H. Kobayashi, *Equitable Monetary Relief Under the FTC Act: An Opportunity for a Marginal Improvement*, 83 ANTITRUST L.J. 645 (2021).

10 If firms are uncertain about the boundary between legal and illegal actions, for a wide variety of cost structures and distributions, they will rationally take too much care to avoid liability. *See* John E. Calfee & Richard Craswell, *Some Effects of Uncertainty on Compliance with Legal Standards*, 70 VA. L. REV. 965 (1984).

These shortcomings are not news; recognition of the deficiencies in the case-by-case enforcement approach is why the FTC has spent the better part of the last twenty years asking Congress for privacy legislation that would grant the FTC the power to issue privacy rules with civil penalty authority. Though there appears to be new momentum on Capitol Hill to provide the FTC with a more robust toolkit to deal with privacy issues,[11] the FTC has taken a newfound interest in its organic rulemaking power, dropping serious hints that it is prepared to pursue rules under its dual authorities to prevent "unfair and deceptive acts or practices" (UDAP) and "unfair methods of competition" (UMC).[12] Indeed, in the fall of 2021, the FTC quietly notified the Office of Information and Regulatory Affairs that it was contemplating rulemaking on "Commercial Surveillance."[13]

But before the FTC discards its enforcement-based approach to privacy, it is important to consider the opportunity costs. While a rule banning certain conduct provides legal clarity and the ability to pursue monetary remedies, it comes at the cost of flexibility. When a practice is widespread, consumers suffer similarly from banned practices, and firms face similar costs to avoid prohibited practices, a rule is likely to provide the same net benefits to most of the covered population. But when consumer harm and prevention costs are heterogenous, a one-size-fits-all rule can create more harm than good by forcing firms to provide meager benefits to some consumers at a steep cost. Exacerbating this problem, rules are far less adaptable to changing circumstances that impact the harm and prevention costs associated with a practice. Of course, rules themselves can be flexible, but as rules start to look more like broad conduct standards – e.g., "take reasonable care" – it is less clear what advantage they might offer over a case-by-case approach.

This chapter addresses the tradeoffs between the certainty of rulemaking and the flexibility inherent to the FTC's current approach in the context of privacy regulation. Part II provides an overview of the FTC's current approach to privacy under its section 5 authority, and examines the pros and cons of rulemaking versus case-by-case enforcement. Parts III and IV form the core of the chapter, exploring the legal boundaries of possible privacy rulemaking paths for the FTC, including under both its UDAP and UMC authorities. Part V concludes.

---

11 *See, e.g.*, S. 2499, 117th Cong. (2021) (would provide the FTC rulemaking authority over consumer privacy); S. 2710, 117th Cong. (2021) (would provide the FTC with the same over consumer privacy as it does under the Federal Trade Commission Act); H.R. 5807, 117th Cong. (2021) (would authorize the FTC to implement regulations for greater consumer privacy).

12 In 1975, Congress explicitly granted the FTC the authority to promulgate consumer protection rules, albeit under the so-called Magnuson-Moss procedures, which are a hybrid between informal and formal APA rulemaking. 15 U.S.C. § 57. The FTC can seek civil penalties for "knowing" violations of these rules and damages.

13 *See* Trade Regulation Rule on Commercial Surveillance, RIN No. 3084-AB69, OIRA (Fall 2021); *see also* Devin Coldeway, *FTC may consider rule curbing algorithmic discrimination and 'commercial surveillance,'* TechCrunch (Dec. 15, 2021), https://techcrunch.com/2021/12/15/ftc-may-consider-rule-curbing-algorithmic-discrimination-and-commercial-surveillance.

II. The Current FTC Approach to Privacy

The FTC was early in recognizing how the collection and use of consumer data in the online world would pose an important consumer protection issue. In 1998, the FTC issued its first privacy report, and in recognition that it lacked authority to require firms to adopt information practices, it called on Congress to pass legislation to allow the FTC to protect children's online privacy.[14] Two years later, the commissioner repeated its call for legislation, but this time urging that it cover all consumers.[15] Nearly a quarter of a century later, the FTC is still waiting for privacy legislation. But the lack of legislative authority to mandate certain information practices has not stopped the FTC from acting to protect consumer privacy. In what is widely seen as the most popular consumer protection measure in the FTC's history, the FTC vindicated consumer privacy by enacting the "Do Not Call Registry" pursuant to its authority under the Telemarketing Sales Act.[16]

The FTC also stepped into the breach left by congressional inaction by enforcing its expansive section 5 power against firms' unfair and deceptive privacy practices.[17] Early FTC actions centered on breaches of express promises related to the collection and use of consumer data, and were pleaded as deception.[18] As the Internet matured, so did the FTC's application of its UDAP powers. For example, consistent with longstanding FTC policy regarding the ability to disclaim representations, in *Sears Holdings*, the FTC found that disclosures made in privacy policies were insufficient to correct an initial impression that certain data would not be collected.[19] Further, the FTC began to focus not only on express promises, but also on implicit representations found in platforms' interfaces,[20] manuals,[21] FAQs,[22] marketing,[23] and blog postings.[24] The FTC has also expanded the use of UDAP beyond deception, finding the collection and use of certain types of sensitive data without adequate consent to be an unfair practice.[25] Importantly, the FTC has yet to litigate a single privacy case

---

14 1998 Privacy Report at 41 (June 1998).

15 2000 Privacy Report at 33 (May 2000),

16 Telemarketing Sales Rule, Final Amended Rule, 69 Fed. Reg. 4580 (Jan. 29, 2003), codified at 16 C.F.R. § 310.

17 45 U.S.C. § 45(a)

18 *See, e.g.*, Geocities, 127 F.T.C. 94

19 *In re* Sears Holdings Mgmt. Corp., No. 82-3099, 2009 WL 2979770, at *5 (F.T.C. Aug. 31, 2009).

20 *See* United States v. Facebook, Inc., No. 19-cv-2184, at 21–26 (D.D.C. 2019).

21 *In re* HTC America Inc., No. C-4406, 2013 WL 3477025, at *6–7 (F.T.C. 2013).

22 United States v. Google Inc., No. 12-04177, at 8–10 (N.D. Cal. 2012).

23 *In re* Snapchat, Inc., 2015-1 Trade Cas. (CCH), 2014 WL 7495798, at *1–2 (F.T.C. Dec. 23, 2014).

24 Complaint at 12, *In re* Facebook, Inc., No. C-4365 (F.T.C. July 27, 2012).

25 *See In re* Google Inc., No. C-4336 (F.T.C. Oct. 13, 2011); *In re* DesignerWare, LLC, No. 112-3151, 2013 WL 1684153 (F.T.C. Apr. 11, 2013).

– this entire body of UDAP law is based on consent decrees, and thus has never been tested in court.[26]

1. Limits to the Current Approach

The creative use of its UDAP authority to address privacy concerns has allowed the FTC to become the nation's leading privacy regulatory, but this approach has some important drawbacks. The goal of any public law regime, like section 5, should be optimal deterrence: creating a set of incentives that lead covered actors to engage in conduct only if it generates consumer benefits in excess of direct costs and external harms. Broadly, there are two approaches an agency can use to accomplish this goal.[27] One approach, akin to strict liability in tort law, does not define any area of forbidden conduct, but instead requires firms to pay for all of the external harm their conduct causes. Forcing firms to internalize their externalities in this way leads to efficient incentives, as firms rationally will forego conduct that creates more harm than benefits. A second approach, akin to a negligence standard in tort law, requires an agency to identify behavior that is on net harmful to society and set penalties sufficiently high to prevent firms from engaging in this proscribed conduct.[28]

The current application of section 5 to privacy is much more like this second approach, where the FTC brings section 5 enforcement actions against firms it believes are engaging in unfair or deceptive data practices; only firms that violate the legal standard are punished. In this way, case-by-case enforcement of section 5 can generate common-law-like rules by mapping out conduct that triggers FTC enforcement.[29] But this quasi-common law approach suffers two important shortcomings in creating economy-wide privacy norms, both related to the FTC's remedial powers.

The most important shortcoming of using section 5 to deter firms from engaging in net harmful privacy practices is a lack of effective monetary remedies. Harm-based remedies can be used to effect optimal deterrence; if firms realize that they will be forced to pay for the harm their practices cause consumers, they will engage only in acts that create more good than harm for society.[30] Unfortunately, the monetary remedies available to the Commission for unfair or deceptive data practices are unlikely to create the needed internalization of consumer harm.

If the FTC brings a case administratively, it can obtain only injunctive relief – requiring the firm to stop engaging in the challenged business practice, and in

---

26 *See* Daniel J. Solove & Woodrow Hartzog, *The FTC and the New Common Law of Privacy*, 114 Colum. L. Rev 583, 619 (2014).

27 Robert Cooter, *Prices and Sanctions*, 84 Colum. L. Rev. 1523 (1984).

28 These penalties need not be equal to consumer harm. A wide range of penalties can deter firms from engaging in proscribed conduct as long as they make the conduct unprofitable.

29 *See* Solove & Hartzog, *supra* note 26.

30 *See* Cooper & Kobayashi, *supra* note 9, at 668–69 (2021).

some instances, requiring the firm to take additional prophylactic measures.[31] These injunctive requirements, which typically run for twenty years, probably place non-trivial costs on defendant firms – especially if it requires major changes in business model or reduces the ability to monetize consumer data. But there is no correspondence between these compliance costs and consumer harm, which is a necessary condition to force firms to internalize the expected harm their data practices cause.

Section 19 of the FTC Act provides the Commission with the ability to obtain equitable relief and damages from companies after a fully litigated administrative proceeding, and only for conduct that a "reasonable [person] would have known… was dishonest or fraudulent."[32] These conditions are unlikely to be satisfied for privacy cases, as to date, all have been settled, and most typically involve misfeasance, not the type of malfeasance that would satisfy section 19. What is more, even if a case were to satisfy the section 19 predicates, the subjective nature of privacy harms likely would make it difficult for the FTC to adequately quantify damages.[33]

Although last year's *AMG* decision, which took away the FTC's ability to obtain equitable monetary relief in federal court for first-time violations of the FTC Act, has had important ramifications for the FTC's ability to remedy fraud-related to the sale of goods and services, it is unlikely to have much of an impact on the FTC's privacy portfolio.[34] The Commission's pre-*AMG* power was limited to obtaining the money that consumers spent on fraudulently marketed products.[35] The Commission's typical privacy case, however, does not involve monetary flows from consumers to the defendant firm, so there is no equitable relief to obtain in the first place. This fact explains why all but one of the FTC's privacy cases that rely on its UDAP power have been brought administratively and settled without any monetary remedies.[36]

---

31 In some cases, the FTC will include so-called fencing-in relief that prohibits conduct not alleged to have violated the FTC Act. *See, e.g.*, Telebrands Corp. v. FTC, 457 F.3d 354, 357 n. 5 (4th Cir. 2006); FTC v. Colgate-Palmolive Co., 380 U.S. 374, 394–95 (1965). For example, the FTC has required in an order certain defendants to obtain "affirmative express consent" from their users before changing their data collection practices, although not alleging that failure to obtain opt-in consent had violate the FTC Act. *Compare In re* Facebook, Inc., Dkt. No. 4365, Decision and Order at Sec. II (July 12, 2012) (requiring Facebook to obtain "affirmative express consent" before using data in a materially different way), *with In re* Facebook, Inc., Dkt. No. 4365, Compl. at ¶29 (Nov. 29, 2011) (failure to obtain "informed consent" for material changes to use of already collected data was unfair practice)

32 15 U.S.C. § 57b.

33 *See, e.g.*, Burns v. Mammoth Media, Inc., 2021 WL 3500964 (C.D. Cal., Aug. 6, 2021) (dismissing a data breach case under 12(b)(1) for lack of standing when the alleged harm is subjective privacy harm).

34 *AMG*, 141 S. Ct. at 1344, 1347–49 (2021). *See also* Bona, *supra* note 6.

35 FTC v. Commerce Planet, Inc., 878 F. Supp. 2d 1048, 1088-90 (C.D. Cal. 2012), *aff'd in part*, 642 F. App'x 680 (9th Cir. 2016), and *aff'd in part, vacated in part, remanded*, 815 F.3d 593 (9th Cir. 2016).

36 The only exception is *VIZIO*, which was brought in federal district court with the New Jersey Attorney General. $1.5 million of the $2.2 million total monetary remedy was paid to the FTC. *See* Fed. Trade Comm'n, Press Release, VIZIO to Pay $2.2 Million to FTC, State of New Jersey to Settle Charges It Collected Viewing Histories on 11 Million Smart Televisions without Users' Consent, FTC (Feb. 6, 2017), https://www.ftc.gov/news-events/news/press-releases/2017/02/vizio-pay-22-million-ftc-state-new-jersey-settle-charges-it-collected-

All of this means that, as a practical matter, the FTC has the ability to obtain monetary remedies for privacy violations only against firms that have agreed to a consent order to settle section 5 charges. Failing to comply with an order – over $44,000 per violation – can be expensive, and the FTC has obtained substantial penalties against Google and Facebook for order violations.[37] The ability to obtain civil penalties for order violations may be effective at securing specific deterrence, but because this remedial power is limited to specific practices that individual companies have agreed to abstain from, it is unlikely to have a major impact on general deterrence.[38]

The second shortcoming of the current approach is due to difficulties in using section 5 enforcement to prohibit or prescribe certain data practices. While the FTC can obtain cease-and-desist orders in administrative and federal court actions, these injunctions must be tied to the allegedly unlawful conduct. For example, if an FTC complaint alleges deception against a company for lying about placing tracking cookies on users' browsers despite expressly or implicitly representing it does not, an FTC order can require the firm to stop lying about the placement of cookies, but *not to stop using cookies*.[39] Thus, a company can resolve the FTC's complaint by continuing to use tracking cookies as long as it is no longer deceiving consumers about the practice – which could include no longer making *any* express or implied representations about the presence or absence of cookies.[40] The upshot is that the FTC's deception authority can be used to define acceptable disclosures

viewing-histories-11-million. The ability to obtain a monetary settlement may have rested on the fact that, unlike most privacy cases, *VIZIO* involved consumer expenditures on a product, which could be refunded.

37 *See, e.g.*, United States v. Facebook, Inc., Stipulated Order for Civil Penalty, Monetary Judgment, and Injunctive Relief, No. 19-cv-2184 (D.D.C. , July 24, 2019) ($5 billion civil penalty); United States v. Google, Inc., Order Approving Stipulated Order for Permanent Injunction and Civil Penalty Judgment, No. CV 12-04177 SI (N.D. Cal., Nov. 16, 2012) ($22.5 million civil penalty).

38 Order provisions can map out how the Commission intends to approach enforcement decisions. But the impact of order provisions on general deterrence is likely to be minimal, given that it is only backed by the possibility of initiating an administrative action, which despite the concomitant costs, is less than civil penalties. The FTC Act also allows the Commission to seek civil penalties from any firm that engages in conduct that the FTC has found to be "unfair or deceptive" in a fully litigated administrative action against another firm, but only if the defendant had "actual knowledge" that their conduct violated the FTC Act. *See* 15 U.S.C. § 45(m)(1)(B). For a full discussion, *see* notes 106-108 *infra*, and accompanying text.

39 *See, e.g., In re* Nomi Technologies, Inc., No. C-4538, at 2 (F.T.C. Aug. 28, 2015).

40 Commissioners Ohlhausen and Wright both make this point in their respective dissents in *Nomi*. Dissenting Statement of Commissioner Maureen K. Ohlhausen In the Matter of Nomi Technologoies, Inc., (Aug. 28, 2015), https://www.ftc.gov/legal-library/browse/cases-proceedings/public-statements/dissenting-statement-commissioner-maureen-k-ohlhausen-matter-nomi-technologies-inc; Dissenting Statement of Commissioner Joshua D. Wright In the Matter of Nomi Technologoies, Inc. (Apr. 23, 2015), https://www.ftc.gov/legal-library/browse/cases-proceedings/public-statements/dissenting-statement-commissioner-joshua-d-wright-matter-nomi-technologies-inc. The FTC can allege that failure to disclose a practice constitutes a deceptive omission, but this cause of action is limited to instances in which the data practice at issue would be so contrary to reasonable consumer expectations as to change the character of the product. For example, failing to disclose that a car is incapable of reaching highway speeds would be a deceptive omission. *See In re* Int'l Harvester Co., 104 F.T.C. 949 (1984); *In re* Lenovo (United States) Inc., No. 152-3134, 2017 WL 4021825 (F.T.C. Sept. 5, 2017). A deceptive omission – a setting in which the defendant has made no representation at all – is distinct from a failure to adequately disclose a material fact that is necessary to prevent an express or implied claim from being misleading. For example, a representation that a website will collect "browsing history" may be deceptive if the website fails to adequately disclose that it will also be collecting sensitive health or financial information that users input into websites they visit. *See In re* Sears Holdings *supra* note 19.

or what constitutes a privacy representation; at bottom, it cannot do much work beyond spelling out a prosaic rule against deceiving consumers about data collection and use. Thus, the FTC is unable to lean on its deception power to effect, for example, a notice-and-choice regime, let alone regulate data collection and use.

The FTC's other enforcement tool – unfairness – can be used to attack specific practices that are likely to cause substantial consumer injury that is unavoidable and is not outweighed by countervailing benefits to consumers or competition.[41] Not surprisingly, given that an unfairness claim requires the FTC to prove (or have a credible threat to prove) more than a deception claim, the FTC has rarely applied an unfairness theory in privacy cases.[42] Because injury under unfairness focuses on tangible monetary or physical harm, moreover, it can be difficult to position pure subjective privacy harms into an unfairness theory.[43] Finally, the ability of the FTC to use unfairness to map out prohibited and required conduct is further limited by the fact that case-specific factors are likely to influence the cost-benefit calculation at the heart of unfairness. Thus, while the FTC might be able to use unfairness to obtain an order preventing one company from engaging in a data practice, this prohibition does not necessarily neatly map onto other firms if they, for example, operate in different industries or serve different customers so that the practice in question generates a different benefit-cost profile.

2. Advantages of Case-by-Case Enforcement: Heterogeneity and Flexibility

Moving to a rules-based regime would change the FTC's privacy toolkit in three important ways. First, a rule would allow the FTC to ban precise conduct that it believes is inherently unfair or deceptive, and additionally to require prophylactic actions to prevent this proscribed conduct from occurring in the first place.[44] Second, it would lower the Commission's costs of bringing enforcement actions by reducing its evidentiary burden in enforcement actions: rather than having to prove (or having a credible threat to prove) the elements of unfairness or deception in each case, it would merely have to show that the conduct at issue was the same as that prohibited by the rule.[45] Third, the FTC would be able to obtain monetary remedies to "redress injury to consumers,"[46] and substantial civil penalties when the defendant acted with "actual knowledge or knowledge fairly implied" that the conduct in question violated a rule.[47]

---

41 *See* 1980 FTC Policy Statement on Unfairness, *supra* note 8.

42 Research indicates that the FTC has used unfairness in eight privacy cases. *See infra* notes 120-131 –, and accompanying text for a detailed treatment of these cases.

43 *See* notes 114-25, *infra*, and accompanying text.

44 15 U.S.C. § 57a(a)(1)(B).

45 *See* Nat'l Petroleum Refiners Ass'n v. FTC, 482 F.2d 672, 674–75 (D.C. Cir. 1973).

46 45 U.S.C. § 57b(b).

47 45 U.S.C. § 45(m).

While rulemaking could be seen as a solution to the limitations of using case-by-case enforcement to achieve optimal deterrence, this path is not costless. What a rule gains in certainty, it loses in flexibility because it treats all covered practices as if they have the same benefit-cost profile. If these profiles are fairly uniform across all possible cases, rules and case-by-case enforcement will arrive at the same outcome most of the time, and rules will do it more efficiently. But when the consumer harm or precaution costs are heterogenous, even if a rule is calibrated to the average case, it will be welfare reducing compared to a case-by-case approach because it will either over- or under-deter most of the population.[48] That is, when there is significant heterogeneity in the covered population, the certainty that a rule provides is a bug, not a feature.

Heterogeneity seems likely in the case of data practices. Consider the use of consumer information to serve tailored online advertisements, which is the subject of a rulemaking petition,[49] and has been flagged by the Commission as a potential subject for rulemaking.[50] No one seriously disputes that all else constant, consumers value their privacy. But not all types of data are the same: a search for dish soap on Google is likely to be less private than a search for incontinence products or birth control, and real-time geolocation data of a child is likely to raise more concerns than cookies designed to track online shopping habits. Importantly, holding the type of information collected constant, different people will suffer different privacy harms. That is, privacy harm varies across individuals and contexts.

The same can be said on the benefit side. Firms monetize consumer data through a variety of mechanisms. It can be used to increase engagement and traffic – for example, by honing a recommendation engine for videos, news, or search, or by producing better content – which increases ad inventory or revenue from subscriptions, if a pay service. It can also be used to target ads – which increases revenues from a given amount of traffic.[51] What is more, this revenue can be poured back into content provision, which in turn drives more traffic.[52] In this manner, tailored advertising based on consumer information plays a key role in facilitating consumers' free access to myriad online content. Further, tools that

48 *See* Steven Shavell, *A Model of the Optimal Use of Liability and Safety Regulation*, 15 RAND J. ECON. 271, 276–77 (1984); James C. Cooper, *Separation Anxiety*, 21 VA. J.L. & TECH. 1, 50–51 (2017).

49 Petition for Rulemaking to Prohibit Surveillance Advertising, Accountable Tech, No. FTC-2021-0070 (Dec. 3, 2021).

50 *See* Remarks of Chair Lina M. Khan As Prepared for Delivery IAPP Global Privacy Summit 2022 (Apr. 11, 2022), https://www.ftc.gov/news-events/news/speeches/remarks-chair-lina-m-khan-prepared-delivery-iapp-global-privacy-summit-2022.

51 Several researchers have studied the impact of moving from targeted to contextual ads and found large reductions in publisher revenue as a result. *See, e.g.*, Avi Goldfarb & Catherine E. Tucker, *Privacy Regulation and Online Advertising*, 57 MANAG. SCI. 57, 57–58, 64 (2011) (65% reduction in revenue); Howard Beales & Jeffrey A. Eisenach, *An Empirical Analysis of the Value of Information Sharing in the Market for Online Content* 11–13 (2014), https://papers.ssrn.com/sol3/papers.cfm?abstract_id=2421405 (66% reduction); Garrett A. Johnson, Scott K. Shriver & Shaoyin Du, *Consumer Privacy Choice in Online Advertising: Who Opts Out and at What Cost to Industry?*, 39 MARK. SCI. 33, 33 (2020) (52% reduction); Deepak Ravichandran & Nitish Korula, *Effect of Disabling Third-Party Cookies on Publisher Revenue*, GOOGLE (Aug. 27, 2019) (64% reduction); *The Value of Personalized Ads to a Thriving App Ecosystem*, FACEBOOK (June 18, 2020) (50% reduction).

52 Beales & Eisenach, *supra* note 51, at 7–8.

allow advertisers more efficiently to reach consumers who are likely to be interested in what they are selling enhances consumer information and spurs competition in product markets, also to consumers' benefit.[53] Note that the monetization process typically requires that there are benefits to consumers – more relevant advertising, better content, more customization. As with the privacy harms, different consumers will value these benefits differently – some may find no value in ads related to recent shopping, whereas others may enjoy the information to discover new products or lower prices.

At the end of the day, how data collection and use impacts individuals is likely to be highly complex and idiosyncratic. It depends on the joint distribution of privacy harms and data collection benefits.[54] In this manner, the range of data practices that would create harm in excess of benefits for most consumers, and thus good candidates for prohibitory rules, might be quite narrow. That rules are far less adaptable to rapidly changing harm and prevention costs only exacerbates this potential problem with rulemaking in a dynamic environment.[55] Of course, rules themselves can be flexible, but as rules start to look more like broad conduct standards, any advantages over a case-by-case approach start to dissipate.

The extent to which rulemaking would better allow the FTC to achieve optimal deterrence is ultimately an empirical question. On the one hand, to the extent that these remedies are calibrated to consumer harm, they can force firms to internalize the external harm they cause.[56] On the other hand, given the extreme difficulty in quantifying privacy harms and the heterogeneity with which these harms are likely suffered, rulemaking could just as easily lead to over- or under-deterrence.

3. Possible Rulemaking Paths

Given some of the drawbacks inherent to the FTC's current approach to constructing economy-wide privacy norms, it should not be surprising that the FTC has signaled that it may be preparing to dust off its rulemaking toolkit. For example, in one of the first actions under the new chair, the Commission modified several Mag-Moss procedures, ostensibly to make rulemaking "more efficient."[57] Further, in its annual

---

53 *See, e.g.*, C. Robert Clark, *Advertising, Restrictions and Competition in the Children's Breakfast Cereal Industry*, 50 J.L. & Econ. 757 (2007); Pauline M. Ippolito & Alan Mathios, *Information, Advertising and Health Choices: A Study of the Cereal Market*, 21 RAND J. Econ. 459 (1990).

54 *See* Daniel P. O'Brien & Douglas Smith, *Privacy in Online Markets: A Welfare Analysis of Demand Rotations* (Fed. Trade Comm'n. Bureau of Econ. Working Paper No. 323, 2014), https://www.ftc.gov/system/files/documents/reports/privacy-online-markets-welfare-analysis-demand-rotations/wp323.pdf.

55 Change to rules require using the notice-and-comment procedure.

56 *See* Cooper & Kobayashi, *supra* note 9.

57 Fed. Trade. Comm'n, Statement of the Commission Regarding the Adoption of Revised Section 19 Rulemaking Procedures 1–3 (July 9, 2021), https://www.ftc.gov/system/files/documents/public_statements/1591786/p210100commnstmtsec18rulesofpractice.pdf. As Beales & Muris note, these changes were adopted based on the fiction that the Reagan administration had adopted procedures to curtail rulemaking. In fact, most of the procedures were already in place prior to the Regan administration, and in any event, were never followed. . Howard Beales III & Timothy J. Muris, *Back to the Future: How Not to Write a Regulation* at 4, American Enterprise Institute (*forthcoming*, 2022).

report to Congress on privacy and data security efforts, the Commission touted its rulemaking power as an important tool "to protect Americans' privacy,"[58] and in its annual Statement of Regulatory Priorities, the FTC stated that it "is particularly focused on developing rules that allow the agency to... seek penalties for firms that engage in data abuses."[59] What is more, the FTC has emphasized the need to approach data and competition issues "holistically," opening the door to the possibility of pursuing privacy rulemaking under its UMC authority. Finally, suggesting that these statements are more than just bluster, in the fall of 2021, the FTC quietly let the Office of Information and Regulatory Affairs know that it was considering rulemaking on the subject of "Commercial Surveillance."[60]

Broadly, there are two ways for the FTC to promulgate a privacy rule. First, the FTC could act on specific authority from Congress. For example, Congress commanded the FTC to promulgate rules to enforce the Children's Online Privacy Protection Act (COPPA).[61] This type of rulemaking is relatively straightforward, as it is limited to the congressional grant of authority.[62] The second path is more complicated and the focus of the next two sections: the FTC could use its organic authority under section 5 to declare certain data practices to be either "unfair or deceptive acts or practices" or "unfair methods of competition." Below, I discuss how both approaches might work in practice.

III. UDAP Rules

1. History and Procedures

Section 5 of the FTC Act provides the FTC with the power to proscribe "unfair and deceptive acts and practices."[63] Although the FTC originally had disclaimed any substantive rulemaking authority, beginning in 1962, it reversed path, discovering this authority in section 6(g), which permits the Commission "[f]rom time

---

58 FTC Report to Congress on Privacy and Data Security 8 (Sept. 13, 2021) [hereinafter "Privacy Report to Congress"], at chrome-extension://efaidnbmnnnibpcajpcglclefindmkaj/https://www.ftc.gov/system/files/documents/reports/ftc-report-congress-privacy-security/report_to_congress_on_privacy_and_data_security_2021.pdf.

59 Fed. Trade. Comm'n, Statement of Regulatory Priorities 1–2 (2021), https://www.reginfo.gov/public/jsp/eAgenda/StaticContent/202110/Statement_3084_FTC.pdf.

60 *See* Trade Regulation Rule on Commercial Surveillance, RIN No. 3084-AB69, OIRA (Fall 2021); *see also* Devin Coldeway, *FTC may consider rule curbing algorithmic discrimination and 'commercial surveillance,'* TechCrunch (Dec. 15, 2021), https://techcrunch.com/2021/12/15/ftc-may-consider-rule-curbing-algorithmic-discrimination-and-commercial-surveillance.

61 15 U.S.C. § 6502.

62 Under this approach, Congress can control the FTC's discretion over the types of practices that would be proscribed or prescribed. *See* Fed. Trade. Comm'n, Prepared Remarks of Commissioner Noah Joshua Phillips FTC Hearing #12: The FTC's Approach to Consumer Privacy 4–6 (Apr. 9, 2019), https://www.ftc.gov/system/files/documents/public_statements/1513177/phillips_-_ftc_hearing_12_remarks_4-9-19.pdf; Noah Joshua Phillips, Prepared Remarks, "Keep It: Maintaining Competition in the Privacy Debate," Internet Governance Forum USA, 4–6 (July 27, 2018), https://www.ftc.gov/system/files/documents/public_statements/1395934/phillips_-_internet_governance_forum_7-27-18.pdf.

63 15 U.S.C. § 45a.

to time... to make rules and regulations for the purpose of carrying out the provisions of this subchapter."[64] The FTC began to exercise its rulemaking muscle slowly at first, promulgating what it called "trade regulation rules" that relied on its UDAP power, but also declaring some conduct to be unfair methods of competition under the theory that deceptive acts diverted business from honest firms.[65]

Two court cases help solidify the Commission's rulemaking power. First, *in FTC v. Sperry & Hutchinson, Co.*[66] – an enforcement action alleging a trading stamp supplier had engaged in an unfair practice by trying to prevent secondary markets for its stamps – the Supreme Court blessed the "unfairness test" that the FTC had developed in the so-called Cigarette Rule, and elements of which survive today.[67] In the second case, *National Petroleum Refiners Association v. FTC*, the D.C. Circuit held that section 6(g) of the FTC Act provides the FTC power to promulgate substantive rules pursuant to both its consumer protection and competition authorities.[68]

In response to these judicial developments, Congress became interested, and ultimately passed the Magnuson-Moss FTC Improvement Act of 1974 ("Mag-Moss").[69] The most important part of this new law was to provide the FTC with explicit authority to promulgate rules under its consumer protection authority. Specifically, the Commission "may prescribe rules which define with *specificity* acts or practices which are unfair or deceptive acts or practices," and also prescribe requirements "for the purpose of preventing such acts or practices."[70]

With this new power, however, came some important guardrails. Cognizant of the breadth of section 5, Congress put procedures in place that were more stringent than standard informal Administrative Procedure Act (APA)[71] rulemaking, and which have been amended over the years in response to subsequent FTC overreach.[72]

First, before it engages in any rulemaking, the FTC is required to publish an advance notice of proposed rulemaking (ANPRM), which must contain "a brief description of the area of inquiry under consideration, the objectives which the

---

64 15 U.S.C. § 46(g).

65 *See* Royce Zeisler, Chevron *Deference and the FTC: How and Why the FTC Should Use* Chevron *to Improve Antitrust Enforcement*, 2014 Colum. Bus. L. Rev. 266, 281 (FTC did not promulgate legislative rules until 1962).

66 405 U.S. 233 (1972).

67 William MacLeod, Elizabeth Brunins & Anna Kertesz, *Three Rules and a Constitution: Consumer Protection Finds Its Limits in Competition Policy*, 72 Antitrust L. J. 943 (2005).

68 482 F.2d 672 (D.C. Cir. 1973).

69 Pub. L. No. 93-637, 88 Stat. 2183 (1975).

70 15 U.S.C. § 57a(a)(1)(B) (emphasis added).

71 5 U.S.C. § 553.

72 *See* MacLeod et al., *supra* note 67; FTC Improvements Act of 1980, Pub. L. No. 96-252, 94 Stat. 374 (1980).

Commission seeks to achieve, and possible regulatory alternatives under consideration by the Commission."[73] The Commission must "invite the response of interested parties... including any suggestions or alternative methods for achieving such objectives."[74] The FTC additionally must provide the ANPRM to its relevant Senate and House oversight committees, and give these committees a copy of a notice of proposed rulemaking (NPRM) at least thirty days before its publication.[75] After these preliminary notices, the Commission is permitted to issue an NPRM to the public "only where it has reason to believe that the unfair or deceptive acts or practices which are the subject of the proposed rulemaking are prevalent."[76] The Commission can base a finding of "prevalence" on previously issued "cease and desist orders regarding such acts or practices," or "any other information available to the Commission [that] indicates a widespread pattern of unfair or deceptive acts or practices."[77]

In addition to the solicitation of public comments, Mag-Moss requires the Commission to hold an "informal hearing," which provides "the opportunity for oral presentations on all issues."[78] Further, "disputed issues of fact," which are "material and necessary to resolve," are subject to "examination, cross-examination, and rebuttal submissions."[79] The Commission appoints a "presiding officer," who runs the rulemaking proceeding, including designating issues of disputed fact, and making a "recommended decision" based on their findings and taking into account the staff report.[80] If the Commission decides to promulgate a rule, it must publish a "statement of basis and purpose," which explains the prevalence of the unfair or deceptive acts or practices and addresses the economic impact of the rule, and a "final regulatory analysis," which describes the "need for" and the "objectives" of the rule, alternatives considered, significant issues raised by parties, and provides a cost-benefit analysis of the rule.[81]

As Beales and Muris note, despite these statutory strictures, the FTC often employed less formal, alternative rulemaking procedures.[82] For example, the FTC has tended to avoid formal hearings in favor of more informal workshops.[83]

---

73 15 U.S.C. § 57a(b)(2)(A)(i).

74 *Id.* § 57a(b)(2)(A)(ii), (B).

75 *Id.* § 57a(b)(2)(B) – (C).

76 *Id.* § 57a(b)(3).

77 *Id.* § 57a(b)(3)(A) – (B).

78 16 C.F.R. § 1.13(d); 15 U.S.C. § 57a(C).

79 16 C.F.R.. § 1.13(d)(1)(i),(5); 15 U.S.C.§ 57a(c)(2)

80 16 C.F.R § 1.13(g); 15 U.S.C.§ 57a(c)(1)(B).

81 *Id.* § 1.14(1) – (2).

82 *See* Beales & Muris, *supra* note 57, at 26–29. The FTC may use "procedures other than those established" in its rules by "announcing those procedures in the Federal Register notice commencing the rulemaking proceeding." 16 C.F.R. § 1.20.

83 *See* Beales & Muris, *supra* note 57, at 30.

Further, 1989 was the last time a presiding officer was used.[84] Indeed, Beales and Muris conclude that the Commission's procedures "have not been followed since the initial wave of rulemaking, with the Commission opting for some form of alternative procedures in every rulemaking proposal since April 1976."[85] Nonetheless, among new FTC chair's first official actions were to amend the Commission's rules governing rulemaking procedures.

Seemingly esoteric, some of these changes could have important impacts. First, the Commission removed the requirement that the statement in its NPRM describe "with particularity" the reasons for the proposed rule, now requiring only a statement "describing the reason for the proposed rule."[86] Second, it limits the role of the presiding officer's report to "explaining [their] proposed resolution of disputed issues of material fact,"[87] and designates the FTC chair, or their designee, as the presiding officer.[88] Third, the Commission in the NPRM will designate "disputed issues of material fact," rather than having interested parties propose such issues to the Commission or the presiding officer.[89] Fourth, the Commission eliminated the final staff report and the post-report comment period.[90] Taken together, these changes appear to be greasing the skids for rulemaking, both making it easier to justify beginning a rulemaking and providing the FTC chair with substantial control over the ultimate substance of any rule that the full Commission will consider.

2. Possible Substance

Having reviewed the Mag-Moss procedures, I now turn to substance. The FTC's power to use rulemaking to proscribe or prescribe data practices is not boundless. The Commission must satisfy two threshold requirements to promulgate a rule. First, the FTC can issue an NPRM only "where it has reason to believe" that the conduct covered by the rulemaking is "prevalent."[91] It appears that this threshold is pretty easily satisfied: as long as the FTC has successfully challenged a practice – either winning in litigation or securing a consent order – more than once, or has access to "any other information" – perhaps from workshops or internal or external studies – indicating a "widespread pattern," it can claim a "reason to believe" a practice is prevalent.[92]

84 *See id.* ("the last appointed presiding officer was in 1989, for a Mail Order Rule Amendment").

85 *Id.* at 33.

86 *Compare* 16 C.F.R. § 1.11(b)(3) (2021) *with* 40 Fed. Reg. 33,966 (Aug. 13, 1975).

87 *Compare* 16 C.F.R. § 1.13(d) (2021) *with* 40 Fed. Reg. 33,967–68 (Aug. 13, 1975).

88 16 C.F.R. §§ 0.8, 1.13(a)(1).

89 *Id.* § 1.13(b).

90 *Compare* 16 C.F.R. § 1.13(d) (2021) *with* 40 Fed. Reg. 33,968 (Aug. 13, 1975).

91 15 U.S.C. § 57a(b)(3).

92 *Id.* § 57a(b)(3)(A) – (B) (reason to believe a practice is prevalent can be found only if the Commission "has issued cease and desist orders regarding such acts or practices, or any other information available to the Commission indicates a widespread pattern of unfair or deceptive acts or practices.").

The potentially more binding constraint on FTC rulemaking is the requirement that any rule "define with specificity acts or practices which are unfair or deceptive."[93] It is easy to see why the specificity requirement is needed; without it, there would be no legal impediment to the FTC promulgating a rule that, for example, defined any deception about the price or quality of a good or service as an unfair or deceptive act or practice. In the limit, the FTC could use its Mag-Moss rulemaking authority to transform any violation of the FTC Act into a rule violation, and thus subject to monetary remedies.

Courts have not had many occasions to address the specificity requirement, and only one has found the FTC failed to meet it. *Katharine Gibbs School v. FTC* concerned a challenge to the FTC's Vocational School Rule.[94] In one of its first Mag-Moss rules, the FTC set out various requirements related to refunds and disclosures designed to stop what the FTC saw as "abusive practices against vocational and home study school students and prospective students."[95] The court, however, struck down the Commission's rule because the Commission failed to "define with specificity" the extant conduct that was "unfair or deceptive."[96] The court faulted the FTC for bootstrapping the specificity requirement by "content[ing] itself with treating violations of [the] 'requirements prescribed for the purpose of preventing' unfair practices [themselves as] unfair practices." That is, rather than explaining why current refund and disclosure practices violated section 5, the FTC mandated new refund and disclosure practices that it thought better than the status quo, and defined violations of the *standards it created* as unfair or deceptive practices. As the court saw it, this put the cart before the horse, as the FTC Act allows the Commission to prescribe practices only "for the purpose of preventing" the conduct that it first has defined as unfair or deceptive.[97]

In the only other two challenges to the specificity requirements – involving the Funeral Rule[98] and the Credit Practices Rule[99] – courts found the Commission had satisfied section 5's requirements. In *Harry and Bryant Co. v. FTC*, the Fourth Circuit perfunctorily explained that because the Funeral Rule "defines unfair practices in the sale of funeral goods and services and prescribes preventative requirements," it clearly falls within the FTC's authority.[100] Similarly, in *American Financial Services v. FTC*, the D.C. Circuit distinguished the Vocational Schools

93 *Id.* § 57a(a)(1)(B). The statement of basis and purposes accompanying any rule must also include "a statement as to the manner and context in which such acts or practices are unfair or deceptive." *Id.* § 57a(d)(1)(B).

94 612 F.2d 658 (2d Cir. 1979).

95 *Id.* at 661.

96 *Id.* at 662.

97 *Id.* ("Requirements designed to prevent unfair practices are predicated upon the existence of unfair practices.")

98 16 C.F.R. § 453 *et seq.*

99 *Id.* § 444 *et seq.*

100 726 F.2d 993, 999 (4th Cir. 1984). *See* Funeral Rule, 16 C.F.R. § 453.2(a) (defining unfair or deceptive pricing practices, including failing to provide "accurate price information disclosing the cost to the purchaser for each of the specific funeral goods and funeral services").

Rule at issue in *Katharine Gibbs* from the Credit Practices Rule, finding that unlike the former, which prescribed requirements designed to prevent "unspecified unfair enrollment advertising and sales practices," the Credit Practices Rule "identifies specific practices... as *per se* unfair."[101]

More recent cases examining the balance that Congress struck when crafting the FTC Act between notice and remedy can also provide some guidance on what specificity might require. The FTC Act is carefully calibrated to allow the Commission to seek monetary remedies only after potentially defendants have been put on notice – through a variety of means under the statute, including enforcement actions and rulemaking – of exactly what type of conduct is unfair or deceptive. Importantly, this balance between knowledge of illegality and remedy played a central role in the Supreme Court's recent *AMG* decision, which held that the FTC lacked power to seek monetary remedies in federal court for first-time violations of the FTC Act.[102]

Recognition of this balance is also on full display in the 11th Circuit's decision in *LabMD v. FTC*, in which the court held that an order that required the defendant to use "reasonable" data security standards was unenforceably vague, because it did not provide the defendant with sufficient notice of what was required of it to avoid the real possibility of substantial civil penalties.[103] The court focused on the parallel between an order and a rule. When the FTC is successful in having conduct judged unfair or deceptive in an enforcement action, it has in effect promulgated a rule, and as such "the concept of specificity is crucial." Further, "given the severity of the civil penalties a district court may impose," the order must state with "clarity and precision" exactly what it prohibits to avoid a denial of due process.[104] The court anchored the order's specificity requirement to the requirements that an FTC complaint must provide a plaintiff sufficient notice of how they violated the FTC Act:

> [A Commission] complaint must contain "a clear and concise factual statement sufficient to inform each respondent with reasonable definiteness of the types of acts or practices alleged to

---

101 767 F.2d 957, 984 (D.C. Cir. 1985). *See* Credit Practices Rule, 16 C.F.R. § 444.2–4 (defining unfair or deceptive practices in extension of credit).

102 593 U.S. __, 141 S. Ct. 1341 (2021). For example, the Court pointed to the fact that the FTC Act allows the Commission to obtain monetary remedies against a party only if it violates a cease-and-desist order, engages in conduct the Commission has already condemned in a fully litigated administrative action, or if the conduct was such that a "reasonable man" would have known that it was "dishonest or fraudulent." *Id.* at 1348–49. *See also* Jarod Bona, *The US Supreme Court rules that the FTC is unauthorized to seek monetary damages in antitrust cases (AMG Capital Management)*, E-COMPETITIONS APRIL 2021, art. No. 103294.

103 894 F.3d 1221 (11th Cir. 2018).

104 *Id.* at 1232, 1235. *See also id.* ("[T]he remedy the complaint seeks must comport with this requirement of reasonable definiteness.") Of note, the court did not challenge the initial unfairness liability standard of unreasonableness as too vague, and this makes sense in the context of the FTC Act's balance between notice and remedy: elucidating what constitutes unreasonable data practices in an administrative proceeding, where the Commission can obtain only a cease-and-desist order, is in line with Congress's vision of the FTC as expert agency using enforcement to provide information to the marketplace about what types of conduct are unfair, deceptive, or anticompetitive. Only after notice is given with some level of specificity beyond "reasonableness" can the FTC then obtain monetary remedies for violations.

> violate the law." It follows that the remedy the complaint seeks must comport with the requirement of reasonable definiteness.[105]

This connection with the complaint finds support in the only judicial review of the FTC's use of what has come to be known as its "penalty offense" authority. In addition to being able to seek civil penalties against firms who are parties to an order, the FTC Act also allows the Commission to seek civil penalties from any firm that engages in conduct that the FTC has found to be "unfair or deceptive" in a fully litigated administrative action, but only if the defendant had "actual knowledge" that its conduct violated the FTC Act.[106] Again, notice is the key to being able to obtain monetary remedies.

The only case to examine this seldom-used FTC authority, *U.S. v. Hopkins Dodge, Inc.*, involved car dealers who admitted to violating Regulation Z of the Truth in Lending Act (TILA), which requires certain disclosures related to consumer lending.[107] The Eighth Circuit held that sending defendants copies and synopses of final orders the FTC had issued against firms involving different industries (e.g., retail meat, beauty products, and real estate) and different practices (e.g., "bait and switch") provided insufficient notice to the defendants to satisfy the "actual knowledge" requirement of section 45(m)(1)(B). Despite the fact that the prior Commission orders sent to defendants involved TILA violations, in none of the appended orders had the Commission found the TILA violation amounted to an "unfair or deceptive" act or practice, and the defendants in *Hopkins Dodge* had not engaged in any of the conduct the synopsized cases involved.[108]

While this relatively thin body of relevant case law fails to provide a precise definition of what "specificity" requires, it does provide some important limiting principles. First, the Commission cannot require practices that it thinks would improve the marketplace (and then define failure to adhere to these prescribed practices as an unfair or deceptive act), without first identifying precisely which elements of the status quo are unfair or deceptive, and why. Second, fealty to the FTC Act's careful balance between notice and remedy requires the FTC to identify proscribed acts and practice with a level of "reasonable definiteness" similar to what would be required in a complaint to satisfy due process requirements.

---

105 *Id.* at 1235 (citation omitted).

106 45 U.S.C. § 45(m)(1)(B). The FTC has used this power only once since *Hopkins Dodge*, both times dealing with false claims related to bamboo clothing by retailers. Stipulated Order and Judgment at 9, United States v. Kohl's, Inc., No. 1:22-cv-00964 (D.D.C. 2022); Stipulated Order and Judgment at 8–9, United States v. Walmart, Inc., No. 1:22-cv-00965 (D.D.C. 2022); Decision and Order, *In re* Pure Bamboo, LLC, No. C-4278 (F.T.C. Dec. 15, 2009); Decision and Order, *In re* The M Group, Inc., No. 9340 (F.T.C. Aug. 7, 2009).

107 849 F.2d 311 (8th Cir. 1988).

108 *Id.* at 314 (of the four cases supplied to defendants, "only *Seekonk* states as a 'conclusion' that respondents 'engaged in false, misleading and deceptive advertising, and *utilized unfair and deceptive acts and practices…*' [,] [b]ut *Seekonk* is basically a 'bait and switch case,'" a practice that "was never utilized by appellees").

With these constraints on Mag-Moss rulemaking in mind, what are some candidates for privacy rules? As explained above, over the past two decades, the FTC has found reason to believe that numerous firms have violated section 5 by making express or implied representations about their data practices that were materially false or misleading to a significant minority of reasonable consumers. The sheer number of cases likely allows the FTC to claim that deception about privacy practices is "prevalent," but a broad rule defining material misrepresentations about privacy practices as a deceptive practice would almost surely fail the specificity requirement. Moreover, because the remedy for such cases is to correct the false representations, not to stop the underlying data practices, it might prove problematic to use a deception theory to issue a prophylactic rule that banned or required certain data practices, something the new chair seems keen to do.[109]

The ability of the FTC to mandate disclosure of data practices is also severely limited. Silence about a latent feature of a product is deceptive in only the narrowest of circumstances: when it so fundamentally alters the product beyond consumer expectations as to essentially make it unfit for its intended use.[110] Of note, although the FTC has alleged that certain express or implied representations gave false impressions that required additional disclosure to make them truthful,[111] the FTC has never pursued a "pure" deceptive omission theory in a privacy case.[112] Finally, it is worth noting that the element of materiality – while presumed in an FTC enforcement action[113] – may prove a more difficult showing in a rulemaking process given the widespread acknowledgment that consumers rarely read privacy policies and the role that privacy plays in consumers' actual market place choices is uncertain at best.[114]

None of this means that deception would have no role to play in privacy rulemaking – only that what it could accomplish with respect to actual data practices may be minimal. For example, a deception theory potentially could form the basis for a rule mandating the *form* of disclosure, such as mandating the size and placement of privacy disclosures, restricting the use of so-called dark patterns to provide notice or obtain consent, or requiring digital platforms

---

109 *See* Khan, *supra* note 50, at 6 ("Going forward, I believe we should approach data privacy and security protections by considering substantive limits rather than just procedural protections ….").

110 *See* Replace with *In re* International Harvester Co., 104 F.T.C. 949, 1058–59 (1984); Deception Statement. *See also* Statement of Acting Chairman Maureen K. Ohlhausen In the Matter of Lenovo, Inc. (Sept. 5, 2017), https://www.ftc.gov/legal-library/browse/cases-proceedings/public-statements/statement-acting-chairman-maureen-k-ohlhausen-matter-lenovo-inc.

111 *See, e.g.*, *Sears Holdings*, 2009 WL 2979770.

112 The upshot is that, in theory, a firm can avoid deception by making no representations regarding its data collection practices at all. *See* Wright's and Ohlhausen's statements in *Nomi*, *supra* note 39. Although in practice, given mandated disclosure requirements stemming from General Data Protection Regulation (GDPR) and state regimes such as the California Consumer Privacy Act (CCPA), this option may be limited.

113 *See* 1983 FTC Policy Statement on Deception , *supra* note 7, at 5.

114 *See, e.g.*, Alessandro Acquisti, Curtis Taylor & Liad Wagman, *The Economics of Privacy*, 54 J. ECON. LIT. 442, 476 (2016).

to make privacy settings more easily understandable so that users are not deceived about how their personal information is being used. Indeed, such an approach to deception-based rulemaking could be found in current FTC guidelines for online and mobile disclosures.[115]

Given the limitations on deception, the FTC would have to rely primarily on its unfairness authority if it wanted to ban certain data practices outright or to mandate a notice-and-choice regime with either opt-in or opt-out consent.[116] For conduct to be unfair, it must cause, or be likely to cause, "substantial consumer injury" that consumers cannot reasonably avoid, and that is not outweighed by "countervailing benefits to consumers and competition."[117] The Commission has used unfairness theories sparingly in its privacy cases, most likely because substantial injury in the context of privacy may be difficult to show. Most injuries involving suspect data practices are subjective, involving disutility from dignitary affronts or loss of autonomy from unwanted observation,[118] but the FTC's Unfairness Policy Statement explicitly states that substantial consumer injury is unlikely to be satisfied by emotional or other subjective harms.[119] To surmount this stricture, the FTC has leaned on potential physical and financial harms that can accompany surreptitious surveillance or unwanted publication of private data.

For example, cases against DesignerWare, TRENDnet, Retina-X, and Support King each center around unwanted surveillance of intimate activity.[120] In *DesignerWare*, the Commission alleged that "consumers are harmed by DesignerWare's unwarranted invasion into their homes and lives and its capture of the private details of individual and family life, including, for example, images of visitors, children, family interactions, partially undressed individuals, and couples engaged in intimate activities."[121] Similarly, *TRENDnet* involved allegedly unsecured feeds for personal webcams, with the Commission alleging that "the exposure of sensitive information through the respondent's IP cameras increases

115 *See, e.g.*, Fed. Trade Comm'n, .com Disclosures: How to Make Effective Disclosures in Digital Advertising (Mar. 2013), https://www.ftc.gov/system/files/documents/plain-language/bus41-dot-com-disclosures-information-about-online-advertising.pdf.

116 *See, e.g.*, Daniel J. Solove & Paul M. Schwartz, *ALI Data Privacy: Overview and Black Letter Text*, 68 UCLA L. Rev. 1252 (2022) (explaining the American Law Institute's *Principles of Law, Data Privacy*, which "breathe new life" into the notice-and-choice-approach).

117 15 U.S.C. § 45(n).

118 *See* Cooper, *supra* note 48 (discussing intrinsic vs. instrumental harms).

119 1980 FTC Policy Statement on Unfairness, *supra* note 8 ("The Commission is not concerned with trivial or merely speculative harms.... Emotional impact and other more subjective types of harm, on the other hand, will not ordinarily make a practice unfair.").

120 The Commission recently brought a case against Zoom for unfair and deceptive data security practices. While styled as a data security case, the alleged injury to satisfy the unfairness count involved the possibility that a Zoom user could be surreptitiously monitored. *See* Complaint ¶ 38, *In re* Zoom Video Communications, Inc., No. C-4731 (F.T.C. Jan. 19, 2021) ("Without the circumvented Safari safeguard, one wrong click could expose consumers to remote video surveillance by strangers through their computers' webcams.").

121 Complaint ¶ 19, *In re* DesignerWare, LLC, No. C-4390 (F.T.C. Apr. 15, 2013).

the likelihood that consumers or their property will be targeted for theft or other criminal activity."[122]

Two recent cases involve the sale of surveillance software. *Retina-X*, for example, concerned software that allowed the purchaser to monitor another person's activities on a mobile device or computer.[123] The Commission's primary concern was that this app, when installed without the device user's knowledge, could facilitate financial harm and harms related to stalking. As the Commission explained, "[s]talkers and abusers... use the information obtained via monitoring to perpetuate stalking and abusive behaviors, which cause mental and emotional abuse, financial and social harm, and physical harm, including death."[124] Similarly, the case against Support King concerned the sale of its "SpyFone" software, which allowed parties to surreptitiously monitor user activity.[125] The Commission alleged that the sale of this software, "without taking reasonable steps to ensure that the purchasers use the monitoring products and services only for legitimate and lawful purposes" was unfair, and like *Retina-X*, with the alleged injury centering around financial and physical harms attendant to stalking.[126]

The case against Facebook straddles the line between pure subjective privacy harm and the potential manifestation of the publication of private data in physical or financial harm. The Commission's original case against Facebook centered around problems with Facebook's privacy settings that led some to believe information on their pages were private when in fact, they were public.[127] Unfairness allegations intimated the potential of physical harm from "unwanted contacts" by those who would be "able to infer [a Facebook user's] locale" based on the newly available information, but the complaint also alleged that the potential disclosure to third parties of information that a user may not want to share constituted injury sufficient to make a practice unfair.[128] Although not explicit, one could also imagine reputational harms emanating from these practices that had the potential to impair employment or business prospects, which moves injury into the more familiar terrain of losses that are capable of being monetized.

Only two cases seem grounded in pure subjective privacy harms. First, *VIZIO*, a case brought jointly with the New Jersey Attorney General, involved the

---

122 *In re* Complaint ¶ 13, *In re* TRENDnet, Inc., No. C-4426 (F.T.C. Feb. 7, 2014).

123 *In re* Retina-X Studios, LLC, No. 172-3118, 2020 WL 1549673, at *1 (F.T.C. Mar. 26, 2020).

124 Complaint ¶ 11, *In re* Retina-X Studios, LLC, No. C-4711 (F.T.C. Mar. 27, 2020).

125 *In re* Support King, LLC, No. C-4756 (F.T.C. Dec. 20, 2021).

126 Complaint at ¶¶ 22–30, Support King, LLC, No. C-4756 (F.T.C. Dec. 20, 2021).

127 *In re* Facebook, Inc. No. C-4365, 2012 WL 3518628 (F.T.C. July 27, 2012).

128 *Id.* at *5. Specifically, the complaint identifies "exposing potentially controversial political views or other sensitive information," "potentially sensitive affiliations, that could, in turn reveal a user's political views, sexual orientation, or business relationships" to "prospective employers, government organizations, or business competitors."

collection and sharing of television viewing data without obtaining adequate consent.[129] The more recent case, *U.S. v. Mortgage Solutions FCS*, involved a mortgage broker posting consumers' sensitive financial information – such as credit history, full names, and health information of family members – in public responses to negative Yelp reviews.[130] The Commission alleged that the ability of the Yelp users to discover this sensitive information and the deprivation of consumer choice as to "whether and to whom they disclosed sensitive information" satisfied the substantial injury prong of its unfairness claim.[131]

So given the Commission's history applying unfairness to privacy, what might a privacy rule based on an unfairness look like? An obvious candidate that flows directly from the FTC's actions is a ban on unconsented surveillance in one's home, or surveillance that otherwise was likely to increase the risk of physical or financial harm. Although the FTC's unfairness standard eschews subjective harm, it specifically allows physical harm and would also consider situations involving emotional effects where "tangible injury could be clearly demonstrated."[132] A rule covering such subject matter could satisfy the specificity requirement as long as it was limited to precise types of data (e.g., video feeds, real-time geolocation, financial or health information) and contexts (e.g., in the home) that increased the likelihood of physical or financial harm, or that otherwise comprised the type of dignitary harm that has been widely recognized to give rise to actional invasions of privacy in common law or public law.[133]

Of course, existing case law is not the limit on what could be promulgated in a privacy rule based on unfairness: prevalence can be based on evidence gathered during the rulemaking process. So a rule could rely on new evidence and an expansive view of "injury" to define a new category of proscribed practices (and concomitant prescribed prophylactic practices). One contender could be a rule that treats "biased algorithms" as an unfair data practice. For example, the FTC recently described algorithmic bias as an area of concern, and at least two commissioners would be willing to find the type of discrimination that violates the Equal Credit Opportunity Act to additionally constitute an unfair practice.[134]

129 Complaint at 4–7, FTC v. VIZIO, Inc., No. 2:17-cv-00758 (D.N.J. 2017).

130 Complaint, United States v. Mortgage Solutions FCS, Inc., No. 4:20-cv-00110 (N.D. Cal. Jan. 7, 2020).

131 *Id.* at ¶ 38. Although one could see how this information may lead to reputational harm that reduces employment or credit opportunities, the FTC's complaint lacked any such intimation.

132 For example, the Unfairness Statement list "harassing late-night telephone calls" as the type of conduct where "emotional effects might possibly be considered as the basis for a finding of unfairness." 1980 FTC Policy Statement on Unfairness, *supra* note 8, at n. 16.

133 *See, e.g.*, 15 U.S.C. § 6502 (COPPA); 45 C.F.R. § 160 *et seq.* (HIPAA Privacy Rule) ; TransUnion LLC v. Ramirez, 141 S.Ct. 2190, 2204 (2021) (explaining that certain common law actions, including "disclosure of private information" and "intrusion upon seclusion" can form a sufficient basis for "injury in fact" for Article III standing purposes).

134 *See* Privacy Report to Congress, *supra* note 58, at 6–7 (describing algorithmic bias as an area of concern); Statement of Chair Lina M. Khan Joined by Commissioner Rebecca Kelly Slaughter In the Matter of Napleton Automotive Group Commission 3–4 (Mar. 31, 2022), https://www.ftc.gov/news-events/news/speeches/joint-statement-chair-lina-m-khan-commissioner-rebecca-kelly-slaughter-matter-napleton-automotive

IV. Unfair Competition Rules

Another potential avenue to privacy rulemaking could be to invoke the FTC's power to proscribe "unfair methods of competition" Indeed, the chair has suggested as much in the recent Privacy Report to Congress, and the Commission is currently considering a petition from an anti-tech advocacy group calling on the Commission to adopt a rule under its UMC authority to ban so-called surveillance advertising – personalized digital advertising based on consumer interests.[135]

There are serious legal and policy problems with this possible approach to privacy rulemaking. First, as a threshold matter, it is unclear whether Congress has even given the FTC the power to promulgate rules under its UMC authority. The only court to address the issue did so fifty years ago,[136] and it is far from certain that its rationale would survive today, especially when one looks at the provision purported to give the FTC such power (section 6(g)) in the context of the entire structure of the FTC Act.[137] Second, leaving aside legal authority to issue UMC rules, there are unlikely to be any privacy-threatening data practices that would fit into the small compartment of behavior that current antitrust laws condemn per se, yet this is precisely what a UMC rule would do. Not only would this misalignment between a UMC rule targeting data practices and modern antitrust precedent signal bad policy, it also suggests that the FTC would have trouble defending such a rule as a "reasonable interpretation" of its organic statute.

1. History and Legal Authority

The first, last, and only word on whether the FTC enjoys the authority to engage in rulemaking under this provision was almost a half-century ago in *National Petroleum Refiners Association v. FTC*, which involved a challenge to the FTC's 1971 Octane Rule. Although the Commission based the Rule on a finding that a failure to disclose octane ratings on pumps was both an "unfair method of competition" and an "unfair and deceptive act and practice," the statement of basis and purpose discusses consumer harm arising from a lack of information about octane levels as the sole rationale, never once making a link between a failure to disclose octane levels and competition.[138]

(explaining how discriminatory practices under the Equal Credit Opportunity Act also satisfied the unfairness standard).

135 Accountable Tech Petition, *supra* note 49. The petition defines "surveillance advertising" as consisting of (i) the collection of personal data; and (ii) "targeting advertisements at users, based on that personal data, as they traverse the internet, including other digital platforms," and it asks the FTC to "issue a rule prohibiting online platforms from using personal data for the purpose of delivering advertisements." *Id.* at 60.

136 *Nat'l Petroleum Refiners Ass'n*, 482 F.2d 672.

137 *See generally AMG*, 141 S. Ct. 1341.

138 *See* 36 Fed. Reg. 23,871 (Dec. 16, 1971). Specifically, the rule expressed concern that lacking information about octane levels, consumers would either (i) purchase gasoline that contained more octane than they needed for their specific engines, thus paying too much for gasoline; or (ii) that they would unknowingly purchase gasoline with too little octane, thus potentially harming their engines. *Id.*

The D.C. Circuit upheld the Commission's authority under section 6(g) to promulgate substantive rules, but importantly did not distinguish between UMC or UDAP theories.[139] In fact, all of the prior rulemaking the FTC engaged in prior to *National Petroleum Refiners* that invoked unfair methods of competition did so under a "diversion of sales" theory[140] – honest competitors were harmed by losing customers to dishonest firms – which is the exact harm that forms the basis for consumer protection remedies.[141] Indeed, such a focus on harm to competitors is inimical to modern antitrust precepts, which are concerned with harm to competition, not harm to competitors.[142]

After *National Petroleum Refiners*, Congress passed the Magnuson-Moss Warranty and Federal Trade Commission Improvement Act, which provided the FTC with explicit consumer protection rulemaking authority.[143] Thus, any claim that the FTC retains authority to engage in rulemaking under its UMC authority must be staked in section 6, which addresses "additional powers" of the Commission, and is primarily concerned with industry investigations and reports, and international cooperation. Tucked away in this part of the Act, section 6(g) provides that the Commission may "[f]rom time to time classify corporations and... to make rules and regulation for the purpose of carrying out the provisions of the [FTC Act]."[144] Although beyond the scope of this chapter, there are sound legal reasons to be skeptical that the FTC actually has power to promulgate rules under its UMC authority.[145]

2. Potential Conflict with Modern Antitrust Principles

Just as UDAP rulemaking requires the conduct in question to be unfair or deceptive within the meaning of the FTC Act, UMC rulemaking would require a link between the proscribed conduct and an adverse effect on competition. What is more, a competition rule would operate in the same manner as a per se rule in antitrust, as it would "narrow the inquiry" from a full accounting of

139 *Nat'l Petroleum Refiners Ass'n*, 482 F.2d at 678.

140 *See* Beales & Muris, *supra* note 57, at 7.

141 Under 13(b) cases brought before *AMG*, the typical remedy sought by the Commission was revenues received by the defendant as a result of the fraud, which necessarily includes revenue that was diverted from honest firms. *See* Cooper & Kobayashi, *supra* note 9, for an exposition of the proper analysis of consumer protection remedies.

142 Brunswick Corp. v. Pueblo Bowl-O-Mat, Inc., 429 U.S. 477, 488 (1977).

143 Magnuson-Moss Warranty–Federal Trade Commission Improvement Act, 15 U.S.C. § 2301.

144 15 U.S.C. § 46(g).

145 For example, a plain reading of this provision, in conjunction with the structure of the FTC Act, would tend to suggest that section 6(g) provides the Commission the power to enact procedural rules necessary to carry out its core enforcement provisions, not the power to issue rules governing competition for the entire economy. *See* Whitman v. Am. Trucking Ass'ns, 531 U.S. 457, 468 (2001) ("Congress... does not alter the fundamental details of a regulatory scheme in vague terms or ancillary provisions – it does not, one might say, hide elephants in mouseholes."). For detailed examinations of these and other arguments *see* Maureen K. Ohlhausen & James Rill, *Pushing the Limits? A Primer on FTC Competition Rulemaking*, U.S. Chamber of Com. (Aug. 12, 2021), https://www.uschamber.com/assets/archived/images/ftc_rulemaking_white_paper_aug12.pdf; *see supra* Alden F. Abbot, *Legal Constraints on FTC Competition Rulemaking*, pp. 129–154.

the competitive impact of a practice to merely determining whether the defendant has engaged in the proscribed conduct.[146] Leaving aside problems with legal authority, from a policy perspective, it is unlikely that any data practices under scrutiny would deserve per se condemnation based on their impact on competition.

For a very limited set of practices that experience and learning have shown "always or almost always tend to restrict competition and decrease output," the antitrust laws allow a plaintiff to circumvent the fact-specific inquiry into market impacts and succeed by merely showing the defendant engaged in the proscribed conduct.[147] Over time, this category has dwindled, and now courts typically will condemn only naked agreements among horizontal competitors to fix prices, reduce output, or divide markets as per se illegal.[148] Significantly, there are *no* unilateral practices that fall into this per se category – indeed, it is well established that the "mere possession of monopoly power, and concomitant charging of monopoly prices, is not only not unlawful; it is an important element of the free-market system."[149]

Yet, the link between competitive harm and privacy is weak at best, and regardless of its direct impact on consumers, there does not appear to be any privacy-intrusive data practice that would come even close to the type of conduct that "always or almost always tend to restrict competition and decrease output." For example, consider the so-called privacy paradox – an empirical finding that actual consumer demand for privacy appears to fall below what their stated preferences (through surveys) would predict.[150] Although the cause of this "paradox" is unclear – it could result from rational decision-making, asymmetric information, behavioral biases, or some combination of all three – if only a small proportion of consumers make marketplace decisions based on privacy, privacy is

---

146 *See Nat'l Petroleum Refiners Ass'n*, 482 F.2d at 674–75.

147 Ohio v. American Express, 138 S. Ct. 2274, 2283–84 (2018) (quoting Business Electronics Corp. v. Sharp Electronics Corp., 485 U.S. 717, 723 (1988)). *See also* Walid Chaiehloudj, *United States: The US Supreme Court rules that the credit card market is a multisided market and that anti-steering clauses do not have anticompetitive effects on this market (American Express)*, Concurrences No. 4-2018, art. No. 88296, pp. 209–212.

148 *Id.*

149 Verizon Comm'ns Inc. v. Law Offices of Curtis V. Trinko, LLP, 540 U.S. 398, 407 (2004). *See also* James E. Scheuermann & William D. Semins, *The US Supreme Court introduces a new method for regulatory antitrust analysis (Trinko / Verizon)*, e-Competitions January 2004, art. No. 43984.

150 *See, e.g.*, Acquisti et al., *supra* note 114, at, 476 ("If anything, the adoption of privacy-enhancing technologies (for instance, Tor, an application for browsing the Internet anonymously) lags vastly behind the adoption of sharing technologies (for instance, online social networks such as Facebook"); Johnson et al., *supra* note 48, at 40 (2020) (finding that 0.23% of display advertising impressions are served to consumers who have opted out of online tracking through the AdChoices program); Susan Athey, Christian Catalini & Catherine Tucker, *The Digital Privacy Paradox: Small Money, Small Costs, Small Talk* (NBER Working Paper No. 23488, June 2017), https://www.nber.org/system/files/working_papers/w23488/w23488.pdf (finding that students were willing to disclose personal contact information for a small incentive, that is, free pizza). Experiments have attempted to determine if privacy education will reduce the gap between revealed preference and stated preference and have found little impact. Lior Jacob Strahilevitz & Matthew B. Kugler, *Is Privacy Policy Language Irrelevant to Consumers?*, 45 J. Legal Stud. S69 (2016); Omri Ben-Shahar & Adam S. Chilton, *Simplification of Privacy Disclosures: An Experimental Test*, 45 J. Leg. Stud. S41 (2016).

unlikely to be a particularly important dimension of competition for most firms.[151] Recent empirical work is consistent with the privacy paradox, finding no statistical link between privacy ratings and market share in the Android app marketplace.[152]

To the extent that consumers understand firms' privacy promises and view them as credible, theoretical work demonstrates that even monopolies have incentives to take only welfare-enhancing actions.[153] This result flows from the fact that, with full information, firms internalize reductions in demand that flow from privacy harms.[154] Although this full information result may not hold in many circumstances, leading to suboptimal levels of privacy protection, it merely highlights the fact that the root of consumer harm is asymmetric information, not anticompetitive conduct.

The most plausible theory linking privacy and reduced competition involves using *deception about a firm's data practices* to attain monopoly power, not the practices themselves.[155] But as discussed in Part III, the Commission already addresses direct consumer harm from deception under its UDAP authority.[156] What is more, although deception can form the basis for an antitrust claim, courts require plaintiffs to satisfy rigorous showing.[157] All of this suggests that

---

151 James C. Cooper & John M. Yun, *Privacy & Antitrust: It's Complicated*, __ ILL. J.L. & TECH. __ (forthcoming, 2022), at 19, https://papers.ssrn.com/sol3/papers.cfm?abstract_id=3871873 (finding no statistical relationship between privacy ratings and market concentration for Android), at 19; ALEX MARTHEWS & CATHERINE TUCKER, PRIVACY POLICY AND COMPETITION, ECON. STUD. BROOKINGS at 8 (Dec. 2019) ("There is little evidence that competition itself appears to enhance privacy.")

152 *See* Cooper & Yun, *supra* note 151, (finding no statistical relationship between privacy ratings and market concentration for Android apps).

153 *See* Joseph Farrell, *Can Privacy Be Just Another Good?*, 10 J. TELECOM. & HIGH TECH. L. 251 (2012).

154 Farrell illustrates this point in a simple model of a firm with market power choosing the profit-maximizing level of privacy. He considers a setting in which the firm charges a positive price for its product, with privacy being one dimension of quality that impacts consumer value of the product. He models the revenue stream from increased access to consumer information as an equivalent reduction in marginal cost. The net impact on welfare depends on whether the increased data revenue streams cause the marginal cost to fall more or less than the value that consumers place on the product falls (due to reduced privacy). *See also* O'Brien & Smith, *supra* note 54. They find that if some consumers find reductions in privacy accompanied by concomitant product quality increases on net beneficial, changes in privacy lead to shifts and rotations in demand. The direction and size of the rotation (clockwise or counter-clockwise), and hence the net impact on welfare, depend on the correlation of the distributions of preferences for privacy and quality improvements.

155 For example, a recent petition of the FTC to engage in competition rulemaking to ban the use of consumer information to tailor online advertisements revolves around alleged *deception about the use* of such tailored advertising, not the use of these advertising techniques themselves. *See, e.g.*, Accountable Tech Petition, *supra* note 49, at 21–30.

156 For example, both Facebook and Google are under FTC orders for alleged deception surrounding their privacy practices, and both have agreed to pay substantial monetary penalties to settle charges that they violated those orders. *In re* Google Inc., FTC File No. 102-3136 (Oct. 13, 2011) (administrative cease and desist order); *In re* Facebook, Inc., FTC File No. 092-3184 (July 27, 2012) (administrative cease-and-desist order); United States v. Google, Inc., No. CV12-04177 SI, Order Approving Stipulated Order for Permanent Injunction and Civil Penalty Judgment (N.D. Cal. Nov. 16, 2012) ($22.5 million civil penalty); United States v. Facebook, Inc., Case No. 19-cv-2194, Complaint for Civil Penalties, Injunction, and Other Relief (July 24, 2019) ($5 billion civil penalty).

157 A district court recently denied Facebook's motion to dismiss a monopolization case that is based in large part on deception about the collection and use of consumer information. *See* Klein v. Facebook, Inc., No. 2 0-CV-08570-LHK, 2022 WL 141561 (N.D. Cal. Jan. 14, 2022). The stated the test to base a Sherman Act claim based on deception: "[A] plaintiff must show that the company made representations about its own

any sensible policy covering the relationship between competition and privacy involves evaluating complex tradeoffs, not per se condemnation, as would be the case under a UMC rule.

That a per se condemnation of firms' data practices is so inconsistent with Sherman Act precedents also casts doubt on the likelihood that such an interpretation of the Commission's UMC power would withstand judicial scrutiny. Even assuming that Congress intended the FTC, and not the courts, to define what constitutes an unfair method of competition,[158] under *Chevron U.S.A., Inc. v. NRDC* the courts defer only to an agency's "reasonable" interpretation of an ambiguity in a statute it administers.[159] Although some courts have paid lip service to the notion that section 5's prohibition of "unfair methods of competition" is somehow broader than conduct the Sherman Act proscribes,[160] what practices actually comprise this set remains a mystery.[161] The FTC has not litigated a case alleging a UMC violation that was not also a Sherman Act violation since 1992, and the last three appellate courts to weigh in on the issue have rejected the FTC's attempts to stretch the reach of section 5 beyond the Sherman Act, each of which involved the unilateral adoption of certain pricing and information sharing practices that were alleged to facilitate tacit collusion.[162]

---

products or its rivals' products that were [1] clearly false, [2] clearly material, [3] clearly likely to induce reasonable reliance, [4] made to buyers without knowledge of the subject matter, [5] continued for prolonged periods, and [6] not readily susceptible of neutralization or other offset by rivals." *Id.* at *23 (internal quotations omitted). Further, the court explained that "[b]ecause fraud is an 'essential element' of a Sherman Act claim based on misrepresentations to buyers, a plaintiff that brings such a claim must satisfy the heightened pleading standard set forth by Federal Rule of Civil Procedure 9(b)." *Id.*

158 The question of deference to FTC interpretation raises what Cass Sunstein has referred to as the "*Chevron* Step Zero" problem. That is, whether *Chevron* applies to an agency interpretation is ultimately a question of congressional delegation; the reviewing court must first determine whether Congress intended to delegate the duty to interpret the statute to the agency in the first place. The answer to this "step zero" question may hinge on whether the interpretation decides an important policy issue or merely concerns a minor ministerial function. *See* Cass Sunstein, Chevron *Step Zero*, 92 VA. L. REV. 187 (2006). Thus, despite a rich legislative history suggesting that Congress intended an expert commission to use section 5 as a vehicle to establish new competition norms, courts may enjoy a veto right over any FTC definition of unfairness – not merely an unreasonable one. *See* Daniel Crane, *Technocracy and Antitrust*, 86 TEX. L. REV. 1159, 1190 (2008). A trio of pre-*Chevron* cases appears to adopt this position. Official Airline Guides v. FTC, 630 F.2d 920, 927 (2d Cir. 1980); E.I. Du Pont de Nemours & Co. v. FTC (*Ethyl*), 729 F.2d 128, 136 (2d Cir. 1984); Boise Cascade Corp. v. FTC, 637 F.2d 573, 581 (9th Cir. 1980). The only post-*Chevron* case to consider the issue is FTC v. Indiana Fed'n of Dentists, 476 U.S. 447, 454 (1986) ("[C]ourts are to give some deference to the Commission's informed judgment that a particular commercial practice is to be condemned as 'unfair'" but "the legal issues presented – that is, the identification of governing legal standards and their application to the fact found – are… for the courts to resolve ….''). Some have argued that *Chevron* does apply to the FTC's determination of its section 5 UMC authority. *See* Rohit Chopra & Lina M. Khan, *The Case for "Unfair Methods of Competition" Rulemaking*, 87 U. CHICAGO L. REV. 357 (2020); Justin (Gus) Hurwitz, Chevron *and the Limits of Administrative Antitrust*, 76 U. PITT L. REV. 209 (2014); Royce Zeisler, Chevron *Deference and the FTC: How and Why the FTC Should Use* Chevron *to Improve Antitrust Enforcement*, 2014 COLUM. BUS. L. REV. 266 (2014).

159 467 U.S. 837 (1984).

160 *See* FTC v. Sperry & Hutchinson Co., 405 U.S. 233 (1972).

161 *See* James C. Cooper, *The Perils of Excessive Discretion: The Elusive Meaning of Unfairness Under the FTC Act*, 3 J. ANTITRUST ENF'T. 87 (2015).

162 *See Boise Cascade Corp.*, 637 F.2d at 581; *Official Airline Guides, Inc.*, 630 F.2d 920; *Du Pont*, 729 F.2d 128. The FTC's last judicially decided section 5 action was in 1992. FTC v. Abbott Labs, 853 F. Supp. 526 (D.D.C. 1994). *See also In re* McWane, Inc. and Star Pipe Prods., Inc., No. 9351 (F.T.C. Jan. 4, 2012) (the administrative law judge (ALJ) ruled against the complaint counsel at the trial level on an invitation to collude

It seems improbable that the FTC, having failed to convince courts to adopt even incremental expansions[163] of its UMC power, could successfully argue that a reasonable interpretation of "unfair methods of competition" includes a blanket ban on data practices that, regardless of their impact on consumer privacy, have no clear connection with diminished competition. Further casting doubt on the reasonableness of such interpretation is that any rule that would make online advertising more difficult in the name of competition would be hard to reconcile with past FTC actions designed to promote the free flow of consumer information: the FTC has brought several landmark antitrust actions challenging restrictions on consumer information flows,[164] stopping restrictions on professional advertising was a focus of early FTC rulemaking,[165] and advocating against restrictions on professional advertising has been a mainstay of the FTC competition advocacy program.[166]

V. Conclusion

The FTC has been the chief U.S. privacy regulator for nearly a quarter of a century without using its broad statute to promulgate a privacy regulation. Instead, the FTC has relied on case-by-case enforcement to proscribe unfair and deceptive acts and practices. This reluctance to use rulemaking appears to be coming to an end. The FTC is not so subtly telegraphing that it intends to put its long-dormant power to use.

While the FTC Act is capacious, the FTC's power to write rules is not.

Given its shaky legal grounds and the tenuous link between privacy practices and anticompetitive conduct, UMC rulemaking seems a particularly bad option,

---

count, and this count was not appealed to the full Commission). Since 1992, the FTC has continued to define section 5's reach internally, through settlements primarily involving two classes of conduct: so-called invitations to collude and breaches of agreements to disclose or to license standard-essential patents (SEPs). In addition to these lines of cases, the FTC has used section 5 in two additional matters: the "*CD MAP*" cases, involving the parallel adoption by major record companies of "minimum advertised price" restrictions; and the suit against Intel for engaging in exclusionary conduct, including deception and certain pricing practices. *See* Cooper, *supra* note 161, at 98–99.

163 *See* Sandeep Vaheesan, *Resurrecting "A Comprehensive Charter of Economic Liberty": The Latent Power of the Federal Trade Commission*, 19 U. Penn. J. Bus. Law. 645, 663 (2017) ("When the Commission has brought standalone Section 5 actions in the intervening years, these cases have represented only marginal extensions of existing Sherman Act precedent.").

164 *See, e.g.*, California Dental Ass'n v. FTC, 526 U.S. 756 (1999); *Indiana Fed'n of Dentists*, 476 U.S. 447; 1-800 Contacts, Inc. v. FTC, 1 F.4th 102 (2d Cir. 2021); Realcomp II, Ltd. v. FTC, 635 F.3d 815, 819 (6th Cir. 2011); Polygram Holding, Inc. v. FTC, 416 F.3d 29 (D.C. Cir. 2005).

165 *See, e.g.*, California State Bd. of Optometry v. FTC, 910 F.2d 976 (D.C. Cir. 1990) (striking down on state action grounds the FTC's Eyeglass II rule which state bans on commercial practice); Am. Optometric Ass'n v. FTC, 626 F.2d 896 (D.C. Cir. 1980) (upholding the FTC's Eyeglass I rule, which required optometrists to provide patients with a copy of their prescription); *see also* 57 Fed. Reg. 18,822 (1992).

166 *See, e.g.*, Fed. Trade. Comm'n, FTC Staff Letter to the Supreme Court of Tennessee, Concerning Proposed Amendments to the Tennessee Rules of Professional Conduct Relating to Attorney Advertising (Jan. 24, 2013), https://www.ftc.gov/legal-library/browse/advocacy-filings/ftc-staff-letter-supreme-court-tennessee-concerning-proposed-amendments-tennessee-rules-professional.

both on legal and policy grounds. While the legal authority for UDAP rules is clear, the FTC Act strikes a careful balance between remedy and notice: any rule must be addressed at specific behavior that is responsible for widespread harm. Whether promulgating such rules would be an improvement over the current case-by-case approach is another question entirely. The answer depends on whether any benefits from greater deterrence – due to potentially increased clarity and a monetary remedy – outweigh costs associated with a one-size-fits-all rule applied to heterogenous consumers and firms. If the FTC proceeds down the privacy rulemaking path, as seems likely, it must be mindful of these tradeoffs to avoid creating more harm than good.

What Happens if the FTC Becomes a Serious Rulemaker?

AARON L. NIELSON*

J. Reuben Clark Law School, Brigham Young University

Abstract

The Federal Trade Commission (FTC) is no one's idea of a serious rulemaker. To the contrary, the FTC is, in many respects, a law enforcement agency that operates through litigation and consent decrees. There are understandable reasons for this absence of FTC rulemaking. Not only has Congress imposed heightened procedural obligations on the FTC's ability to promulgate consumer protection rules, but it is far from clear that the FTC even has statutory authority to promulgate substantive rules relating to unfair methods of competition (UMC). Yet things may be changing. It appears that the FTC is preparing to begin using rulemaking more aggressively, including for substantive UMC regulations. The FTC's ability to use rulemaking this way will undoubtedly prompt sharp and important legal challenges.

This short essay, however, considers the question of FTC rulemaking from a different angle: What if the FTC has broad rulemaking authority? And what if the FTC begins to use that authority for controversial policies? Traditionally, the FTC operates in a case-by-case fashion that attempts to apply familiar principles to the facts of individual matters. Should the FTC begin to make broader policy choices through rulemaking, however, it should be prepared for at least three unintended consequences: (i) more ossification, complete with judicial challenges and perhaps even White House oversight; (ii) more zigzagging policy as new FTC leadership, in response to changes in presidential control, moves to undo what the agency has just done; and (iii) to more often be the target of what has been called "administrative

---

* Professor, J. Reuben Clark Law School, Brigham Young University.

law as blood sport," by which political actors make it more difficult for the agency to function, for example by delaying the confirmation process. The upshot would be an agency that could in theory (and sometimes no doubt in fact) regulate more broadly than the FTC does now, but also one with a different character. In short, the more the FTC becomes a serious rulemaker, the more the FTC will change as an institution.

I. Introduction

The Federal Trade Commission (FTC) is many things, but a serious rulemaker it is not. As Daniel Crane has documented, when it comes to antitrust, the FTC has promulgated "virtually no substantive rules" at all in its more than 100-year history.[1] And although the FTC "has issued some consumer protection rules in the last few decades," even in that space, "rulemaking remains a very limited portion of its docket."[2] Indeed, the FTC does not even engage in much in-house adjudication.[3] Instead, the FTC is largely a law enforcement agency that operates through consent decrees and, if necessary, litigation in federal court.[4] And as a law enforcement agency, the FTC generally assesses the facts of individual matters against (relatively) consistent legal principles.[5]

It is possible to make educated guesses why to date the FTC has not been a serious rulemaker. One possibility may be path dependency. Because the FTC does not have much experience with rulemaking, those running the agency may be reluctant to try something new. Beyond path dependency (or perhaps a reason for that path dependency), it is also disputed whether the FTC even has substantive rulemaking authority relating to unfair methods of competition (UMC).[6] Rather than investing resources in a rule that may fail in court, the FTC might prefer to act through other means, especially if the agency feels those other means over the years have generally been satisfactory. The FTC may also be gun-shy. When the agency tried to use rulemaking aggressively for consumer protection issues in the 1970s, Congress responded by mandating a more

1 Daniel Crane, *Debunking* Humphrey's Executor, 83 Geo. Wash. L. Rev. 1835, 1839 (2015).

2 *Id.*

3 *See id.* ("A new empirical study... shows that the FTC's predominant mode of law enforcement is through consent decrees, which involve no adjudication, and that the FTC is more prone to sue in federal district court as a plaintiff than to adjudicate matters administratively in the event there is adjudication.")

4 *See id.*

5 *See, e.g.*, LabMD, Inc. v. FTC, 894 F.3d 1221, 1227–29 (11th Cir. 2018) (describing the lengthy evolution of the FTC's approach to what makes a practice "unfair"). To be sure, although the agency's guiding principles may be generally familiar, the FTC is sometimes accused of failing to provide fair notice of how those principles will be applied. *See, e.g.*, Woodrow Hartzog & Daniel J. Solove, *The Scope and Potential of FTC Data Protection*, 83 Geo. Wash. L. Rev. 2230, 2243 (2015) (collecting citations).

6 *See, e.g.*, Stephanie Kanwit, 1 Fed. Trade Comm'n. § 5:6 (2021) ("If... the FTC does promulgate rules in [the competition] area, it will amount to nothing less than a legal revolution – it will mean a determination *before* adjudication whether a particular act covered by the rule constitutes an unfair method of competition under § 5 [15 U.S.C. § 45(a)]. Debate in legal journals on both sides of this topic has been fierce.").

procedurally rigorous process – known as Magnuson-Moss (or just Mag-Moss) rulemaking – than what the Administrative Procedure Act (APA) requires.[7] Now that those more rigorous procedures are firmly in place for consumer protection rules, it may be that the FTC would prefer to proceed without rulemaking rather than navigate those procedures.[8]

Today, however, some would like to see the FTC become a serious rulemaker – including Lina Khan, the current FTC chair. Khan has argued the FTC has the power to promulgate substantive UMC rules[9] and, as chair, has urged the agency to use that authority.[10] Whether she is correct about the FTC's rulemaking authority will surely be the subject of fierce litigation. On the one hand, in 1973, the D.C. Circuit held in *National Petroleum Refiners v. FTC* that the FTC can promulgate substantive rules – in that case, rules regarding the retail sale of gasoline.[11] On the other hand, the D.C. Circuit's statutory interpretation in *National Petroleum Refiners* is far removed from how courts – including perhaps especially the U.S. Supreme Court – read statutes today.[12] Indeed, Richard Pierce predicts that if the FTC relies on *National Petroleum Refiners*, the Supreme Court will reject that case as "a relic from a bygone era of statutory interpretation."[13] Others disagree.[14] It is safe to say, however, that the federal judiciary will be watching this issue closely.

The scope of the FTC's rulemaking authority – perhaps most importantly whether that authority extends to substantive UMC rules – is an important question. But it is not the only question. Assume for argument's sake that the FTC does

7 *See, e.g.*, Stephen Calkins, *FTC Unfairness: An Essay*, 46 Wayne L. Rev. 1935, 1953–54 (2000) ("The Commission redirected its efforts away from case-by-case adjudication to the crafting of sweeping rules with the force of law.... The combination of unfairness and rule-making was deadly: the over-stimulated Commission reached too far; the press and business interests pilloried the agency as the 'National Nanny' after it proposed a rule regulating advertising to children; Congress passed legislation cutting back on the FTC's jurisdiction over a wide swath of the economy and preventing 'unfairness'-based regulation of commercial advertising, and the Commission strategically (and hastily) retreated."). *See also* Jeffrey S. Lubbers, *It's Time to Remove the "Mossified" Procedures for FTC Rulemaking*, 83 Geo. Wash. L. Rev. 1979, 1983–84 (2015) (describing the additional procedures).

8 *See* Lubbers, *supra* note 7, at 1985 (explaining that the FTC has issued a relatively small number of rules following the enactment of these Mag-Moss requirements).

9 *See, e.g.*, Rohit Chopra & Lina M. Khan, *The Case for "Unfair Methods of Competition" Rulemaking*, 87 U. Chi. L. Rev. 357 (2020).

10 *See, e.g.*, Memo from Chair Lina M. Khan to Commission Staff and Commissioners Regarding the Vision and Priorities for the FTC (Sept. 22, 2021) (urging greater use of the FTC's "full set of tools and authorities – including rulemaking"), https://www.ftc.gov/legal-library/browse/cases-proceedings/public-statements/memo-chair-lina-m-khan-commission-staff-commissioners-regarding-vision-priorities-ftc.

11 482 F.2d 672 (D.C. Cir. 1973).

12 *See supra* Maureen K. Ohlhausen & Ben Rossen, *Dead-End Road: National Petroleum Refiners Association and FTC "Unfair Methods of Competition" Rulemaking,* pp. 31–48. Thomas W. Merrill & Kathryn Tongue Watts, *Agency Rules with the Force of Law: The Original Convention*, 116 Harv. L. Rev. 467, 586 (2002) (arguing that the reasoning from *National Petroleum Refiners* does "considerable violence to actual congressional intent").

13 *See supra* Richard Pierce, *Can the Federal Trade Commission Use Rulemaking to Change Antitrust Law?* pp. 101–128. (quoting Food Mktg. Inst. v. Argus Leader Media, 139 S. Ct. 2356, 2364 (2019)).

14 *See, e.g.*, Kacyn H. Fujii, National Petroleum Refiners *Is (Still) Correctly Decided*, Yale J. on Regul. Notice & Comment (Mar. 28, 2022), https://www.yalejreg.com/nc/national-petroleum-refiners-is-still-correctly-decided-by-kacyn-h-fujii (defending the court's decision).

have broad rulemaking authority, including for high-stakes UMC rules.[15] And assume further that the FTC decides to start using that authority for consequential policies, such as, for example, a new test for predatory pricing or a ban on non-compete clauses in employment contracts.[16] In other words, assume that the FTC becomes a serious rulemaker. What will happen?

This question may seem strange; obviously, if the FTC becomes a serious rulemaker, it will pursue bolder policies.[17] The ability to regulate more aggressively and with broader scope is no doubt one reason why many proponents of FTC rulemaking find it attractive. This question, however, is important because it prompts consideration of unintended consequences. In reality, the rulemaking process is complicated – and is becoming increasingly so. Those who focus on the FTC may think that rulemaking is straightforward because they do not often focus on it.[18] To the extent that the FTC becomes more like other regulators, however, general trends in administrative law will become more important for the FTC. More bluntly, the more serious the FTC becomes about rulemaking, the more the agency will have to confront some of the complications of rulemaking.

If the FTC becomes a serious rulemaker, for example, it may experience what scholars have dubbed "ossification."[19] Although rulemaking may not be difficult when it comes to low-stakes, non-controversial policies, rulemaking for the most significant policies may be a different story. Although the notice-and-comment process may appear simple enough, in application it can be difficult. By way of illustration, the Supreme Court requires agencies to consider important aspects of an issue before promulgating a regulation.[20] This duty of reasoned decision-making is intended to produce higher quality rules, but it also makes the rulemaking process more burdensome for agencies that must attempt to predict – and preemptively address – those issues that a court years later may conclude are important.[21] Agencies seeking to promulgate rules also need to engage in a robust notice-and-comment process, including responding to all material comments.[22] This too can slow rulemaking down, especially for significant rules that can prompt mountains

15 In other words, assume the correctness of *National Petroleum Refiners* and, further, that the FTC has the ability to regulate broadly without running afoul of the major questions or nondelegation doctrines. Of course, it is possible to disaggregate these issues – to imagine a world in which the FTC has substantive UMC rulemaking authority but not for significant policies. Indeed, rulemaking qua rulemaking may be better than case-by-case adjudication – *see, e.g.*, Kristin E. Hickman & Aaron L. Nielson, *Narrowing* Chevron*'s Domain*, 70 Duke L. J. 931, 965–66 (2021) – even if broad delegated authority is concerning.

16 *See, e.g.*, Pierce, *supra* note 13.

17 *Cf.* Lina M. Khan, *Amazon's Antitrust Paradox*, 126 Yale L.J. 710 (2017) (arguing for more aggressive antitrust review).

18 *See, e.g.*, Richard J. Pierce, Jr., *The Rocky Relationship Between the Federal Trade Commission and Administrative Law*, 83 Geo. Wash. L. Rev. 2026, 2040–41 (2015).

19 Aaron L. Nielson, *Sticky Regulations*, 85 U. Chi. L. Rev. 85, 91 (2018).

20 *See, e.g.*, Motor Veh. Mfrs. Ass'n v. State Farm Ins., 463 U.S. 29, 43 (1983).

21 Nielson, *supra* note 19, at 98 (discussing *State Farm*, 463 U.S. at 43).

22 *See id.* at 97–98.

of comments. And when agencies act aggressively, litigation almost always follows. The more the FTC uses rulemaking for significant policies, moreover, the more likely it is that the White House will subject the FTC's rules to cost-benefit review by the Office of Information and Regulatory Affairs (OIRA).[23] Thus far, presidents have been reluctant to subject "independent" agencies like the FTC to OIRA review,[24] but the more policy that the FTC creates through rulemaking, the stronger the case becomes for OIRA to step in to foster inter-agency coordination and ensure that the FTC's analysis is sound.[25]

Likewise, if the FTC becomes a serious rulemaker, the agency's most significant rules sometimes may not have much staying power. Instead, policy may zigzag along with changes in White House control. The FTC's cousin, the Federal Communications Commission (FCC), is a good example of this. In recent decades, the FCC's approach to "net neutrality" has been marked by flip-flopping; when a Republican is in the White House, the agency uses a "light touch" regulatory approach that attempts to encourage greater investment in broadband infrastructure, but when a Democrat is in charge, the FCC imposes heavier regulations that are designed to encourage greater investment by content providers.[26] The result is that neither broadband providers nor content creators can invest with confidence because everyone knows that whatever the current FCC's policy happens to be, that policy is likely to have a short shelf life.[27] Ironically, the best check against such regulatory whiplash may be the ossification of the rulemaking process – which, as noted, presents its own challenges. But the key point is that if the FTC begins making major policy changes through rulemaking, it should also expect to begin unmaking those major policy changes through rulemaking in a few years.

Finally, the more serious the FTC becomes about rulemaking, the more it should be prepared for what Thomas McGarity has provocatively dubbed "administrative law as blood sport."[28] Especially in a polarized society, agency attempts to regulate are increasingly met by political opposition. This opposition may appear within the ordinary rulemaking process (for example, those who dislike the regulation may file negative comments and then pursue litigation if the agency disagrees), but can also emerge outside of that process, as political actors attempt to prevent the agency

---

23 *See generally* Cass R. Sunstein, *The Office of Information and Regulatory Affairs: Myths and Realities*, 126 Harv. L. Rev. 1838 (2013) (describing OIRA).

24 *See, e.g.*, *id.* at 1839 n. 3 ("The so-called independent agencies are not subject to OIRA review, though President Barack Obama did issue an important executive order asking such agencies to follow many of the principles that govern executive agencies.").

25 *See, e.g.*, *id.* at 1840 (discussing these aspects of OIRA's role).

26 *See, e.g.*, Richard J. Pierce, Jr., *The Combination of* Chevron *and Political Polarity Has Awful Effects*, 70 Duke L.J. Online 91, 99 (2021); Aaron L. Nielson, *Sticky Regulations and Net Neutrality Restoring Internet Freedom*, 71 Hastings L.J. 1207 (2020).

27 *See, e.g.*, Pierce, *supra* note 26, at 99.

28 Thomas O. McGarity, *Administrative Law as Blood Sport: Policy Erosion in a Highly Partisan Age*, 61 Duke L.J. 1671 (2012).

from acting at all. Applied here, for example, if the FTC becomes a serious rulemaker, the confirmation process for FTC commissioners may become nastier and the agency's relationship with Congress and the public more strained. Along similar lines, greater use of the FTC's rulemaking authority may also invite structural separation of powers challenges. Whether the FTC will remain an "independent" agency, for example, is already questionable given recent Supreme Court cases.[29] If the FTC also becomes a serious rulemaker, the Supreme Court may be more willing to conclude that the agency's powers should be subject to presidential control.

Simply put, if the FTC becomes a serious rulemaker, it will be able to pursue more significant policies, but its character will also change. The FTC will find itself devoting considerable resources to rulemaking and litigation, and may ultimately fall within the domain of OIRA. The FTC may also become an entity that makes and unmakes policies when political winds shift, and one that is subject to sharp and sophisticated political attacks. To be sure, the benefits of serious rulemaking might outweigh these costs, but the costs will not disappear. Each of these unintended consequences is addressed in greater detail below.

II. Ossification

Rulemaking is understandably attractive to those who would like to see the FTC begin regulating more aggressively. Rulemaking's appeal is intuitive; although agencies can create policy through adjudication, one of the benefits of rulemaking is the ability to address entire categories of situations at once.[30] Logically, however, rulemaking's attractiveness should be tied to how easy it is for agencies to navigate the rulemaking process; the more difficult rulemaking is, the less valuable it should be. This observation is relevant because although rulemaking may look easy enough, in the real world, it can be challenging.

One of the most important questions in administrative law concerns the concept of "ossification," i.e., the notion that it takes too much time and too many resources for agencies to use notice-and-comment rulemaking.[31] Many scholars lament ossification, and have been doing so for decades.[32] Others challenge

---

29 *See infra* Daniel A. Crane, *FTC Independence after Seila Law*, pp. 271–297.

30 *See, e.g.*, John F. Manning, *Constitutional Structure and Judicial Deference to Agency Interpretations of Agency Rules*, 96 Colum. L. Rev. 612, 665 (1996).

31 *See, e.g.*, Nielson, *supra* note 19, at 88; *see also id.* at 94 ("At bottom, the ossification thesis argues that although rulemaking is used frequently, it should be used even more frequently. Rulemaking is not used as often as it should be, the thesis goes, because all three branches of the federal government have imposed onerous procedural requirements on rulemaking."). Needless to say, the label "ossification" is debatable; not all delay is bad. *See, e.g.*, Aaron L. Nielson, *Optimal Ossification*, 86 Geo. Wash. L. Rev. 1209 (2018). The term "ossification" is helpful as a label, however, because the term is so commonly used in the literature.

32 *See, e.g.*, Richard J. Pierce, Jr., *Seven Ways to Deossify Agency Rulemaking*, 47 Admin. L. Rev. 59, 60 (1995); Thomas O. McGarity, *Some Thoughts on "Deossifying" the Rulemaking Process*, 41 Duke L.J. 1385, 1385 (1992) ("During the last fifteen years the rulemaking process has become increasingly rigid and burdensome. An assortment of analytical requirements have been imposed on the simple rulemaking model, and evolving judicial doctrines have obliged agencies to take greater pains to ensure that the technical bases for rules are capable of withstanding judicial scrutiny.").

whether the rulemaking process actually is ossified.[33] Part of the empirical difficulty is that not all rules are equal – it is possible (and perhaps even likely) that ossification is not a major factor for minor rules, but for important ones, it is. According to Richard Pierce, for example, "[o]ssification is a problem only in the context of the much smaller number of rulemakings that raise controversial issues where the stakes are high."[34] In other words, perhaps agencies can move through the rulemaking process relatively painlessly – or even sometimes skip it altogether[35] – for low-level issues, but must spend much more time and effort on those issues that make headlines.

Some evidence supports the theory that ossification is most significant for the most significant rules. Numerous examples demonstrate that it can take a great deal of an agency's time (and treasure) to complete "economically significant rulemakings," i.e., the ones with the most economic consequences.[36] Although agencies promulgate thousands of rules every year, most do not attract much public attention. By contrast, although the number of significant rules is relatively small, they can receive an extraordinary amount of attention. For example, the Environmental Protection Agency (EPA) – an agency that knows a thing or two about high-stakes rulemaking – received more than four million comments after it proposed to "reduc[e] carbon pollution from power plants."[37]

It is also easy to see why the rulemaking process could be ossified for the most significant rules. On its face, the APA does not appear to mandate an onerous rulemaking process, at least for informal (or notice-and-comment) rulemaking.[38] Under the APA, all an agency must do is publish a "[g]eneral notice of proposed rule making" that provides the public with details of any public hearing (if any), identifies the legal basis for the proposed rule, and provides "either the terms or substance of the proposed rule or a description of the subjects and issues involved."[39] The agency must also "give interested persons an opportunity to

33 *Compare, e.g.*, Jason Webb Yackee & Susan Webb Yackee, *Testing the Ossification Thesis: An Empirical Examination of Federal Regulatory Volume and Speed, 1950–1990*, 80 Geo. Wash. L. Rev. 1414 (2012) (challenging the ossification thesis), *with* Richard J. Pierce, Jr., *Rulemaking Ossification Is Real: A Response to* Testing the Ossification Thesis, 80 Geo. Wash. L. Rev. 1493 (2012) (defending it).

34 *See, e.g.*, Pierce, *supra* note 33, at 1498.

35 *See, e.g.*, Connor Raso, *Agency Avoidance of Rulemaking Procedures*, 67 Admin. L. Rev. 65, 68 (2015) (claiming that agencies "avoid rulemaking procedures more frequently as the threat of a successful lawsuit challenging that avoidance declines").

36 *See, e.g.*, Pierce, *supra* note 33, at 1498 ("*Every* study of economically significant rulemakings has found strong evidence of ossification – a decisionmaking process that takes many years to complete and that requires an agency to commit a high proportion of its scarce resources to a single task.").

37 *See* Environmental Protection Agency, Fact Sheet: Clean Power Plan by the Numbers, https://archive.epa.gov/epa/cleanpowerplan/fact-sheet-clean-power-plan-numbers.html.

38 *See* Nielson, *supra* note 19, at 95 (discussing seemingly limited requirements of 5 U.S.C. § 553). Of course, the formal rulemaking process can be more demanding, as can be the process for forms of hybrid rulemaking (such as Mag-Moss rulemaking). *See, e.g.*, Aaron L. Nielson, *In Defense of Formal Rulemaking*, 75 Ohio St. L.J. 237, 270 (2014). Whether or not these procedures result in higher quality rules (another subject of debate), the reality is that formal rulemaking is largely extinct and has been for nearly fifty years. *See generally* Kent H. Barnett, *How the Supreme Court Derailed Formal Rulemaking*, 85 Geo. Wash. L. Rev. Arguendo 1 (2017).

39 5 U.S.C. § 553(b).

participate in the rule making through submission of written data, views, or arguments" and, after considering those submissions, prepare "a concise general statement of [the final rule's] basis and purpose."[40] Just reading the APA, the rulemaking process does not seem too difficult.

Like much of administrative law, however, the rulemaking process has become more complicated since Congress enacted the APA in 1946. Indeed, all three branches have contributed to the complexity of modern rulemaking. Congress, for example, has imposed additional procedural requirements, such as those found in the Paperwork Reduction Act or the National Environmental Policy Act.[41] Congress also sometimes requires agencies to pay special attention to the effects of their proposed rules on, say, small business, or to consider whether regulations impose unfunded mandates.[42] Congress presumably imposes these duties to improve the technical quality and fairness of regulations, but they do make it harder for agencies to act.

All the while, courts have broadly read some of the APA's rulemaking requirements. For example, not only must agencies prepare notices of proposed rulemaking (which the APA explicitly requires), but they also generally must release any data or other material information that they intend to rely on (which the APA does not explicitly require).[43] Similarly, to enable more meaningful comments, the logical outgrowth doctrine requires that a final rule not depart too much from a proposed rule.[44] Agencies thus must spend more time preparing the notice of proposed rulemaking. Perhaps more significantly, rules also need to survive arbitrary-and-capricious review in court. As interpreted, this means that agencies must take a "hard look" at the important aspects of an issue, which may also require them to expend significant resources upfront to demonstrate that they have sufficiently contemplated each "important aspect of the problem."[45] Accordingly, especially when an agency anticipates litigation, officials must do a lot before seeking public comment. Furthermore, some speculate that fear of ossification can be a self-fulfilling prophecy, as the agency's efforts to prepare for ossification may itself lead to delay.[46]

---

40 *Id.* § 553(c).

41 *See, e.g.*, Nielson, *supra* note 19, at 100–01.

42 *See id.*

43 *See, e.g.*, Nielson, *supra* note 19, at 96–97 (explaining the rule from Portland Cement Ass'n v Ruckelshaus, 486 F.2d 375, 393 (D.C. Cir. 1973)).

44 *See id.* at 97–98 (citing, inter alia, Phillip M. Kannan, *The Logical Outgrowth Doctrine in Rulemaking*, 48 Admin. L. Rev. 213 (1996)).

45 *State Farm*, 463 U.S. at 43; *see also* Nielson, *supra* note 19, at 99 ("Hard-look review, perhaps more than anything else, is blamed for ossification. The doctrine 'require[s] agencies to offer detailed explanations for their decisions, to provide strong justifications for any departures from past decisions, to permit widespread public participation in the rulemaking process, and to consider alternative regulatory measures to those proposed.'") (quoting Yackee & Yackee, *supra* note 33, at 1426).

46 *Cf.* Cristina M. Rodríguez, *Foreword: Regime Change*, 135 Harv. L. Rev. 1, 97 n. 359 (2021) ("We need not 'prove' the ossification thesis regarding notice-and-comment rulemaking, for example, to appreciate that the perception of litigation risk by agencies cognizant of hyperproceduralism makes promulgating legislative rules enormously costly and complicated.").

After the agency has sought public comment, moreover, the process can still take considerable time. This is because courts have concluded that not only must agencies solicit public comments, but they must also respond to all material comments.[47] This requirement may not be burdensome in a rulemaking with only a handful of comments. But for the most significant rules, agencies may receive millions of comments. Identifying which comments are material and then responding to them can be a challenge.

Additionally, at least for those agencies and rules subject to the relevant executive orders, the White House has also imposed additional rulemaking requirements beyond those in the APA, including cost-benefit analysis.[48] In conjunction with those requirements, agencies may need to submit their proposed rules to OIRA, which also takes time. To date, the White House has not imposed those requirements on independent agencies like the FTC, but the Department of Justice has concluded that the White House has the authority to do so.[49]

When all of these procedural obligations are combined, it is unsurprising that rulemaking can take a long time, especially for the most momentous and controversial rules.

If the FTC wishes to become a serious rulemaker, it needs to be prepared to operate in a world with ossification (at least to the extent that the ossification thesis is accurate). The FTC thus will be forced to shift time and effort to rulemaking, especially because the sorts of substantive UMC rules that may be on the table appear to be significant.[50] This reallocation of staff should include a greater emphasis on litigators because broad rules almost inevitably face significant challenges in court. To be sure, the FTC already has talented litigators. But if the FTC were to become a serious rulemaker, it is hard to see how more litigation would not follow, and of a different sort than what the FTC typically engages in. Lawyers that defend agency rules must be more focused on principles of administrative law than litigators who attempt to prove facts in court. Thus, the more the FTC promulgates rules, the more it needs to do to prepare for litigation, and the more it should expect to be in court.

If Pierce is right, moreover, that ossification is most significant for the most significant rules, the FTC might not be able to promulgate as many significant

---

47 *See* Nielson, *supra* note 19, at 97–98.

48 *See* Nielson, *supra* note 19, at 99 ("President Ronald Reagan issued Executive Order 12291 – and later Executive Order 12498 – which forced executive agencies to submit many proposed rules to the White House before they could go into effect, plus 'major rules' became subject to cost-benefit analysis. Although President Bill Clinton rescinded these orders, he issued an Executive Order of his own – Number 12866 – that in many respects required the same things. These procedures, moreover, largely remain in effect today.").

49 *See, e.g.*, Richard J. Pierce, Jr., *Introduction to the OIRA 30th Anniversary Conference*, 63 Admin. L. Rev. 1, 6 (2011) ("[T]he Office of Legal Counsel in the Department of Justice in both Republican and Democratic administrations has consistently concluded that the President has the power to authorize OIRA review of rules proposed by independent agencies. The only reason this has not yet happened is because presidents of both parties have been unwilling to suffer the political consequences of such an action.").

50 *See supra* Alden F. Abbott, *Legal Constraints on FTC Competition Rulemaking*, pp. 131.

rules as it would like. The FTC's experience with consumer protection rules may provide a useful analogy. Under Mag-Moss rulemaking, the FTC must complete a complicated process to promulgate even relatively low-profile rules, including analyzing the proposed regulation's economic effects and explaining why the agency chose the rule over alternatives.[51] Because of those procedural requirements, it appears that the FTC is reluctant to use rulemaking at all, even though Congress has expressly authorized rulemaking for consumer protection rules.[52] To the extent that an ossified rulemaking process is akin to the heightened Mag-Moss rulemaking process, the FTC may also be reluctant – or perhaps even realistically unable – to begin the rulemaking process. In other words, the FTC may have to carefully pick its battles. Even if agency leadership would like to pursue many major policies at once, resource constraints may stand in the way.

Finally, ossification may be relevant in another sense. As of now, the White House does not require the FTC to send proposed rules to OIRA. As a practical matter, this is not a major issue currently because the FTC does not engage in a large volume of rulemaking. Should the FTC begin using rulemaking to address significant issues, however, the White House may change its mind about the FTC's relationship with OIRA. As Cass Sunstein has explained, OIRA review facilitates greater policy consistency across agencies and helps ensure that agencies carefully consider the benefits and the costs of their regulations.[53] Logically, the more the FTC looks to create policy that implicates the need for inter-agency consistency and sound cost-benefit analysis, the more OIRA review of FTC rules makes sense. Politically, moreover, the more powerful the FTC becomes, the more pressure presidents may feel to bring the agency's activities under White House control. Suffice it to say, if the FTC becomes subject to OIRA review, the FTC's rulemaking process will be further slowed (though hopefully for reasons that increase the quality of the FTC's rules), and the prospect of review from OIRA's team of experts will "undoubtedly affect the design of rules presubmission."[54]

III. Zigzagging Policy

Ossification is not the only feature of modern rulemaking that may be relevant to the FTC. If the FTC opts to use rulemaking for major policies, a different issue may emerge: zigzagging regulation. In particular, what an agency does under one administration can be undone when the White House flips hands and a new president's nominees take over. In a polarized age in which Republicans and Democrats have sharply opposing views, the upshot can be rules with short shelf lives. As Justice Neil Gorsuch has observed, "these days it sometimes seems

51 *See, e.g.*, Lubbers, *supra* note 7, at 1982–85.

52 *See id.*

53 *See* Sunstein, *supra* note 23, at 1840.

54 *Id.* at 1865.

agencies change their statutory interpretations almost as often as elections change administrations."[55]

Although not the only one, a familiar example of zigzagging regulation is the FCC's inconsistent approach to so-called net neutrality. For decades, the FCC has been yo-yoing back and forth between a "light touch" to internet regulation, which may encourage internet service providers (ISPs) to invest in broadband infrastructure, and a heavier touch, which prevents ISPs from favoring certain content by blocking or slowing internet traffic. The pattern is not pretty:

> The history is as neck-snapping as a tennis match. The FCC in 2004 adopted open internet principles that encouraged, but did not require, internet service providers to provide an open internet. In 2010, during President Obama's administration, the FCC opted for more formal rules. Those rules were struck down in 2014 for exceeding the FCC's authority. In 2015, the FCC adopted even stronger rules classifying providers as "common carrier" utilities. But in 2017, after President Trump took office, the FCC rescinded those 2015 rules. Now the FCC is preparing to adopt a perhaps even more stringent set of regulations than the 2015 rules, which the FCC will presumably rescind when a Republican returns to the White House.[56]

When agencies promulgate rules with broad political consensus, there is less flip-flopping. The same would be true if one political party were able to control the White House for a long time. But in today's world, where many policies are not broadly supported and one party does not consistently control the White House, flip-flopping is possible because administrative law (generally) "makes no distinction... between initial agency action and subsequent agency action undoing or revising that action," i.e., an agency generally does not need to make a greater showing to undo a regulation than to promulgate it in the first place.[57] Indeed, where an agency has policymaking discretion, not even a prior judicial decision necessarily will bar the agency from changing its mind and undoing an old policy.[58]

Zigzagging policy has considerable downsides. For example, "flip-flopping between net neutrality and deregulation of internet service providers every time the White House changes hands discourages all investments in the internet."[59] Neither ISPs nor content creators can fully rely on the incentives

55 Guedes v. Bureau of Alcohol, Tobacco, Firearms & Explosives, 140 S. Ct. 789, 790 (2020) (statement of Gorsuch, J.).

56 Aaron Nielson, *It's Time for Congress to Set Internet* Policy, Bloomberg Law (Apr. 29, 2022), https://news.bloomberglaw.com/us-law-week/its-time-for-congress-to-set-internet-policy.

57 FCC v. Fox Television Stations, Inc., 556 U.S. 502 (2009).

58 *See* Nat'l Cable & Telecomms. Ass'n v. Brand X Internet Servs., 545 U.S. 967 (2005); *see also* Jonathan Masur, *Judicial Deference and the Credibility of Agency Commitments*, 60 Vand. L. Rev. 1021 (2007) (explaining why an agency's ability to disagree with a prior judicial reason results in greater regulatory instability).

59 Pierce, *supra* note 26, at 99.

that the FCC is trying to create – at least for long-term investment decisions – because the policy is likely to change.[60] As Justice Antonin Scalia once observed, "[t]here are times when even a bad rule is better than no rule at all."[61] A "rule" that constantly changes is not much better. Thus, Pierce reports:

> attend[ing] many conferences in which utility executives said that, while they oppose the issuance of a strict limit on mercury emissions, they would much prefer issuance of such a limit to continued uncertainty. They explained that they did not know which of two alternative sets of major investments in generating technology they should make until they knew what EPA was going to do with respect to mercury emissions. As a result, they were deferring many important investment decisions.... The same analysis applies in each of the hundreds of contexts in which Democrats and Republicans have opposing and uncompromising preferences with respect to policy issues on which investment decisions depend.[62]

In other words, when an agency's rules vacillate, regulated entities – rationally – cannot fully rely on those rules. This is bad for business, obviously, but it is also bad for consumers, who benefit from investment. And it is bad for regulators, too, who cannot focus on long-term priorities but instead must spend time and resources undoing what the agency has just done. Because of these downsides, Pierce has soured on strong deference to agency decisions.[63] The cause of zigzagging regulation, however, is not just deference, but instead springs more generally from the fact that agencies can change policy. To be sure, some flip-flops are no doubt a good thing (elections have consequences and old policies sometimes can be improved upon), but they also have costs.[64]

Ironically, the best solution to the problem of zigzagging rules may be the very ossified rulemaking process discussed above.[65] After all, the harder it is for an agency to make policy through rulemaking, the harder it is for that agency to

---

60 *See id.* ("Whether net neutrality is a good or bad policy, we have chosen the worst possible policy in this context. Net neutrality discourages investment by internet service providers by subjecting them to strict regulation, but it encourages investment by content providers by assuring them of equal access to the internet. Conversely, deregulation of the internet discourages investment by content providers because they cannot be confident that they will have access to the internet on fair and impartial terms, but it encourages investment by internet service providers by assuring them that they will have the freedom to use the assets in which they invest in ways that maximize the return on their investments.... [Thus, the FCC's inconsistency] discourages investment by both content providers and internet service providers.")

61 Antonin Scalia, *The Rule of Law as a Law of Rules*, 56 U. Chi. L. Rev. 1175, 1179 (1989).

62 Pierce, *supra* note 26, at 100.

63 *See id.* at 110 ("*Chevron* is not capable of producing acceptable results in today's political environment.").

64 *See, e.g.*, Nielson, *supra* note 26, at 1218–23 (explaining costs and benefits of various reforms that could reduce zigzagging regulation).

65 *See, e.g., id.* at 1219–20 (explaining how ossification can be a commitment mechanism against change). There are other solutions, too, but each has costs. For example, flip-flopping may be a signal that an issue is too important for an agency to resolve. *See id.* at 1221–22. The law could put a heavy thumb in favor of the first mover – though that may create perverse incentives. *See id.* at 1220–21. And if the current rulemaking process is not ossified enough to prevent policy shifting, more procedures could be added. *See id.* at 1221.

unmake policy. Thus, at least at the margins, the prospect of an ossified rulemaking process may lead some officials to decide it is too much trouble to undo a prior rule and that scarce agency resources should instead be devoted to new issues.[66] The FCC's experience, however, suggests that ossification may not be a meaningful check on zigzagging, at least for the most significant regulations. When the stakes are high, it appears that agencies are willing to expend the resources to undo the work of a prior administration, even if it requires navigating an ossified rulemaking process.

The emergence of zigzagging regulation is relevant to FTC rulemaking because those who favor greater use of such authority presumably want the FTC to tackle big issues. The FTC, however, may struggle to do that because big issues tend to be divisive. In this current age of polarization, regulatory efforts to address divisive issues may not work well because what an agency does under one administration can be undone in the next administration. Thus, the end result may be policy that exists under some administrations but not others. Indeed, the FTC's recent slew of party-line votes suggests that if the FTC begins using rulemaking for controversial policies, it will look to undo those rules when the political balance flips.[67] Of course, not all FTC rules will vacillate – there are not enough resources to undo everything, especially as agencies confront new issues. But if the FTC becomes a serious rulemaker, at least some zigzagging likely will occur. By contrast, there is less risk of zigzagging if the FTC acts through the fact-specific application of established standards.

IV. Administrative Law as Blood Sport

Finally, experience from other agencies suggests that the FTC should expect pushback if it becomes a serious rulemaker. This pushback likely will not be limited to what happens in the rulemaking process itself but will include outside attacks.

Politics has always been a rough business, and that includes agency efforts to make policy through administrative law. In recent decades, however, rulemaking has been subjected to what McGarity has dubbed "administrative law as blood sport."[68] In particular, McGarity identifies numerous ways that political actors interfere with rulemaking, including "strategies aimed at indirectly disrupting the implementation of regulatory programs by blocking Senate confirmation of

66 To be sure, this analysis may be more complicated when sunk costs are involved. Imagine that a regulator of a relatively stable industry promulgates a new rule that requires manufacturers to invest in new technology that, once installed, does not change the marginal costs of production. Such a regulator may not worry too much about zigzagging regulation because, even if policy were to flip under a new administration, the manufacturers would be unlikely to change their behavior. It is likely that the FTC's rulemaking efforts would impose some sunk costs (e.g., long-term contracts premised on a particular regulatory scheme).

67 *See generally*, Crane *supra* note 29.

68 McGarity, *supra* note 28.

new agency leaders, cutting off promised funding for agencies, introducing rifle-shot riders aimed at undoing ongoing agency action, and subjecting agency heads to contentious oversight hearings."[69]

There are many reasons for the rise of blood-sport tactics. One explanation, however, relates to divided public opinion. In an age of political polarization, it is difficult for Congress to enact legislation. Accordingly, presidents – looking to accomplish their goals – increasingly turn to the administrative state for policy priorities.[70] Agencies may seek to repurpose old grants of delegated authority to address new issues or, when applicable, rely on statutory language enacted when one party overwhelmingly controls Congress.[71] Courts sometimes disallow agency efforts to repurpose old statutes for new policies.[72] Additionally, as discussed above, rules promulgated under these circumstances may be unmade by the next administration. Beyond that, though, policies that do not command deep legislative support trigger strong feelings and political responses, which may prompt efforts to stop the agency from acting in the first place. And, unsurprisingly, the more that political actors do this, the better they become at it, and their level of comfort with disruption increases. Thus, in the rough-and-tumble process that is federal policymaking, it is unsurprising that as rulemaking becomes a more important policymaking tool, enterprising actors look outside of the rulemaking process to limit agency authority.

It does not take much work to find real-world examples of the use of blood-sport tactics. Look no further than the confirmation process. Getting confirmed by the Senate can be brutal, especially when the White House and the Senate are controlled by different parties (and sometimes even when they are controlled by the same party).[73] Thus, as McGarity demonstrates, to thwart agency rulemaking, the Senate – sometimes due to the effort of a single senator – may refuse to confirm agency officials, or at least slow-walk the confirmation process; senators may also exact policy concessions as the price of support.[74] Congress

69 *See id.* at 1672.

70 *See, e.g.*, Aaron L. Nielson, *Deconstruction (Not Destruction)*, 150 Dædalus 143, 147 (Summer 2021) (citing Elena Kagan, *Presidential Administration*, 114 Harv. L. Rev. 2245, 2248 (2001)).

71 For example, McGarity focuses on blood-sport responses to rulemaking under a 2010 amendment to the Dodd-Frank Wall Street Reform and Consumer Protection Act. *See* McGarity, *supra* note 28, at 1681–82. That amendment was passed during a short period of almost supermajority control of Congress by the Democrats.

72 *See, e.g.*, Nat'l Fed'n of Indep. Bus. v. Dep't of Lab., Occupational Safety & Health Admin., 142 S. Ct. 661, 666 (2022) ("It is telling that OSHA, in its half century of existence, has never before adopted a broad public health regulation of this kind – addressing a threat that is untethered, in any causal sense, from the workplace."); Utility Air Regulatory Grp. v. EPA, 573 U.S. 302, 324 (2014) (rejecting an agency's assertion of "newfound authority" to address a policy issue that Congress did not clearly address in the statute).

73 *See, e.g.*, Matthew C. Stephenson, *Can the President Appoint Principal Executive Officers Without a Senate Confirmation Vote?*, 122 Yale L.J. 940, 942 (2013) (explaining "the widely shared belief that our system for appointing senior federal officials is a mess, and seems to be getting worse").

74 *See* McGarity, *supra* note 28, at 1714–16.

has also used the Congressional Review Act – which, under certain circumstances, allows Congress to undo an agency rule through an expedited process – much more often since 2016 than before it.[75] Agencies engaged in rulemaking (again, especially regarding controversial subjects) also need to be prepared for "rifle-shot amendments" to prevent particular rules, as well as aggressive public-relations campaigns.[76]

One can debate whether the benefits of these tactics outweigh their costs. What is less debatable, however, is that the FTC would be subjected to such tactics should it become a serious rulemaker. The FTC's own history illustrates the point. As explained above, when the FTC began regulating aggressively in the 1970s, Congress responded by requiring Mag-Moss rulemaking for consumer protection rules. Today, even if it would be difficult for Congress to pass such broad legislation, it is not hard to imagine efforts to hobble the FTC, including rifle-shot amendments in omnibus legislation. The confirmation process for FTC commissioners is already not a cakewalk, but – as has happened with the Supreme Court confirmation process – could be even more vicious. And especially if one branch of Congress is controlled by a different party than the FTC, it is no stretch to imagine intense oversight hearings. The key point is that when controversial policies are on the table, the FTC must be prepared for sharp-elbowed politics.

Moving beyond politics, moreover, the FTC may be susceptible to another type of attack: constitutional litigation. Since 2010, the Supreme Court has begun viewing independent agencies with considerable skepticism. In a series of cases, the Supreme Court has held that the president must be able to fire agency heads so that the White House can more fully control how agencies use executive power.[77] As Crane has explained, this development is relevant to the FTC because the primary precedent that proponents of independent agencies rely on is *Humphrey's Executor v. United States*, which concerned the FTC.[78] It is challenging to reconcile the logic of the Supreme Court's recent precedent with *Humphrey's Executor*.[79] In fact, it appears that perhaps the only reason why the Supreme Court has not overruled *Humphrey's Executor* is stare decisis.[80] If, however, the Supreme Court comes to believe that the FTC is addressing controversial issues without sufficient political control – in other words, if the Supreme Court concludes that the FTC, as a "headless fourth branch of government," poses the sort of threat to liberty that presidential removal is designed to prevent – it will be harder for the FTC to

75 *See id.* at 1716–18.

76 *See id.* at 1708, 1718.

77 *See, e.g.*, Aaron L. Nielson & Christopher J. Walker, *Congress's Anti-Removal Power*, __ Vand. L. Rev. __ (forthcoming 2023).

78 *See* Crane, *supra* note 29, at 274–278 (discussing 295 U.S. 602 (1935)).

79 *Id.*

80 *See, e.g.*, Nielson & Walker, *supra* note 77.

defend *Humphrey's Executor*.[81] To the extent this account is accurate, the more serious the FTC is about rulemaking, the greater the risk that the Supreme Court will conclude that the FTC cannot operate outside of direct presidential control.[82] This would be a generational change for the FTC as an institution and administrative law generally.

V. Conclusion

The extent of the FTC's rulemaking authority is an important question. But it is not the only question that matters. If the FTC has broad rulemaking authority, other questions must also be answered, including what the FTC should do with that authority. The truth is that rulemaking can be challenging, especially for significant policies. When trying to do controversial things, agencies struggle to navigate an ossified process. And after an agency has finished that process, sometimes that same agency turns around and undoes what it just did – especially, again, for the most controversial issues. And the more an agency attempts to use rulemaking for such policies, the more that the agency should expect to face political opposition. Given all of this, answering whether the FTC has broad rulemaking authority is not enough. We also need to think about what will happen if the FTC becomes a serious rulemaker.

81 To be sure, the fact that the FTC is an enforcement agency by itself may raise constitutional concerns. *See, e.g.*, Crane, *supra* note 1. In *Seila Law v. CFPB*, however, the Supreme Court emphasized that the Consumer Financial Protection Bureau has broad rulemaking authority. *See* 140 S. Ct. 2183, 2191 (2020) (emphasizing the agency's "vast rulemaking, enforcement, and adjudicatory authority over a significant portion of the U.S. economy").

82 *See, e.g.*, Aaron L. Nielson, *Is the FTC on a Collison Course With the Unitary Executive?*, Yale J. on Regul. Notice & Comment (July 2, 2021), https://www.yalejreg.com/nc/is-the-ftc-on-a-collison-course-with-the-unitary-executive.

FTC Independence after *Seila Law*

Daniel A. Crane*
University of Michigan

Abstract

The FTC's status as an independent agency is in jeopardy from both political and constitutional forces. Politically, the Biden administration has given indications that it expects the FTC to follow a blueprint for competition policy directed by the White House. While the President may not currently have the power to compel the Commission's acquiescence, the constitutional bedrock of the FTC's independence – the Supreme Court's landmark 1935 Humphrey's Executor decision – is hanging on by a thread. The Supreme Court's recent unitary executive decisions show that at least a plurality, and likely a majority, of the justices are disposed to overrule Humphrey's and hold that the President has the power to remove commissioners of agencies that wield essentially executive powers, which is certainly true of the FTC. If the FTC loses its insulation from the President's removal power, it will have lost a good bit of its functional independence, with significant short- and long-term implications.

---

* Frederick Paul Furth, Sr. Professor of Law, University of Michigan. Many thanks to Aaron Nielsen, Dick Pierce, and the other participants at the Gray Center FTC Roundtable for invaluable comments.

I. Introduction

Nominally, the Federal Trade Commission is the quintessential example of a Progressive Era agency – multi-partisan, expert, and politically independent from the White House and Congress. Yet the days of the FTC's independence may be numbered. Never mind legislative initiatives like Senator Josh Hawley's that would sweep the FTC into the executive branch[1] and have very little chance of succeeding. The threats to the FTC's independence come mildly from the executive branch, and strongly from the judicial branch.

From the executive branch: In this moment of intensive political focus on antitrust reform, the Biden administration has appointed an FTC chair intent on dramatically overhauling U.S. antitrust law in a considerably more interventionist direction. But, to accomplish a comprehensive overhaul of competition policy, the administration is calling for a "whole-of-government competition policy" that requires coordination among the various institutions of the administration, including independent agencies like the Federal Reserve System, the FTC, the Securities and Exchange Commission, and the Federal Communications Commission.[2] The administration has created a White House Competition Council including the secretaries of various executive branches, with an open invitation for participation by the heads of various independent agencies, including the FTC chair. The Executive Order purports to give directions to the heads of the various agencies with competition policy powers – they "*shall* consider using their authorities to further the policies set forth in section 1 of this order." Further, the FTC is "encouraged" to consider revisions to the horizontal and vertical merger guidelines. Most strikingly, the "[c]hair of the FTC is encouraged to consider working with the rest of the Commission to exercise the FTC's statutory rulemaking authority under the Federal Trade Commission Act to curtail the unfair use of non-compete clauses and other clauses or agreements that may unfairly limit worker mobility." This admonition precedes, and is subtly distinct, from a separate admonition for the FTC chair in her "discretion" to consider whether to exercise the FTC's statutory rulemaking authority with respect to a laundry list of competitive topics, including data collection and surveillance, third-party or self-repair, restrictions on biosimilar entry in the pharmaceutical industry, unfair competition in major Internet marketplaces, occupational licensing, and real estate listing services. Apparently, the FTC chair should consider herself to have "discretion" as to the longer list of rulemaking topics, but not as to labor non-competes.

The Biden Executive Order does not go so far as to give the FTC direct orders (as it does with respect to executive branch departments or agencies), but it leaves

---

1 https://www.hawley.senate.gov/overhauling-federal-trade-commission.

2 Executive Order on Promoting Competition in the American Economy (July 9, 2021), https://www.whitehouse.gov/briefing-room/presidential-actions/2021/07/09/executive-order-on-promoting-competition-in-the-american-economy.

no doubt that the White House expects compliance. Now, in practical terms there is little doubt that the FTC chair, who was selected to carry out this sort of mandate, will be willing to comply. Further, the administration gets to select a replacement for Commissioner Chopra, who is heading over to the (newly non-independent) Consumer Financial Protection Board, and will enjoy the advantage of a Democrat majority on the five-member Commission, so the likelihood of a confrontation between the Commission and the administration is low. But the administration's directions to the FTC set the stage for confrontation with another branch that, while the "least dangerous" in principle, poses the greatest danger to the FTC's independence.

From the judiciary: In *Humphrey's Executor v. United States*,[3] the United States Supreme Court paved the way for the modern administrative state by holding that Congress could constitutionally limit the President's power to remove FTC commissioners for political reasons.[4] The Court held that President Franklin Roosevelt's removal of Federal Trade Commissioner William E. Humphrey without cause contravened the Federal Trade Commission Act,[5] which constitutionally limited the President's removal power to "for cause" termination.[6] Since *Humphrey's Executor*, the FTC has been assumed to be politically independent from the President's control.

However, *Humphrey's Executor*'s vision for independent agencies has long been under attack, with the drumbeat intensifying in recent years. Then-Judge Brett Kavanaugh launched a vigorous assault on *Humphrey's Executor*, arguing that the decision deserved the same overruling as the company it kept during the 1935 term.[7] The Supreme Court continued to retrench on agency independence, holding unconstitutional provisions of the Sarbanes-Oxley Act creating accounting oversight board where members of the board could only be removed for cause by the Securities and Exchange Commission, whose commissioners also could only be removed for cause.[8]

And then came the not-quite *coup de grâce*, *Seila Law LLC v. Consumer Financial Protection Bureau*,[9] where the Court held that the for-cause restriction of the President's executive power to remove CFPB's single director violated the constitutional separation of powers. To be sure, the Court distinguished *Humphrey's Executor* as a different case – one concerning an agency performing only "quasi-legislative" and "quasi-judicial functions," and not said to exercise any executive power. That was a fair enough report on what the Court *said* about the FTC in *Humphrey's Executor*, but fantasy as to what the FTC actually *does*. In fact,

3 Humphrey's Ex'r v. United States, 295 U.S. 602 (1935).

4 *Id.* at 629.

5 15 U.S.C. §§ 41–58 (2012).

6 *See id.* § 41; *Humphrey's Ex'r*, 295 U.S. at 629.

7 *In re* Aiken Cnty., 645 F.3d 428, 441–42 (D.C. Cir. 2011) (Kavanaugh, J., concurring).

8 Free Enter. Fund v. Pub. Co. Accounting Oversight Bd., 561 U.S. 477, 492 (2010).

9 591 U.S. ___, 140 S. Ct. 2183 (2020).

as I have shown in previous work,[10] in its antitrust capacity the FTC has historically done relatively little "judicial" work and virtually no "legislative" work, but has instead become a thoroughly executive agency, enforcing the antitrust laws against alleged violaters. Taking *Seila Law*'s analytical framework and applying it to the actual facts concerning the FTC, it seems that *Humphrey's Executor* and, with it, the FTC's independence from the White House are hanging by a thread.

This article proceeds in three parts. Part II recalls the *Humphrey's Executor* decision and its implications for the FTC and the administrative state more broadly. Part III analyzes the implications of *Seila Law* and two follow-up Supreme Court decisions – *Arthrex*[11] and *Collins*[12] – for the FTC's continuing independence. Part IV contemplates the immediate and longer-run parameters of a post-independence world.

II. *Humphrey's Executor* and the Progressive Vision for Commission Independence

The FTC was a Progressive Era creation designed fundamentally to alter the modalities of political control over firms and markets. As a commentator noted a decade after the Commission's creation, the FTC Act represented "a steady extension of legal control" reflecting "[t]he vast changes wrought . . . during the nineteenth century" – particularly "the introduction of new mechanical forces, the penetrating influence of science, large scale industry and progressive urbanization."[13] Against these forces, the conventional modalities of executive law enforcement and common law adjudication were seen as ineffective. The Progressives believed that a Commission, unlike the courts and executive branch, could be proactive rather than reactive to these sprawling social and economic problems. As Justice Brandeis, a chief architect of the FTC, noted in a later dissenting opinion, FTC enforcement "was to be prophylactic. Its purpose in respect to restraints of trade was prevention of diseased business conditions, not cure."[14]

The Progressives also believed that the Commission would be superior to executive branch enforcement before generalist judges due to the expertise of the commissioners. For instance, the Senate Committee on Interstate Commerce emphasized:

> The work of this commission will be of a most exacting and difficult character, demanding persons who have experience in the problems to be met – that is, a proper knowledge of both the public requirements and the practical affairs of industry. It is manifestly desirable that

10 Daniel A. Crane, *Debunking* Humphrey's Executor, 83 Geo. Wash. L. Rev. 1836 (2015).

11 U.S. v. Arthrex, Inc., 141 S. Ct. 1970 (2021).

12 Collins v. Yellen, 141 S. Ct. 1761 (2021).

13 Gerard C. Henderson, The Federal Trade Commission: A Study in Administrative Law and Procedure v (Yale University Press 1924).

14 FTC v. Gratz, 253 U.S. 421, 435 (1920).

> the terms of the commissioners shall be long enough to give them an opportunity to acquire the expertness in dealing with these special questions concerning industry that comes from experience.[15]

The expertise claim came straight from the Progressive-technocratic playbook, which called for the separation of politics from economic and social administration and the entrustment of decision-making to neutral experts – economic engineers capable of improving the performance of the market through planning based on objective scientific principles.[16] As Woodrow Wilson famously put it, regulators would be experts in the "science of administration" that operated "outside the proper sphere of *politics*."[17]

To achieve this vision, Congress vested the FTC with trappings of technocratic independence. The Commission would have five members, not more than three of whom could be of the same party, with staggered seven-year terms. Most significantly, the FTC Act allowed the President to dismiss an FTC commissioner only for "inefficiency, neglect of duty, or malfeasance in office." In other words, although the President could nominate commissioners and thereby control the FTC's composition (with the advice and consent of the Senate) *ex ante*, the President would not have the power to steer the Commission's conduct *ex post*. Given the length of the commissioners' terms of office, their bipartisan composition, and their bent on technocratic expertise, the Commission would thereby become detached from ordinary politics.

While the Progressive's vision for the FTC was clear, its constitutionality was not. Did Congress have the power to create an independent agency free from the President's control? Earlier unitary executive decisions like *Myers v. United States* suggested a negative answer.[18] In *Myers*, Chief Justice Taft – a great defender of the common law and traditional executive enforcement of the law – held that the President enjoyed the constitutional power unilaterally to remove a postmaster appointed by the President with the advice and consent of the Senate. The Court reasoned that the President's constitutional obligation to take care that the laws be faithfully executed necessarily assumed the power to remove executive officers for whose performance the President had ultimate responsibility.[19] *Myers* articulated a hierarchical vision of the executive branch with the President atop, wielding plenary removal powers over officers of the United States.[20]

---

15 *Humphrey's Ex'r*, 295 U.S. at 624–25 (quoting S. Rep. No. 63-597, at 10–11 (1914)).

16 *See* William E. Akin, Technocracy and the American Dream: The Technocrat Movement, 1900–1941 ix–xi (University of California Press 1977) (summarizing the rise and fall of the technocratic movement); *see also* James M. Landis, The Administrative Process 7–8 (Yale University Press 1938) (arguing for technocratic-administrative solutions to improve over the laissez-faire economic system).

17 Woodrow Wilson, *The Study of Administration*, 2 Pol. Sci. Q. 197, 197, 210 (1887).

18 Myers v. United States, 272 U.S. 52, 176 (1926).

19 *Id.* at 117 (holding that the President must have some "power of removing those for whom he cannot continue to be responsible").

20 *See id.*

The test case that became *Humphrey's Executor* arose from President Roosevelt's firing of Commissioner Humphrey, who had flagrantly defied the Commission's New Deal orientation, on October 7, 1933.[21] Roosevelt made clear that the reasons for his firing here were political, and not grounded in the statutory cause criteria.[22] Humphrey died, but his executor brought a case for back pay on the theory that Humphrey's firing was wrongful. The case's paltry economic stakes were overshadowed by its tremendous consequences for agency independence and the constitutional charter of the administrative state.

The Supreme Court ruled in favor of Humphrey, establishing the principle that the President may not remove FTC commissioners for political reasons, but only for good cause.[23] Justice Sutherland's opinion rests on a quartet of observations about the nature of the FTC that ostensibly distinguish the Commission from executive branch departments. According to the Court, the FTC is (i) nonpolitical and nonpartisan, (ii) uniquely expert, (iii) "quasi-legislative," and (iv) "quasi-judicial," rather than executive.[24] Together, these four qualities ostensibly lent the FTC a character different from that of ordinary law enforcers, hence the legitimacy of insulating commissioners from the President's constitutional responsibility to "take Care that the Laws be faithfully executed."[25] At its core, *Humphrey's Executor* rests on the assertion that the FTC is something other than a conventional law enforcement agency and thus merits a different position in the political order than executive departments like the Justice Department that also enforce laws concerning antitrust and consumer protection.

First, the Court characterized the FTC as a politically independent and nonpartisan body. According to the Court, the FTC is "a body which shall be independent of executive authority, *except in its selection*, and free to exercise its judgment without the leave or hindrance of any other official or any department of the government."[26] The FTC's independence, the Court asserted, stemmed in part from its nonpartisan nature, emphasizing that "[t]he commission is to be non-partisan; and it must, from the very nature of its duties, act with entire impartiality."[27] In addition to its composition, the FTC's statutory mandate was devoid of partisan taint, as "[i]t is charged with the enforcement of no policy except the policy of the law."[28]

---

21 *Humphrey's Ex'r*

22 *Id.*

23 *Id.* at 619.

24 *Id.* at 628.

25 U.S. Const. art. II, § 3.

26 *Humphrey's Ex'r*, 295 U.S at 625–26.

27 *Id.* at 624.

28 *Id.* For discussion on congressional intent that the FTC be insulated from politics, *see* Robert E. Cushman, The Independent Regulatory Commissions 188–95 (Octagon Books 1972).

In addition to being politically neutral, it mattered to the Court that the FTC commissioners were *experts*. "Like the Interstate Commerce Commission, [the FTC's] members are called upon to exercise the trained judgment of a body of experts appointed by law and informed by experience."[29]

Finally, in contrast to executive branch agents that merely enforced the law, the FTC was not a law enforcement agency at all: "Its duties are neither political nor executive, but predominantly quasi-judicial and quasi-legislative."[30] Because the FTC was not acting as a law enforcer, but instead as a judge and legislator, the President did not need to control FTC commissioners in order to perform his constitutional obligation to see that the laws were faithfully executed.

A piece of important context concerns the company that the *Humphrey's Executor* decision kept. The decision was announced on Roosevelt's "Black Monday," May 27, 1935, in the midst of a sweep of cases in 1935–1936 in which the conservative Supreme Court waged combat against Roosevelt,[31] and on the same day as the *Schechter Poultry*[32] decision, which invalidated crucial aspects of the National Industrial Recovery Act on nondelegation and commerce clause grounds.[33] It is striking that this decision, ostensibly reflecting the "heyday of the progressive model within the judiciary,"[34] came from a predominantly conservative Court intent on reigning in the power of the New Deal presidency.[35] The conventional account has the Progressive takeover of the Supreme Court beginning in 1937 with the repudiation of the classical liberal and laissez-faire doctrines favored by the Sutherland wing of the Court,[36] so it is odd to think of *Humphrey's Executor* as symbolizing the heart of Progressive-technocratic ideology. The *Humphrey's Executor* decision was unanimous (as was *Schechter Poultry*), with McReynolds writing separately only to point back to his dissenting opinion in *Myers*,[37] which had argued from a constitutional history standpoint for limitations on the President's removal power.[38] That Justices Stone, Cardozo, and Brandeis joined without comment points to an anticentralization ideological strand in the decision – the Court's progressives in 1935 remained more in the Jeffersonian-Jacksonian camp that feared large aggregations of power, whether

---

29 *Humphrey's Ex'r*, 295 U.S. at 624 (quoting Illinois Cent. R.R. Co. v. Interstate Commerce Comm'n, 206 U.S. 441, 451 (1907)) (internal quotation marks omitted).

30 *Id.*

31 *See generally* Miller, *infra* note 40, at 92–94 (discussing context of *Humphrey's Executor* decision).

32 A.L.A. Schechter Poultry Corp. v. United States, 295 U.S. 495 (1935).

33 *Id.* at 541–42, 550–51.

34 Lawrence Lessig & Cass R. Sunstein, *The President and the Administration*, 94 Colum. L. Rev. 1, 100 (1994).

35 *See* Christopher S. Yoo, Steven G. Calabresi & Laurence D. Nee, *The Unitary Executive During the Third Half-Century, 1889–1945*, 80 Notre Dame L. Rev. 1, 88 (2004).

36 *See generally* Richard A. Epstein, How Progressives Rewrote the Constitution 13 (Cato Institute 2006).

37 *Humphrey's Ex'r*, 295 U.S. at 632.

38 *See generally Myers*, 272 U.S. at 178–239 (McReynolds, J., dissenting).

in the private sector or government, than later New Deal appointees who were more comfortable with the expansion of the federal government and executive branch power.[39]

Because the coalition that decided *Humphrey's Executor* was a mixed bag of conservative classicists and populist anticentralizationalists, it is perhaps best to understand the decision as accidentally or opportunistically Progressive rather than embodying true-belief Progressivism. Nonetheless, the decision articulated the heart of the Progressive vision for administrative agencies – politically detached and independent, uniquely expert and objective, and acting through a combination of political decisional modes, particularly those conventionally associated with legislatures and courts. Broadly speaking, *Humphrey's Executor* served to legitimize the modern regulatory state and remains one of the iconic judicial pillars of the technocratic, independent administrative system.[40] As Geoffrey Miller has put it, the decision serves as the "fundamental constitutional charter of the independent regulatory commissions."[41]

III. *Seila Law* and its Consequences

1. From *Humphrey's Executor* to *Seila Law*

Unitary executive proponents and critics of the modern regulatory state have sharply criticized the Court's assumptions in *Humphrey's Executor*. They have argued that, contrary to the Court's assertion, the FTC serves quintessentially executive functions[42] and that it impairs the President's ability to cohesively and consistently enforce the laws.[43] But despite its symbolic importance as an expression of Progressive-technocratic values, the importance of *Humphrey's Executor*'s four-prong justification as a matter of constitutional law has eroded

---

39 An anecdote recounted by Peter Irons concerning the day of the *Schechter Poultry* and *Humphrey's Executor* decisions is telling: "Before Tommy Corcoran could depart, a Supreme Court page tapped him on the shoulder and said that Justice Brandeis would like to see him in the justices' robing room. Brandeis wanted Corcoran to convey a message to the White House: 'This is the end of this business of centralization, and I want you to go back and tell the President that we're not going to let this government centralize everything. It's come to an end.'" Peter H. Irons, The New Deal Lawyers 104 (Princeton University Press 1982).

40 *See, e.g.*, Frank H. Easterbrook, *Formalism, Functionalism, Ignorance, Judges*, 22 Harv. J.L. & Pub. Pol'y 13, 17 (1998) (asserting that *Humphrey's Executor* "ratifies the Administrative State"); Larry Kramer, *What's a Constitution for Anyway? Of History and Theory, Bruce Ackerman and the New Deal*, 46 Case W. Res. L. Rev. 885, 926 (1996) (calling *Humphrey's Executor* one of the "administrative state's main support beams"); Geoffrey P. Miller, *Independent Agencies*, 1986 Sup. Ct. Rev. 41, 94 (1986) ("*Humphrey's Executor* has long been viewed as the fundamental constitutional charter of the independent regulatory commissions."); Richard H. Pildes, *Separation of Powers, Independent Agencies, and Financial Regulation: The Case of the Sarbanes-Oxley Act*, 5 N.Y.U. J.L. & Bus. 485, 520 (2009) (calling *Humphrey's Executor* "truly the seminal decision of the modern administrative state").

41 Miller, *supra* note 40, at 94; *see also* Kirti Datla & Richard L. Revesz, *Deconstructing Independent Agencies (and Executive Agencies)*, 98 Cornell L. Rev. 769, 778 (2013) (observing that "[t]he constitutional status of independent agencies stems . . . from . . . *Humphrey's Executor*") at 778–79.

42 Miller, *supra* note 40, at 93 ("It was nonsense to assert that the FTC did not act in an executive role.").

43 Justice Scalia has been a particularly sharp critic of *Humphrey's Executor*. *See, e.g.*, Morrison v. Olson, 487 U.S. 654, 724–27 (1988) (Scalia, J., dissenting) (describing *Humphrey's Executor* as "six quick pages devoid of textual or historical precedent").

over time. In subsequent cases, the Supreme Court expanded *Humphrey's Executor* well beyond the limited frame presented in the 1935 opinion, seemingly calling into doubt the importance of *Humphrey's* analytical framework.

The first important decision was *Wiener v. United States*,[44] a 1958 decision involving President Eisenhower's removal of a Truman appointee to the War Claims Commission ("WCC").[45] Unlike the FTC tenure statute, which limited removal to for-cause situations, the WCC statute was silent on removal.[46] Nonetheless, finding the War Claims commissioner's three-year terms to imply protection against political removal, Justice Frankfurter's unanimous opinion for the Court held the President's removal unlawful.[47] The opinion pivoted from *Humphrey's Executor*, which had treated *Myers* as the background rule and articulated tailored reasons for departing from it. *Wiener* suggested instead that *Myers* was a "short-lived" and narrow aberration and that *Humphrey's Executor*'s flexible and functional approach should be understood as the more general rule.[48] Only a duo – political independence and adjudicatory functions – of the *Humphrey's Executor* quartet made appearances to justify the commissioner's tenure in office.[49]

Unitary executive proponents saw a glimmer of hope for *Myers* in 1986 with the Court's decision in *Bowsher v. Synar*,[50] which held that the Gramm-Rudman-Hollings Act's[51] delegation of budget-reduction duties to the comptroller general, over whom Congress held the removal power, was unconstitutional on separation of powers principles.[52] *Myers* re-emerged as favored, along with a renewed focus on the executive character of the removed actor: "Congress cannot reserve for itself the power of removal of an officer charged with the execution of the laws except by impeachment."[53] But the glimmer was short-lived, as just two years later in *Morrison v. Olson*,[54] the Court cast *Bowsher* as a case about congressional self-aggrandizement rather than presidential prerogative.[55]

---

44 Wiener v. United States, 357 U.S. 349 (1958).

45 *Id.* at 349–50.

46 *Id.* at 350.

47 *Id.* at 350, 356.

48 *Id.* at 352.

49 *See id.* at 354–55 (discussing the commissioners' political independence from the executive and legislative branches and discussing the Commission's judicial functions).

50 Bowsher v. Synar, 478 U.S. 714 (1986).

51 Balanced Budget and Emergency Deficit Control Act of 1985, Pub. L. No. 99-177, 99 Stat. 1038 (codified as amended at 2 U.S.C. §§ 900–907d, 922 (2012)).

52 *Bowsher*, 478 U.S. at 726.

53 *Id.*

54 Morrison v. Olson, 487 U.S. 654 (1988).

55 *Id.* at 685–86.

Morrison, in which the Court upheld the constitutionality of the independent counsel provisions of the Ethics in Government Act of 1978,[56] cast serious doubt on the continuing relevance of the *Humphrey's Executor* quartet.[57] Prosecution is manifestly a core executive function,[58] so the central thrust of *Humphrey's Executor* – recasting the FTC as something other than a law-enforcement agency – had to be abandoned. On the statute's restriction of the attorney general's power to remove the independent counsel, Justice Rehnquist's opinion explicitly jettisoned the "quasi-legislative, quasi-judicial" criteria:

> We undoubtedly did rely on the terms "quasi-legislative" and "quasi-judicial" to distinguish the officials involved in *Humphrey's Executor* and *Wiener* from those in *Myers*, but our present considered view is that the determination of whether the Constitution allows Congress to impose a "good cause"-type restriction on the President's power to remove an official cannot be made to turn on whether or not that official is classified as "purely executive."[59]

Rather than the *Humphrey's Executor* quartet, removability analysis would turn on whether the removal restriction "unduly interfer[es] with the role of the Executive Branch."[60]

The Supreme Court's decision in *PCAOB* renewed unitary executive theorists' hopes of a *Myers* revival – indeed, in contradistinction to *Wiener*, which attempted to bury *Myers*, Justice Roberts's opinion in *PCAOB* refers to *Myers* as a "landmark case."[61] The 5-4 decision invalidated the Public Company Accounting Oversight Board's ("PCAOB") "dual for-cause" limitation, which gave for-cause removal of PCAOB members to the Securities and Exchange Commission ("SEC") and gave for-cause removal of SEC commissioners to the President.[62] The Court distinguished *Humphrey's Executor* as a case that, unlike *Morrison* and *PCAOB*, did not involve "inferior officers" of the United States.[63] The opinion focused on the multiple layers of protection issue, declined to reconsider *Humphrey's Executor*,[64] and left untouched its quartet of rationales.

---

56 Ethics in Government Act of 1978, Pub. L. No. 95-521, 92 Stat. 1824 (codified as amended in scattered sections of 2, 5, and 28 U.S.C.)

57 *Morrison*, 487 U.S. at 689–91.

58 *See id.* at 706 (Scalia, J., dissenting) ("[P]rosecution of crimes is a quintessentially executive function.").

59 *Id.* at 689 (majority opinion).

60 *Id.* at 693.

61 Free Enter. Fund v. Pub. Co. Accounting Oversight Bd., 561 U.S. 477, 492 (2010).

62 *See id.* at 486–87.

63 *Id.* at 493.

64 *Id.* at 483 (explaining that none of the parties had asked the Court to reconsider *Myers*, *Humphrey's Executor*, *Morrison*, or United States v. Perkins, 116 U.S. 483 (1886), and that the Court would not do so on its own initiative).

Prior to *Seila Law*, then, the continuing relevance of *Humphrey's Executor*'s constitutional reasoning was in substantial doubt. *Seila Law* put *Humphrey's Executor* squarely back on the table.

2. *Seila Law*

In the wake of the 2008 financial crisis, Congress took up a proposal from then-Professor (now Senator) Elizabeth Warren and established the Consumer Financial Protection Bureau (CFPB) and tasked it with ensuring that consumer debt products are safe and transparent. "Congress also vested the CFPB with potent enforcement powers. The agency has the authority to conduct investigations, issue subpoenas and civil investigative demands, initiate administrative adjudications, and prosecute civil actions in federal court."[65]

The CFPB sits as an independent regulator within the Federal Reserve System. In establishing the CFPB's institutional arrangement, "Congress deviated from the structure of nearly every other independent administrative agency in our history. Instead of placing the agency under the leadership of a board with multiple members, Congress provided that the CFPB would be led by a single Director, who serves for a longer term than the President and cannot be removed by the President except for inefficiency, neglect, or malfeasance."[66] This unusual arrangement set the stage for a challenge to the CFPB's constitutionality – could Congress create an independent agency wielding "vast rulemaking, enforcement, and adjudicatory authority over a significant portion of the U.S." without the head of that board being accountable to the President's removal power?[67] Per Chief Justice Roberts, the Court answered no.

Promisingly for unitary executive theorists, the Court began its analysis with constitutional history, George Washington, and the pronouncement that "[t]he entire 'executive Power' belongs to the President alone."[68] In this scheme, "lesser officers must remain accountable to the President, whose authority they wield."[69] Hence, "[t]he President's removal power has long been confirmed by history and precedent,"[70] as confirmed importantly in *Myers*, and more recently in *PCAOB*.

Nonetheless, *PCAOB* had "left in place two exceptions to the President's unrestricted removal power."[71] The second one – protections for "inferior officers" "with limited jurisdiction and tenure and lacking policymaking or significant

65 *Seila Law*, 140 S. Ct. at 2193.

66 *Id.* at 2191.

67 *Id.*

68 *Id.* at 2197.

69 *Id.*

70 *Id.*

71 *Id.* at 2198.

administrative authority"[72] – is not germane to the FTC, so we can pass it quickly. The first one is *Humphrey's Executor* itself.

The Court began its analysis of *Humphrey's Executor* with the caveat that the case was "decided less than a decade after *Myers*,"[73] the sort of observation that often precedes the idea that the subsequent case is less deserving of stare decisis respect.[74] *Humphrey's Executor* announced a limited exception to *Myers* that depended "on the characteristics of the agency before the Court."[75] Chief Justice Roberts then observed that "[r]ightly or wrongly, the Court viewed the FTC (as it existed in 1935) as exercising 'not part of the executive power.'"[76] Two implications jump out: First, the Court was unwilling to endorse the *Humphrey's Executor* Court's institutional understanding of the FTC. Second, the "as it existed in 1935" proviso suggests that the Court would be willing to reconsider the FTC's constitutional status as it exists *today*.

The Court then proceeded to repeat the views of the FTC that had legitimated its independence from the President's removal power:

> [I]t was "an administrative body" that performed "specified duties as a legislative or as a judicial aid." It acted "as a legislative agency" in "making investigations and reports" to Congress and "as an agency of the judiciary" in making recommendations to courts as a master in chancery. "To the extent that [the FTC] exercise[d] any executive *function*[,] as distinguished from executive *power* in the constitutional sense," it did so only in the discharge of its "quasi-legislative or quasi-judicial powers."
>
> The Court identified several organizational features that helped explain its characterization of the FTC as non-executive. Composed of five members – no more than three from the same political party – the Board was designed to be "non-partisan" and to "act with entire impartiality." The FTC's duties were "neither political nor executive," but instead called for "the trained judgment of a body of experts" "informed by experience." And the Commissioners' staggered, seven-year terms enabled the agency to accumulate technical expertise and avoid a "complete change" in leadership "at any one time."
>
> In short, *Humphrey's Executor* permitted Congress to give for-cause removal protections to a multimember body of experts, balanced

72 *Id.* at 2199 (citation omitted).

73 *Id.* at 2198.

74 *See, e.g.*, *Continental TV, Inc. v. GTE Sylvania, Inc.*, 433 U.S. 36, 48 (1977) (overruling restrictions *United States v. Arnold, Schwinn & Co.*, 388 U.S. 365 (1967) as an "abrupt and largely unexplained departure from *White Motor Co. v. United States*, 372 U.S. 253 (1963), where only four years earlier the Court had refused to endorse a *per se* rule for vertical restrictions").

75 *Seila Law*, 140 S. Ct. at 2198.

76 *Id.*

> along partisan lines, that performed legislative and judicial functions and was said not to exercise any executive power.[77]

The Court thus allowed the FTC to remain distinguished from the CFPB on the terms of *Humphrey's Executor*. The FTC, being "a mere legislative or judicial aid" that did "not wield substantial executive power" could remain constitutionally insulated from the President's removal powers.[78]

The majority opinion thus allowed *Humphrey's Executor* to linger on its own ostensible terms. Concurring in part, Justices Thomas and Gorsuch would apparently have gone further and overruled *Humphrey's Executor*, which they found "an unfortunate example of the Court's failure to apply the Constitution as written."[79] In their view, "*Humphrey's Executor* laid the foundation for a fundamental departure from our constitutional structure with nothing more than handwaving and obfuscating phrases such as 'quasi-legislative' and 'quasi-judicial.'"[80] "It is hard to dispute that the powers of the FTC at the time of *Humphrey's Executor* would at the present time be considered 'executive,' at least to some degree.'"[81]

The only possible surprise about Justices Thomas and Gorsuch's concurrence is that Justice Kavanaugh did not join it given his explicit call for overruling *Humphrey's Executor* while on the D.C. Circuit. Perhaps he felt that such a step was unnecessary, since the majority opinion had already so undermined the prior opinion's rationale.

The *Seila Law* dissenters – Justice Kagan joined by Justices Ginsburg, Breyer, and Sotomayor – also understood the stakes for *Humphrey's Executor*. They emphasized that the CFPB statute was "identical" to the FTC Act and that in *Humphrey's Executor* nothing turned "on any of the agency's organizational features."[82] They observed the majority's suggestion "that the FTC was a different animal when this Court upheld its independent status," and stressed that, even in 1940, the Commission had powers that were effectively executive, such as running investigations, bringing administrative charges, and conducting investigations.[83] The dissenters also stressed that the relevant point of comparison was "the present-day FTC, which remains independent even if it now has some expanded powers."[84] Or, they might have said, it remains independent *for now*.

---

77 *Id.* at 2199 (citations and footnote omitted).

78 *Id.* at 2200.

79 *Id.* at 2212 (Thomas, J., concurring in part and dissenting in part).

80 *Id.* at 2216.

81 *Id.* at 2217.

82 *Seila Law*, 140 S. Ct. at 2234.

83 *Id.* at n. 10.

84 *Id.*

3. *Collins* and *Arthrex*

Two more Supreme Court opinions handed down at the end of the 2020–21 term suggest further implications for the FTC's constitutional independence from the executive branch. *Collins* involved the Federal Housing Finance Agency (FHFA), "an independent agency" tasked with regulating the Fannie Mae and Freddie Mac mortgage financing companies.[85] Like the CFPB, the FHFA has a single director, appointed by the President with the advice and consent of the Senate, whom the President could remove only for cause.[86] Justice Alito's majority opinion found that *Seila Law* made "all but dispositive" the unconstitutionality of the removal restriction.[87] "The FHFA (like the CFPB) is an agency led by a single Director, and the Recovery Act (like the Dodd-Frank Act) restricts the President's removal power."[88] None of the following facts was sufficient to distinguish the FHFA from the CFPB: the FHFA had more limited authority than the CFPB; the FHFA acts as a receiver or conservator and hence somewhat like a private party; the regulated entities were federally chartered; or the FHFA statute offered only modest tenure protection. The President's removal power over the FHFA must be plenary.

Unlike *Seila Law* and *Collins*, *Arthrex* involved an Appointments Clause issue rather than the removal power, but it drew heavily on *Seila Law* and *PCAOB* to continue the trend of cases asserting the constitutional imperative of Presidential power over officials performing executive functions. At issue was the constitutionality of the Patent Trial and Appeal Board, which consists of administrative patent judges (APJs) who conduct *inter partes* reviews of patent validity.[89] Arthrex argued that APJs were principal officers and that their appointment by the Secretary of Commerce, rather than by the President with the advice and consent of the Senate, was therefore unconstitutional.[90] Per Chief Justice Roberts, the Supreme Court agreed. Although Congress had designated APJs as inferior officers, the Court found this designation inconsistent with "the nature of their responsibilities."[91] Because APJs had the power to issue final decisions on behalf of the United States without review by their nominal superior or any other principal officer, they were exercising the powers of principal officers.[92] The availability of judicial review in Article III courts could not save the APJ system: "The activities of executive officers may 'take "legislative" and "judicial" forms,

85 *Id.* at 1770.

86 *Id.*

87 *Collins*, 141 S. Ct. at 1783.

88 *Id.* at 1784.

89 *Arthrex*, 141 S. Ct. at 1977.

90 *Id.* at 1978.

91 *Id.* at 1980.

92 *Id.* at 1981.

but they are exercises of – indeed, under our constitutional structure they must be exercises of – the "executive Power,'" for which the President is ultimately responsible."[93]

4. Implications for the FTC

Are *Seila Law* and its progeny the handwriting on the wall for the FTC's independence? If the answer turns on head counting, the magic number is five and we are already at three. Another way of answering the question is by matching the characteristics attributed to the FTC in *Humphrey's Executor* and called out again in *Seila Law* and asking whether they remain genuine characteristics of the Commission. Here, the answer is mixed but leans decidedly toward no.

A key distinction between CFPB and FTC, raised by the *Seila Law* majority and dismissed by the dissenters, is its organizational structure. Whatever the similarity in their functions, the FTC's multi-partisan, multi-member, long-term and staggered term nature marks it as different from the CFPB. If formal organizational structure marks a genuinely dispositive line, then the FTC's independence seems to remain secure.

On the other hand, if the organizational question is functional rather than formal, it remains far from clear that the FTC qualifies for independence even on organizational terms. As I argued in a prior article, cited twice in Justice Thomas's concurring opinion, the FTC has been anything but a nonpartisan and independent agency in fact.[94]

Although the Commission is operationally independent from the President, it has shown itself largely subservient to Congress's purse strings in important ways,[95] as Congress deliberately structured it to be.[96] Empirical work shows that Congress exerts its influence to control the FTC's ideological trajectory, to push it in particular enforcement directions.[97] For example, an empirical study analyzing FTC enforcement during the 1969–1979 period found that the FTC consistently chose policy programs that followed the expressed will of the FTC's oversight

---

93 *Id.* at 1982.

94 Crane, *supra* note 10, at 1852–1856.

95 William E. Kovacic, *Congress and the Federal Trade Commission*, 57 Antitrust L.J. 869, 881–88 (1988); William E. Kovacic, *The Federal Trade Commission and Congressional Oversight of Antitrust Enforcement*, 17 TULSA L. J. 587 (1982) [hereinafter Congressional Oversight]; Roger L. Faith, Donald R. Leavens & Robert D. Tollison, *Antitrust Pork Barrel, in* Public Choice and Regulation: A View from Inside the Federal Trade Commission (Robert J. MacKay, Bruce Yandle & James C. Miller III, eds., Hoover Institution Press 1987).

96 Kovacic, *Congressional Oversight, supra* note 95, at 612. As Senator Albert Cummins, a leading backer of the FTC Act, explained, the FTC was to be "a commission at all times under the power of Congress" and "always subordinate to Congress."

97 Barry R. Weingast & Mark J. Moran, *Bureaucratic Discretion or Congressional Control? Regulatory Policymaking by the Federal Trade Commission*, 91 J. Pol. Econ. 765, 788, 792 (1983). *But see* Terry M. Moe, *An Assessment of the Positive Theory of 'Congressional Dominance,'* 12 Legis. Stud. Q. 475, 476–77 (1987) (criticizing Weingast & Moran study); Timothy J. Muris, *Regulatory Policymaking at the Federal Trade Commission: The Extent of Congressional Control*, 94 J. Pol. Econ. 884, 884–89 (1986) (same).

committees in Congress, particularly by embarking on more aggressive enforcement programs in response to congressional pressure.[98] Another study found that case dismissals at the FTC were nonrandomly concentrated on defendants headquartered in the home districts of members of Congress on committees and subcommittees with budgetary and oversight jurisdiction over the FTC, suggesting that influential members of Congress leveraged their budgetary power over the FTC to shield powerful constituents from enforcement actions.[99]

The same goes for the idea that the FTC is distinguished from other organs of government by its unique expertise. As I showed previously, the FTC cannot claim any expertise advantage over its closest executive branch analog – the Justice Department's Antitrust Division – except in particular market sectors, where the expertise comes from the FTC's historical experience based on an informal market-division arrangement with the Antitrust Division.[100] Historically, FTC commissioners have not been leading experts in their fields when appointed and have not stayed at the Commission long enough to acquire expertise.[101] Bill Kovacic's comprehensive study of the FTC commissioners over time found a striking "paucity" in the quality of the appointments.[102] Kovacic found that only a handful of appointees to the FTC had distinguished experience or training in competition or consumer protection.[103]

All of that is to say that any serious inquiry into the FTC's actual functioning as opposed to its organizational chart would find that it is not apolitical, genuinely independent, or comparatively expert. But, as the *Seila Law* dissenters observed, those claims about the FTC's organizational status may have been little more than window dressing in *Humphrey's Executor*, and to the *Seila Law* majority as well. Far more important were the agency's *functions* – whether the Commission acts as "a mere legislative or judicial aid" that did "not wield substantial executive power –"[104] a point repeated in *Arthrex*, where the Court again emphasized the importance of looking at an agency's actual functions.[105]

If whether the Commission acts as "a mere legislative or judicial aid" that does "not wield substantial executive power" is the test, then game, set, match, the FTC's independence from the President's removal power is unconstitutional. It cannot be seriously maintained today that the FTC is anything like a legislative aid to Congress

98 Kovacic, *Congressional Oversight*, *supra* note 95, at 631–634, 645–648, 669–670.

99 Faith, Leavens & Tollison, *supra* note 95, at 19, 22, 26.

100 *See* Fed. Trade Comm'n, The Enforcers, http://www.ftc.gov/tips-advice/competition-guidance/guide-antitrust-laws/enforcers (last visited Oct. 17, 2015).

101 *See* Richard A. Posner, *The Federal Trade Commission: A Retrospective*, 72 Antitrust L.J. 761, 768 (2005).

102 William E. Kovacic, *The Quality of Appointments and the Capability of the Federal Trade Commission*, 49 Admin. L. Rev. 915, 917 (1997).

103 *Id.* at 916–17.

104 *Seila Law*, 140 S. Ct. at 2200, 2211.

105 141 S. Ct. at 1980.

or a judicial aid to the Justice Department, or that it does not "wield substantial executive power." As I showed previously, the FTC is neither primarily legislative nor adjudicatory, but instead acts primarily as an executive law enforcement agency.[106]

On the "legislative" side, two different things could be meant. One is that the original design for the FTC envisioned that the Commission would serve as a legislative helper to Congress by conducting investigations and rendering reports that could become blueprints for future legislation. It is probably in that sense that the *Seila Law* Court referred to the Commission's function as a legislative "aid." To be sure, the Commission does conduct market investigations and prepare reports, which some people in Congress may sometimes read, but that is a very small part of the Commission's overall workload. Read the FTC 2021 Budget request to Congress.[107] In 185 pages justifying the agency's existence, you will find nary a reference to preparing reports as legislative blueprints for Congress. Rather, you will find a detailed account of the Commission's *law enforcement* activities against bad guys.

A second sense of "legislative" would be the Commission's rulemaking authority. Its chartering statute in 1914 gave the FTC the authority to "make rules and regulations for the purpose of carrying out the [FTC Act's] provisions,"[108] but it remained unsettled until 1973 whether this general provision applied only to procedural or noninvestigatory rulemaking, or whether it also applied to substantive rules fleshing out the open-ended prohibition of section 5 of the FTC Act.[109] In 1973, the U.S. Court of Appeals for the D.C. Circuit held that section 46(g) gave the FTC the power to promulgate trade regulation rules with the effect of substantive law.[110] Two years later, the Magnuson-Moss Warranty–Federal Trade Commission Improvement Act of 1975 ("Magnuson-Moss")[111] gave the FTC the power to frame substantive trade regulation rules in furtherance of its consumer protection mission, although with heightened notice and comment procedural requirements.[112]

Despite the Progressive ambitions for an actively legislative agency and eventual affirmation by the federal courts of its substantive rulemaking power, the FTC's

---

106 Crane, *supra* note 10, at 1867–1868.

107 Fed. Trade Comm'n, Press Release, FTC Submits Annual Budget Request, Performance Plan and Performance Report to Congress (May 28, 2021), https://www.ftc.gov/news-events/news/press-releases/2021/05/ftc-submits-annual-budget-request-performance-plan-performance-report-congress.

108 15 U.S.C. § 46(g) (2012).

109 *E.g.*, Thomas W. Merrill & Kathryn Tongue Watts, *Agency Rules with the Force of Law: The Original Convention*, 116 Harv. L. Rev. 467, 551–55 (2002).

110 Nat'l Petroleum Refiners Ass'n v. FTC, 482 F.2d 672, 673, 698 (D.C. Cir. 1973).

111 Magnuson-Moss Warranty–Federal Trade Commission Improvement Act, Pub. L. No. 93-637, 88 Stat. 2183 (1975) (codified as amended at 15 U.S.C. §§ 2301–2312 (2012)).

112 *See id.*

substantive rulemaking activity has been quite limited.[113] For its first forty-nine years, until the passage of Magnuson-Moss, the FTC issued a few rules mostly related to discrete, industry-specific statutory grants of rulemaking authority under such statutes as the Wool Products Labeling Act of 1939,[114] the Fur Products Labeling Act of 1951,[115] and the Textile Fiber Products Identification Act of 1958.[116] It promulgated few substantive rules related to its core mission under section 5 of the FTC Act.[117] Following Magnuson-Moss, the FTC embarked on a temporary surge of rulemaking activity regarding consumer protection, but continued to ignore completely its power to pass substantive antitrust rules.[118]

The antitrust side is arguably more relevant when evaluating the assertions made in *Humphrey's Executor*, because the FTC only had antitrust powers at the time the case was decided and would not receive its consumer protection mandate until the Wheeler-Lea Amendments three years later.[119] Over the course of its first century, the FTC promulgated exactly one substantive antitrust rule (in 1968),[120] which it apparently never enforced.[121] In its original capacity and only capacity at the time of *Humphrey's Executor*, the FTC has not been quasi-legislative at all.

On the consumer protection side, the FTC has been more active in rulemaking, although with important qualifications. The FTC has issued twenty rules pursuant to specific Acts of Congress authorizing the FTC to regulate particular industries or practices, such as the sale of wool products or automotive fuel ratings.[122] These include some of its most popularly known rules, such as the Do-Not-Call Registry

---

113 The FTC may issue both substantive rules and those controlling procedural matters internal to the agency. *See* FED. TRADE COMM'N, OPERATING MANUAL ch. 7.

114 Wool Products Labeling Act of 1939, ch. 871, 54 Stat. 1128 (1940) (codified as amended at 15 U.S.C. § 68 (2012)); 16 C.F.R. pt. 300 (2015).

115 Fur Products Labeling Act, ch. 298, 65 Stat. 175 (1951) (codified as amended at 15 U.S.C. § 69 (2012)); 16 C.F.R. pt. 301 (2015).

116 Textile Fiber Products Identification Act, Pub. L. No. 85-897, 72 Stat. 1717 (1958) (codified as amended at 15 U.S.C. § 70 (2012)); 16 C.F.R. pt. 303 (2014).

117 *See* Mark E. Budnitz, *The FTC's Consumer Protection Program During the Miller Years: Lessons for Administrative Agency Structure and Operation*, 46 CATH. U. L. REV. 371, 415–16 (1997) (noting the "trivial" rules made before Magnuson-Moss).

118 *See id.* at 416–17 (noting that the FTC used its rulemaking ability to address unfair and deceptive practices, not antitrust).

119 *See* Ira M. Millstein, *The Federal Trade Commission and False Advertising*, 64 COLUM. L. REV. 439, 453–54 (1964).

120 Discriminatory Practices in Men's and Boys' Tailored Clothing Industry, 16 C.F.R. pt. 412 (1968); C. Scott Hemphill, *An Aggregate Approach to Antitrust: Using New Data and Rulemaking to Preserve Drug Competition*, 109 COLUM. L. REV. 629, 678 (2009). Max Huffman argues that the FTC's petroleum market manipulation rule, 16 C.F.R. pt. 317 (2015), promulgated in November 2009, could also be understood in part as an antitrust rule. Max Huffman, *Gen Next Antitrust? Reviewing Daniel Crane*, The Institutional Structure of Antitrust Enforcement, ANTITRUST & COMPETITION POL'Y BLOG 1, 3 (Sept. 19, 2011), http://papers.ssrn.com/sol3/papers.cfm?abstract_id=2201067.

121 Royce Zeisler, Chevron *Deference and the FTC: How and Why the FTC Should Use* Chevron *to Improve Antitrust Enforcement*, 2014 COLUM. BUS. L. REV. 266, 281 (2014).

122 *See* 16 C.F.R. subchapter C (2015).

Rule[123] and the Children's Online Privacy Protection Rule.[124] It has also promulgated a batch of rules concerning the Fair Credit Reporting Act, also pursuant to a specific delegation from Congress.[125] The FTC has promulgated only sixteen trade regulation rules – rules designed to implement the agency's core organic mission to prevent deceptive and unfair trade practices and unfair methods of competition. Six of these rules were promulgated from 1965 to 1979,[126] including five during the 1970s, a period that corresponded with the passage of Magnuson-Moss and optimism that the FTC could address broad swaths of the consumer protection landscape through regulation.[127] In the late 1970s, the FTC's rulemaking agenda suffered a serious setback as the ordinarily friendly *Washington Post* labeled the agency the "national nanny"[128] over a series of proposed consumer protection rules, culminating in its proposed "kidvid" rules relating to advertising to children.[129] As political will turned sharply against the kidvid rules, the FTC was forced to back down.[130] Following the kidvid debacle, the pace of trade regulation rulemaking slowed. The FTC promulgated four rules during the 1980s,[131] three rules during the 1990s,[132] and only three rules since 2000.[133]

But maybe this will now change. FTC Chair Lina Khan has made no secret of her desire to proceed with unfair methods of competition rulemaking.[134] Despite the D.C. Circuit's *National Petroleum Refiners* decision, whether the FTC in fact has that power remains subject to question. At a minimum, it seems unlikely that the FTC will begin to issue unfair methods of competition rules at a pace

123 Telemarketing Sales Rule, 16 C.F.R. § 310.1 (2015) (implementing Telemarketing and Consumer Fraud and Abuse Prevention Act, 15 U.S.C. §§ 6101–6108 (2012)).

124 Children's Online Privacy Protection Rule, 16 C.F.R. § 312.1 (2015) (implementing Children's Online Privacy Protection Act of 1998, 15 U.S.C. §§ 6501–6506 (2012)).

125 16 C.F.R. §§ 310.4, 313.16 (2015).

126 Unfair or Deceptive Advertising and Labeling of Cigarettes in Relation to the Health Hazards of Smoking, 16 C.F.R. pt. 408 (1965); Deceptive Advertising as to Sizes of Viewable Pictures Shown by Television Receiving Sets, 16 C.F.R. pt. 410 (1971); Use of Prenotification Negative Option Plans, 16 C.F.R. pt. 425 (1973); Power Output Claims for Amplifiers Utilized in Home Entertainment Products, 16 C.F.R. pt. 432 (1975); Preservation of Consumers' Claims and Defenses, 16 C.F.R. pt. 433 (1977); Labeling and Advertising of Home Insulation, 16 C.F.R. pt. 460 (1979).

127 15 U.S.C. §§ 2301–2312.

128 Editorial, *The FTC as National Nanny*, Wash. Post, Mar. 1, 1978, at A22.

129 Children's Advertising, 43 Fed. Reg. 17,967 (Apr. 27, 1978); *see also* J. Howard Beales III, *Advertising to Kids and the FTC: A Regulatory Retrospective that Advises the Present*, 12 Geo. Mason L. Rev. 873, 878–79 (2004).

130 Beales, *supra* note 129, at 879–80 (describing termination of rulemaking by FTC in response to political pressure).

131 Care Labeling of Textile Wearing Apparel, 16 C.F.R. pt. 423 (1983); Credit Practices, 16 C.F.R. pt. 444 (1985); Used Motor Vehicle Trade Regulation Rule, 16 C.F.R. pt. 455 (1985); Retail Food Store Advertising and Marketing Practices, 16 C.F.R. pt. 424 (1989).

132 Ophthalmic Practice Rules, 16 C.F.R. pt. 456 (1992); Funeral Industry Practices, 16 C.F.R. pt. 453 (1994); Cooling-Off Period for Door-to-Door Sales, 16 C.F.R. pt. 429 (1995).

133 Disclosure Requirements and Prohibitions Concerning Franchising and Business Opportunity Ventures, 16 C.F.R. pt. 436 (2007); Mail or Telephone Order Merchandise, 16 C.F.R. pt. 435 (2011); Disclosure Requirements and Prohibitions Concerning Business Opportunities, 16 C.F.R. pt. 437 (2011).

134 Rohit Chopra & Lina M. Khan, *The Case for "Unfair Methods of Competition" Rulemaking*, 87 U. Chi. L. Rev. 357 (2020).

that would justify the view that its primary character can be described as "quasi-legislative."

On the "quasi-judicial" side, there are also two possible meanings. What the *Seila Law* majority focuses on, which was also the primary sense in which this concept was used in *Humphrey's Executor*,[135] is section 7 of the FTC Act, which allows district courts to refer Department of Justice antitrust cases to the FTC to sit as a "master in chancery" and determine the appropriate form of relief.[136] Several related powers, alluded to more indirectly in *Humphrey's Executor*,[137] include section 6(c), which calls for the FTC to monitor compliance with antitrust decrees obtained by the Justice Department,[138] and section 6(e), which allows the attorney general to request that the FTC "make recommendations for the readjustment of the business of any corporation alleged to be violating the antitrust Acts in order that the corporation may thereafter maintain its organization, management, and conduct of business in accordance with law."[139]

While these chancery-like powers make the FTC "quasi-judicial" in theory, practice has been entirely different. The powers simply have not been used, largely because the FTC and Justice Department have become rival enforcement agencies that have little interest in ceding power to one another. Indeed, the only instance of the use of the equity power of which I am aware is a 1962 letter to the chairman of the FTC, referring a decree matter to the FTC under section 6(c), in which the attorney general stated that the section had been "virtually unused since its enactment in 1914."[140] To this author's knowledge, that power has been unused again since that time.

The FTC's other "quasi-judicial" capacity concerns its power to hear matters administratively. Under its original statutory mandate, which was still in place at the time of *Humphrey's Executor*, the FTC had no power to sue in federal district court.[141] It could bring only administrative actions and then seek to have those orders enforced by a court of appeals.[142] Conversely, defendants who lost before the Federal Trade Commission could seek vacatur of the Commission's order in a court of appeals.[143] The *Humphrey's Executor* Court was thus correct in observing that the FTC wielded quasi-judicial powers in principle.

---

135 *See Humphrey's Ex'r*, 295 U.S. at 621.

136 15 U.S.C. § 47 (2012).

137 *See Humphrey's Ex'r*, 295 U.S. at 621.

138 15 U.S.C. § 46(c).

139 *Id.* § 46(e).

140 United States v. Int'l Nickel Co. of Can., 203 F. Supp. 739, 741 (S.D.N.Y. 1962).

141 Federal Trade Commission Act of 1914, Pub. L. No. 63-203, 38 Stat. 717, 719–20 (1914).

142 *Id.*

143 *Id.*

Legislative changes within three years of the *Humphrey's Executor* decision began a trend that gradually reduced the FTC's adjudicatory character significantly. The Wheeler-Lea Amendments of 1938 granted the FTC new powers to act as a party litigant in federal district court.[144] The thrust of the FTC's new power under section 13 was to seek a preliminary injunction maintaining the status quo pending the filing of an administrative complaint.[145] Thus, a preliminary injunction obtained under section 13 dissolves automatically if, within the time specified by the district court (not to exceed twenty days), the FTC fails to file an administrative complaint.[146] Writing immediately in the wake of the Wheeler-Lea Amendments, the eminent trade scholar Milton Handler believed that, although the statutory language was unclear, "an injunction can not be sought independently of a proceeding by the Commission."[147] In time, however, the FTC would obtain new statutory authority to seek injunctions without going through administrative proceedings at all. In 1973, section 13 was amended to add a proviso that, with time, would become the rule rather than the exception: "[I]n proper cases the Commission may seek, and after proper proof, the court may issue, a permanent injunction."[148] Eventually, the courts interpreted the language of section 13(b) to permit a district court to grant a permanent injunction even though the Commission never brought an administrative action.[149]

Two years later, in 1975, Congress granted the FTC additional powers to seek monetary relief, primarily for consumer protection violations.[150] The Commission could seek consumer redress in federal court for "dishonest or fraudulent" practices, but only after an administrative proceeding.[151] However, the Commission soon fell into the habit of obtaining effective monetary relief without administrative action by suing in federal district court seeking asset freezes and mandatory injunctions requiring the defendant to return assets to defrauded consumers.[152] This use of the federal courts' injunctive power became known as the "Section 13(b) Fraud Program."[153] In combination with other institutional pressures and strategic

---

144 15 U.S.C. § 53(a).

145 *Id.* § 53(b).

146 *Id.*

147 Milton Handler, *The Control of False Advertising Under the Wheeler-Lea Act*, 6 LAW & CONTEMP. PROBS. 91, 106 (1939).

148 15 U.S.C. § 53(b).

149 United States v. JS & A Group, Inc., 716 F.2d 451, 457 (7th Cir. 1983) ("[W]e hold that section 13(b) of the FTC Act authorizes the Commission to seek, in a proper case, and the court to grant, after proper proof, permanent injunctive relief, irrespective of whether a Commission proceeding regarding the alleged violations is pending or contemplated."); FTC v. H. N. Singer, Inc., 668 F.2d 1107, 1110–11 (9th Cir. 1982); United States v. Nat'l Dynamics Corp., 525 F. Supp. 380, 381 (S.D.N.Y. 1981).

150 15 U.S.C. § 57b; *see also* J. Howard Beales III & Timothy J. Muris, *Striking the Proper Balance: Redress Under Section 13(b) of the FTC Act*, 79 ANTITRUST L.J. 1, 1–2 (2013) (detailing the events leading up to the 1975 amendments to the FTC Act).

151 15 U.S.C. § 57b(a).

152 Beales & Muris, *supra* note 150, at 3.

153 *Id.*

considerations, it had the effect over time of shifting the FTC's enforcement activities in the consumer protection field from internal adjudication to executive enforcement in federal district court.[154]

Due to various reasons I have described elsewhere,[155] agency adjudication has become a smaller part of the FTC's work in recent decades. My prior empirical project studied FTC enforcement action in recent decades and found that 1,183 cases proceeded in federal court and 909 before the agency.[156] In total, 1,524 cases ended in consent decrees without any adjudicatory activity at all, whether in court or before the agency, and 475 cases saw adjudicatory activity in federal district court. Over the eighteen-year period studied, only 79 cases of agency adjudication were identified – just over four a year. It concluded that adjudication is a vanishingly small aspect of what the FTC does.

So if the FTC is not primarily involved in legislation (whether as an aid to Congress or as an independent rulemaking agency) or adjudication (whether sitting as a special master in equity to aid the Justice Department or adjudicating its own cases internally), what is it doing? The answer is given plainly in the FTC's 2022 budget request to Congress, when the Commission described how its 1,140 employees were deployed. Five hundred twelve of them were tasked to "identify and take actions to address deceptive or unfair practices that harm consumers," and another 453 to "identify and take actions to identify anticompetitive mergers and practices that cause harm to consumers." That is to say, 85% of the Commission's staff are involved in traditional law enforcement. The two other categories of full-time equivalent ("FTE") assignment – conducting research or consumer outreach, and collaborating with domestic and international partners – also contain elements of enforcement. They do not describe a primarily legislative or adjudicatory agency. The *Seila Law*'s recitation of *Humphrey's Executor* view of the FTC – that it "performed legislative and judicial functions and was said not to exercise any executive power"[157] – bears zero resemblance to the actual FTC.

Any pretense that the FTC is not primarily a law enforcement agency recently was given the lie by Judge Boasberg's decision rejecting Facebook's argument that FTC Chair Lina Khan should have been recused from voting out a complaint against Facebook because of her work in compiling anti-Facebook evidence in the House Judiciary Committee and her prior academic writing.[158] Judge Boasberg observed that Chair Khan was acting as *a prosecutor* rather than a judge with

154 *Id.* at 4 (describing the increasing use of the "Section 13(b) Fraud Program" and increasing amount of redress ordered); *id.* at 22 (explaining that the FTC could have accomplished asset freezes in the district court and then returned to the administrative forum, but there was little reason to use such a clunky procedure).

155 Crane, *supra*, note 10, at 1867.

156 *Id.*

157 *Seila Law*, 140 S. Ct. at 2199.

158 FTC v. Facebook, Inc., 2022 WL 103308, at*18 (Jan. 11, 2021).

respect to her vote on authorizing the filing of an amended complaint, and therefore that the neutrality standards applicable to adjudicators did not apply.[159] "Prosecutor" is an apt description of the commissioners' role most of the time.

One final point of potential distinction between the FTC and the CFPB that bears analyzing concerns the *Seila Law* Court's observation that the CFPB has the authority to "seek restitution, disgorgement, and injunctive relief, as well as civil penalties up to $1,000,000 (inflation adjusted) for each day that a violation occurs."[160] Thus, the CFPB director has "the power to seek daunting monetary penalties against private parties on behalf of the United States in federal court – a quintessentially executive power not considered in *Humphrey's Executor.*"[161]

True enough, at the time of *Humphrey's Executor*, the FTC's powers were solely equitable – and essentially limited to equity's injunctive power to order defendants to comply with the law. Further, the Supreme Court recently ruled that the FTC lacks power under section 13(b) of the FTC Act to seek disgorgement as an equitable remedy.[162] The *AMG* decision has, for now, frustrated the FTC's ability to seek the billions of dollars in disgorgement that it has sought (and obtained) in some recent cases, but that does not mean that the FTC today lacks the power to seek significant monetary penalties. The FTC has significant civil penalty authority in its consumer protection capacity, as evidenced by the $5 billion fine it recently meted on Facebook for violations of consumer privacy.[163] From 2000 to 2018, the Commission secured over $400 million in civil fines for consumer protection violations.[164] Moreover, the House of Representatives has passed the Consumer Protection and Recovery Act (H.R. 2668), which would give the FTC the disgorgement authority that the Supreme Court denied it in *AMG*. With or without that authority, the FTC is already in a position to demand significant sums of money from companies that violate consumer protection law.

In short, very little of what the *Humphrey's Executor* Court said about the FTC was true at the time, and most of it that was arguably true at the time is no longer true. The FTC is for all intents and purposes an executive law enforcement agency. Under the logic of *Seila Law*, it should not be divorced from the President's removal power.

---

159 *Id.* at *20.

160 *Seila Law*, 140 S. Ct. at 2193.

161 *Id.* at 2200.

162 AMG Capital Management, LLC, et al. v. FTC, 593 U.S. ___ 141 S. Ct. 1341 (2021). *See* Steven A. Reed, Scott A. Stempel & Daniel S. Savrin, *The US Supreme Court holds that the FTC lacks the authority to seek equitable monetary relief in cases brought in federal court under FTC Act Section 13(b) (AMG Capital Management)*, e-Competitions April 2021, art. No. 100669.

163 Fed. Trade Comm'n, Press Release, FTC Imposes $5 Billion Penalty and Sweeping New Privacy Restrictions on Facebook, https://www.ftc.gov/news-events/news/press-releases/2019/07/ftc-imposes-5-billion-penalty-sweeping-new-privacy-restrictions-facebook.

164 Fed. Trade Comm'n, Data Sets, https://www.ftc.gov/policy-notices/open-government/data-sets.

IV. FTC Independence Going Forward

So now what? For now, the FTC remains constitutionally independent from the President's removal power because the Court declined to say otherwise in *Seila Law*. But, of course, it was the CFPB, not the FTC, that was actually before the Court, and it said plenty to cast doubt on *Humphrey's Executor.* A bet on *Humphrey's Executor's* survival should come with a significant premium for risk. What would be the effects on the FTC's independence and enforcement agenda should the Supreme Court finally discard *Humphrey's Executor* and hold that FTC commissioners are removable by the President for political reasons? The effects, both short-run and long-run, could be considerable.

1. Short-Run Remedial Risks

An immediate effect of *Seila Law* is to cast a pall over FTC enforcement actions. Should the Supreme Court ultimately rule that the FTC must be accountable to the President's removal power, the party that successfully brought that challenge (and others currently bringing such a challenge) might be entitled to dismissal of the case or *vacatur* of any prior decisions. Remedy was a secondary issue in *Seila Law* – whether the civil investigative demand at issue should be quashed, or whether it had been sufficiently ratified by a director accountable to the President.[165] Following remand, the CFPB's new Director Kraninger, "now removable by the President without cause," ratified the Board's past action against Seila Law.[166] En banc, the Ninth Circuit held that post-hoc ratification was sufficient to overcome the unconstitutional taint of the prior Board action, but four judges of the court dissented.[167] In the dissenters' view, the prior CFPB's unconstitutional structure rendered the enforcement action irremediably tainted.

In *Seila Law*, the Supreme Court declined to address the ratification question because it "turn[ed] on case-specific factual and legal questions not addressed below and not briefed" before the Court.[168] The Supreme Court returned to that question in *Collins*, holding that the subsequent ratification of the prior decision by a director (acting director, in the facts of *Collins*) who was removable at the will of the President could remove the constitutional taint of the prior decision made by a director insulated from removal except for cause, at least if the harm to the defendant had not yet been completed at the time of the new director's ratification.[169] Subsequent ratification by a constitutionally legitimate (in the

165 *Seila Law*, 140 S. Ct. at 2211.

166 Consumer Financial Protection Bureau v. Seila Law LLC, 997 F.3d 837, 842 (9th Cir. 2021) (Bumatay, J. dissenting from denial of rehearing en banc).

167 *Id.*

168 *Seila Law*, 140 S. Ct. at 2208 (plurality opinion).

169 *Collins*, 141 S. Ct. at 1781 ("If the statute does not restrict the removal of an Acting Director, any harm resulting from actions taken under an Acting Director would not be attributable to a constitutional violation.").

sense of removable at the will of the President) director thus seems to limit the potential disruptive effect of *Seila Law* on ongoing agency business.

But much remains unresolved. In both *Collins* and *Seila*, the subsequent ratification was by a newly appointed director (or acting director, in *Collins*). Would the taint of unconstitutionality have been removed if the same director who had issued the prior decision simply reissued it after the judicial decision on removability? There is no clear answer. Presumably, the injury in fact suffered by the subject of an adverse agency decision by a decision-maker unconstitutionally insulated from the President's removal power is that, if the decision-maker had been properly subject to the removal power, her decision might have been different. Having already made the prior adverse decision, should the decision-maker be counted on to consider a new decision without the overhang of her prior decision? The Supreme Court considered a similar question in *Lucia v. SEC*,[170] deciding that an unconstitutionally appointed administrative law judge (ALJ) should not be assigned to hear the same matter again even if after a new, constitutional appointment. Justice Kagan observed that the ALJ "cannot be expected to consider the matter as though he had not adjudicated it before" and that "the old judge would have no reason to think he did anything wrong on the merits."[171] On the other hand, in dialogue with Justice Breyer's concurring opinion, she also noted that a new officer may not be required for "every Appointments Clause violation" and that if "the Appointments Clause problem is with the Commission itself, so that there is no substitute decisionmaker, the rule of necessity would presumably kick in and allow the Commission to do the rehearing."[172] In support of this proposition, Justice Kagan cited *FTC v. Cement Institute*,[173] in which the Court held that the same Commission could conduct industry-wide investigations and subsequently engage in proceedings against a defendant on the same legal and factual questions since there was no practical way of separating the Commission's investigatory and adjudicatory functions.

So maybe this means that, if the Supreme Court should overrule *Humphrey's Executor* and hold FTC commissioners removable by the President, the Commission simply has to ratify its prior decisions and get on with business. Since that issue was not squarely presented in *Lucia* – Justice Kagan's comments were dicta – the issue remains formally unresolved. But even if subsequent ratification by the same commissioners revives a previously unconstitutional order, there is no guarantee that the Commission will ratify its prior decisions. Years would pass from the moment of a constitutional challenge to a Commission decision to the final decision on the constitutional question. In the interim, vacancies or changes in the Commission's composition could make it impossible

170 138 S. Ct. 2044 (2018).

171 *Id.* at 2055, 2055 n. 5.

172 *Id.* at 2055 n. 5.

173 333 U.S. 683, 700–03 (1948).

for the Commission staff to secure subsequent ratification from a Commission majority, particularly given the current, deeply partisan division on the Commission.

The upshot is that every company or individual against whom the FTC takes enforcement action is walking around with a potential "get out of jail free" card in their pocket. At a time when the Commission is apparently embarking on a considerably more aggressive enforcement agenda, *Seila Law* and its progeny could represent a major roadblock to the FTC's agenda.

2. Long-Run Institutional Consequences

Beyond the short-term remedial issue, there are important questions about what it would mean for the FTC to become accountable to the President's removal power. Perhaps it would not change much at all. Some commentators have argued that the focus on removal power as the fulcrum of independence or control is misplaced, since presidents face practical and political constraints on removing even executive officers whom they have the clear right to remove.[174] Witness President Trump's seemingly odd reluctance to fire Cabinet officers like Attorney General Jeff Sessions, whom the President characterized as incompetent, disloyal, and out of step but allowed to linger on in office.[175] On the other hand, President Biden's firing of Social Security Commissioner Andrew Saul, a Trump holdover who refused to resign, suggests that the President's newfound removal powers may be wielded aggressively even in nakedly political cases.[176]

On the other hand, giving the President removal powers over the commissioners on a multi-member, multi-partisan commission could affect the Commission's dynamics by permitting the President to remove holdover commissioners from the opposite party and replace them with a more pliable "loyal opposition." This power could be particularly useful to avoid Commission stalemates resulting from vacancies – a situation that has occurred with some frequency in recent decades and has, at times, disabled the Commission from advancing the chair's agenda. For example, consider a period during which the Commission is down to four members – two of the President's party and two of the other party – and is therefore at a stalemate. Further assume that the opposing party controls Congress and therefore may delay or refuse confirmation of the President's same-party nominee to fill the fifth seat. In such a circumstance, the opposing party essentially holds a veto over the Commission doing any business of a controversial nature. With the removal power, the President could remove one of the two opposition

174 Lisa Schultz Bressman & Robert B. Thompson, *The Future of Agency Independence*, 63 VAND. L. REV. 599, 628 33 (2010).

175 Rebecca Savranksy, *Trump does not intend to fire Sessions: report*, THE HILL (June 8, 2017), https://thehill.com/homenews/administration/336885-trump-does-not-intend-to-fire-sessions-repor.

176 *See* Lisa Rein, *Biden fires head of Social Security Administration, a Trump holdover who drew the ire of Democrats*, WASH. POST (July 11, 2021), https://www.washingtonpost.com/politics/andrew-saul-social-security-/2021/07/09/c18a34fa-df99-11eb-a501-0e69b5d012e5_story.html.

commissioners, thus breaking the stalemate immediately and creating bargaining leverage for the appointment of the new same-party commissioner.

Beyond partisan issues, affording the President a removal power over FTC commissioners could result in more fluid coordination on antitrust matters between the FTC and Justice Department's Antitrust Division, which share a considerably overlapping mandate. At times, the agencies have bickered significantly and publicly, most recently when the Antitrust Division filed an amicus curiae brief opposing the FTC's monopolization case against Qualcomm.[177] Although the removal power would not eliminate all inter-agency strife, it would likely reduce the likelihood that the agencies would take publicly opposing positions.

Clarifying that the FTC works for the President – which is, after all, the symbolic and perhaps practical meaning of the removal power – would also make sense of directives like President Biden's Executive Order on Competition, which is where this article began. At present, it is questionable practice for the President to issue directions to an agency over which he has no control.[178] Granting the President the removal power would clarify the President's authority to direct the activities of the FTC,[179] which in turn could facilitate the sort of coordination on competition policy that President Biden's Executive Order envisions.

But, of course, the price of presidential control would be the loss of FTC independence. The *Humphrey's Executor* narrative envisioned Commission independence as a powerful force for the superior administration of the law. Neutral expertise, political detachment, and technocratic continuity are the ostensible virtues that stand to be lost with the assertion of presidential control. If they ever existed.

V. Conclusion

Seila Law is significant for taking *Humphrey's Executor* at face value – as Chief Justice Roberts wrote, by "tak[ing] the decision on its own terms, not through gloss added by a later Court in dicta."[180] If the accuracy of the *Humphrey's Executor* Court's description of the FTC's institutional arrangement and functions is the necessary condition for its continuing independence, then that independence is in significant peril. No one could seriously argue that the FTC is anything like a mere legislative and judicial aid to Congress and not a law enforcement agency performing executive functions. If *Seila Law* means what it says, the President may soon have removal power over FTC commissioners.

---

177 Brief of the United States of America as Amicus Curiae in Support of Vacatur, No. 19-16222 (9th Cir. 2019).

178 *See* Adrian Vermeule, *Conventions of Agency Independence*, 113 Colum. L. Rev. 1163, 1216–17 (2013); Extending Regulatory Review Under Executive Order 12866 to Independent Regulatory Agencies, Office of Legal Counsel (Oct. 8, 2019).

179 Neomi Rao, *Removal: Necessary and Sufficient for Presidential Control*, 65 Ala. L. Rev. 1205 (2014).

180 *Seila Law*, 140 S. Ct. at 2200 n. 4.

Table of Contents

Dead-End Road: *National Petroleum Refiners Association* and FTC "Unfair Methods of Competition" Rulemaking

Maureen K. Ohlhausen and Ben Rossen

The Constitutional Revolution That Wasn't: Why the FTC Isn't a Second National Legislature

Berin Szóka and Corbin Barthold

Policing Anticompetitive Practices and Protecting the Competitive Process through Adjudication vs. Rulemaking

Henry C. Su

Can the Federal Trade Commission Use Rulemaking to Change Antitrust Law?

Richard J. Pierce, Jr.

Legal Constraints on FTC Competition Rulemaking

Alden F. Abbott

Pushing the Limits? A Primer on FTC Competition Rulemaking

Maureen K. Ohlhausen and James F. Rill

Regulatory Rents: An Agency-Cost Analysis of the FTC Rulemaking Initiative

Jonathan M. Barnett

Case-by-Case Rules! Old Statutes and New Tech at the FTC

Neil Chilson

What Happens if the FTC Becomes a Serious Rulemaker?

Aaron L. Nielson

FTC Independence after Seila Law

Daniel A. Crane

CPSIA information can be obtained
at www.ICGtesting.com
Printed in the USA
JSHW042131100622
26832JS00001B/1

9 781954 750869